THE COIN-INSCRIPTIONS
AND EPIGRAPHICAL ABBREVIATIONS
OF IMPERIAL ROME

The Coin-Inscriptions and Epigraphical Abbreviations of IMPERIAL ROME

By

HENRY COHEN
J.C. EGBERT, Jr.
R. CAGNAT

ARES PUBLISHERS INC.
CHICAGO   MCMLXXVIII

THE EPIGRAPHICAL ABBREVIATIONS
OF THE LATIN INSCRIPTIONS
J.C. EGBERT, Jr. & R. CAGNAT

LEXICON OF THE LATIN INSCRIPTIONS ON THE
REVERSES OF ROMAN IMPERIAL COINS
H. COHEN

© Copyright 1978
ARES PUBLISHERS INC.
612 N. Michigan Avenue
Chicago, Illinois 60611
Printed in the United States of America
International Standard Book Number:
0-89005-227-1

PREFACE

This manual, *Coin-Inscriptions and Epigraphical Abbreviations of Imperial Rome*, is intended to serve at least two desiderata of classical scholars and students: (1) As a reference and research tool, this manual will enable one to use and interpret Roman Imperial coins and tables of coin inscriptions. (2) As a collection of *inscriptions on the reverses of Roman Imperial coins*, this manual makes readily available the content of Imperial coins. It is not only for numismatists but also for all the scholars and students who are interested in the political and socio-moral history of the Roman Empire that this manual has been compiled.

To a scholar who has neither the time nor the opportunity to consult the extant collections of Imperial coins scattered throughout the world, the alphabetized list of *inscriptions on the reverses of Roman Imperial coins*, contained in this manual, will afford at a glance a panoramic view of the ethical ideals of the Empire, the political platforms and propaganda slogans of the emperors, and, in general, the moral and social conditions of this turbulent era. A glance at this list suggests that our Western culture, past and present—with its coinage, its ethical system, its tendency toward propaganda, its attitude toward war and foreigners, its manipulation of religion, and its aspirations—is a direct continuation of the Roman Empire.

The alphabetized list of *inscriptions on the reverses of Roman Imperial coins*, reprinted in this manual, was originally published by H. Cohen as an Appendix to the eighth volume of his *Description historique des monnaies frappées sous l'empire romain*, a work many times reprinted but now out of print.

The two complementary tables of epigraphical abbreviations reprinted in this manual were originally published by R. Cagnat in *Cours d' Epigraphie Latine* and by J.C. Egbert, Jr. in *Latin Inscriptions*, both works now out of print.

For many scholars and students these tables of Latin abbreviations will prove to be *sine qua non* tools for reading the inscriptions on stone as well as those on Roman Imperial coins with efficiency and ease. These tables, moreover, will enable one to read and use in research the extensive number of *inscriptions on the reverses of Roman Imperial coins* which makes up the main part of this manual.

In compiling this manual, *Coin-Inscriptions and Epigraphical Abbreviations of Imperial Rome*, I was guided by two principles: economy and usefulness to classical scholars and students. The result I wanted was a manual that would prove to be the most efficient short cut to the understanding and the control of the rich, exciting, and revealing contents of Imperial coinage.

Without the generous and indispensable help given to me by Professor Al. N. Oikonomides, this manual would not exist. I am grateful to the Ares Publishers, Inc. for the privilege of being invited to complete and bring this manual to you.

Ladislaus J. Bolchazy

Table of Archaisms

ai and ae; *ae* is found replacing *ai* in some words in *S. C. de Bacchanalibus* (186 b.c.), alongside of the earlier spelling. It is the established form for the *Lex Bantina* (133–118), the *Lex Repetundarum* of 123–122 b.c. The transition form, *aei*, appears about the close of the second century b.c. The archaic spelling was restored in the reign of Claudius.

oi for oe and ū; about 200 b.c. *ū* begins to replace *oi* and *oe*. *ū* is found in the Scipio epitaph of the beginning of the second century b.c. and in the Mummius inscription of 146 b.c. *oi* and *oe* continue to be used, especially in official inscriptions, even to the Ciceronian period.

ou and ū; *ū* replaces *ou* about 100 b.c. It appears for *ou* in *Lucius* in the Scipio epitaph, dating not later than 200 b.c. Both are seen in *Lex Bantina* (133–118 b.c.), *Lex Repetundarum* (123–122 b.c.), but *ou* is disregarded entirely in *Lex Cornelia* (81 b.c.).

ei and ī; *ei* represents in the inscriptions either original *ei*, as in *deico*, or stands for the long *i*. The first is found in the early inscriptions, and appears in the *S. C. de Bacch.* (186 b.c.). The spurious diphthong *ei* is found in *audeire* in *Lex Repetundarum* of 123–122 b.c., and in *ameicitiam* of *Lex Agraria* of 111 b.c.

Aspiration of Consonants; see page 29.

Final s and m; the letters *s* and *m* are frequently omitted in early inscriptions, but this omission ceases about 130 b.c.

Final d; this final letter of the ablative case is written in the *S. C. de Bacch.* (186 b.c.), but is not found in the decree of Aemilius Paulus of 189 b.c. It may be said to have disappeared from use a little after 200 b.c.

xs for simple x; this spelling does not occur before its appearance in the *S. C. de Bacch.* (186 b.c.). It then is found particularly in inscriptions of 130–120 b.c., and again in the Augustan period, and later.

Double Consonants; see page 29.

Double Vowels; see page 30.

-os and -om; these forms were reduced to *-us* and *-um* except after *u* and *v* in the nominative and accusative cases of *o*-stems about 234 b.c.

-ēs, -eis, -īs; these endings mark the nominative case plural of *o*-stems of the close of the second century b.c., and of the beginning of the first.

-us, genitive; the *-us* ending of consonant stems is found in early inscriptions, as in the *S. C. de Bacch.* (186 b.c.), also in the *Lex Agraria* (111 b.c.) and the *Epistula ad Tiburtes* (100 b.c.), but ceases about 100 b.c.

Table of Legions

II. *Augusta.* Formed by Augustus, 27 B.C. Quartered in Egypt, in Moesia (5 A.D.), on the Rhine (9), with Germanicus (15–16), Britain (43).

III. *Augusta P(ia) V(index).* Formed by Augustus, 27 B.C. Service in Africa, surnamed *Liberatrix* by Galba, in Numidia, surnamed *Pia Vindex* by Septimus Severus, against the Parthians (216 A.D.), disbanded by Gordian III, re-formed by Valerian, in wars against Formus (373) and Gildon (398).

III. *Cyrenaica.* Formed by Lepidus in Africa. Service in Egypt (66), with Vespasian in 69, in the East with Trajan.

III. *Gallica.* Formed by L. Munatius Plancus in Gaul. Service with M. Antonius against the Parthians, in Moesia (5 A.D.), with Corbulo in Armenia, in Moesia (58), in Syria under Vespasian and Domitian, with Trajan in the East, with Hadrian in Judea and Phoenicia.

IV. *Macedonica.* Formed probably by Brutus in Macedonia. Quartered in Spain in time of Augustus, in Mauretania under Caligula, in Germany (Moguntiacum) in 43, favored Vitellius (68), disbanded by Vespasian.

IV. *Scythica.* Formed by M. Crassus in 29 B.C. Quartered in Syria (27 B.C.), in Moesia (5 A.D.), in Germania Inferior (47), with Corbulo in the East (58), surrendered to Vologeses (62), in Syria (63), with Trajan in Judea (114).

V. *Alauda.* Formed by Julius Caesar. Quartered in Spain (27–24 B.C.), in Germany, in Pannonia (6–9 A.D.), in Britain with Claudius, in Moesia in time of Vespasian, destroyed by Sarmates (84) or disbanded by Vespasian.

V. *Macedonica.* Formed by Brutus in Macedonia. Service in Syria up to 5 A.D., then in Moesia, with Corbulo in the East (62), in Judea with Titus, defeated Sarmates (84), in Dacia, in Moesia.

VI. *Victrix P(ia) F(elix).* In Spain after the reign of Augustus, on the Rhine (70 A.D.), in Germania Inferior up to time of Hadrian, in Britain (120). Trajan gave the name *Pia Felix.*

VII. *Claudia P(ia) F(idelis).* Quartered in Macedonia, about 10 A.D. sent to Dalmatia, to Pannonia by Nero, recalled to Italy (68), sent to Moesia by Galba, to Germany under Mucianus, in Moesia (71). Claudius gave the name *Claudia Pia Fidelis.*

VIII. *Augusta.* Formed by Augustus. Quartered in Pannonia, in Moesia in time of Claudius (47), called to Italy (68), in Moesia in time of Galba, in Germany under Mucianus.

IX. *Hispana.* On the Danube in time of Augustus, sent to Africa (20 A.D.), to Spain (24), to Britain (43), destroyed by the Britons (120).

X. *Gemina P(ia) F(idelis).* Formed by Augustus in 27 B.C. under name *X Augusta.* Quartered in Spain, lost its name in 19 B.C., named *Gemina* after 5 A.D., sent to Germany in 58, to Spain in time of Galba, in Germany in time of Vespasian until reign of Trajan, in Dacia with Trajan, in Pannonia.

XI. *Claudia P(ia) F(idelis).* In Pannonia in time of Augustus, then in Dalmatia, called to Italy (68), in Germania Superior (70), in Moesia in time of Trajan.

XII. *Fulminata.* Formed by Augustus. Quartered in Egypt, sent to Syria (18 A.D.), with Corbulo (62), in Armenia, surrendered to Vologeses, in Syria, in Cappadocia.

XIII. *Gemina P(ia) F(idelis).* Formed by Augustus in 27 B.C. Service in Pannonia, with Germanicus in Germany, in Pannonia, called to Italy (68 A.D.), at Bedriacum and Cremona, sent to Pannonia by Vespasian, in Dacia. Nero probably gave the name *Pia Fidelis.*

XIV. *Gemina Martia Victrix.* Formed by Augustus in 27 B.C. Service in Germany with Tiberius and with Germanicus, in Britain (43 A.D.), summoned by Nero (68), opposed Vitellius, after Bedriacum returned to Britain (69), sent to Pannonia (92). Nero gave the name *Martia Victrix.*

XV. *Apollinaris.* Formed by Augustus. Service in Pannonia (6–9 A.D.), with Corbulo in the East (63), in Judea with Vespasian and Titus, in Egypt and Pannonia, with Trajan in the East.

XVI. *Gallica.* Sent to the Danube by Augustus, in Germany after disaster of Varus, disbanded by Vespasian.

XVII. *Gallica.* Destroyed with Varus at Teutoburg Forest (9 A.D.).

XVIII. *Gallica.* The same as the above.

XIX. *Gallica.* The same as the above.

XX. *Valeria Victrix.* Formed in 27 B.C. by Augustus, quelled insurrection in Pannonia (6 A.D.), and received name *Valeria Victrix,* with Germanicus, in Britain (43), fought under Agricola.

VI. *Ferrata.* Formed by Augustus in Syria (5 A.D.). Service with Corbulo in Armenia (58 and 62), in Syria in time of Vespasian, with Trajan against the Parthians, after Hadrian in Judea.

X. *Fretensis.* Formed by Augustus in Syria (5 A.D.), with Corbulo in Armenia (62), in Egypt in time of Nero (65), in Judea with Vespasian and Hadrian.

I. *Germanica.* Formed hastily in 9 A.D. after destruction of Varus, sent into Germany, disbanded by Vespasian (71).

XXI. *Rapax.* Formed in 9 A.D. Service in Germany, fought for Vitellius at Bedriacum, in Illyria, in Germany against Civilis, in Moesia in 101.

XXII. *Deiotariana.* Formed 9 A.D. Quartered in Egypt, supported Ves-

pasian (69), in Judaea with Titus, annihilated in an ambuscade by the Parthians (162).

XXII. *Primigenia P(ia) F(idelis).* Formed in 43 A.D., sent to Moguntiacum, in Italy (69), favored Vitellius against Galba, sent to Illyria, to Pan-nonia, returned to Germany (91). Hadrian gave the name *Pia Fidelis.*

I. *Italica.* Formed by Nero in Italy, sent into Gaul, after Cremona sent to Illyria, then to Moesia.

XV. *Primigenia.* Formed probably in time of Claudius. Service in Pan-nonia, called to Italy by Nero (68), sent to Pannonia by Galba, dis-banded by Vespasian because of revolting to Civilis.

I *Adiutrix.* Formed by Nero for the fleet (68), enrolled as legion by Galba, sides with Otho, after Bedriacum sent to Spain by Vitellius, in Germany, in Moesia, 86–91, and in time of Trajan, in Pannonia.

VII. *Gemina F(elix).* Formed by Galba in Spain under name *Galbiana* or *Hispana* (68 A.D.), in Pannonia. Vespasian gave the name *Gemina F(elix),* in Spain.

II. *Adiutrix P(ia) F(idelis).* Enrolled under Vespasian from the fleet at Ravenna, on the Rhine with Mucianus, on the Danube (85), in Pannonia after 107. Vespasian gave the name *Pia Fidelis.*

IV. *Flavia F(elix).* Formed by Vespasian (71 A.D.), sent to Dalmatia, to Pannonia, in Moesia, in Dacia under Domitian and Trajan. Hadrian gave the name *Felix.*

XVI. *Flavia P(ia) F(idelis).* Formed by Vespasian (71 A.D.). Service in Cappadocia, against the Parthians. Trajan gave the name *Pia Fidelis.*

I. *Minervia P(ia) F(idelis).* Formed by Domitian (85 A.D.). Service in Lower Germany (91), in Moesia, in Germany (107), Trajan gave the name *Pia Fidelis.*

XXX. *Ulpia Victrix.* Formed in 101 by Trajan. Service in Germany, in Mesopotamia, under Constantius II.

II. *Traiana Fortis.* Formed in 105 A.D. by Trajan. Stationed at Alexan-dria, in Parthia (114), sent to Alexandria by Hadrian, where it received the name *Fortis* (137).

II. *Italica.* Formed by M. Aurelius before 170 A.D. In Noricum in time of Alex. Severus.

III. *Italica.* Formed by M. Aurelius before 170 A.D. In Rhaetia in time of Alex. Severus.

I. *Parthica.* Formed by Septimius Severus. Quartered in Mesopotamia, in Arabia, and at Palmyra.

II. *Parthica P(ia) F(idelis).* Formed by Septimius Severus. Quartered at Alba in Italy. Elagabalus gave name *Pia Fidelis.*

III. *Parthica.* Formed by Septimius Severus. Quartered in Mesopotamia

THE MEMBERS OF THE IMPERIAL FAMILY

The following list includes all the members of the Imperial Family, from Augustus to Constantine, whose names appear in inscriptions Those that were honored after death with the title DIVVS, DIVA are marked with *. Those whose memory was execrated, and whóse names are erased from the monuments, are designated by †. For names of the Emperors themselves see Chronological Table, p. 123.

*AVGVSTVS

1. OCTAVIA, sister of Aug.; wife (1) of M. Antonius, (2) of C. Marcellus.

2. ANTONIA (MINOR), daughter of M. Antonius and Octavia; wife of Drusus (16).

3. MARCELLA (MAIOR), daughter of C. Marcellus and Octavia.

4. MARCELLA (MINOR), daughter of C. Marcellus and Octavia.

5. SCRIBONIA, first wife of Aug.

6. IVLIA, daughter of Aug. and Scribonia; wife (1) of M. Marcellus, (2) of M. Agrippa, (3) of Tiberius (15).

7. M. VIPSANIVS AGRIPPA, second husband of Julia; son-in-law of Aug.

8. *LIVIA DRVSILLA (also called IVLIA AVGVSTA), wife (1) of Ti. Claudius Nero, (2) of Aug.

9. M. LIVIVS DRVSVS CLAVDIANVS, father of Livia.

10. ALFIDIA, mother of Livia.

11. C. CAESAR, son of M. Agrippa and Julia; grandson of Aug.

12. L. CAESAR, son of M. Agrippa and Julia; grandson of Aug.

13. AGRIPPINA I., daughter of M. Agrippa and Julia; wife cf Germanicus (18).

14. M. AGRIPPA (POSTVMVS) (also called PVPVS AGRIPPA and AGRIPPA IVLIVS), son of M. Agrippa and Iulia.

15. TIBERIVS, son of Ti. Claudius Nero and Livia; adopted son of Aug.; husband (1) of Vipsania Agrippina, (2) of Julia (6).

16. NERO CLAVDIVS DRVSVS, son of Ti. Claudius Nero and Livia; husband of Antonia Minor (2).

17. DRVSVS IVLIVS, son of Tiberius and Vipsania Agrippina; husband of Livia, the sister of Germanicus and Claudius.

18. GERMANICVS CAESAR, son of Drusus (16) and Antonia Minor (2); husband of Agrippina (13).

19. *CLAVDIVS, son of Drusus (16) and Antonia Minor (2).

20. C. CAESAR, infant son of Germanicus (18) and Agrippina (13).

21. TI. CAESAR, infant son of Germanicus (18) and Agrippina (13).

22. — CAESAR, infant son of Germanicus (18) and Agrippina (13).

23. NERO CAESAR, son of Germanicus (18) and Agrippina (13).

24. IVNIA, daughter of Q. Caecilius Metellus Creticus Silanus; bride of Nero Caesar.

25. Drvsvs Caesar, son of Germanicus (18) and Agrippina (13).
26. †CALIGVLA, son of Germanicus (18) and Agrippina (13).
27. †Agrippina II., daughter of Germanicus (18) and Agrippina (13) ; fourth wife of Claudius.
28. *Ivlia Drvsilla, daughter of Germanicus (18) and Agrippina (13).
29. Ivlia Livilla, daughter of Germanicus (18) and Agrippina (13).
30. Medvllina, bride of Claudius.
31. Drvsvs, infant son of Claudius and Plautia Urgulanilla.
32. Antonia, daughter of Claudius and Aelia Petina.
33. †Valeria Messalina, third wife of Claudius.
34. Octavia, daughter of Claudius and Messalina; first wife of Nero.
35. Ti. Clavdivs Caesar Britannicvs, son of Claudius and Messalina.
36. †NERO, son of Cn. Domitius Ahenobarbus and Agrippina II. (27).
37. *Poppaea Sabina, second wife of Nero.
38. Cn. Domitivs Ahenobarbvs, husband of Agrippina II. (27); father of Nero.
39. *VESPASIANVS
40. Flavia Domitilla, wife of Vespasian.
41. *TITVS, son of Vespasian and Domitilla.
42. †DOMITIANVS, son of Vespasian and Domitilla.
43. *Flavia Domitilla II., daughter of Vespasian and Domitilla ; wife of Flavius Sabinus.

44. Flavia Domitilla III., daughter of Flavius Sabinus and Domitilla II. ; grandchild of Vesp.
45. *Ivlia Avgvsta, daughter of Titus.
46. Domitia Longina, daughter of Cn. Domitius Corbulo ; wife of Domitian.
47. Cn. Domitivs Corbvlo, father of Domitia Longina.
48. *NERVA
49. Sergia Plavtilla, daughter of Sergius Laenas ; mother of Nerva.
50. *TRAIANVS
51. *M. Vlpivs Traianvs, father of Trajan.
52. *Plotina, wife of Trajan.
53. *Marciana, sister of Trajan.
54. *Matidia (Maior), daughter of Marciana ; niece of Trajan.
55. *Vibia Sabina, daughter of L. Vibius and Matidia Maior; wife of Hadrian.
56. Matidia (Minor), daughter of L. Vibius and Matidia Maior.
57. *HADRIANVS
58. Domitia Pavlina, sister of Hadrian.
59. L. Aelivs Caesar, adopted son of Hadrian.
60. Ceionia Plavtia, daughter of Aelius Caesar.
61. *ANTONINVS PIVS
62. Arria Fadilla, mother of Antoninus Pius.
63. *Annia Galeria Favstina (Maior), sister of L. Aelius Caesar ; wife of Antoninus Pius.
64. M. Avrelivs Fvlvvs Antoninvs, infant son of Antoninus Pius and Faustina.

35. M. GALERIVS AVRELIVS ANTONI-
NVS, infant son of **Antoninus**
Pius and Faustina.

66. AVRELIA FADILLA, daughter of
Antoninus Pius and Faustina.

67. *ANNIA FAVSTINA (MINOR),daugh-
ter of Antoninus Pius and Faustina; wife of M. Aurelius.

68. *M. AVRELIVS

69. ANNIVS VERVS, father of M.
Aurelius.

70. DOMITIA LVCILLA, mother of
M. Aurelius.

71. T. AVRELIVS ANTONINVS, infant
son of M. Aurelius and Faustina Minor.

72. T. AELIVS AVRELIVS, infant son
of M. Aurelius and Faustina
Minor.

73. DOMITIA FAVSTINA, daughter
of M. Aurelius and Faustina
Minor.

74. M. ANNIVS VERVS, son of M.
Aurelius and Faustina Minor.

75. VIBIA AVRELIA SABINA, daughter of M. Aurelius and Faustina Minor.

76. *L. VERVS, son of Aelius Caesar
(59); adopted son of Antoni-
nus Pius.

77. ANNIA LVCILLA, daughter of M.
Aurelius and Faustina Minor;
wife of L. Verus.

78. *†COMMODVS, son of M. Aurelius and Faustina Minor.

79. BRVTTIA CRISPINA, wife of Com-
modus.

80. *PERTINAX
81. †CLODIVS ALBINVS
82. *SEPTIMIVS SEVERVS
83. PACCIA MARCIANA, first wife of
Septimius Severus.

84. *IVLIA DOMNA, second wife of
Septimius Severus; aunt of
Julia Soaemias (93).

85. *CARACALLA, son of Septimius Severus and Julia
Domna.

86. †GETA, son of Septimius Severus and Julia Domna.

87. †FVLVIA PLAVTILLA, daughter of
C. Fulvius Plautianus; wife
of Caracalla.

88. †C. FVLVIVS PLAVTIANVS, father
of Fulvia Plautilla.

89. †MACRINVS
90. †DIADVMENIANVS, son of
Macrinus.

91. †ELAGABALVS
92. SEX. VARIVS MARCELLVS, father
of Elagabalus.

93. †IVLIA SOAEMIAS BASSIANA,
mother of Elagabalus.

94. *†IVLIA MAESA, mother of Julia
Soaemias; sister of Julia
Domna (84).

95. IVLIA CORNELIA PAVLA, wife
of Elagabalus.

96. †SEVERVS ALEXANDER,
cousin of Elagabalus.

97. †IVLIA AVITA MAMMAEA, sister
of Julia Soaemias; mother of
Severus Alexander.

98. GNEIA SEIA HERENNIA SALLVS-
TIA BARBIA ORBIANA, wife of
Severus Alexander.

99. †MAXIMINVS
100. *CAECILIA PAVLINA, wife of
Maximinus.

101. †MAXIMVS, son of Maximinus
and Paulina.

102. *GORDIANVS I.
103. *GORDIANVS II., son of Gordian I.

148. **Flavivs Clavdivs Constan-**
tinvs (Ivnior), son of Con-
stantine the Great and Fausta.
149. †**Flavivs Ivlivs Constans**, son
of Constantine the Great and
Fausta.

150. **Flavivs Ivlivs Constantivs II.,**
son of Constantine the Great
and Fausta.
151. **Flavivs Delmativs,** nephew of
Constantine the Great.

Abbreviations (Notae, later Sigla).
It has already been seen from what has preceded that initial letters and various other abbreviations of words enter very largely into
the language of the inscriptions, and that consequently a familiarity
with the most common of these forms is essential to facility in
reading. The student is referred to the very complete table given
on p. 417 ff., which has been obtained from the *Cours d'Épigraphie
Latine* of Professor Réne Cagnat.

Certain general principles[1] will be found of advantage in the
interpretation of abbreviations.

1. Words written in abbreviated form consist either of the initial
letter (*si(n)g(u)la*) or of a continuous group of letters more or less
restricted in number. In the latter case the final letter of the
abbreviation is the first consonant of a syllable, but this is not an
exact rule. T = *Titus;* TIB = *Tiberius;* CLAVD, CLAV, CLA =
Claudia; QVIR, QVI, Q = *Quirina.*

2. If a word is composed of several members, the above rule
applies either to the word treated as a whole or to each of the component parts regarded as individual words. Thus *signifer* may be
abbreviated synthetically SIG or SIGN, or analytically SIGF for
signum and *fer*, so BENEFIC, BENEF, B, or again B · F = *beneficiarius,* DVMTAX or D · T = *dum taxat,* Q · Q · V = *quoquoversus,*
P · Q = *populusque.*

This in theory is the system of abbreviations up to the end of
the third century A.D.

When a disregard of these principles first made itself felt in the
formation of abbreviations cannot be exactly determined, but it is
probable that ignorance or a misunderstanding of the second rule,

---

[1] R. Mowat, *Sigles et Autres Abréviations* in *Bulletin Épigraphique,* IV., p. 127.

combined with a lack of knowledge of the component parts of words as determining the abbreviated forms, led to the violation of the principle of continuity of the letters, so that we find PD = *pedes*, MN = *minus*, PBL = *publicus*, LG = *legio*, VT = *vixit*, MM = *memoriae*, DPS = *depositus*, etc.

3. Again, we find in the inscriptions a peculiar form of abbreviation[1] occasioned by the repetition of the terminating consonant. This probably arose from the collocation of several *praenomina*, as in the designations of the patrons of *liberti*. This system appeared in Rome about the beginning of the Christian era, and was limited in the first century to the initial letters of *praenomina*. COSS for *consules* appears for the first time in two Christian inscriptions of the year 107 and 111.

a) This form indicates two, three or four individuals, the exact number being defined by the number of repeated letters. AVGG = *duo Augusti*, CCC = *Gaii tres*, DDDD · NNNN = *domini nostri quattuor*, VI · VIR · AVGG = *seviri Augustales duo*, FLL · P · P = *flamines perpetuo duo*.

b) The doubling of the last letter, however, may denote simply the plural number. PROCC = *procuratores*, PONTIFF = *pontifices*, CAESS = *Caesares*, HERR = *heredes*.

In some instances other letters have been doubled, and the following forms are the result:

NNOBB = *nobilissimi duo*, AAVVRR = *Aurelii*, EEQQRR = *equites Romani*.

It is necessary to mention here also certain special signs which are used to mark abbreviations and to distinguish them from other letters in the inscriptions.[2]

1) A line of differentiation is placed over the letter or group of letters[3]; *e.g.* AVG = *Augustus*, D · N = *dominus noster*, N = *natione*, QQ = *quinquennalis*, V · C = *vir clarissimus*, COS = *consul*.

Sometimes the line crosses the letter; *e.g.* Ꞃ=*beneficiarius*, Ꝺ=*dicit*, or *dies*, or *domo*, ꝳ = menses, Ꝋ = *obiit* or *obitus*, Ꞥ = *nummum*.

---

[1] C. Jullian, *Des Lettres Redoublées* in *Bulletin Épigraphique*, IV., p. 170.

[2] E. Hübner, *Exempla Scripturae Epigraphicae*, p. lxxii.

[3] This custom becomes prevalent from the beginning of the second century.

2) The bar may be replaced by an apex or circumflex, a custom common from the third century on; e.g. D́ · Ḿ = *diis manibus*, F́F́ = *felix fidelis*, Ī · Õ · M̃ = *Iovi Optimo Maximo*, AED̃ = *aedilis*, COH́ · PŔ = *cohors praetoria*.

3) Some letters serving as abbreviations are reversed; e.g. Ɔ = *Gaia*, standing for *mulier*, ꟼ = *puella*, Ɔ = *caput*(?), or *conductor*, or *contra*, or *corona*(?).

TABLE OF ABBREVIATIONS

A

A	absolvo, absolvito
A	accipiet
A	actum, actarius
A	aedilis
A	aeternus, aeterna
A	Africa, Afer
A	ala
A	anniculus ?
A	annona
A	annus, anno, **annum, annos,** annis
A	Antoninus
A	Aprilis
A	ara
A	armatura
A	as, assibus
A	augur ?
A	Augustus, Augusta
A	Aulus
A	Aurelius, Aurelia
A	auro
A·A	Aponus ? Augustus ?
A·A	Aquae Aponi
A·A	Auli duo
A·A·A·F·F	aere argento auro flando feriundo
AAAGGG	Augusti (tres)
A·A·C	agri accepti Cirtensium
AAGG	Augusti (duo)
AAVVGG	Augusti (duo)
A B	a balneis
A·B	amicus bonus
A BA	a balneis
AB AEG	ab aegris
A BAL	a balneis
A BIB	a bibliotheca
AB EPIST	ab epistulis
A·B·F·S·S·S	amico bene (merenti) fecit sepulcrum supra scriptum
AB INST, INSTRVM	ab instrumentis
A·B·M	amico bene merenti, amicis bene merentibus

ABN, ABNEP	abnepos
AB VIN	ab vineis
A BYB	a bibliotheca, bibliothecis
A·C	absolvo condemno
AC	actarius
A·C	aere collato
A·C	armorum custos
A CAD	a caducis
ACC	accipiet, accepit, acceperunt, accipiendus etc.
A‾CENS	a censibus
A COGNIT	a cognitionibus
A COM, COMM, COMMENT	a commentariis
A COM·COS	a commentariis consularis
A COMMENT· CVST	a commentariis custodiarum
A CORIN	(procurator) a Corinthiis
A C·PR	a commentariis praefecti
ACT	actarius, actor, actus, **actum**
ACT·AMB	actu ambitu
ACT·LEG	actarius legionis
ACT·PVB, PVBL	actor publicus
A CVBIC	a cubiculo
AD	Adiutrix (legio)
AD	adlectus
A·D	ante diem
A·D·A	agris dandis adsignandis
A·D·A·I	agris dandis adsignandis iudicandis
AD AVGVST TEM·C·P	ad Augusti templum comprobatum pondus[1]
AD B	ad balneas
AD B·DAMNATORVM	ad bona damnatorum
ADF	adfinis
AD FAL·VE– GET[2]	(procurator) ad Falernas (vites) vegetandas
ADI	adiutor, Adiutrix (legio)
ADIABEN	Adiabenicus
ADI·P·F	adiutrix pia fidelis (legio)
ADIVT·PRAEF, PROC, TABVL	adiutor praefecti, procuratoris, tabulariorum

[1] Orelli, 784.   [2] *C. I. L.* II. 2029.

ADI·VI·P·	Adiutrix sextum pia sextum fidelis
VI·F	(legio)
ADL	adlectus
ADL·AER, AERA	adlectus aerario
ADLEC	adlectus
ADLEC·IN·DEC,	adlectus in decurias, in quin-
IN·V·D, DEC	que decurias
ADN, ADNEP	adnepos
ADOP	adoptivus
AD·P·F	Adiutrix pia fidelis (legio)
ADQ	adquiescit
AD QS	ad quaestiones
A·D·S	ager divisus Sigensibus
ADSOR [1]	adsessor
ADVOC·PVB, PVBL	advocatus publicus
A·E	actum esse
AE	Aelius
AEC, AECVR,	Aecorna, Aecurna (dea)
AEQVOR	
AED	aedes
AED	aedilis
AED	aedituus
AED·CER	aedilis cerialis
AED·COL	aedilis coloniae
AED·CVR	aedilis curulis
AEDD	aediles (duo)
AEDD·QQ	aediles quinquennales
AED·EQ	aedilitas equestris
AED·ET·PR·SAC·	aedilis et praetor sacris Vol-
VOLK·FAC	cano faciundis
AED·HAB·IVR·	aedilis habens jurisdictionem
DIC·Q·PRO·	quaestoris pro praetore
PRAET	
AEDIC	aedicula
AED·I·D	aedilis jure dicundo
AEDIF	aedificavit
AEDIT	aedituus
AED·IVR·DIC	aedilis jure dicundo
AED·LVSTR	aedilis lustralis
AED·P	aedilicia potestate
AED·PL	aedilis plebi
AED·PL·CER	aedilis plebis cerialis
AED·PRO·Q	aedilis pro quaestore
AED·Q·P	aedilis quaestoriciae potestatis
AED·V·A·S·P·	aedilem viis aedibus ? sacris ?
P·V·B·D·R·	publicis ? procurandis ? virum
P·O·V·F	bonum dignum republica ora-
	mus ut faciatis
AED·POT	aedilicia potestate
AEG	Aegyptus
AEL	Aelius, Aelia
AEM	Aemilia (tribus et regio)
AEMI, AEMIL, AEMILI	Aemilia (tribus)
AE·PI·F·FI	aeterna pia felix fidelis
AER	aera
AER	aerarium

AER	aereus
AER	aera (= stipendia)
AER·COLL	aere collato
AER·MIL	aerarium militare
AER·S, SAT	aerarium Saturni
AEST	aestimatus
AET	aeternus, aeterna
AEV [2]	evocatus
AF, AFR	Africa
A FRVM	a frumento
A FRVM·CVB	a frumento cubiculariorum
AG	ager
AG	Agonalia
AGIT	agitator
AGO, AGON	Agonalia
AGONOTH	agonotheta
AGR	agraria
AGR·DAND·	agris dandis adtribuendis iudi-
ADTR·IVD	candis
A·G·T	augustus
AG·V·P·P	agens vices praefectorum praetorio
A·G·IV·C·P	arborum genera quattuor cetera
	privata
A·H·N·P	ad heredem non pertinet
A·I·A	agris iudicandis adsignandis
AID	aidilis
AID·CVR	aedilis curulis
AID·PL	aedilis plebis
AID·SEN·COP	aedilis senator cooptatus
A·IN·C	area in circuitu ?
A·L	actarius legati
A·L	(et si qui) alii liberti (erunt).
A·L·F	animo libens fecit
A·L	Augusti, Augustae libertus, liberta
A·L·XXXIII	area lata (pedes) xxxiii
ALAMANN	Alamannicus
ALB·VET	album veteranorum
A·L·F	animo libente fecit
A LIB	a libris
ALIM	alimenta
ALIMENT	alimentarius
ALLECT·ARK	allector arcae
ALLEC·IN V	allectus in quinque decurias
DECVR	
ALP	Alpini (cohors)
A·L·P	animo libens posuit
ALT	altus
ALV·TIB·ET·RIP·	(curator) alvei Tiberis et ri-
ET·CLOAC·VRB	parum et cloacarum urbis
AM·B·M	amico bene merenti
A·M·C	amicis memoriae causa
A MIL	a militiis
AMP	amphora
AN	annus, anno, annum, annorum,
	annis, annos
AN	Aniensis (tribus)

[1] *C. I. L.* VIII. 2777.

[2] *C. I. L.* VIII. 4197.

AN	Annius
AN·D	ante diem
ANI, ANIE, ANIEN, Aniensis (tribus)	
ANIENS, ANIES	
ANN	Aniensis (tribus)
ANN	annona
ANNI	Aniensis (tribus)
ANN·FR	annona frumentaria
ANN·V·R	annona urbis Romae
AN·P	anno provinciae
ANT	Antonius
ANTESIGN	antesignanus
AN·XV·PR	annorum quindecim progressus
H·O·C·S	hostem occidit civem servavit
A·O	amico optimo
A·O·F·C	amico optimo faciundum curavit
A·P	aedilicia potestate
A·P	animo pio ?
A·P	anno provinciae
AP	Apollinaris (legio)
AP	Apollo
A P	(tribunus militum) a populo
AP	Appius
AP	Aprilis
A·P	arca publica
A·P	argenti pondo
A·P·C	ager publicus Cirtensium
A·PL·M·IVG	agri plus minus iugera
APOL, APOLLIN	Apollinaris (legio)
A POP	(tribunus militum) a populo
APP	appellationes
APP	Appius
A·P·R	aerarium populi Romani
APR	Aprilis
A·P·R·C	anno post Romam conditam
A·PV	argento publico
AQ	aqua, aquarius
A Q	a quaestionibus
AQ·CO	aquarius cohortis
A Q·P, PR	a quaestionibus praefecti
AQ·STA	Aquae Statiellae
AQV	aquilifer
AQV, AQVA	aquarius
A Q·E·R·P·	(ei) ad quem ea res pertinet, perti-
PR·L	nebit recte licet
AQVIL	aquilifer
AQVIT	Aquitani (cohors)
A R	a rationibus
AR	arietes
AR	Arnensis (tribus)
AR	artifex
AR	Aruns
ARAB	Arabicus
A RAT, A RATION	a rationibus
ARB, ARBITR	arbitratu
ARC	area, arcarius
ARC	archimimus
ARC	architectus

ARCHIG	archigallus
ARCHIG	archigybernes
ARCHIT	architectus
ARC·MVST	archimista
ARG	argentarius
ARG	argenteus
ARG	argentum
ARG·P	argenti pondo
ARG·PVB	argento publico
ARG·P·V·	argenti p(ondo) V pecunia sua
P·S·P	posuit
ARK	arca, arcarius
ARM	armamentarium
ARM	armatura
ARM [1]	armatus or armiger (Mars)
ARM	Armenia
ARM	armilustrium
ARMATV	armatura
ARM	armorum (= armorum custos)
ARM·CVST	armorum custos
ARMEN, ARMENIAC	Armeniacus
ARMO	armorum (custos)
ARN, ARNE, ARNEN, Arnensis (tribus)	
ARNENS	
ARNI, ARNIEN, ARNN	Arniensis (tribus)
ARV	Arvalis
A·SA	ala Sabiniana
A S	a sacris
A S	a senatu
A S	a solo
ASC	ascia
ASC	Asclepiades
A S·F, F·C	a solo fecit, fecerunt, faciendum
	curavit, curaverunt
ASP	aspritudines
AST	(h)astatus (prior, posterior)
AST	Astures (ala)
A SVBSCR	a subscriptionibus
ATR, ATRI	atriensis, atriarius
AT	Atta or Attus
A·V	aediles vici
A·V	argenti unciae
A·V	ave or ave vale
AV	Augustus, Augusta
AV	Aulus
AV	Aurelius
AVCT	auctoritate
A·V·F·O·D·	aediles vici Furfensis opus de vici
V·S·C	scitu curarunt [2]
AVG	augur
AVG	augustalis
AVG	Augustus, Augusta
AVGG	Augusti (duo)

[1] Brambach. 996.

[2] Wilmanns (*Exempla*, p. 712) thinks this is corrupted from the earlier *M(agistri) v(ici) f(aciundum) c(urarunt) d(e) v(ici) sc(itu).*

AVGGG   Augusti (tres)
AVGG NN Augusti nostri (duo)
AVG·L   Augusti libertus
AVG·MAX· augur maximus augurum (Cirta
AVG   and Cuicul)
AVG·N   Augustus noster
AVG·P·AN Augusta Pannoniorum Antonini-
         ana (ala)
AVG·P·F Augusta pia fidelis (legio)
AVG·P·F·CO Augusta pia fidelis Commoda
AVG·PP   augustalis perpetuus
AVG·PVB· augur publicus populi romani Qui-
P·R·Q   ritium
AVGVS   Augustus (mensis)
AVGVST   augustalis, augustalitas
AVGVST   Augustalis (sodalis) Claudialis
CLAVDIAL
AVGVST·PERP augustalis perpetuus
A·V·L   agens vices legati
AVN¹   avunculus
A·V·P   agens vices praesidis
AVR   aurariae
AVR   Aurelius
AVR   Auriana (ala)
AVRR   Aurelii (duo)
AVTHEM   authemerum
AYG²   Aegyptus

B

B   Badius
B   beneficiarius
B   Belinus
B³   beteranus = veteranus
B   bixit = vixit
B   bonus, a
B   bos
B   brachium (secundum, tertium)
         etc.⁴
₿   beneficiarius
BAD   badius
BAL   balneator
B·A·S ; B·AVG·S Bacaci Augusto sacrum
BASIL, BASSIL basilica
BB   beneficiarii
B·B   bonis bene
B·B·ET·MAL·B bonis bene et malis bene
BB·FF   beneficiarii
B·B·M·B bonis bene, malis bene
B·B·M·M bonis bene, malis male
BB·MM   bene merenti
BB·VV   boni viri
BB·VV·QQ boni viri quinquennales
₿₿   beneficiarii
B·COS, CONS beneficiarius consularis

B·D   Bona dea
B·D·M   bene de (se) merenti ?
B·D·S·M bene de se merenti
BE   beneficiarius
BE·DE·S·M bene de se merenti
BEL   Belgae (cohors)
BE·ME   benemerenti
B·E·M·M·FECI bene merenti memoriam fecit
BENE·D·S·M bene de se merenti
BENEF   beneficium
BENEM   benemerenti
BENIF   benificiarius = beneficiarius
BE·ME·DE bene merenti de (se)
BE·ME·DE·S bene merenti de se
BE·ME·FEC bene merenti fecit
BENEFIC, BENIF⁵ beneficiarius
BEN·M   benemerenti
BEN·MER bene merenti
BEN·M·M·F bene merenti memoriam fecit
BE·TR   beneficiarius tribuni
B·F, BF beneficiarius, beneficiatus
B·F   Bona Fortuna
B·F   bonum factum ?
B·F   bos femina
₿F, ₿F   beneficiarius
B·F·A·IVNCT boves feminae auro junctae
BF·COS   beneficiarius consularis
BF·LEG·LEG beneficiarius legati legionis
BF·SEXM beneficiarius (tribuni) semestris
BIB   bibes
BIP   bipedalis
BIS   bisellarius
BIS F   bis fusum (vinum)
BIS·VI·AVG bisellarius sevir Augustalis
BIX·PRI bixellarius (= vexillarius) princi-
         palis
B·K·M   beteranus classis Misenensis
B·M   bene merenti
B·M   bona mens
B·M   bonae memoriae, or bene memo-
         rius
B·M   bos mas
B·M·D   bene merenti de (se)
B·M·D·S bene merenti de se
B·M·D·S·F bene merenti de se fecerunt
B·M·F   bene merenti fecit
B·M·F   bonae memoriae femina
B·M·F·C bene merenti faciundum curavit
         or curaverunt
B·M·F·D·S bene merenti fecerunt de suo
B·M·FEC bene merenti fecit
B·M·FF   bene merenti fecerunt
B·M·M·P bene merenti memoriam posuit
B·M·P   bene merenti posuit
B·M·P   bonae memoriae puella
B·M·P·C bene merenti ponendum curavit

---

¹ *Ephem. Ep.* III. 158.   ² *C. I. L.* III. 35.
⁴ *C. I. L.* X. 749.   ⁴ See page 334.   ⁵ *C. I. L.* III. 1956.

B·M·R	bonae memoriae religiosa	
B·M·S	bonae memoriae sacrum	
B·M·V	bonae memoriae vir	
BN	bene	
B·N·M	bene merenti	
B·N·M	bonae memoriae	
B·OPIF	bona opifera	
B·P	bonus puer (deus)	
B·PR	beneficiarius praefecti	
B·PR·PR	beneficiarius praefectorum praetorio	
B·Q	bene quiescat *or* quiescant	
BR	Breuci (cohors), Britones (cohors)	
BR	Britannia	
BRAC	Bracaraugustani (cohors)	
BRITO	Britones (numerus)	
BRIT	Bruttium	
BRITT	Britones (numerus)	
B·R·N	bono rei publicae natus	
B·R·P·N	bono rei publicae natus	
B·S	bonus suis ?	
B·S, SEC	brachium secundum	
B·SPR	beneficiarius subpraefecti	
B·TR	beneficiarius tribuni	
B·V	bene vale	
BV, BVC, BVCC BVCIN	buccinator	
BVL	buleuta	
BV·SIG	bucranium signavit	
B·VIX	bene vixit	
BV SV	buccinator supra (numerum)	
B·V·V	balnea, vina, Venus	

C

C	cacus, capsarius
C	Caesar
C	Gaius
C	Kalendae
C	candidatus
C	castrum, castra
C	cedit
C, C¹	centurio
C	censuere
C	cicatrices
C	cineres
C	circiter
C	circus, circenses (ludi)
C	citra
C	civis, civitas
C	claritas
C	classiarius
C	Claudius, Claudia (tribus)
(QVN) C· (VINSIN)² (cum) co (vixi)	
C	codicillarius
C	cohors
C	colonia, colonus

Ↄ	comitialis (dies)
Ↄ	communis (hora)
Ↄ	compos (voti)
Ↄ	condemno, condemnato
Ↄ	condidit
Ↄ	congius
Ↄ	coniux (*m.* or *f.*)
Ↄ	consule, consulibus
Ↄ	constans (legio)
Ↄ	crocodes
Ↄ	cuneus
Ↄ	curator, curavit *or* curaverunt, curante *or* curantibus
Ↄ	curia
Ↄ	caput ?
Ↄ	centurio
Ↄ, 7, Ꝼ	Gaia = femina
Ↄ	conductor
7	contra (legem, retiarius, etc.)
Ↄ, 7	contrascriptor
7	conventus
Ↄ	coronarum in inscriptions of gladiators
CA	candidatus
CA	carcerarius
CA	carissimo
C·A	curam agens *or* curam egit
C·A	custos armorum
C·A·A·A	colonia Aelia Augusta Aeclanum
C·A·AQ	colonia Aurelia Aquensium
C·A·D·A·I	colonis agrorum dandorum adsignandorum jus
CAEL, CAELT	Caelestis (dea)
CAES	Caesar
CAES	caesura
CAESARIBB	Caesaribus (duobus)
CAES·N	Caesar noster
C·AGENT	curam agente
CAL	Calabria
CAL	caligo
CALAB	Calabria
CALC	calciator
CAM	Camilia (tribus)
CAMD	campidoctor
CAMIL	Camilia (tribus)
CAMP	Campania
CAMP	campestris (cohors)
CAMPED³	campidoctor
CAN	canabae, canabenses
CAN	Canatheni (cohors)
C·A·N	colonia Augusta Nemausus
CAND, CANDID	candidatus
CANN	Canninefates (ala)
CAP, CAPIT	capitalis
C·AQ	civis Aquensis
CAR	carcerarius

CAR	Carmentalia
CAR	Carpicus
CAR·M	Carpicus maximus
CARC	carcerarius
CAS	castra, castris (*oriundus*)
CATER	Caterenses = Cattherenses (numerus)
CATTHR	Cattharenses (numerus)
C·B	colonia Beneventana
C·B	compos boti?
C·B	coniux bona
C·BEL	civis Bellovacus
C·B·F	coniugi bonae fecit
C·B·M	conjugi bene merenti
C·B·M·F	conjugi bene merenti fecit
C·B·M·P	coniugi bene merenti posuit
CC	Caesares (duo)
CC	Gaii duo
C·C	censuerunt cuncti
C·C	certa constans (legio)
C C	cives C...
C·C	collegium centonariorum
C·C	colonia Claudia
C·C	coloni coloniae
C·C	constans Commoda
C·C	(agens) curam carceris
ꓛꓛ, Ɛ, ꝛ	Gaiae (= feminae) duae
CCA	Caesaribus (duobus)
C·C·A	colonia Caesaraugusta
C·C·A·A·A	coloni coloniae Augusta Alexandrianae Abellinatium
C·C·C	coire convocari cogi
C·C·C	colonia Copia Claudia
C·C·C	tres Gaii
C·C·C	cum consilio collocutus
ꓛꓛꓛ	Gaiae (= feminae) tres
C·C·C·AVG·LVG	colonia Claudia Copia Augusta Lugudunum
C·C·C·D	cum consilio collocutus dixit
C·C·C·IVL	coloni coloniae Claritatis Iuliae
C·CENT	collegium centonariorum
C·C·I·K	coloni coloniae Iuliae Karthaginis
C·C·I·V·C·S·N	coloni coloniae Iuliae Veneriae Cirtae Siccae nostrae
C·C·N	coloni Castri Novani
CC·NN	Caesares nostri
C·C·R	curator civium Romanorum
C·C·R·CON·HE	curator civium Romanorum conventus He[lvetici]
CC·SS	consulibus
CC·VV, C·C·V·V	clarissimi viri
ꓛꓛ EXSERC	centuriones (duo) exercitatores
C·D	compos dat
C·D	consulto decurionum
C·D·D	creatus decreto decurionum
C·E	curam egit
C·E·B·Q	cineres eius bene quiescant
CEL	cella

CEN	censor
CEN	centurio
CENS	censitor
CENS	censor, censores
CENS	censuit, censuerunt
CENS·ACC	(legatus Augusti) censibus accipiendis
CENT	centenarius
CENT	centonarii
CENT	centurio
CENTO	centonarii
C·E·Q	cineres ei quiescant *or* curam egit, Quintus
CER	Cerealia
CES	censor, censores
C·F	clarissima femina
C·F	clarissimus filius
C·F	coniux fecit
C·F·C	censores faciundum curarunt
C·F·C·C	collegium fabrum centonariorum Comensium
C·F·C	coniux faciendum curavit
C·F·F	carissimae filiae fecit
C·F·N	conductor ferrariarum Noricarum
ꓸFR	centurio frumentariorum
C·G	civis gratissimus?
C·G·P·F	cohortes germanicae piae fideles
CH	c(o)hors
CHELID	chelidonium
CHO, CHOR	c(o)hors
C·I	clarissimus iuvenis
C·I	colonia Iulia
C·I·A·A	colonia Iulia Augusta Apollinaris
C·I·C	colonia Iulia Carcaso
CIC, CICA	cicatrices
CICATRI·V	cicatrices veteres
C·I·F·S	colonia Iulia Felix Sinope
C·I·K	colonia Iulia Karthago
C·I·P·C·N·M	colonia Iulia Paterna Claudia Narbo Martius
C·I·P·A	colonia Iulia Paterna Arelate
CIRT	Cirtenses (cohors)
C·I·S	colonia Iulia secundanorum
CIV	civis, civitas, civitate (*oriundus*)
CIV·AQV	civis Aquensis
CIVI·SVMA	civitate Sumalocenna
CIVIT	civitas
C·IVL·N	colonia Iulia Numidica (Simitthus)
C·K	coniux karissima
C·K·F	coniugi karissimae fecit
C·L	Gaii libertus, liberta
C·L	cives Latini?
CL	clarissimus, claritas
CL	classis
CL	Claudius, Claudia, Claudialis
CL	Clustumina (tribus)
C·L	colonia Lambaesitana
C·L	conliberti?

ƆꞏL	mulieris libertus, liberta
LꞋƆ	mulieris liberta
CLA	Claudia (tribus)
CLAꞏBRI	classis Britannica
CLꞏALIS	Claudialis ?
CLA	claritas
CLAR	clarissimus, clarissima
CLARꞏET	clarissima et inlustris femina
INLꞏFEM	
CLARI	claritas
CLASꞏBRIT	classis Britannica ·
CLASꞏPR	classis praetoria
CLASS	classicus
CLAV, CLAVD	Claudia (tribus)
CLAVD	Claudialis (flamen)
CLꞏBR, CLꞏBRIT	classis Britannica
CLꞏGꞏPꞏF	classis Germanica pia fidelis
CLꞏPR	classis praetoria
CLꞏPRꞏM, MIS	classis praetoria Misenensis
CLꞏPRꞏRAV,	classis praetoria Ravennas
RAVEN	
CLꞏV	clarissimus vir
CLV, CLVS, CLVST	Clustumina (tribus)
CꞏM	civitas Mattiacorum
CꞏM	collegium or corpus mensorum
CꞏMꞏF	clarissimae memoriae femina
CꞏMꞏP; CꞏMꞏV	clarissimae memoriae puer, vir
CꞏN	Caesar noster
CN	Gnaeus
CꞏC	civitas or colonia Nemausensium
CN	consulatus
CNAT	natus
CNS	consulatus
CNTA	cognata ?
CO	codicillarius
CO	cohors
CO	coniux
CꞏO	coniugi optimo
CO	Coventina (dea)
COꞏCA	coniugi carissimo
COD	codicillarius
CODꞏTR	codicillarius tribuni
COER	coeravit = curavit
COGNꞏSACR	cognitiones sacrae
COH	cohors
COHERR	coheredes
COHH	cohortes
COHꞏIꞏCꞏR	cohors I civium Romanorum
COHꞏEQꞏ∞	cohors equitata miliaria
COHꞏIꞏFꞏPED	cohors I Flavia peditata
COHꞏIꞏFL	coh. I Flavia miliaria equitata
∞EQꞏSAG	sagittariorum
COHꞏIꞏPꞏC	cohors I pia constans
COH· .. PR	cohors praetoria
COH· .. VIG	cohors vigilum
COHꞏIꞏVLP	cohors I Ulpia...Antoniniana
.. ANT	
COHꞏVRB	cohors urbana

COINQ	coinquendi
COIR	coirarunt = curarunt
COL	collegium, collega
COL	Collina (tribus)
COL	colonia, coloni, colonicus ?
COL	columbarium
COLꞏBEN	colonia Beneventum
COLꞏCENT	collegium centonariorum
COLꞏCOL	coloni coloniae
COLꞏCONC·	colonia Concordia Ulpia (Hadrume-
VLP	tum)
COLꞏFAB	collegium fabrum
COLꞏFꞏIꞏA·	colonia Faventia Iulia Augusta
PꞏBARC	Pia (Barcino)
COLꞏFLꞏAVG	colonia Flavia Augusta
COLꞏHORR	coloniae horrearius
COLꞏIVLꞏG	colonia Iulia Gemina
COLꞏIꞏVꞏT	colonia Iulia Victrix Triumphalis
COLꞏKAL	collocatum Kalendis...
COLL	collapsum
COLL	collegium
COLL	coloniae
COLLIB	collibertus
COLꞏLIB	coloniae libertus
COLLꞏAER	collegium aerariorum
COLLꞏCENT	collegium centonariorum
COLLꞏDENDR	collegium dendrophorum
COLLꞏFAB, FABR	collegium fabrum
COLLꞏFAB·	collegium fabrum et centonario-
ETꞏCENT	rum
COLLIN	Collina (tribus)
COLꞏL, LIB	coloniae libertus, liberta
COLLꞏSꞏS·	collegium suprascriptum
COLONꞏG·	colonia Gallieniana (?) Augusta Fe-
AꞏFꞏMED	lix Mediolanum
COLꞏSARNꞏMIL	colonia Sarniensis Milev
COLꞏSEP	colonia Septimia
COLꞏSER	coloniae servus
COLꞏVAL	colonia Valentia
COLꞏVEN	colonia Veneria
COLꞏVENꞏCOR	colonia Veneria Cornelia
COLꞏVLP	colonia Ulpia
COM	Commageni (cohors)
COM	comes
COM	commanipularis
COM	commentariensis
COM	commune
CꞏOꞏM	cum omnibus meis
COMꞏAVG	comes Augusti
COMꞏL	commentariorum loco
COMM, COM-	commentaria, commentariensis
MEN	
COMMIL	commilito
COMꞏSꞏBꞏM	commilitoni suo bene merenti
COMꞏSꞏC	comes sacri consistorii
COMTAR	commutare
CON	coniux
CON	constat

CON	consul
CON	contubernalis
CON·B·M	coniugi bene merenti
CON·CELL	contubernalis cellarius
COND	conductor
CON·FER· N·P·D	conductor ferrariarum Norici, Pannoniae, Daciae ?
COND·P·P	conductor publici portorii
COND·P·P·ILL– YRIC·ET R·T	conductor publici portorii Ill- yrici et ripae Thraciae
CONDVC	conductor
COND·IIII· P·AFR	conductor quatuor publicorum Af- ricae
CON·FER· N·P·D	conductor ferrariarum Noricarum partis ? dimidiae ?
CONG	coniugi
CON·KAR	coniugi carissimo
CONL	conlatus
CONL	conlegium
CON·M·F	coniugi merenti or memoriam fecit
CONNSS	consulibus
CON·R·F·C	coniugi rarissimo faciundum cura- vit
CONS	consensu
CONS	conservus
CONS	consistens
CONS	Consualia
CONS	consul, consulibus, consularis, con- sulatus
CONS·MEM·V	consularis memoriae vir
CONS·ORD	consul ordinarius
CONS·P	consularis provinciae
CONS·P·S	consularis provinciae Siciliae
CONSS	consules
CONS·S·S	consulibus supra scriptis
CONT	contarii (ala)
CONVEC	convectio
CONV	convenerunt
COOPT	cooptatus
CO·P	coniugi pientissimae
COR	cohors
COR	Cornelia (tribus)
COR	cornicen, cornicularius
COR	corpus, corporati
COR	curavit
COR	corona
CO·RA·FE	coniugi rarissimo fecit
COR·ANAL	corona analempsiaca
COR·AVR	corona aurea
COR·CLASS	corona classica
COR·FAB	corpus fabrum
COR·MVR	corona muralis
CORN, CORNIC	cornicen, cornicularius
CORP·CVST	corporis custos
CORPOR	corporati, corporis
CORPOR·C	corporatus Caesariensis
CORP·N·RHO	corpus nautarum Rhodanicorum

COR·PR	cornicularius praefecti
CORR	corrector
COR·S·PR	cornicularius subpraefecti
COR·T, TRIB	cornicularius tribuni
COR·VALL	corona vallaris
COS	consul, consules, consularis
COS·A·A·S· E·V	consules alter ambove si eis vide- retur
COS·AD LEG	consistentes ad legionem
COS·AMPL	consul amplissimus
COSE	consensu
COSOB·CVR·EGI	consobrinus curam egit
COS·ORD	consul ordinarius
COSS	consules
CO·TR	codicillarius tribuni
COVET	Coventina (dea)
CO·VI·CE·P	cohors sexta, centuria prima
C·P·C	cacus praefecti cohortium
C·P	Castor (et) Pollux
C·P	castra praetoria
C·P	censoria potestate
C·P	clarissimus puer
C·P, C·Q	clarissima puella
C·P	comprobatum pondus
C·P	coniugi pientissimae or posuit
C·P	cui praeest
C·P·C	cacus praefecti cohortium
C·P·EST	cui praeest
C·P·F	Claudia pia fidelis (legio)
C·P·L	civitas Pictonum Limonum
C·P·M	classis praetoria Misenensis
C·P·M·P	coniugi pientissimae memoriam posuit
C·P·P	conductor publici portorii
C·P·Q·K	clarissimus puer quaestor candi- datus
C·Q	cum quo or cum qua (vixit)
C·Q·V	cum quo or qua vixit
C·Q·V·A	cum quo or qua vixit annis
C·R	civis Romanus ; cives Romani ; civitas Romana
CREM	cremavit
CRET·ET C	Creta et Cyrenae
7 RET	contraretiarius
CRIOB	criobolium
C·R·M	cives Romani Mogontiaci
C·R·P	curator rei publicae
CRV, CRVST	Clustumina (tribus)
CRVST, CRVSTVL	crustulum
CS	Caesar
C·S	carissimus sibi
C·S	carus or cara suis
C·S	coniugi sanctissimae
C·S	coniugi suae
C·S	(de) conscriptorum (?) sententia
CS	consularis
C·S	cum suis
O·S	contrascriptor

C·S·B·M	coniugi suae ? benemerenti
C·SC	genas scissas (on an oculist's stamp)
OSC or 7SC,	SCR contra scriptor
C·S·P·N·C	consularis sexfascalis provinciae Numidiae Constantinae
C·S·N	civitas saltus Nucerini
C·S·O	cum suis omnibus
C·T	civitas Tolosa
CT [1]	catabolensis
C·T, TR	codicillarius tribuni
C·TR, 'I RE	civitas Treverorum
O TRA	contra
C·V	civitas Ulpia
C·V	clarissimus vir
C·V	colonia Viennensis, coloni Viennenses
CV	cura, curator
CVB, CVBIC, CVBICV cubicularius	
C·V·I·B	colonia Victrix Iulia Baeterrae
CVI·PR	cui praeest
CVLT	cultores
C·V·M·P	cum ? uxore ? memoriam posuit
CVN	cuneus
CVNC [2]	concubina
CVN̄S [3]	consul
CVR	cura, curavit, curante or curantibus, curator
CVR	curia
CVR	curulis
C·V·R·A	coloni veteres ? Reienses Apollinares
CVRA	curavit
CVR·AER	curator aerarii
CVR·AG	curam agens
CVR·ALV·TIB curator alvei Tiberis	
CVR·ANN	curator annonae
CVRAT	curator
CVR·COL	curator coloniae
CVR·F·P	curator frumenti publici ?
CVR·IVV	curator iuventutis
CVR·KAL	curator kalendarii
CVR·MIN	curator Miniciae
CVR·P·P	curator pecuniae publicae
CVR·R·P	curator rei publicae
CVRR	curatores
CVR·SCO	curator scolae
CVR·VIAT	curator viarum
CVR· ✗·FL	curator denariis flandis
CVS·BASIL custos basilicae	
CVST	custos
CVST·TABVL custos tabularii	
C·V·T·P	colonia Ulpia Traiana Poetovio
CYMBAL	cymbalistria

[1] *C. I. L.* VIII. 2403.
[2] Orelli, 2463.
[3] *C. I. L.* XII. 2384 (year 491).

CYR, CYREN	Cyrenaica (legio, cohors)
CYR, CYRIN	Quirina (tribus)

D

D	Dalmatia ?
D	dat, donum
D	decurio
D	deus, dea
D	decem
D	December (mensis)
D	Decimus
D	decessit
D	decimanus
D	decretum
D	decurio, decuriones, decuria
D	dedit, dederunt, datum
D	defunctus
D	denarius
D	designatus
D	Diana
D	dies, die, diebus
D	dignus
D	dispensator
D	divus
D	dixit
D	doctor
D	dominus, domina
D	domo
D	donavit, donaverunt, donat, donant, donatus
D	duumvir
D	duplarius, duplicarius
D	dux
Ð	defunctus, dicit, dies, domo
DA	Daci (cohors)
D·A	defunctus annorum
D·A	discens aquiliferum
DAC	Dacicus
DAC·APVL	Dacia Apulensis
DAC·MALV	Dacia Malvensis
DAC·POROL	Dacia Porolissensis
D·ACC	de acceptore
DA·M	Dacicus maximus
DAMAS	Damasceni (cohors)
D·AQ	discens aquiliferum
D·AR	discens armaturam
D·A·R·ARCAR discens a rationibus arcarii	
DAT·COLL·S·S datum collegio supra scripto	
D·B·M	de (se) bene merenti ?
D·B·S	d(iis ?) b(onis) sacrum
D·C	decreto conscriptorum or decurionum consulto
D·C	decurio civitatis, or coloniae
DC	decessit
DC	decurio
D·C	decurionum consensu or decreto conscriptorum

D·C·D	de conscriptorum decreto
D·COL	de collegis
D·C·R·MOG	decurio civium Romanorum Mogontiaci
D·C·S	de conscriptorum sententia
D·C·S	de consilii sententia
D·C·S	de collegii sententia
D·C·S·C	de conscriptorum sententia curaverunt
DCSM	dulcissimae
D·COLL·S	de collegii sententia
D·C·S·T	decurio civitatis saltus Taunensis
D·D	damnas damnates
D·D	dare debebit, dare debeto
D·D	dea Dia
D·D	dea Diana
D·D	decreto decurionum
D·D	dedit dedicavit *or* donum (dono) dedit, *or* dedicavit (dedicatus, dedicante)
DD¹	defensor?
DD	devoti
D·D	dextra decimanum
D·D	dii deae
D·D	domini duo
D·D	domus divina
D·D·D	· datum decreto decurionum
D·D·D	deo donum dedit
D·D·D	dedit dedicavit?
D·D·D	domini tres
D·D·D	dono dedit dedicavit; *or* dedit dedicavit
D·D·D·ADL·ADLECT	decreto decurionum decurio adlectus
D·D·D·D	datum de decreto decurionum?
D·D·D·D	donum dat dicat dedicat
D·D·D·D·L·M	donum dat dicat dedicat libens merito
D·D·D·E·S	dare damnas damnates esto sunto
D·D·D·L	donum dat dedicat libens?
D·D·D·N	datus decreto decurionum Nemausensium
DDDNNN	domini nostri tres
DDD · NNN· FFFLLL	domini nostri Flavii (tres)
D·D·E	dare damnas esto
D:DEL·S	de delectorum sententia
D·D·H·C	decreto decurionum hic consacravit
D·D·I	dis deabus immortalibus?
D·D·L	donum dedit libens?
D·D·L·D·	dono dedit *or* dedit dedicavit
D·D	loco dato decreto decurionum
D·D·L·M	donum dedit libens merito
D·D·M·C·F	decreto decurionum municipii Celeiani facta

¹ *C. I. L.* X. 7017.

DD·MM	Diis Manibus
D·D·N·N, DD·NN	domini nostri (duo)
DD·NN·NOBB·	domini nostri (duo) nobilissimi
CAESS	Caesares
D·D·O	dis deabus omnibus
D·D·O	donum dato o?..
D·D·P	decurionum decreto publice
D·D·PEC·PVB	decreto decurionum pecunia publica
D·D·P·P	decreto decurionum pecunia publica
D·D·P·P·P	decreto decurionum pecunia publica posuerunt
D·D·Q	dedicavit que
D·D·S	de decurionum sententia
D·D·S·F·C	de decurionum sententia faciundum curavit, curaverunt
DDS	dedit *or* dederunt de suo
D·D·S·P	dedit de sua pecunia?
D·D·S·S	deus dominus sanctissimus Saturnus
D·D·V·L·L·M	dono dedit votum laetus libens merito
D·D·V·S·L··L·M	dono dato votum solvit libens laetus merito
DE	dea
DE	decem
DE	December (mensis)
D·E	decurio
DE	devotus
DEC	December
DEC	decemiugis
DEC	decessit
DEC	Decimus
DEC	decretum
DEC	decurio, decuriones, decurionatus; decuria, decurialis
DECC	decuriones (duo)
DEC·C·A	decurio coloniae Agrippinensis
DEC·COS·ET·PR	decuria consularis et praetoria
DEC·DEC	decurialis decuriae
DEC·DEC, DECR	decurionum decreto
DEC·N·M·M	decurio numeri militum M..
DE CONL·SENT	de conlegii sententia
DEC·POP·Q	decuriones populus que
DECR	decretum, decrevit
DECR·DEC	decreto decurionum
DE C·S	de consilii sententia
DECV	decurio
DEC·VIAT	decuria viatorum
DED	dedit *or* dedicavit, dedicatus
DED	deductus
DEDC	dedicatus
DE·D·D·L	Deanae? donum dat libens
DED·XX·P·	deducta vigesima populi Romani
R·D	dedit

DEF	defunctus
DEF·ANN	defunctus annorum (tot)
D·E·F·V·L	decuriones et familia villae Lucul- lanae ?
DEIOT	Deiotariana (legio)
DEL	delator
DELIC	deliciaris
DELM	Dalmatae (cohors)
DEND, DENDR	dendrophori
DENDROPHORR	dendrophori
DEP	depositus
DE PAG·SEN	de pagi sententia
DE PAG·SEN· FAC·COER	de pagi sententia faciundum coerarunt
DE PEQ·POB	de pequnia poblica
DE PVB	de publico
D·EQ	discens equitem
D·E·R	de ea re
D·E·R·I·C	de ea re ita censuere
D·E·R·Q·D·R·A	de ea re qua de re agetur
DES	designatus
DESCR	descriptum
DE·SEN·SENT	de senatus sententia
DESIG, DESIGN	designatus
DE S·P	de sua pecunia
DE S·S, DE S·SEN, DE SEN· SENT, DE SENA·SEN	de senatus sen- tentia
DEST	destinatus
DE SVA PEQ, DE SVA PECVN	de sua pecunia
DESVLT	desultores
DEV·N·M· Q·EIVS	devotus numini maiestatique eius
DE V·S, DE VI·S, DE VIC·S	de vici scito
DE V DEC	de quinque decuriis
D·F	dare facere
D·F	decima facta
D·F	de figlinis
D·F	defunctus
D·F	duplarius frumentarius ?
D·F	dulcissimae filiae
D·F·P	dare facere praestare
D·F·P·EFFE· RVNDVM CENS	(hunc) decuriones funere pub- lico efferundum censuerunt
DI	dimachaerus
DIA	diatheses
DIABSOR	diabsoricum
DIACHO	diacholes
DIAGLA	diaglaucen
DIALEP	dialepidos
DIAPSOR·OPO	diapsoricum opobalsamatum
DIAZMYR	diazmyrnes
DIC	dictator
DIC·N·M·Q· EIVS	dicatus numini maiestatique eius
DICT	dictator
DIE S	die solis

DIFF	diffusor
DIG	dignus
D·I·M	deus invictus, invictus ? Mithras
D·I·M	deus invictus Mithras
DIM	dimidia
D·I·M	dis inferis Manibus
DI·MA	Di(is) Manibus or D(iis) i(nferis) Manibus
DI·N	dierum numerus
D·INV·M	deus invictus Mithras
DIS	dispensator
DIS	dispunctor
DIS·I·MA	Diis inferis Manibus
DIS·M, MA, MAN, MANI	Diis Manibus
DIS·MAN·MEM	Diis Manibus memoriae
DISP	dispensator
DISP	dispunctor (particularly in Mauretania)
DISPEN, DISPES	dispensator
DISP·P·S	dispensator provinciae Sardiniae
DISP·RAT·COP·	dispensator rationis copiarum
EXPED·FEL· GERM	expeditionum felicium Ger- manicarum
DISP·REIP	dispunctor rei publicae
DISSIGN	dissignator
D·L	dedit libens
D·L·M	dedit lubens merito
D·L	deus Liber
D·L	die Lunae
D·M	dea magna or deum mater
D·M	deus Mithras
D·M	decurio municipii
D·M	devotae memoriae ?
D·M	Diis Manibus
D·M	divino mandatu
D·M	dolus malus
D·M·A·E· I·C	dolus malus abesto et ius civile or iurisconsultus
D·M·E	devotus maiestati eius
D·M·ET M	Diis Manibus et memoriae
D·M·I	dea magna Idaea
D·M·I	Dis Manibus inferis
D·M·ID	dea magna Idaea or (mater) deum magna Idaea
D·M·IN	Dis Manibus inferis
D·M·S	deo Mithrae sacrum
D·M·S	diis Manibus sacrum
D·M·V·F	diis Manibus vivus fecit
D·N	Dea Nehallenia
D·N	dominus noster
D·N·M·E	devotus numini maiestatique eius
D·N·M·Q	devotus numini maiestatique
D·N·M·Q·E	devotus numini maiestatique eius
D·N·P·E	devotus numini pietatique ? eius
D·O	dari oportet
DO	domino
DO	donum, donatus ?
DO·AF	domo Africa

DOC·EQ·AC P¹ doctor equitum ac peditum
DOL   doliaris
DOL   Dolichenus
D·O·M²   deo optimo maximo?
DOM·NOSTR   dominus noster
DON   donavit
DON·POS   donum posuit
D·P   de proprio
D·P   deus patrius
D·P   diis Parentibus
D·P   donum posuit
D·PAG·S   de pagi scitu or sententia
D·P·D   de proprio dedit
D·P·D·M³   Diti patri, Diis Manibus
D·P·E   devotus pietati eius
D·P·P   dii Penates publici
D·P·P   de pecunia publica
D·P·S   de pagi scitu or sententia
D·P·S   de pecunia sua, or de parcimonio
               suo, or de peculio suo, or de
               proprio suo
D·P·S·D   de pecunia sua dedit
D·P·S·D·D   de pecunia sua dono dedit or dedit
               dedicavit
D·P·S·D·L·   de pecunia sua dedit; loco dato
D·P   publice
D·P·S·F   de pecunia sua fecit
D·P·S·F·D   de pecunia sua factum (factam)
               dedit
D·P·S·P   de pecunia sua posuit
D·Q·F³   Decimi quondam? filia?
D·Q   decurio quaestor
D·Q·A   de qua agatur
D·Q·L·S·T·T·L dic qui legis : sit tibi terra levis
D·R·P   dignum republica
D·R·S   deae Romae sacrum
D·S   de suo
D·S   deus sanctus, dea sancta
D·S   deus Saturnus
D·S   deus Silvanus
D·S   disces signiferum
D·S   (Silvano) domestico sacrum
D·SANCT·SATVR dominus sanctus Saturnus
D·S·B·M   de se bene meritus
D·S·D   de sententia decurionum
D·S·D   de suo dedit (dat)
D·S·D·D   de suo donum dedit or dedicavit
D·S·EX·V·P de suo ex voto posuerunt
D·S·F   de suo fecit
D·S·F·C   de suo faciendum curavit
D·S·I·IMP   deus Sol invictus imperator
D·S·I·M   deus sol invictus Mithras
D·S·L·L·M   de suo laetus libens merito

¹ *C. I. L.* IX. 952.
² *C. I. L.* XII. 1069. Not a Christian inscription.
³ Orelli, 1470.

D·S·L·M   de suo libens merito
D·S·M   de se meritus
D·S·M   Diis sacrum Manibus
D·S·P   de sua pecunia or de suo posuit
D·S·P·C   de suo ponendum curavit
D·S·P·D   de sua pecunia dedit
D·S·P·D·D   de sua pecunia dono dedit
D·S·P·EX·   de sua pecunia ex decreto decuri-
D·D   onum
D·S·P·F   de sua pecunia fecit
D·S·P·F·C   de sua pecunia faciendum curavit
D·S·P·L·D·   de suo posuit loco dato decreto
D·D   decurionum
D·S·P·P   de sua pecunia posuit
D·S·P·R   de sua pecunia restituit
D·S·P·R·C   de sua pecunia reficiendum curavit
D·S·R   de suo restituit
D·S·S   de senatus sententia
D·S·S   de suo sibi?
D·S·S·C·F   de suo sibi coniugi filius?
D·S·S·F·C   de senatus sententia faciendum
               curavit
D·S·V   decreto senatus Vocontiorum
D·S·V·L   de suo vivus libens
D·T   dumtaxat
D·T   de thesauro
D·T·S   dii te servent
D·V   duovir, duumvir
D·V·V·A·S·   duumvir viis aedibus sacris pub-
P·P   licis procurandis? (from Pom-
               peii)
DVC   ducenarius
DVC·DVC   duce ducenario?
D·V·I·D   duum vir iure dicundo
D·V·L·M   dedit? or Dianae? votum? libens
               merito
DVM·T, TAX dum taxat
DVPL   duplarius, duplicarius
DVPLI, DVPLIC duplicarius
D·V·S   de vici scitu
D·V·S·F·C·   de vici scitu faciundum curarunt
I·Q·P   idemque probarunt
D·X·PRIM·   duplarius decem primus p...
P·P   p....
D·XX·P·R   deducta vigesima populi Romani

E

E   eius
E   (h)eres
E   est
E   evocatus
E   exsculpsit
E·A·CA   exactum ad Castoris
E·A·E   eques alae eiusdem
E·C   eius causa?
ECD   ecdicus
ED   (a)ediculam

EE·QQ   equites
E·E·Q·Q·R·R equites Romani
EE·VV   egregii viri
EE·VV, EE·MM·VV eminentissimi viri
EG·M·V   egregiae memoriae vir
E·H·L·IVS· ex hac lege ius potestasque esto
POT
E·H·L·N·R eius hace lege nihilum rogato
E·I   eius index
EID   eidus
EIQ   eique
EIS·Q·I·S·S eis quae infra scriptae sunt
E·L·P   e lege Papiria, Petronia
EM   emeritus
E·M   ex monitu
EM·B   emeritus beneficiarius
E·M·D·S·P·F e monitu de sua pecunia fecit [1]
E·M·V   egregiae memoriae vir
EM·V   eminentissimus vir
EN   endotercisus (dies)
E·O·B·Q   ei ossa bene quiescant
EP   Eppius
EPIP   epiphorae
EQ   eques, equestris, equitata
EQ   Equirria
EQ·CATAF   equites cataphractarii
EQ·C·R   equitata civium Romanorum (co-
           hors)
E·Q·D·D   eademque dedicavit
EQ·EX·N   eques ex numero
EQ·G   equitum gradus [2]
EQ·P   equo publico
EQ·P·EXOR equo publico exornatus
EQ·PVB, PVBL equo publico
EQQ   equites
EQ·R   eques Romanus
EQ·R·E·M· eques Romanus egregiae memoriae
V   vir
EQ·R·E·P, eques Romanus equo publico
EQ·PVBL
EQ·R·F   equitis Romani filius
EQ·S·(SING)·D·N eques singularis domini nostri
E·R   ea res
ER   (h)eres
E R·P   e re publica
EX I·P   ex imperio posuit
E R·P·V   e re publica videri
E·R·A   ea res agitur
E·R·C   (cum) ea res consuletur
E R·P   e re publica
ER·TESTAME (h)eredes testamento
E S·C·R·C e senatus consulto reficiendum
           curavit
E·S·F·S·F·L ei sine fraude sua facere liceto

[1] Orelli, 2467.
[2] From the theatre at Orange (*C. I. L.* XII.
1241).

ESQ, ESQVIL Esquilina (tribus)
E·S·R   exemplum sacri rescripti ?
ESS, ESSE essedarius
ESSE·LIB   essedarius liberatus
E·T   ex testamento
E·T·F   ex testamento fecit
E·V   egregius vir, *more rarely* eminen-
           tissimus vir
EV   evocatus
E·V·L·M·P ex voto libens merito posuit
EVOC, EVOK evocatus
EVOC·AVG   evocatus Augusti
E·V·S   ex voto suscepto
EX   exceptor
EXAC   exactor, exactus
EX A·C   ex aere conlato
EX·A(AD) CAS, CAST exactum ad Castoris
EX A·P   ex argento publico
EXAR   exarchus
EX ARG   ex argento
EX AVC, AVCT ex auctoritate
EXC   exceptor
EXC·PR, T exceptor praefecti, tribuni
EX C·C   ex conscriptorum consulto
EX CC   ex ducenario
EX CCC   ex trecenario
EX COM·DOM ex comite domesticorum
EX CONS   ex consensu *or* consulto
EX D   ex devotione
EX D·D   ex decreto decurionum
EX D·D·   ex decreto decurionum ex pecunia
EX P·P   publica
EX D·D·P· ex decreto decurionum pecunia
P   publica
EX DEC·C· ex decreto centum virorum pe-
PEC·SEV   cunia Severiana
EX DEC·DECRET ex decurionum decreto
EX D·ORD   ex decreto ordinis
EX D·P·A   ex decreto provinciae Africae
EXER·PAN·INF exercitus Pannoniae Inferioris
EXERC   exercitator
EXERC   exercitus
EX F·B   ex fide bona
EX FIG, FIGL ex figlinis
EX·G(GER)INF exercitus Germaniae Inferioris
EX H·L·EX· ex hac lege, exve decreto decuri-
VE·D·D   onum
EX H·L·N·R ex hace lege nihilum rogato
EX IMP·IPS ex imperio ipsius
EX IV, IVS ex iussu
EX IVS·IPSA ex iussu ipsarum
EX IVSS·E ex iussu eius
EX IV·V·S· ex iussu votum solvit libens merite
L·M
EX N   ex nomine
EXO   exodiarius
EX O   ex ovo
EX OF, OFF ex officina

EX PAGI·D ex pagi decreto
EX P·D   ex pagi decreto
EX PEQ·PVB ex pecunia public
EXPL   exemplum
EX P·L   ex pecunia legata
EXPLIC   explicarius
EX P·D   ex parte dimidia ?
EXPL·BAT   exploratores Batavi
EX P·P   ex pecunia publica
EX P·P·F·C ex pecunia publica faciundum
           curavit
EX PR   ex praediis
EX PR   exceptor praefecti
EX PR·C·C· ex praediis coloniae copiae Clau-
C·C   diae curatum ?
EXPVRG   expurgatio
EX R   ex ratione
EX R·P   ex responso posuit
EX R·VRB   ex ratione urbica
EX S·C   ex senatus consulto
EXSERC·   exercens artem cretariam
ART·CRET
EX S·P·F·C ex sua pecunia faciendum curavit
EXS TEST·F exs testamento fecit
EX S·VOTO ex suscepto voto *or* exs voto
EX·T, EXC·TR exceptor tribuni
EXT   exterus
EX T   ex testamento
EX T·F·I·C ex testamento fieri iussit, faciun-
           dum curavit
EX T·P   ex testamento posuit
EX TR   ex tributario
EX T·T·F· ex testamento titulum fieri iussit ;
I·H·F·C   heres faciundum curavit
EX V   ex voto
EX VIK   ex vicario
EX V·L·M   ex voto libens merito
EX V·L·S· ex voto libenter suscepto solvit
S·M   merito
EX VO (VOT) L·POS ex voto libens posuit
EX V·P   ex voto posuit
EX V·P·L· ex voto posuit libens laetus merito
L·M
EX V·S·L·A ex voto solvit libens animo
EX V DEC   ex quinque decuriis

F

F   fabri
F   faciunt, fecit, fecerunt, factus, fa-
           ciendum
F   Falerna (tribus)
F   fanum ?
F   fastus (dies)
F   feliciter
F   feriae
F   fida
F   fidelis (legio)

F   figlinae
F   filius, filia
F   fines
F   fiscus
F   fiunt
F   flamen
F   Flavius, Flavia (legio) Flaviensis
F   Fortuna
F   Fretensis (legio)
F   functus
F   fundus
E   filia, femina
FAB   Fabia (tribus)
FAB   fabrica
FAB   fabri, fabrum (praefectus)
FAB·COS,   PR (praefectus) fabrum consularis,
(PRAET)   praetorius
FABR·CENT fabri centonarii
FABR·TIG, TIGN fabri tignarii
FAC   faciebat
FAC·COER·EIDEMQ· faciundum coerarunt ei-
PROB   demque probarunt
FAC·CVR ; FACIV· faciundum curavit, cura-
CVR   runt
FAC·LOCAR·EIDEMQ· faciundum locarunt
PROB   eidemque probarunt
FACT   factio
FAL   Falerna (tribus)
FAL, FALA Falernae (vites)
FALC   Falcidia (lex)
FALE, FALL Falerna (tribus)
FAM   familia
FAM·GLAD   familia gladiatoria
F·A·PERP   flamen Augusti perpetuus
FARMAC·PVBLIC farmacopola publicus
FAS   fascia
FAVS   Faustianum (vinum)
F·B·F   filio bono fecerunt
F·B·M   filio, filiae bene merenti
F·C   faciendum curavit *or* curaverunt
FC   fecit *or* fecerunt
F·C   fisci curator
F·C   frumenti curator ?
F·C·A   Forum Claudii Augusti
FCC   faciundum curaverunt ?
F·C·EIDQ·PRO, faciundum curarunt eidemque
PROB   probarunt
F·C·I·P   faciendum curavit idem probavit
F·C·I·Q·P faciundum curarunt idemque pro-
           barunt
F·COIR   faciendum coiravit *or* coiraverunt
F·C·P   fulgur conditum publice
FCT   fecit
F·D   fecit dedicavit
F·D   filio dulcissimo *or* filiae dulcissimae
FD   fundus ?
F·D·EX·   (praefectus) frumenti dandi ex
S·C   senatus consulto

F·D·F	filiae dulcissimae fecerunt
FD·IVB	fide iubere
F·D·N	feliciter domino nostro ?
F·D·Q	fecit dedicavitque
F·D·S	fecerunt de suo
F·D·S·S·C	faciundum de senatus sententia curaverunt
FE	Februarius (mensis)
FE	fecit
FE	feliciter
FEB	Februarius
FE·B·B	feliciter bonis bene
FEBR	Februarius (mensis)
FEC	fecit, fecerunt
FECR	fecerunt
FEL	felix (legio)
FELIC	felicitas
FER	Feralia
FER LAT	feriae Latinae
FERR	ferrariae
FERR	Ferrata (legio)
FERT	Fertor
F·ET·D	fecit et dedicavit
F·ET·F	filii et filiae
F·EX S·C· Q·E·D	feriae ex senatus consulto quod eo die, etc.
FF	fecerunt or fecit ?
F·F	fecit feliciter ?
F·F	felix fidelis
F·F	fieri fecit ?
FF	filii
F·F	filius or (filia) fecit or filii fecerunt
F·F	fiscus frumentarius
F·F	Flavia felix firma fidelis (legic)
F·F	(viam) Flaviam fecit
F·F·B·M	filii fecerunt bene merenti
FF DD	fundi ?
FFLL	Flavii
FF·PP	flamen perpetuus
F·F·P·P·P	fidelis frater ? pro pietate posuit (??)
FI	filius
F·I	fieri iussit
FID	fidelis (legio)
FID	fidicen
FIG, FIGL	figulinae, figlinae
FIL·K·F	filius karissimus fecit or filio karissimo fecit
FIL·PAT	filius patroni ?
FIR·IVL· SECVND	(colonia) firma Iulia Secundanorum
FISC STAT· HEREDITATI	fiscus stationis hereditatium
F·IVS	fieri iussit
F·K	filio karissimo
F·K·F	filio karissimo fecit
FL	flamen, flaminica, flamonium
FL, FLA	Flavius, Flavia

FLAM	flamen, flaminica, flamonium
FLAM·AVG	flaminica Augustae
FLAM·CLAVD	flamen Claudialis
FLAM·DIALIS	Flamen Dialis
FLAM·MART	flamen Martialis
FLAM·PERP	flamen perpetuus
FLAM·P, PR	flamen provinciae
FLAM·QVIR	flamen Quirinalis
FLAM·ROM· ET AVG	flamen Romae et Augusti
FL·F	Flavia felix, firma, fidelis
FL·FEL	Flavia felix (legio)
FLL	flamines
F·LOC	faciundum locarunt
FL·P	flamen perpetuus
F·LIB·ET PEC	fiscus libertatis et peculiorum
F·L·P	funus, locum publice
FL·PP	flamen perpetuus or flamonium perpetuum
FL·SACR·PVB	flamen sacrorum publicorum
F·L·S·P· D·D	funus locum statuam — or sepulturae — publice decuriones decreverunt
F·M	filio merenti or filio mater
F·M·F	filio mater fecit
F·M·P	filius matri posuit
FO	Fortuna
FORD	Fordicidia
FORT	Fortenses
FORT·HORR	Fortuna horreorum
F P	? (See p. 367.)
F P	filio piissimo or filio posuit or posuerunt
F·P	filii posuerunt
F·P	filius pientissimus
F·P	flamen perpetuus
F·P	Fortuna Praenestina or Primigenia
F·P	frumentum publicum
F·P	funus publicum
F·P·A·D·X· TCXL K·C	frumentum publicum accipit d... X, t... CXL, k... C
F·P·C	filius ponendum curavit
F·P·D·D	Fortunae Primigeniae donum dant
F·P·D·M·P	filius patri dulcissimo matri piissimae or filius parentibus de (se) merentibus posuit
F·P·F	fili pii or patri fecerunt
F·P·F	filius patri fecit
F·P·M·F	filii pientissimi or patri merenti fecerunt
F·P·P	fecit pro pietate
F·P·P	filia patri piissimo or filio piissimo posuit
F·P·P	fratri pio or frater pius posuit
F·P·P·M	filii posuerunt patri merenti
F·P·PR	Fortuna Primigenia Praenestina
F·P·VET	fundus possessoris veteris

F·N	fuerunt *or* fiunt numero
F·Q	faciundum curavit
F·Q·E·E·V	fideque ei esse videbitur
FR	frater
FR	Fretensis (legio)
FR	frumentarius
FRA	frater
FRANC	Francicus
FR·ARV	frater Arvalis
FRAT·O·P	fratri optimo posuit
FRET	Fretensis (legio)
FR·D·	fronte dextra
FR·KA	fratres karissimi
FRONT	Frontoniana (ala)
FR·S	fronte sinistra
FRT	fronte *or* fratri
FRV	frumentarius, frumentum
FRV·EMV	(ad) frumentum emundum
FRVM	frumentarius, frumentum
FRVMENT	frumentarius
FRVMM	frumentarii
F·S	filii sui, filio suo
F·S	fecit sibi
F·S	femina sanctissima?
F·S	Fortunae sacrum
F·S·A	Flavia singularium Antoniniana (ala)
F·S·ET·S	fecit sibi et suis
F·S·ET·S·L·	fecit sibi et suis libertis libertatus
L·P·Q·E	posterisque eorum
F·S·S	fiunt supra scripti (ae, a)
F·V·L	familia villae Lucullanae
FVL·CON·P	fulgur conditum publice
FVLM·FVL	Fulminator Fulgurator
FVLM, FVLMI·C·C[1]	Fulminata certa constans (legio)
F·V·P	filiae vivus posuit
F·M·P·P	filii matri piae posuerunt

G

G	Gaius
G	Galeria (tribus)
G	Galli (cohors)
G	Gallica (legio)
G	Gallienus, Galliena
G	garum
G	Gemina (legio)
G	gener
G	Genius
G	gens (in Africa)
G	centuria [2]
GA	Galeria (tribus)
GAL	Galatia
GAL	Galeria (tribus)

GAL	Gallia, Gallica (legio)
GALER	Galeria (tribus)
GALL	Gallica (legio)
GAR·CAST	garum castum
G·C·D	Genius collegii dendrophororum
G·C·N	Genius Gaii nostri
G·D	Genius domus?
G·D·A·S	Genio D....Augusto sacrum
G·D·N	Genius Decimi nostri
G·D·N	Genius domini nostri
G·D·S	Germanicus Dacicus Sarmaticus
GE	Gemina (legio, cohors)
GE	genitura [3]
GEM	Gemina (legio)
GEM·P·F	Gemina pia fidelis
GEM·SEV	Gemina Severiana
GEN·ET·HON	Genius et Honor
GEN	genitrix
GEN	gentilis
GENAR·CICA	genarum cicatrices
GER, GERM,	Germania, Germanicus
GERMA	
GER, GERM·	Germania Inferior *or* Superior
INF *or* SVP	
GERM·SVP	Germania Superior
G·F	garum factum
G·F	Gemina felix (legio)
G·H·L	Genius huius loci
GIL	gilvus
G·L	Genius loci
GL	gladiatores
GLAD	gladiarius, gladiator, gladiatorius
GLA·PRIM·	gladiatores primi Campaniae
CAMP	
G·M	gens M....
G·M	Genius municipii
G·M·S	Genius municipii Satafensis
G·M·V	gemina Martia victrix (legio)
GN	Gnaeus
GN	gnatus
GOR	Gordianus
GOT, GOTHIC	Gothicus
G·P·AVG	Genius patriae Augustus
G·P·A·S	Genio pagi A...sacrum
G·P·F	Gemina pia fidelis (legio)
G·P·R	Genius populi Romani
G·P·R·F	Genio populi Romani feliciter
G·Q·N	Genius Quinti nostri
G·R	Gallica rapax (legio) [4]
G·R	Germani Raeti
GRAMM	grammaticus
GRAN	granatum *or* granianum (vinum) [5]
GRAT	gratuitus
GREG·VRB	gregis urbani
G·S	Germania Superior

---

[1] *Ephem. Ep.* V. p. 32, n. **61.**
[2] *C. I. L.* XIV. 2278.

[3] *C. I. L.* V. 5020.   [4] Orelli, **441.**
[5] *C. I. L.* IV. 2565.

G·T·N	Genius Titi nostri	H·C·E	hic conditus est *or* crematus? est
GYBER, GYBERN	gybernator	H·C·E·C·E·	hic conditus est; cineres ei bene
		B·Q	quiescant

H

		H·C·I·R	honore contentus impensam remisit
H	habens, habet	H·C·P	heres curavit ponendum?
H	hic, haec	H·C·S·P·P	honore contentus sua pecunia posuit
H	hastatus		
H	haustum	HD	Hadrianus
H	Hercules	H·D·S	heredes de suo
H	heres	H·D·S·P	heres de suo posuit
H	hic	HE	herus?
H	Hispana (legio), Hispani (cohors)	H·E	hic est
H	homo, homines	H·E·B·P	hic est bene positus?
H	horrearius	H·E·B·Q	hic est; bene quiescat
H	hora	HE·ES	heic est
H	Horatia (tribus)	H·E·F	heres ejus fecit *or* heredes ejus fecerunt
H·A	Herculaneus Augustalis		
HAB	habens	HEL	Helvetia
H·A·B·Q	hic a... bene quiescat	HELIOP	Heliopolitanus
HABT	habeant	HELV	helvetia
HAD	Adiutrix (legio)	HEM, HEMAES, HEMES	Hemeseni (cohors)
H·ADQ	hic adquiescit	H·E·N·H	heredem exterum non habebit
HADR	Hadrianus	H·E·N·S	heredem exterum non sequetur
H·A·H·N·S	haec ara heredem non sequetur	H·E·P	hic est positus
H·A·I·R	honore accepto impensam remisit	H·E·P·C	heres ejus ponendum curavit
H·AQ	hic adquiescit	HER	heres, hereditates
HAR	haruspex	HER	Herius
HARM[1]	armorum (custos)	HER·BEN·MER	heres bene merenti
HARN	Arnensis (tribus)	HERC·SAX, SAXAN	Hercules Saxanus
HAR·PRIM·	haruspex primus de sexaginta	HERC·V	Hercules Victor
DE·LX		HERED, HEREDIT	hereditates
H·P	hastatus prior	HERED·NON·SEQ	heredes non sequetur
H·A·S·A·H·	habet aedes Salutis Augustae hoc	HER·FIDVC	heres fiduciarius
L·L·Q·D·	loco leges quas Dianae Romae in	HER·PON·C	heredes ponendum curaverunt
R·IN·A	Aventino	HER·POS	heres posuit
H·A·S·F·C	heres a se faciundum curavit	HERR	heredes
HAS	hastatus	HERVC	Herucina (Venus)
HAS·P, PR,	PRI; hastatus prior, posterior	H·E·S	hic est situs, sita *or* sepultus, sepulta
PO, POST			
HAST	hastatus	HE·S·EST·	heic? situs est; ossa bene quiescant
HAST·POST,	POSTER hastatus posterior	OS·B·Q	
HAST·P, PR,	PRI hastatus prior	H·E·T	heredes ex testamento
H·B	homo bonus	H·E·T·F	heres ex testamento fecit
H·B·C	hic bene cubet	H·E·T·F·C	heres ex testamento faciendum curavit.
H·B·F	homini bono fecit		
H·B·M·F	heres bene merenti fecit	H·E·V·O	hic est; volo? ossa
H·B·Q	hic bene quiescat	H·EX T, TT	heredes ex testamento
H·C	hic conditus *or* hic cubat	H·F	heres fecit *or* heredes fecerunt
H·C	Hispania Citerior	H·F	honestissima femina
H·C	honoris causa	H·F	honore functus
H·C	honore contentus	H·F·C	heres faciendum curavit, heredes faciendum curaverunt
H·C	horrearius cohortis		
H·C·D·D	honoris causa dedit dedicavit•	HII	heredes
H·C·D·N·S	honoris causa Dianae Nemorensi sacrum?	H·H·F	homini honestissimo fecerunt?
		H·H·M·NON·S	heredem hoc monumentum non sequetur
	[1] *C. I. L.* X. 3395.	H·H·P·R	homines hostes populi Romani?

H·H·Q	heres heredesque
H·I	Hercules invictus
HI	Hispani (cohors)
HIEROF	hierofanta
H·I·E·S	hic intus est situs?
H·INNOC	homo innocens
HIS	Hispania, Hispanus, **Hispani**
HI·SP	hic sepultus
HISP	Hispania, Hispanus, **Hispani**
нIST	Histria
H·L	haec lex
H·L	hic locus
H·L·A·N	hunc locum alienari nolo?
H·L·D·M·A	huic loco dolus malus abesto
H·L·ET·M· H·N·S	hic locus et monumentum heredem non sequentur
H·L·H·N·S	hic locus heredem non sequetur
H·L·I·R·Q	hac lege ius ratumque (esto)
H·L·O	(uti) hac lege oportebit
H·L·R	(ante) hanc legem rogatam
H·L·S·E	hoc loco sepultus est
H·L·S·H·N· S	hic locus sepulturae heredem non sequetur
H·L·T·C·S	hunc locum tessellavit cum suis
H·M	hoc monumentum
H·M	homo merens
H·M	(dimissis) honesta missione
H·M	honeste missus
H·M·A·H·N· P	hoc monumentum ad heredem non pertinet
H·M·A·M·R	hoc monumentum apud meos remanebit?
H·M·C·P	(nihil ultra crudelius) hoc monumento cernere potes?
H·M·D·M·A	huic monumento dolus malus abesto
H·M·D·M·A· B·M·M·C	huic monumento dolus malus abesto; bene merenti memoriae causa
H·M·E·H·N· S	hoc monumentum exterum heredem non sequetur
H·M·E·N·S	hoc monumentum (h)eredem *or* exterum (heredem) non sequetur
H·M·ET L· H·N·S	hoc monumentum et locus heredem non sequentur
H·M·ET L· S·H·N·S	hoc monumentum et locus sepulturae heredem non sequentur
H·M·F	honestae memoriae femina
H·M·F·C·ET S·A·D	hoc monumentum faciundum curavit et sub ascia dedicavit
H·M·H·E·N· S	hoc monumentum heredem exterum non sequetur
H·M·HER· FIDVCI- AR·N·S	hoc monumentum heredem fiduciarium non sequetur
H·M·H·H·	hoc monumentum heredes heredis (non sequetur)

H·M·H·M· N·S	hoc monumentum heredem meum non sequetur
H·M·H·N·C	hoc monumentum heredi non cedit
H·M·H·N·S	hoc monumentum heredem non sequetur
H·M·H·N·S· N·H·H	hoc monumentum heredem nor. sequetur nec heredes heredis
H·M·H·N·S· NEQ·LIB· ....EROS	hoc monumentum heredem non sequetur neque libertos [eius neque post]eros
H·M·H·N·S· N·L·S	hoc monumentum heredem non sequetur nec locus sepulturae
H·M·H·S	hoc monumentum heredes sequetur
H·M·I·A	huic monumento itus actus
H·M·L·S·AB	huic monumento, loco sepulturae, abesto (dolus malus)?
H·M·M	honesta missione missus
H·M·M	honor magisterii Mercurialium
H·M·N·S	heredem monumentum non sequetur
H·M·S·D·M	hoc monumentum sine dolo malo
H·M·S·L·H· N·S	hoc monumentum sive locus heredem non sequetur
H·M·S·S·E· F·C	hoc monumentum sive sepulcrum est faciendum curaverunt
H·M·S·S·E· H·H·N·S	hoc monumentum sive sepulcrum est heredes non sequetur
H·M·S·S·E· H·M·N·S	hoc monumentum sive sepulcrum est heredem meum non sequetur.
H·M·S·S·E· H·N·S	hoc monumentum sive sepulcrum est heredem non sequetur.
H·M·S·S·E· N·N·S	hoc monumentum sive sepulcrum est n....? non sequetur
H·M·S·S·E· N·S	hoc monumentum sive sepulcrum est non sequetur
H·M·S·S·H· H·EX·N·S	hoc monumentum sive sepulcrum hoc heredem exterum non sequetur
H·M·S·S·H· M·N·S	hoc monumentum sive sepulcrum. heredem? meum non sequetur
H·M·S·S·H· N·S	hoc monumentum sive sepulcrum heredem non sequetur
H·M·S·S· VSTRIN	hoc monumentum sive sepulcri ustrinum
H·M·S·V·L· N·S·Q	hoc monumentum sive locus non sequetur
H·M·S·V·S· E·H·N·S	hoc monumentum sive sepulcrum est heredem non sequetur
H·M·V	honestae memoriae vir
H·N·S	heredem non sequetur
H·N·C	Hispania Nova Citerior
H·N·S·N· L·S	heredem non sequetur nec libertos suos
HO	horrearius
H·O·B·Q	hic ossa bene quiescant
HOC MON·	hoc monumentum sive hoc se-

SI·HO·SE·	pulcrum heredem non sequetur
HR·NO·SEQ	
H·O·E·B	hic ossa ei bene
HON	honor
HON	honoratus
HON·F	honoribus functus
HON·M	honesta matrona
HOPL	hoplomachus
HOR	hora
HOR	Horatia (tribus)
HOR	horrea
HOROL	horologium
HORR	horrearius
H·O·S	hic ossa sita
H·O·T·B·Q	hic ossa tibi bene quiescant
H·O·V·B·Q	hic ossa volo or vobis bene quiescant
H·P	heres posuit
H·P	hic positus or heredes posuerunt
H·P	homo probus ?
H·P·C	heres ponendum curavit
H·P·D	Herculi ? Primigenio ? dedit ?
H·PR	hastatus prior
H·P·R	hostes populi Romani
H·Q	hic quiescat
H·Q·B	hic quiescat bene
HRD	heredes
H·R·I·R	honore recepto impensam remisit
H·S	hic situs, sita ; sepultus, sepulta
H·S·A	hic situs a....
H·S·B·P·E	hic situs bene positus ? est
H·S·B·Q	hic situs bene quiescat
H·S·D·M·A	huic sepulcro dolus malus abesto
H·S·E	hic situs, sita est or hic sepultus, sepulta est
H·S·E·B·Q	hic situs est ; bene quiescat
H·S·E·H·EX	hic situs est ; heres ex testamento
T·F·C	faciundum curavit
H·S·E·H·F	hic situs est ; heres fecit
H·S·E·H·P	hic situs est ; heredes posuerunt
H·S·E·O·T·	hic situs est ; ossa tua bene quiescant
B·Q	cant
H·S·E·O·V·	hic situs est ; ossa volo bene quiescant
B·Q	escant
H·S·E·S·T·T·L	hic situs est ; sit tibi terra levis
H·S E·T·F·	hic situs est ; titulum fieri iussit ;
I·H·F·C	heres faciundum curavit
H·S·E·T·F·I	hic situs est ; titulum fieri iussit ;
H·P	heres posuit
H·S·EX S	heres secundus ex semisse ?
H·S·H	hic situs, heredes ?
H·S·H·A·	hoc sepulcrum heredibus abalienare non licet
N·L	nare non licet
H·S·H·E	hic situs, heredes eius
H·S·H·N·S	hoc sepulcrum heredem non sequitur
H·S·L·P	hoc sepulcrum libens posuit ?
H·S·N·S	heredem secundum non sequetur

H·S·O·B	hic situs ; ossa bene
H·S·O·T	hic situs ; ossa tibi
H·SP	hic sepultus ?
H·SP·E	hic sepultus est
H·S·Q	hic situs ; quiescat
H·S·S	hic siti or sepulti sunt
H·S·S·H·T·B·	hic situs sepultus ; hic tibi bene
Q·H·E·S	quiescat ; heredes ? eius ? s...
H·S·S·S·V·T·L	hic siti sunt. Volo terra levis
H·S·T	hic situs ; tibi
H·S·T·F·I	hic situs ; testamento fieri iussit
H·T	hic tu
H·T·B	hic tu bene
H·T·B·C	hic tu bene cubes ?
H·T·B·Q	hic tu bene quiescas ; or tumulatus bene quiescas
H·T·F·C	heredes testamento fieri curaverunt
H·T·H·N·S	hic tumulus ? heredem non sequetur
H·T·O·B·Q	hic tibi ossa bene quiescant
H·T·V·P	heres testamento vivus posuit
H·V	Hercules victor
H·V	honore usus
H·V·F	heres vivus fecit
H·V·I·R	honore usus impensam remisit
H·V·O·B·Q	hic volo ossa bene quiescant
H·V·S·R	honore usus sumptum remisit
H·V·S·R·L·	honore usus sumptus remisit ;
D·D·D·	loco dato decreto decurionum
H·V·V·S	Herculi victori votum solvit

I

I	Ianuarius (mensis)
I	invictus (Mithras)
I	itur
I	Iulius, Iulia
I	iunior
I·A	in agro
IA, IAN	Ianuariae
I·A·P	in agro pedes
I·C	in Capitolio
I·C·A	ius civile (or iuris consultus) abesto
ID·IAN	Idus Ianuariae
I·D	invictus deus
I·D	Iupiter Dolichenus
I·D	iure dicundo
IDB	Idibus
I·D·D·D	Iovi Dolicheno dono dedit
ID E	id est
I·D·P	iure dicundo praeesse
I·D·Q·C·P	iure dicundo quinquennalis censoriae potestatis
I·D·Q·Q	iure dicundo quinquennalis
IDQ·P	iidemque probaverunt
ID·QVOT·D·F	idem quotannis divisio fiat

I·E	Iudex esto
I·E·V·Q·I· S·S	in ea verba quae infra scripta sunt
I·F	in fronte
I·F·P	in fronte pedes
I·HER	invictus Hercules
I·H·M·I·A· S·C·F	in hoc monumentum itum aditum sacrorum causa facere
IIMMPP·CC- AA EESS	(duobus) imperatoribus Caesaribus
I·L·H	ius liberorum habens
ILL	illustris
IM	imaginifer
IM	imperator
I·M	invictus Mithras
IMA	imaginifer
IMAG	imaginifer
IM·C	imaginifer cohortis
IMM	immolaverunt
IMM	immunis
IMMAG [1]	imaginifer
IMMV	immunis
IMP	imperator, imperatum ?, imperium
IMP	impetus
IMP·D·N	imperator dominus noster
IMPE	imperator
IMPER	imperator
IMPET·LIPPIT	impetus lippitudinis
IMP·N	imperator noster
IM·PP	immunis perpetuus
IMPP	imperatores (duo)
IMPP·CC	imperatores Caesares (duo)
IMPP·DD·NN	imperatores (duo) domini nostri
IMP·P·Q·R	imperium populusque Romanus
IMP·S	impensa sua
IN	(pater) infelicissimus
IN A, IN AG, IN AGR	in agro
IN CAL	in caliga
IN C·D·C·D	in cujus dedicatione cenam dedit ?
INC·FR·PVBL	incisus frumento publico
INCOMP	incomparabilis
IND	indictio
IN E·V·Q· I·S·S	in ea verba quae infra scripta sunt
IN F, FR	in fronte
INF·S·S	infra subscripti or scripti sunt
ING	ingenua
IN H·D·D	in honorem domus divinae
IN HO	in honorem
IN K·S	in capita singula
INL	inlustris
INPP	imperatoribus (duobus)
INP·S	impensa sua
IN QVINQ	in quinquennium
IN R	in retro
IN T	in tergo

INS	instante, instantia
IN SING·H	in singulos homines
IN·S·S	infra scripti or scripta sunt
INSTA	instante, instantia
INST·TAB	instrumentum tabulariorum
IN SVO CONST, E	in suo constituit, erexit
INTER	interrex
INT	intulit
INV, INVI	invictus
IN V·R·P·VE V·R·P·M	in urbe Roma propius ve urbi Romae passus mille
I·O·C	Iupiter optimus Capitolinus
I·O·D	Iupiter optimus Dolichenus
I·O·D·E	Iupiter optimus Dolichenus E...
I·O·M	Iupiter optimus maximus
I·O·M·A·D	Iupiter optimus maximus Augustus Dolichenus
I·O·M·B	Iupiter optimus maximus Balmarcodes
I·O·M·C	Iupiter optimus maximus conservator
I·O·M·C·O· D·I	Iupiter optimus maximus ceterique omnes dii immortales
I·O·M·CVL	Iupiter optimus maximus culminalis
I·O·M·D	Iupiter optimus maximus depulsor
I·O·M·D	Iupiter optimus maximus Dolichenus
I·O·M·F	Iupiter optimus maximus fulminator
I·O·M·F·F	Iupiter optimus maximus fulminator fulgurator
I·O·M·H	Iupiter optimus maximus Heliopolitanus
I·O·M·H·A	Iupiter optimus maximus Heliopolitanus Augustus
I·O·M·I·R· M·T·M	Iupiter optimus maximus Iuno regina, Minerva, Terra mater
I·O·M·S	Iupiter optimus maximus, Suessulanus
IOVR·DIC	iure dicundo
I·O·S·INVI ...R·N	Iupiter optimus Sol invictus... rupe natus
I·O·S·P·D	Iupiter optimus Sol praetantissimus dignus
I·P	iter prohibitum
I·P·AVG	Ianus pater Augustus
I·P·QVE	ius potestasque (esto)
I·Q·S·S·S	ii qui supra scripti sunt
I·Q·P	idemque probavit
I·R	Iuno Regina
I·S	infra scriptus
I·S·E	(h)ic situs est
I·S·M·R	Iuno sospes magna regina
I·S·P	impensis suis posuit
ISPEC [2]	(i)speculator

[1] *C. I. L.* III. 1583.

[2] *C. I. L.* VIII. 2833.

ISTAN	instante, instantia
ISTR [1]	(i)strator
I·S·V·P	in suo vivi posuerunt
IT	item
IT	iterum
ITAL	Italica (legio)
I·T·M·F·C	idem testamento monumentum faciendum curavit
IT·V·S·M	ita votum solvam meritis ?
IVD	iudicans, iudicandus, iudex
IVD·DEC ; IVD·	iudex decuriae, iudex de
DE V·DEC	quinque decuriis
I·V·E·E·R·	ita utei eis e re publica fideve sua
P·F·S·V·E	videbitur esse
IVG	iugera
IVL	Iulius, Iulia
IVL·TEP·MAR	Iulia Tepula Marcia
IVN	iunior
IVN·REG	Iuno regina
IVR	iuridicus
IVR·DIC	iure dicundo ; iuris dictic
IVRID	iuridicus
IVS·SA	iussione sacra
IVV	iuvenes (collegium iuvenum)

K

K	Kaeso
K	kalendae [2]
K	kalendarium
K	calumnia
K	candidatus
K	caput
K	castellum, castellani, castrum, castra
K	coniux
K	cardo
K	carissimus, carissima
K	casa
K	corpus ?
M	castra
KAL	kalendae
KANAL	canaliclarius
KAND, KANDID	candidatus
KAR	carissimus, carissima
KARC	carcerarius
KARM	Carmentalia
KAS, KAST	castra
KAST·PER	castra peregrina
K·K	calumniae causa
KK	castra
K L	caput legis
KLM [3]	Clementis

[1] *C. I. L.* VIII. 2757.
[2] Wilmanns remarks (*Exempla*, p. 123) that this abbreviation is very common before 180 A.D. and rare after. We find then generally KAL.
[3] *C. I. L.* XIV. 308.

K·O	cannophori Ostienses
K·Q	Kalendae quinctiles
KRS	carissimus, carissima
KRSMAE	carissimae
K·S	carus suis
KVR	Cyrenaïca (legio)

L

L	latum
L	legio
L	leuga
L	lex
L	liberatus
L	libertus, liberta
L	librarius
L	ligatum [4]
L	lippitudo
L	locus, loculus
L	longum
L	Lucius
L	luna
L·A	libens animo
LA·B	laudabilis bonus ?
LAC	lacus
L·A·D	libens animo dedit
L·A·D·D	libens animo donum dat, dederunt, dedicat
LANIS	lanista
LAP	lapis
LAPID	lapidarius
LAR	Larentinalia
L·AR·E	librarius arcarii evocatus ?
LAR·ET IMAG	Lares et imagines
LAR·MIL	Lares militares
LAT	laticlavius
LAT·FVER	Latinae fuere
LARG	largus
L·A·SOL	libens animo solvit
LATIC, LATICL	laticlavius
LAV·LAV	Laurens Lavinas
LAVR·LAV	Laurens Lavinas
L·B	libertus bonus
L·B·S	libens solvit
L·C	laticlavius
L·C	librarius capsarius ?
L·C	liber condicione ?
L·C	librarius cohortis ?
L·C	locus concessus
LC	Lucius
L·C·D·D	locus concessus decreto decurionum
L·O·IX	liberatus coronarum novem
L·D	(votum) libens dat
L·D	libere damno
L·D	locum dedit, loco dato, locus datus, locum donavit

[4] *C. I. L.* V. 6414.

L·D·A REP	locus datus a re publica
L·D·D	libens donum dedit
L·D·D·C	locus datus decreto collegii
L·D·D·C·F·C	locus datus decreto collegii fabrum centonariorum
L·D·D·C·V	locus datus decreto centumvirum
L·D·D·CRE·C	locus datus decreto centumvirum
L·D·D·D	locus datus decreto decurionum
L·D·D·D·D·D	loco dato decreto decurionum, dono dederunt
L·D·D·D·P	locus datus decreto decurionum publice
L·D·DEC·N·R	loco dato decreto nautarum Rhodanicorum
L·D·D·P· COND	loco dato decreto pagi Condatium
L·D·D·PA	locus datus decreto paganorum
L·D·D·S·V	locus datus decreto senatus Vocontiorum
L·D·D·V	locus datus decreto utriclariorum vicanorum
L·D·EX D·D	locus datus ex decreto decurionum
L·D·EX D·PAG	locus datus ex decreto pagi
L·D·G	legio decima Gemina
L·D·P	locus datus publice
L·D·P·C	locus datus permissu collegii
L·D·P·D·D	locus datus publice decreto decurionum
L·D·P·P· D·D	locus datus pecunia publica, decreto decurionum
L·D·PVB· D·D	locus datus publice decreto decurionum
L·D·S·C	locus datus senatus consulto
LE	lene
LE·A·L	lene ad lippitudinem
LEG	legatus
LEG	legavit
LEG	legio
LEG·AVG	legatus Augusti
LEG·AVG·CENS· ACC	legatus Augusti censibus accipiendis
LEG·AVGG· PR·PR	legatus Augustorum duorum pro praetore
LEG·AVG·P·P	legatus Augusti pro praetore
LEG·AVG· PR·PR, PRAE	legatus Augusti pro pratore
LEG·COR	iege Cornelia
LEG·IVR	legatus iuridicus
LEG·LEG	legatus legionis
LEG·PL·VE· SC·S·VE·C	leges plebeive scitum senatusve consultum
LEG·PROCOS	legatus proconsulis
LEG·PRO·Q	legatus pro quaestore
LEG·S·C	legatus senatus consulto
LEMO, LEMON	Lemonia (tribus)
LEM	Lemonia (tribus)
LEM	Lemuria

L·ET F·D·D	libertis, or Laribus et familiae donum dederunt
L·ET L	liberti et libertae
LEV	leucoma
L·F	Latinae fuerunt
L·F	laudabilis femina
L·F	liberti fecerunt
L·F	librarius fisci ?
L·F·D·D	Laribus familiaribus donum dederunt
L·F·D·D	ludos fecerunt decurionum decreto
LG	legio
L·H·N·S	locus heredem non sequitur
LI	libertus ?
LIB	libellus
LIB	liber
LIB	liberatus
LIB	liber, liberalitas
LIB	libertus, liberta
LIB	librae
LIB	librarius
LIB	liburna
LIB	Libya
LIB·AGON	Liberalia Agonalia
LIB·AN	libens animo
LIBB	liberti
LIB·COS	librarius consularis ?
LIBEL	libella
LIBER	libertas (dea)
LIBER	libertus
LIB·LIBERTABVSQ· SVIS·P·E	libertis libertabusque suis posterisque eorum
LIB·LIB·Q·P(POST)· EOR	libertis libertabusque posterisque eorum
LIBR	libertus
LIBR, LIBRA	librarius
LIBR·COMM ST· HER·T·K	librarius commentariorum stationis hereditatium tabularii ? kastrensis ?
LIBTIS	libertatis
LIC	licet
LI·E·P·OP·N	liberti eius patrono optimo nostro
L·I·F·P IIII· R·P·IIII	locus in fronte pedes IIII; retro pedes IIII
LIG	Liguria
LI·M·V·S·L	libens merito votum solvit laetus
L·IN·CIR	ludi in circo
L·IN·LA	locus in latitudinem
LINT	lintiarius
LIP, LIPP	lippitudo
LIQV	liquamen
L·L	Laurens Lavinas
L·L	legatus legionis
L·L	libens laetus
L·L	liberti libertae
L·L	librarius legati or legionis
L·L	Lucii (duo)
L·LIB	locus libertorum ?

L·LIBERT·POSTE-	libertis libertabusque po-
RIS Q·EOR	sterisque eorum
L·L·L·L·L·M [1]	laeti libentes? merito
L·L·P·E	libertis libertabus posterisque eo-
	rum
L·L·L·P·O·	libertis libertabusque... posteris-
M·S	que omnibus monumentum sta-
	tuit?
L·L·M	laetus libens merito
L·L·P·E	libertis libertabus posterisque eo-
	rum
L·L·P·D	laetus libens p... dedit
L·L·P·Q·E	libertis libertabus posterisque eo-
	rum
L·L·P·S	libertis libertabus posterisque suis
L·L·Q	libertis libertabusque
L·L·T	librarius (tribuni) laticlavii
L·L·V·S	laetus libens votum solvit
L·M	libens merito
L·M	libertus meus
L·M	locus monumenti
L·M·A·P	locus monumenti ante? pedes
	(XX)
L·M	ludus magnus
L·M·D	libens merito dedit
L·M·F	libens merito fecit
L·MIL	Lares militares
L·M·P	libens merito posuit
L·M·S	libens merito solvit
L·N	Lucius noster
LO	locus
LOC	locator
LOC·ACCEP·	loco accepto decreto decurionum
D·D	
LOC·ACCEP·DED	loco accepto dedit
LOC·D	locus datus
LOC·DAT·D·D	locus datus decreto decurionum
LOC·EMPT	locus emptus
LOC·EMP	locus emptus
LOC·H·S·P	loco hoc sibi permisso senatus
S·C·P·S	consulto pecunia sua [2]
LOC·LIB	locus libertorum?
LOC·MONVM	locus monumenti
LOC·P·P	locorum publicorum persequendo-
	rum
LOC·PVB	loco publico
LOC·PVBL·	locorum publicorum persequendo-
PERSEQ	rum
LOC·SEP	locus sepulturae
LON	longus
L·P	lex Petronia?
L·P	locus pedum, *or* latus (longus)
	pedes
L·P	Liber pater
L·P	libertus patrono
L·P	libens *or* libertus posuit

L·P·D·A·P	lege Papiria de aere publico?
L·P·D·D·D	locus publice datus decreto decu-
	rionum
L·P·I	libens poni iussit (?)
L·P·IT	legio prima Italica
L·P·M	legio prima Minervia
L·P·P	locorum publicorum persequendo-
	rum
L·P·P·P	loco publico pecunia publica
L·P·Q	locus pedum quadratorum
L·Q	locus quadratus
L·P·S	libertis posterisque suis?
L·R·P	legas rogo praeteriens
L·S	libentes solverunt
L·S	locus sepulturae
L·S·D	locum sibi dante?
L·S·D·	locus sepulturae datus decurionum
D·D	decreto
L·SE·H	locus sepulturae heredem non se-
N·S	quetur
L·S·M	locus sepulturae monumentique?
L·S·PR	librarius subpraefecti
LT	laticlavius
L·T, L·TR	librarius tribuni
LV	Lucius
LVB·MER	lubens merito
LVC	Lycia
LVD·F	ludos fecit
LVD·MAT	ludus matutinus
LVN·VET	Lunense vetus
LVP, LVPERC	Lupercalia, Lupercus
L·V·S	libens votum solvit
LVSTR·MON·SAC	lustratio montis sacri
LYC	Lycaonia
L·V	luna quinta

M

M	Macedonica (legio)
M	magister
M	maiestas
M	maiora
M [3]	manipularis
M	Manes
M	manu
M	Marcus
M	marmora
M	Martia (legio)
M	mas (bos)
M	maritus
M	Mars
M	mater
M	Matres *or* Matronae
M	Mauretania (Caesariensis, Siti-
	fensis)
M	maximus

---

[1] Brambach, 1315.   [2] Orelli, 1450 = 4712.

[3] C. I. L. X. 3595.

M	memoria
M	mensis, menses, mensibus
M	Mercurius
M	merens, meritus
M	metalla
M	(votum solvit bona) mente ?
M	miles, militavit
M	mille, milia
M	Minervia (legio)
M	Minerva
M	minus
M	missus (ex legione)
M	modius
M	moneta
M	monumentum
M	mortuus
M	muliebris
M	municipium
M	murmillo
M	menses
⋏⋏	Manius
Ⅱ	mortuus ?
MA	manu
M·A	Mercurius Augustus
M·A	militavit annos
M·A	municipium Atria
M·A·A	municipium Aurelium Apulum
MAC, MACED	Macedonia ; Macedonica (legio)
MACH	machinarii
M· AD M· PRAEN	magister ad Martem Praenestinum
MAE, MAEC	Maecia (tribus)
MA·ET PA	mater et pater
MAG	magister, magistri, magisterium, magistratus
MAG·AVG	magister Augustalis
MAG·C·D	magister c... dedit
MAG·COL	magister collegii
MAG·EQ	magister equitum
MAG·FIG	magister figulorum
MAGG	magistri, magistratus
MAG·FAB	magister fabrum
MAGN	magnarius
MAG·PAG AVG·F·S· PRO LVD· EX D·D	magistri pagi Augusti felicis surburbani pro ludis ex decreto decurionum [1]
MAG·P, PERP, PP	magister perpetuus
MAG·PR	magister primus
MAG·PR	magister privatae
MAG·PRIVAT· AEG·ET LIB	magister privatae Aegypti et Libyae
MAG·PROVE	magistratus prove magistratu
MAG·P·R	populi Romani
MAG·QQ	magister quinquennalis
MAG·QVIN	magister quinquennalis

[1] *C. I. L.* X. 852.

M·A·G·S	memor animo grato solvit
MAG·VIC	magister vici
MAG·IIII F	magister quartum factus
MAI	Maius (mensis)
MAI, MAIC	Maecia (tribus)
MAIES·D	majestas divina
MAM	Mamercus
MAN	manipularis
MANC	mancipium
MAN·ET CIN	Manibus et cineribus ?
MANI	Manibus
MANIP, MANIPL, MANP [2]	manipularis
MAR	Marcia (aqua)
MAR	margaritarius
MAR	marinus
MAR	maritus
MARG	margaritarius
MARM	marmoreus
MART	Martius (mensis), Martia (legio)
MART·VIC, VICT	Martia victrix (legio)
MANB [3]	manibus (see page 273)
MANIPLR	manipularis
MAR	marsus
MAT	mater
MAT	Matres *or* Matronae
MAT·B	mater bona
MATER·D· M·I·D	Mater deum magna Idaea Dindymena ? [4]
MAT·F·F·CAR	mater fecit filio carissimo
MATR	Matres *or* Matronae
MAV	Mavortius
MAV	Mauri (cohors)
MAVR·CAES *or* SITIF *or* TINGIT	Mauretania Caesariensis *or* Sitifensis *or* Tingitana
MAVRET	Mauretania
MAX	maximus
M·B	municipium Bergomatium
M·B·M·F	maritus bene merenti fecit
M·B·D·D·D	magistrae Bonae Deae donum dederunt ?
M·C	mater castrorum
M·C	Mauretania Caesariensis
M·C	memoriae causa
M.CA	Mauretania Caesariensis
M·C·D·S	momentum condiderunt ? de suo
M·C·F	memoriae causa fecit
MCP	municipium
M·C·P·M	miles classis praetoriae Misenatis
M·CL·PR	miles classis praetoriae
M·C·P·S·I	Mithras Cautus Pater Sol invictus ?
M·C·T·R·N	memoriae causa titulum renovavit ?
M·D	Manibus Diis ?
M·D	mater deum
M·D	mater dulcissima

[2] *C. I. L.* X. 3535.   [3] *C. I. L.* VII. 1336, 585.
[4] Boissieu, *Insc. de Lyon*, p. 24.

M·D	municipium Dianensium
M·D·A·N	metalla domini Augusti nostri
M·D·M	Mater deum magna
M·D·M·A	monumento dolus malus abesto
M·D·M·I	Mater deum magna Idaea
ME, MEC	Maecia (tribus)
M·E	merita eius
ME	Mesogites (vinum)
MED	Medicus
MED	medicus
MED	Meditrinalia
MED·LVD·MAT	medicus ludi matutina
MED·ORD	medicus ordinarius
MED·TVC [1]	Medixtuticus
MEM	memoria
MEM·COL	(ad) memoriam colendam
MEN	Menenia (tribus)
MEN	mensis
MEN	mensor
MENEN	Menenia (tribus)
MENS·AGRAR,	mensor agrarius, agrorum
AGROR	
MENSS	menses
M·EQ	miliaria equitata (cohors)
MER	Mercurius
MER	meridianus (gladiator)
MER	merita, merens, meritus
MERC	Mercurialis
MERC·CAN	Mercurius Canetonensis
MERK	mercatus
MER·S	Mercurio sacrum
MES	mensis
MES	mensor
MES	Mesogites (vinum)
MESOP	Mesopotamia
MET	metalla
METR, METROP	metropolis
M·F	magister fani
M·F	mater fecit
M·F	monumentum fecit *or* memoriam fecit
M·F	miles factus
M·F	munere functus
M·F	(omnibus honoribus) municipalibus functus
M·F·A	municipium Flavium Arvense
M·FE·SV	memoriam fecit suis
M·F·F·M	mater fecit filio merenti *or* memoriam fecit, etc.
M·F·L·A	magister fani Larum Augustorum
M·F·V	municipium Fabrateria vetus
M·H·F·C	memoriam *or* monumentum heres faciendum curavit
M·H (HON)·	M (MISS) missus honesta missione
M·H·N·S	monumentum heredem non sequetur

M·I	magna Idaea (Mater)
MI	Maecia (tribus)
MI	Mithras
MIL	miles, militavit, militia
MIL	milia, miliaria
MILL	milia
MILT	militavit
MILTS	militis
MIL·P	milia passuum
MIL·PETIT	militiae petitor
MIN	Minatius *or* Minius
MIN	Minervia (legio)
MIN	Minicia
MIN	minister, ministri
MIN	minor
MINER	Minerva (legio)
MINER·MEM	Minerva memor [2]
MINIS	minister
MIS	missio, missicius, missus
MISS·HON·M	missus honesta missione
M·K	mater castrorum
M·L	miles legionis
ML	miles
M·L	municipium Lambiriditanum
W, WW, WV, ≶·L	mulieris libertus, liberta
M·M	magister Mercurialis
M·M	malis male
MM	Marci duo
M·M	Mater magna
MM	memoriae
M·M	municipes municipii
M·M·F	marito monumentum fecit
M·M·F	memoriam fecit
M·M·F·A	municipes municipii Flavii Arvensis
M·M·I	Mater magna Idaea
M·M·P·OR	magister militiae per Orientem
M·M·P·F	marito merenti pia fecit
MMR	memoria
M·M·V	municeps municipii Vicetiae
M·N	Mars Nabelcus
M·N	metalla nova *or* Numidica
M·N	milia nummum
MN	minus
M·N	municipium Novaria
M·O	matri optimae
MO	Montani (cohors), Montanae (deae)
MO	monumentum
MOL	mulier
MOLIN	molinarius
MON	monetalis
MON	monumentum
MONEM	monumentum
MON·H·M·	monumentum heredem meum non
N·S	sequetur
MONIM	monumentum

[1] Orelli, 3804.

[2] Orelli, 1427.

MON·SAC	monitor sacrorum
MONT·P·C	Montanorum pia constans (cohors)
MONT	monumentum
M·N	municipium Novensium
M·P	magister pagi
M·P	maior pars
M·P	mater posuit
M·P	memoriam posuit
M·P	mille passus, milia passuum
M·P	municipium Placentia
M·P (PO)· D·M	monumentum positum Diis Manibus
M·P·F	Minervia pia fidelis (legio)
M·P·P	matri piissimae posuit *or* maritus pius posuit
M·P·V·L	Marci, Publii, Vibii libertus
M R	merens
M·S	Moesia superior
M·S	Mars suus
MS	mensis
M·S	merito solvit
M·SEP·APVL	municipium Septimium Apulum
M·S·P	maritus sua pecunia
M·S·S	Mithrae Soli sacrum
M·S·S·E·H· N·S	monumentum sive sepulcrum est heredem non sequetur
M·T	municipium Thibilitanum
M·T·F	memoriae titulum fecit
M·TRIVMPH	municipium Triumphale
M·V	municipium Verulanum
MV	Murtites (vinum)
M·V·F	monumentum vivus fecit, *or* uxori fecit, *or* maritus uxori fecit
M·VIC	municipium Vicetia
MVL	mulier
MV·L	municipium Lamasba
MVL·LIB	mulieris libertus *or* liberta
MVL·XX	multis (votis) vicennalibus
MVN	municipium
MVNER	munerarius
MVN·NAP	municipium Napoca
MVN·SEPT APVL	municipium Septimium Apulum
M·V·P·P	maritus uxori piissimae posuit
MVR	murmillo
MVR·SCAEV	murmillo scaeva
M·V·S	memor voti solvit
M·VX·P	maritus uxori posuit

N

N	natalis
N	natione
N	naturalis ?
N	natus
N	navarchus, nauta
N	nefastus (tristis)
N	Nemesis ?
N	nepos

N	Neronianus
N	niger
N	nomine
N	Nonae
N	Noricum
N	noster
N	novus, novicius
N	noxia (hora)
N	numerat
N	Numerius
N	numero, numerus
N	Numidia
N	numen
N, N̄ *or* Ꞃ	nummi
N	Nymphae
NA	naturalis (pater)
NA	natione, natus
N·A	nauta Araricus
NAOFYL	nauphylax
N·ARARIC	nautae Ararici
NARB	Narbonensis
N·A·S	numini Augusti sacrum
NAT	natione
N·ATR	nautae Atr...
NAV	navicularius, nauta
NAVF	nauphylax
N·AVG	numen Augusti
NAVIC	navicularius
NAV·LIG	nautae Ligerenses
N·BRIT	numerus Britonum
N·C	Numidia Constantina
N·C·INFER...	ne cui ? inferre (liceat ?)
N·D	numen deorum
N·D·A·N·M	nullum dolorem accepit nisi morte
NE [1]	nemini
NE	Neronianus
NEG	negotiator
NEG·FRV	negotiator frumentarius
NEGOT	negotiator
NEG·PAENVL	negotiator paenularius
NEG·STIP·ARG	negotiator stipis argentarii
NEP	nepos
NER	Neronianus
N·E·S·D	numini eius semper devotus
N·EXPLOR·BREM *or* BREMEN	numerus exploratorum Bremeniensium
NϜ	nefastus (hilaris)
N·F·F·N·S·N·C	non fui, fui, non sum, non curo
N·F·N·S·N·C	non fui, non sum, non curo
N·I	natione Itala
N·LIC	non licet
N·M	numerus militum
N·M·Q	numini maiestatique
N·M·Q·E·D	numini maiestatique eius dicatissimus
N·M	Noricum mediterraneum

[1] *Ephem. Ep.* IV. 236.

N·M·V	nobilis memoriae vir
N N	nostri (duo)
N·N	numerus noster
NNOBB·CAESS	nobilissimi Caesares (duo)
NNNOOOBBB·	nobilissimi Caesares (tres)
CAESSS	
NO	nobilissimus
NO	Novius
NOB·CAES	nobilissimus Caesar
NOB·FEM	nobilissima femina
NOB¹	November
NOBB·CAESS	nobilissimi Caesares
NOMI	nomine
NON	Nonae
NONAGEN	nonagenarius
NORICO	Noricorum (ala)
NOT	notarius
NOV	November
NOV	Novius
N·P	natione Pannonius ? Ponticus ?
NP	nefastus (hilaris)
N P	Neptunus
N P	nobilissimus puer
N·P²	(si fato meliore filias) non pepe-
	rissent
N·R	natione Raetus ?
N·R, RHOD	nauta Rhodanicus
NRIS	nostris
N·S	nomine suo
N·S·S·I·M	numen sanctum Solis invicti Mi-
	thrae
N·STAT	numerus statorum
N·T·M	numerus ? tegularum minorum ³
N·V	nobilissimus vir
NVB	numinibus
NVM	numerarius, numerus, numero
NVM	nummum
NVM·AVG	numen Augusti
NVM·BAT·SEN	numerus Batavorum seniorum
NVM·DAL·	numerus Dalmatarum Diviten-
DIVIT	sium
NVMM, NVMMVL	nummularius, nummularia
N·VRSARIEN	numerus Ursariensium
NYMP	nymphaeum

O

O	Olus
O	officina
O	hoplomachus
O	optio
O, Ꝑ	horae
O	ovum
O, Ō, Ꙩ, Ꙩ, ☉	obiit, obitus
O·B	optio balnearii

¹ Boissieu, *Insc. de Lyon*, p. 97.
² *C. I. L.* V. 2956.
³ **Brambach**, *Insc. Rhen.* 112.

O·B	ossa bene
OB	obiit *or* obitus
OB	obiit *or* obitus
O·B·C	ossa bene cubent ?
OB H, HON	ob honorem
OB M·E	ob merita eius, memoriam eius
O·B·Q	ossa bene quiescant
O·B·Q·T	ossa bene quiescant tibi
OBR	obrysum
O·C	opus constat
O·C·S	ob cives servatos
OCT	octogenarius
OCT, OCTO, OCTOB	October
O·D	opus doliare
O·D·D·F·D·	opus doliare de figlinis Domitiae
L·F	Lucillae ; figlinae
O·D·S·M	optime de se merito
O·E·B	ossa ei bene
O·E·B·Q	ossa ei bene quiescant
OF	Oufentina (tribus)
OF	officina
OF·AVR	officina Aureliana
OFE, OFEN, OFENT,	Oufentina (tribus)
OFENTIN	
OFF	Oufentina (tribus)
OFF	officina, officinator
OFF	officium
OFF·CORN	officium corniculariorum
OFFENT	Oufentina (tribus)
OFFI, OFFIC	officina
OFF·PA, PAPI	officina Papiri
OFF·PRAETER,	officium praeteritorum, rati-
RAT	onum
OFF·S·R	officina summae rei *or* summarum
	rationum
OFI, OFIC	officina
O·H	ossa hic ?
O·H·F	omnibus honoribus functus
O·H·Q·B	ossa hic quiescant bene
O·H·S	ossa hic sita
O·H·S·S	ossa hic sita sunt
OIA	omnia ⁴
OL	olla
OLL·D or D·S·D	ollas dedit *or* de suo dedit
OL·PO·V	olei pondo V
O·L·S·T	opto levis sit terra
O·L·T	opto levem terram
O·M	ob memoriam
O·M	optime meritus
O·M	optimus maximus
O·M·C·P·F·	oppidum municipium colonia prae-
V·C·C·T	fectura forum vicus conciliabu-
	lum castellum territorium
O·M·D·S	optime meritus de se
O·M·V	ordo municipii V ...
O·N·F	omnium nomine faciundum

⁴ Orelli, 6041.

TABLE OF ABBREVIATIONS

O·O·D	ornatus ornamentis decurionalibus
OP	optimus
OP	optio
OP·A, ARK	optio arcarii
OP·B	optio balnearii
OP·C, CA	optio carceris
OP·CO	optio cohortis
OPAL	Opalia
OP·C, CA	optio carceris
O·P·C	ollam Publius dedit ?
OP·CO, COH	optio cohortis
OP·D, OP·DO, OP·DOL	opus doliare
OPER·PVB	opera publica
OP·EQ	optio equitum
OPETR, OPI	Opiter
OPIC	Opiconsiva
OPL	hoplomachus
OPO	opobalsamatum
OP·PEC·S·F	opus pecunia sua fecit
OP·PR, PRI	optio principis
O·P·Q	ordo populusque
OPSON	opsonator
OPT	optimus, optima
OPT	optio
OPT·B	optio balnearii
OPT·C	optio carceris
OPT·COH	optio cohortis
OPT·PR	optio principis
OP·VAL	optio valetudinarii
ORA, ORAT	Horatia (tribus)
ORD	ordinarius
ORD·N	ordo noster
O·REST	orbis restitutor
ORN	ornatus, ornamenta
ORN·DEC	ornamenta decurionalia
OR·P	hora prima
O·S	ossa sita
OS·B·C	ossa bene cubent ?
OS·B·Q	ossa bene quiescant
OS·TIB·B·Q·S.	ossa tibi bene quiescant
OS·T·B·Q	ossa tibi or tua bene quiescant
OS·T·B·N·Q	ossa tibi bene quiescant
O·S·T·T·L	opto sit tibi terra levis
O·T·B	ossa tibi bene
O·T·B·C	ossa tibi bene cubent ?
O·T·B·Q	ossa tibi bene quiescant
O·TIB	ossa tibi
O·T·Q	ossa tibi quiescant
OV	Ovius
O·V	oro vos
O·V	ornatus vir
O·V·B·C	ossa volo bene cubent
O·V·B·Q	ossa volo bene quiescant
OVF	Oufentina (tribus)
O·V·F	oro vos faciatis
O·V·F·D·R· P·O·V·F	oro vos faciatis, dignum re publica, oro vos faciatis
OVFENT, OVFF	Oufentina (tribus)

P

P	pagina
P	pagus
P	Pannonii (cohors)
P	Papiria, Pollia (tribus)
P	parentes
P	pars
P	passus
P	pater
P	patria
P	patrimonium
P	patronus, patrona
P	pausarii ?
P	peregrina ?[1]
P	Parthica (legio)
P	pecunia
P	pedatura ?, pedes
P	per
P	periit
P	pius or pie, piissimus pientissimus
P	(lex) Plautia ? Papiria ? Pompeia ?
P	pondo
P	populus
P	posuit or posuerunt
P	posteri
P	praefectus
P	praeses
P	praetor
P	praetoria (cohors)
P	Primigenia (legio)
P	primus, prima
P	princeps
P	pro
P	probum
P	proconsul
P	procurator
P	provincia
P	Proxumae (deae)
P	publicus, publica
P	Publius
P	pugnarum
Ϙ	puella
PA	pagani
PA	Palatina, Papiria (tribus)
PA	pater
PA	patronus
P·A	pondo argenti
P·A	provincia Africa
P·A	publicum argentum
PAC	Pacuius
PA·ET MA	pater et mater
PA·FECE	parentes fecerunt
PAG	pagus, pagani
PAG	pagina
P·AG	piisimus Augustus
PAL	Palatina

[1] Brambach, 163.

PAL	palatium
PAL	pallium
PAL	Palmyreni (numerus)
PALAT,	Palatinus (Salius), **Palatina** (tri-
PALATIN	bus)
PAN·INF	Pannonia inferior
PANN	Pannonia, Pannonii (cohors)
PANNO	Pannonii (cohors)
PAP	Papiria
PAPHLAG	Paphlagonia
PAQ	Paquius
PAR	parentes
PAR	Parilia
PAPER, PAPI. PAPIR Papiria (tribus)	
P·AREL	pausarius Arelatensis
PARENT	Parentalia
PAR·M	Parthicus maximus
PART, PARTH Parthicus, Parthica (legio)	
PASS[1]	passiva (venatio)
PAT	pater
PAT	patricius
PAT	patronus
PAT·COL	patronus coloniae
PAT·ET CVR patronus et curator	
PAT·F·P·P	pater filiae piisimae posuit
PAT·MVN	patronus municipii
PATR	patronus, patronatus
PATR·C	patronus centuriae
PATR·COL	patronus coloniae
PATR·COL·	patronus coloniae rei publicae
R·P·R	Riciniensis
PATRIM	patrimonium
PATR·MVN	patronus municipii
PATRN	patronus
P·A·V	provincia Africa vetus
PAVIMEN	pavimentarius
P·B·F	(filii) patri bono fecerunt ?
PBL	publicus
P·B·M	parentes bene merenti
P·B·M	patrono bene mèrenti
P·B·P, P·B·PR principalis beneficiarius praefecti	
P·BR·S	plumbum Britannicum signatum
	or publicani Britanniae sanctae ?
P·C	patres conscripti
P·C	patronus civitatis, coloniae, col-
	legii, corporis
PC	pecunia
P·C	pia constans (legio cohors)
P·C	pietatis causa
P·C	ponendum curavit
P·C	post consulatum
P·C	potestate censoria
P·C·ET S·A (AS, ponendum curavit et sub	
ASC)·D	ascia dedicavit

[1] *C. I. L.* X. 3704, where it is wrongly explained as *Pass(erum)*. The word is found in full in *Notizie Degli Scavi*, 1888, p. 237.

P·C·N	patronus collegii (corporis) nostri
P·C·O	publicum coloniae Ostiensis
P·COL	patronus coloniae
P·COND	pagus Condatium
PCS	post consulatum
P·D	posuit dedicavitque
P·DAT·D·D publice datum decurionum decreto	
P·D·D	posuit dedicavitque
P·D·D	publice decreto decurionum
P·D·D·E	populo dare damnas esto
P·D·D·P·P	posuerunt decreto decurionum pe-
	cunia publica
P·D·NON·F (misellas in) perpetuum dolorem	
	non funerassent [2]
PE	Percennius *or* Pescennius
PEC	pecunia, pecuniosus
PEC	pequarius
PED	pedatura, pedes
PED	pedites, peditata (cohors)
PEDIS, PEDISEQ, PEDISQ[3] pedisequus	
PED·SING	pedes singularis
PEL	pellis
PEQ	pecunia
P·EQ·R·M	patronus eques Romanus muni-
	cipii
PER	Percennius
PER	peregrinus (praetor)
PER	permissu
PERP	perpetuus
P·E·S·C	publice e senatus consulto
PET	Petriana (ala)
PET II	patronus et heres
PERS	Persicus
PESC	Pescennius
PET	Petro
P·F	pater fecit *or* parentes fecerunt
P·F	pater filio
P·F	pia femina ?
P·F	pia fidelis
P·F	pius felix
PF	praefectus
P·F	(in kalendas Februarias quae) prox-
	imae fuerunt
P·F·C·R	pia fidelis civium Romanorum
	(cohors)
P·FE·FILIE parenti (or parentibus) fecerunt	
	filiae
P·FEL	pius felix
P·F·F	parentibus fili fecerunt ?
P·F·F	pia felix fidelis (legio)
P·F·F·AET pia felix fidelis aeterna (legio)	
P·F·K·F	pater filio karissimo fecit
P·F·P, P·FI·P parentibus filii posuerunt ?	
P·F·V	pius felix victor
PG	Primigenia
P·G·D	Petra genetrix domini

[2] *C. I. L.* V. 2956.   [3] *C. I. L.* X. 6638.

P·G·N	provincia Gallia Narbonensis
P·G·S	provincia Germania Superior
PHAL	phalerae
P·H·C	provincia Hispania Citerior
P·H·O·ADQ E·R·P·V	placere huic ordini atque e re publica videri
PI	pius
P·I	poni iussit
PIC	Picenum
P·I·D, PR·I·D	praefectus iuri dicundo
PI·F·F	pia felix fidelis
PIL·PR, POST	pilus prior, posterior
P·I·S	pius in suos
P·K	praetor candidatus
P·L	patrono libertus *or* patronus liberto
PL	placuit
PL	Plancus
PL	Plautus ?
PL	plebs, plebis (aedilis, tribunus)
PL	plumbum
P·L	provincia Lugdunensis
PLA	Plancus
PLA	Plautus
PLAT·DEXT·E·N [1]	platea dextra eunti Nidam
PLB	plumbarius
PL·C	plebs collegii
PL·CER	plebis Cerialis (aedilis)
P·L·L	posuit laetus libens
P·L·L [2]	pro ludis luminibus
PL·M	plus minus
P·L·M	posuit libens merito
PL·MIN	plus minus
P·L·P	patrono liberti posuerunt
P·L·P	praefecti lege Petronia ?
P·L·S·F	patronus liberto suo fecit ?
PLS·MINS	plus minus
PL·SC	plebi scitum
PL·VE·SC	plebive scita
P·M	patronus municipii
P·M	patronus municipii
P·M	plus minus
P·M	pontifex maior
P·M	pontifex maximus
P·M	(et) post mortem (nihil)
P·M	pro meritis
P·M·C	provincia Mauretania Caesariensis
P·MIS	parentes miserrimi
P·M·F	patri merenti fecit
P·M·V	patronus municipii Verulani
P·N	(conservatori) patrimonii nostri
P·N	praeses noster *or* Numidiae
P·N	provincia Numidia
P·N·C	provincia Numidia Constantina
PO	Poblilia (tribus)

PO	Poblius = Publius
P·O	post obitum
PO	posuit
P O	praetorio
P·O	princeps optimus
POB	Poblilia (tribus)
P·O·C	primi ordinis comes
POL	polio
POL	Pollia (tribus)
P·O·M	patrono optime merito
POM, POMEN, POMENT, POMI, POMP	Pomptina (tribus)
POMP	Pompeius
POMT	Pomptina (tribus)
PON·CENS	ponendum censuerunt
PON·CVR	ponendum curavit
PONDER	ponderarius
PONT	Pomptina (tribus)
PONT, PONTIF	pontifex
PONTIFF	pontifices
PONT·MAX	pontifex maximus
PONT·M·M	pontifex municipum municipii
POP	Pompo *or* Popidius
POP	Poblilia (tribus)
POP	populus
POPIN	Popinia (tribus)
POPLIF	Poplifugium
POR, POROL	Porolissensis (Dacia)
POR·PVBLIC	portorium publicum
POS	Postumus
PORT	porticus
PORT	Portunalia
POS	posuit
POS·AED·CAS	post aedem Castoris
POS·CONS	post consulatum
POS·D·S	posuerunt de suo
POSE	poseit = posuit
POS·P·P	posita (statua) pecunia publica
POST	Postumus
POST CONS, CON, COL, CNS	post consulatum
POST H·L·ROG	post hance legem rogatam
POSV	posuit
P·P	pater patriae
P·P	pater patrum (Cult of Mithras)
P·P	pater posuit
P·P	pater piissimus
P·P	parentes pientissimi
P·P	patronus pientissimus
P·P	patronus perpetuus
P·P	pecunia posuit
P·P	pecunia publica
P P	Penates publici ?
P·P	pendens pondo
P·P	permissu proconsulis [3]
P·P	perpetuus
P·P	pius *or* pia posuit

[1] Brambach, 1311 et 1312.
[2] *C. I. L.* X. 856 ; cf. 855 et 857.

[3] Very uncertain, occurs in Africa alone

P·P	piissimo, piissimae, posuit *or* posuerunt
P·P	populo postulante
P·P	populus Parmensis
P·P	portorium publicum
P·P	praepositus
P·P	praeses provinciae
P·P	primus pilus *or* primipilaris
P·P	pro parte
P·P	pro pietate
P·P	propria pecunia
PP	proprio
P·P	(aere) proprio posuerunt
P·P	provincia Pannonia
P·P	publicani provinciae
P·P	publice positus
P·P·A·A·V·V·G·G	perpetui Augusti (duo)
P·P·ANN	praepositus annonae
P·P·AVGG	perpetuis Augustis (duobus)
P·P·BRI· LON	publicani provinciae Britanniae Londinienses
P·P·C	pientissimo ponendum curavit
P·P·D·D	pecunia publica decreto decurionum
P·P·F	patri piissimo fecerunt
P·P·F	Primigenia pia fidelis (legio)
P·P·F·C	pecunia publica faciundum curavit
P·P·F·D·D	pecunia publica fecerunt dedicarunt
P·P·FL· VIEN	praeses provinciae Flaviae Viennensis
P·PI [1]	primipilus
P·P·INFER	provincia Pannonia inferior
P·P·K	praepositus kastris
P·P·L	Publiorum duorum libertus
P·P·M·S	praeses provinciae Mauretaniae Sitifensis
P·P·N NVM	praeses provinciae Numidiae
P·P·O	posuit patrono optimo
PPO	praefectus praetorio
P·P·P	pater pius posuit *or* parentes pii posuerunt
P·P·P	patri piissimo posuit *or* posuerunt
P·P·P	proconsul pater patriae
P·P·P	pro pietate posuit
P·P·P	propria pecunia posuit *or* posuerunt
P·P·P·C	primipilaris patronus coloniae
P·P·P·F	(filii) pii patri pio *or* patri pro pietate fuerunt
PPP·FFF· AAA·GGG	Pii Felices Augusti (tres)
P·P·R	praeses provinciae Raetiae
P·P·R	(forma) publica populi Romani
P·PR·BR	publicani provinciae Britanniae
P·PR·LON	publicani provinciae Londinienses

P·P·R·Q	Penates populi Romani Quiritum
PP·RROM	pontifices Romani
P·P·S	posuit pecunia sua
P·P·S	pro parte sua?
P·P·S	provincia Pannonia superior
P·P·STAT	praepositus stationis
P·P·S	pro pecunia sua
PP·VV	perfectissimi viri
P·P ⌣ ⌣	pro parte tertia
P·Q	pedes quadrati
PQ	pequarius
P·Q	(petitio) persecutio que (esto)
P·Q	populusque
P·QVOQVE VERS	pedes quoque versus
P·Q·Q·V	pedes quoquoversus
P·Q·R	populusque Romanus
P·Q·S	posterisque suis
PR	parentes
P·R	populus Romanus
P·R	post reditum *or* pro reditu
PR	praedium
PR	praefectus
PR	praetor, praetorium, praetorius
PR	praepositus
PR	pridie
PR	Primigenia (legio)
PR	Primus (praenomen)
PR	primus, prior
PR	princeps, principalis
PR	privata (ratio)
PR	pro
PR	probante
PR	Proculus
PR	procurator
PR	promotus
PR	pronepos
PR	provincia
PR	provinciae (anno provinciae, in Mauretania)
P·R	provincia Raetia
P·R	publice restituit?
PRAE, PRAEF	praefectus
PRAEF·AEDIL POT	prafectus aedilicia potestate
PRAEF·AER	praefectus aerarii
PRAEF·AER·SAT	praefectus aerarii Saturni
PRAEF·COH	praefectus cohorti
PRAEF·C·A·V [2]	praefectus centuriae accensorum velatorum
PRAEFEC	praefectus
PRAEF·EQ	praefectus equitum
PRAEFF	praefecti
PRAEFF·PR·	praefecti praetorio
PRAEF·F·D	praefectus frumenti dandi
PRAEF·I·D, IVR·DIC	praefectus iure dicundo

[1] *C. I. L.* XII. 2210.

[2] *C. I. L.* VI. 9219.

PRAEF·MIN	praefectus Miniciae
PRAEF·NVM	praefectus numeri
PRAEF·P·	praefectus puerorum pedisequo-
PEDISIC	rum
PRAEF·PRAET	praefectus praetorio
PRAEF·TIR	praefectus tironum
PRAEF·TVR	praefectus turmarum
PRAEF·VEX, VEXIL	praefectus vexillationi
PRAE·N·H·	praepositus numero Herculis An-
ANT	toniniano
PRAEP	praepositus
PRAEPO [1]	praepositus
PRAEP·P·	praepositus publici frumenti *or*
FRVM	pecuniae frumentariae
PR·AER	praefectus aerarii
PRAES	praesentes
PRAET	praetor, practorius
PRAETT	praetoriae (cohortes)
PR·BR·LON	provinciae Britanniae Londinienses
P·R·C·ANN	post Romam conditam anno
PR·CER·I·D,	praetor cerialis iure dicundo
IVR·DIC	
PR·C·R	praetoria civium Romanorum
	(cohors)
PREC	precari
PREF	praefectus
P·R·F [2]	praefectus
PR·GER·SVP	provincia Germania Superior
PR·G·N	princeps gentis Numidarum
PR·H·O·C·S	progressus hostem occidit civem
	servavit
PRI	pridie
PRI	Primus (praenomen)
PRI	princeps
PRI	primus, prima
PR·I·D	praefectus *or* praetor iure dicundo
PRID	pridie
PRIM	primarius
PRIM·IN·C	(Fortunae) Primigeniae in colle
PRIM, PRIMIG	Primigenia (legio)
PRIMOP [3]	primipilus
PRIMO·V	primo (*dative*) unquam
PRIN	princeps
PRINC	princeps, principalis
PRIN·COL	princeps coloniae
PRINC·PEREG	princeps peregrinorum
PRINC·PRAET	princeps praetorii
PR·IN PED	principales in pedatura
PR·IV	princeps iuventutis
PR·IVV	praetor iuventutis
PR·IVVEN	princeps iuventutis
PR·K	praetor candidatus
PR·K·TVT	praetor candidatus tutelaris
PR·LV·LV·	pro ludis luminibus

[1] *Ephem. Ep.* VII. 362.
[2] *C. I. L.* VII. 450.
[3] *C. I. L.* VIII. 9045.

PR·L·V·P·F	praetor ludos Victoriae **primus**
	fecit
P·R·N	patrimonium? regni Norici
PRO	proconsul
PRO	procurator
PRO	proficisceretur
PRO	pronepos
PRO	protector
PRO	provincia
PROB	probavit, probaverunt, probante,
	probatus
PROC	proconsul
PROC	procurator
PROC·AD B	procurator ad bona
PROC·AVG	procurator Augusti
PROC·AVG·	procurator Augusti quadragesi-
XXXX	mae (Galliarum)
PROCC	procuratores
PROC·CA–	procurator capiendorum vectiga-
PIEND·VEC	lium
PROC·K	procurator kastrensis [rum
PROC·M·N	procurator marmorum Numidico-
PROC·VECT	procurator vectigalis (Illyrici)
PROC·IIII	procurator quattuor publicorum
P·AFR	Africae
PROCO	proconsul
PROCONSS	proconsulatus
PRO·COS, PROCOS	pro consule, proconsule
PROCOS	proconsul, proconsulatus
PRO·D	provincia Dacia
PRO DOM	protector domesticus
PRO LVD·LVM	pro ludis luminibus
PRO·M	processum meritus
PROM	promotus
PRO MAG	promagister
PRON, PRONEP	pronepos
PROP·P·C	propria pecunia curavit
PRO PR	pro praetore
PRO PR·	pro praetore ex senatus **consulto**
EX S·C	
PRO Q	pro quaestore
PROR	proreta
PRO S	pro salute
PRO S·D·N	pro salute domini nostri
PROT	protector
PROV	provincia
PROV	provocator
PROX	proximus (rationum, tabulario-
	rum)
PROX·CIPP	proximus cippus
PR·M	praepositus militum
PRM·FEL·	Primani Felices Iustiniani (nu-
IVST	merus)
PROV	provincia
PRP	propriis
PR·PER	praetor peregrinus
PR·P·F	Primigenia pia fidelis (legio)
PR·POS, POST	princeps posterior

PR·PR	praefectus praetorio
PR·PR	praeses provinciae
PR·PR	pro praetore
PR·PRAET	princeps praetorii
PR·POST, PR	princeps posterior, prior
PR·P·V	praetoria pia vindex (cohors)
P·R·Q	populus Romanus Quiritium
PR·REL[1]	praepositus reliquationis
P·R·S	procurator rationum summarum?
PR·S	profecturus sit
PR·SAC	praetor sacrorum
PR·SAC·VOLK· FAC	praetor sacris Volcano faciendis
PR·SEN·CONS	praetor senatum consuluit
PR·S·P·S	pro salute posuit
PR·STA	praepositus stationis
PR·VIG	praefectus vigilum
PR·VRB	praefectus urbi or praetor urbanus
PR·II VIR	praetor duo vir
PR·XX LIB	procurator vigesimae libertatis
P·S	Pannonia Superior
P·S	Parthica Severiana (legio II)
P·S	pater sacrorum
P·S	pecunia sua
P·S	pius, pia suis?
PS	posuerunt
P·S	praeses Samnii
P·S	proprio sumptu
P·S	pro salute
P·S	proximis suis
P·S·D·D	pro salute domus divinae
P·S·D·N	pro salute domini nostri
P·S·F	pecunia sua fecit
P·S·F·C	pecunia sua faciundum curavit
P·S·I	pro salute imperii
P·S·P	pecunia sua posuit
P·S·P·D	pecunia sua posuit dedicavit
P·S·P·L·L	pecunia sua posuerunt laeti libentes
P·S·P·L·L	pro salute posuit laetus libens?
P·S·R	pecunia sua restituit
P·S·R	procurator summarum rationum
P·S·S[2]	Pannonia Secunda Savia
P·S·S	pro salute sua
P·S·S·P	pro salute sua posuit or posuerunt
P·S·S·S	pro salute sua suorumque?
P·ST	posuit
PST CONSLTO	post consulatum
P·S·V	parentibus suis vivis
PT	pater
P·T	posuit testamento?
P·T·M	posuit titulum memoriae
PTR	patronus

1 *Ephem. Ep.* III. p. 311.
2 *Ephem. Ep.* II. 884.

P·V	perfectissimus vir
P·V	pia vindex (legio)
P·V	portus uterque
P·V	praefectus urbi
P·V	provincia utraque
PV	publice
V·q	pupilla
P·V·A	pius vixit annos or annis
PVB	publicus, publica, publice
PVB	Publilia (tribus)
PVBCO	publico
PVB·FAC	publice factum
PVBL	publicus, publica, publice
PVBL	publicanus
PVBL·COL	publicum coloniae
PVBLI, PVBLIL	Publilia (tribus)
PVBL·MVN	publicum municipii
P·V·B·P·R·Q	publicus populi Romani Quiritium
PVG	pugnarum
PVP	Pupinia (tribus)
PVP	pupillus
PVP	Pupus
PVPI, PVPIN	Pupinia (tribus)
P·V·PHILIP	pia vindex Philippiana (legio)
PV·PO	publice positus
PV·PV·L	duorum puporum libertus, liberta
PVR	purpureus
P·V·S	posuit volo soluto

Q

Q	quaestiones
Q	quaestor, quaestoricius
Q	quando
Q	que
Q	qui, quae, quod
Q	Quinquatria
Q	quinquennalis
Q	Quintus
Q	Quirina (tribus)
Q, Ꝗ	quondam
Q·A	quaestor aerarii
Q·A	quot annis
Q·AER·P	quaestor aerarii publici
Q·AL, ALIM	quaestor alimentorum
Q·A·V	qui annos or annis vixit...
Q B[3]	quaestor beneficiarius??
Q·B·F·F	quod bonum faustum felix (sit)
Q·C·A	quorum curam agebat
Q·C·C·R·M NEG·MOG· C·T[4]	quaestor curator civium Romano- rum Mogontiaci, negotiator Mo- gontiacensis, civis Taunensis
Q·CONT	qui continet
Q·C·P	quinquennalis censoria potestate
Q·C·R	quei cives Romani (erunt)
Q·C·V	quaestor coloniae Viennae

3 Brambach, 24.   4 Brambach, 756.

Q·D	quaestor designatus
Q·D	quondam
Q·D·A	quo, qua *or* quibus de agitur
Q·D·E·R·F·P·	quid de ea re fieri placeret, de
D·E·R·I·C	ea re ita censuerunt
Q·D·R	qua de re
Q·D·R·A	qua de re agitur
Q·E	qui, quae, quod est
Q·E·C·F	(votum libens animo posuit) quo-ius eum compotem fecit
Q·E·D	quod eo die
Q·F	qui, quae, quod fuit *or* qui faciunt *or* quod factum *or* quo facto
Q·F·P·D·E·	quid fieri placeret, de ea re ita cen-
R·I·C	suerunt
Q·F·IVG	quod facit iugerum
Q·H·C·I·R	quo honore contentus impensam remisit
Q·HH·S·S	qui heredes scripti sunt
Q·H·N·S	quod heredem non sequetur
Q·I·D·P	qui iure dicundo praeerit
Q·INF·S·S	qui(quae)infra scripti (scripta) sunt
QIQE [1]	quinque
QIR	Quirina (tribus)
Q·I·S·S	qui (quae) infra scripti (scripta) sunt
Q·K	quaestor kandidatus
Q·L·S·V·T·L	(dicite) qui legitis sit vobis terra levis
Q·M	qui militavit
Q·M	quo minus
Q·M·C	qui militare coeperunt
Q·MIL	qui militavit
Q·N·S·S·S	quorum nomina supra scripta sunt
Q·P	quaestoria potestate
Q·P	quadrati pedes
Q·P·A	quaestor pecuniae alimentariae
Q·P·A·P	quaestor pecuniae alimentorum publicorum
Q·P·F	qui primi fuerunt
Q·P·P	quaestor pecuniae publicae
Q·PR·PR	quaestor pro praetore
Q·Q	quaestores
Q·Q	quicquid
Q·Q	quinquennalis
Q·Q	Quinti duo
Q·Q·C·F·	quinquennalis corporis fabrum na-
NAV	valium
Q·Q·C·P	quinquennalis censoria potestate
Q·Q·P	quoquoversus pedes
Q·Q·PER, Q·	quinquennalis perpetuus *or* quin-
Q·P·P	quennales perpetui
Q·P·P·C·M	quinquennalis perpetuus corporis mensorum
Q·Q·S·S·S	quam qui supra scripti sunt
QQ·TT	quaestores

[1] Boissieu, *Insc. de Lyc*

Q·Q·V	quoquoversus
Q·Q·V·L·P	quoquoversus locus pedum...
Q·Q·V·P	quoquoversus pedes...
Q·Q·V·P·Q	quoquoversus pedes quadratos .
Q·R·C·F	quando rex comitiavit fas, *or* quando rex comitio fugit (see page 367)
QR	Quirina (tribus)
Q·R·P	quaestor rei publicae
Q·R·P·A	quaesturam rei publicae agens ?
Q·R·S·H·F·	?
H·T·T·V [2]	
QS	quiescant ?
Q·S	qui, quae, quod supra
Q·SAC·P·	quaestor sacrae pecuniae alimenta-
ALIM	riae
Q·S·F·E	quod supra factum est
Q·S·P·P·S	qui sacris publicis praesto sunt
Q·S·S·S	qui (quae) supra scripti (scripta) sunt
Q·ST·D·F	quando stercus delatum fas (see page 367)
QT	quot
Q·V	quoquoversus
QV	quinque
QV	Quintus
QV	Quirina (tribus)
Q·V	qui vixit
Q·V	qui vocatur
Q·V·A	qui vixit annis *or* annos
QVAD	quadrans
QVADR	quadrigae
QVAE, QVAES	quaestor
QVAESIT·IVD	quaesitor iudex
QVAES·RET	quaestum rettulit
QVAEST·SAC	quaestor sacrae pecuniae ali-
P·ALIM	mentariae
QVAIST	quaestor (archaic)
QVANTI E·	quanti ea res erit tantam pecuniam
R·E·T·P	
QVAR	Quartus (praenomen)
Q·V·F·S·I·O	quod verba facta sunt in ordine
QVI	Quinctilis
QVI [3]	Quintana ? (ara)
QVI	Quirina (tribus)
QVIB·EX·	quibus ex senatus consulto coire
S·C·C·P	permissum (est)
QVI·I·D·P	qui iure dicundo praeest
QVIN	Quinquatria
QVIN	quinquennalis
QVINCT	Quinctilis
QVINQ	quinquennalis
QVINQ	quinquies

[2] Gruter, 886, 3, explains: *Qui retro scripti heredes fecerunt hunc titulum. Titulo usi.* —It is probable that the abbreviations have not been correctly copied.   [3] Bramb. 1446.

QVIR	Quirina (tribus)
QVIR	Quirinalia
QVIR	Quirinalis (flamen)
QVIRI, QVIRIN	Quirina (tribus)
Q·VIX	qui, quae vixit
QVO F	quo facto
QVOT	quotannis
Q·V·P	quoquoversus pedes
Q·V·P·Q	quoquoversus pedes quadratos
Q·VR, VRB	quaestor urbanus
QVR	Quirina (tribus)

R

R	Raetia, Raeti (cohors)
R	Rapax (legio)
R	ratio
R	recessus
R	regnum
R	restituit
R	retiarius
R	retro
R	Retus (praenomen)
R	revocatus
R	Romanus
R	rubrica, rubrum
R	Rufus
R	ratio, Romanus (eques), rubrica
RAP	Rapax (legio)
RAS[1]	rarissimo
RAT	rationalis
RAT·CASTR	ratio castrensis
RAT·PRIV	ratio privata
RAT·S·R	rationalis sacrarum remunerationum ?[2]
R·C	reficiendum curaverunt
R·D·A	ratio dominica Augusta
RE	Regina
REC	reciperator, reciperatorius
RECT·PROV	rector provinciae
RED·IN C	redactus in colonicum ?
RED·AB AER	redemptor ab aerario
REF, REFE, REFEC	refecit, refecerunt, refectus
REFIC·COER	reficienda coerarunt (archaic)
REFIC·D· C·S·C	reficiendas de conscriptorum sententia curaverunt
REG	Regina
REG	regio
REIP, REIPVB	rei publicae
RE·P	rei publicae
REP	reparari
REPLET	repletio
RES	restituit
RES P·C·	res publica coloniae Lambaesitanae
L·F	fecit

REST, RESTIT	restituit, restituerunt
RET	retiarius
RET	rettulit
REVOC	revocatus
RHOD	Rhodanici (nautae)
R·IN C	redactus in colonicum ?
R·L	recte licet, licebit
R·M·F	reverentissimae memoriae femina ?
R·N	regnum Noricum
ROB	Robigalia
ROM	Romanus
ROM, ROMIL, ROMVL	Romilia (tribus)
ROS	rosalia
R·P	ratio privata
R·P	res publica, rei publicae, re publica
R·P·B	res publica Bovillensium
R·P·C	rei publicae constituendae
R·P·C	res publica Carsiolorum
R·P·C·A	rei publicae caussa abesse
R·P·C·L	res publica coloniae Lambaesitanae
R·P·D	rei publicae dedit
R·P·M·D	res publica municipii Dianensium
R·P·N	res publica nostra
R·P·P	res publica Philippensium
R·P·P·D·D	res publica Phuensium decreto decurionum
R·P·R	res publica Reatinorum
R·P·R	res publica Ricinensis
R·P·R	res publica restituit
R·P·RS·RTA[3]	re publica Romanis restituta
R·P·S·S	res publica suprascripta
RR	rarissimae ?
R·R·PROX· CIP·P	recto rigore proximo cippo pedes...
R·T	ripa Thraciae
R·T, TIB	ripa Tiberis
RV·I	rudis prima
RVSS	Russata (factio)

S

S	sacerdos
S	Servius
S	servus
S	sestertium
S	Severiana (legio or cohors)
S	Severus
S	sextarius
S	Sextus
S	si
S	Sicilia
S	sacerdos, sacrum
S	saeculum
S	saltus
S	salve or salutem
S	Saturnus

---

[1] *C. I. L.* VIII. 4037.   [2] Orelli, 1090.   [3] *C. I. L.* VIII. 10298.

S	scriba, scripsit, scriptus	S·A·F	Saturnus Augustus Frugifer
S	se, sibi	SAG	sagittarii (cohors)
S	secundae	SAL	Salius
S	secutor	SAL	Salvius
S	semis	SAL	salve *or* salutem
S	sententia	S·AL	Severiana Alexandriana (legio *or*
S	sepultura		cohors)
S	signavit, signator	SALA	salararius
S	singuli	SALARI·SOC	salarius sociorum
S	Silvanus	SAM	Samnis
S	singuli, singularis	SAR	Sarmaticus
S	situs *or* sepultus	SAR	Sardinia
S	sol ?	S·ARK	servus arcarius
S	solvit	SARM, SARMAT	Sarmaticus
S	soror ?	S·A·S	Saturno *or* Silvano Augusto sa-
S	Spurius		crum
S	stipendia	SA·SAT	sacerdos Saturni
S	studiosus [1]	S·AS·D	sub ascia dedicavit
S	sunt	SAT·AVG	Saturnus Augustus
S	suus, sui	SATVR	Saturnus
S	suppurationes	SB·P·Q·S	sibi posterisque suis
S	quinarius	SB·D	sub die
S	servus, Sextus,[2] scriba ?[3]	SC [4]	sacerdotium
SA	sacerdos	S·C	sacra cognoscens
S·A	(procurator) saltuum Apulorum ?	SC	scaenicus
SA	salve *or* salutem	S·C	senatum consuluerunt
SA	Salvius	S·C	senatus consulto
S·A	Salus Augusta ?	SC	(plebi) scitum
S·A	Severiana Alexandriana (legio co-	S·C	singularis consularis
	hors)	S·C	scribendum (curaverunt)
S·A	Silvanus Augustus	S·C	sub cura
S·A	somnus aeternalis	S·C·F·C	senatus consulto faciendum cura-
SAB, SABATI, SABATIN Sabatina (tribus)			vit
SAC	sacer, sacrum, sacerdos, sacerdo-	SCA	scabillarii
	talis, sacravit	SC·ADF	scribendo adfuerunt
SACC	sacerdotes	SCAP, SCAPT	Scaptia (tribus)
S·AC·D	sub ascia dedicavit	SCAPTINS	Scaptiensis (of the tribus Scaptia)
SACER	sacerdos	SCAT	Scaptia (tribus)
SACERD·CER	sacerdos Cereris	S·C·C	senatus consulto curavit, curave-
S·M·P·XV	sacerdos matris Deum quindecim-		runt
V	viralis	S·C·D·D	socii cultores domus divinae
SAC·P	sacerdos publicus	S·C·D·D·	s... creatus decreto decurionum
SAC·P·A·A	sacerdos provinciae Africae anni...	SC·D·M	sciens dolo malo
SAC·PHRYG·	sacerdos Phrygius maximus	S·C·D·T	senatus consulto de thesauro
MAX		S·C·E	servo conserva eius ?
SACR	sacrum	SCEN	scaenicus
SACR·FAC	sacris faciundis	S·C·F·C	senatus consulto faciundum cu-
SAC·SVP	sacerdos superior ?		raverunt
SAC·VRB	sacerdos urbis	SC·HR	secundus heres
S·A·D,D·D	sub ascia dedicavit	S·C·P	sacerdos Cererum publica
		S·C·P·R	senatus consultum populi Romani
		S·C·Q·ANN	sui cuiusque anni
		SCR	scriba, scripsit
		SCR·ADF	scribendo adfuerunt
		S·C·R·C	senatus consulto restituendum cu-
			raverunt

[1] *C. I. L.* III. 4876.

[2] The explanation "*Secutor*" suggested by Hübner (*Exempl. script. epigr.* p. lxxiii), for n°s 2441 and 2547 of the VI volume of the *Corpus* appears to Cagnat very doubtful. We can in these two cases interpret as, *Sextus*.

[3] *Bull. Épigr.* 1889, p. 94.

[4] *C. I. L.* VI. 736.

SCRI	scriba, scripsit
SCRIB·ADF	scribundo adfuerunt
SCRIB·LIBR·Q	scriba librarius quaestorius
SCRIB·Q·VI PR	scriba quaestorius sexprimus
SCRIB·R·P	scriba rei publicae
S·CRI·VLL	sine crimine ullo
SCRP	scripuli
SCR·CER	scriptus cerarii
SCRVT ·	scrutarius
SCS	sacerdos
SCVR	scurra
SCVT	Scutata (cohors)
SCYT, SCYTH	Scythica (legio)
S·D	sancta dea
S·D	Serapis? deus
S·D	Silvanus deus
S·D	sinistra decumanum
S·D	Sol deus
S·D·L·S·D	sacerdos dei Liberi, sacerdos deae
S·D·M	sacrum Diis Manibus
S·D·M	sine dolo malo
S·D·N	(pro) salute domini nostri
S·DO·M	sine dolo malo
S·D·S	Saturno deo or domino sacrum
S·D·S	Silvano domestico sacrum
S·D·S·D	Silvano deo sancto domestico?
SE	secutor
SE	secunda
SE	sestertius
S·E	situs est
SEB	Sebasteni (ala)
SEBAC	sebaciaria
SEC	secundae
SEC	secutor
SEC·H	secundus heres
SEC·TR	secutor tribuni, trierarchi
SEI V·E	sei videatur eis
SEIVG	seiuge
SEM	semel
SEM, SEMEN, SEMENS	semestris
SEN	senatus
SEN	senior
SEN·SEN	senatus sententia
SEP	September
SEP	Septimius
SEP	sepultura
SEPT	September
SEPT	Septimius
SEQ	Sequana (dea)
SEQ	secutor
SER	Sergia (tribus)
SER	Servius
SER	servus, serva
SER·AEQ·MONET	servus aequator monetae
SERG	Sergia (tribus)
SERT	Sertor
SER·7SC	servus contrascriptor
SER·VIL	servus vilicus

SER·V·LIBER·V	servus vovit, liber solvit
S·E·S·F	sibi et suis fecit
SESQ, SESQVIPL	sesquiplicarius
SE·TR	secutor tribuni
S·ET S	sibi et suis
S·ET S·L·L·P·Q·E,	sibi et suis libertis, liberta-
or LIB·LIB·POST·	bus posterisque eorum
Q·EOR	
SEV·AVG	sevir Augustalis
SEX	sexmestris (tribunus)
SEX	sextilis
SEX	Sextus
SEXM	sexmestris (tribunus)
SEXTIL	Sextilis (mensis)
S·F	sacris faciundis
S·F·S	sine fraude sua
S·H	secundus heres ?
S·H	semihora
S·H	signum Herculis ?
S·H	sita hic ?
S·H	summa honoraria
S·H·F·C	secundus heres faciendum curavit
S·I	stlitibus iudicandis
S·I·D	Sol invictus deus
SI·E	situs est
SIF	sifonarius
SIG	signifer
SIGF	signifer
SIGN	signator, signavit
SIGN	signum, signifer
SIGNF	signifer
SIL·SILV	Silvano silvestri
S·I·M	Sol invictus Mithras
SING	singularis, singuli
SING·COS	singularis consularis
SINGVL	singularis
S·I·N·M	Sol invictus n... Mithras
S·IV	sanctissimus iuvenis ?
SL·IVDIK	stlitibus iudicandis
S·L·L·M	solvit laetus libens merito
S·L·M	solvit libens merito
S·L·P	sibi libertis posterisque
S·L·R	(votum) susceptum libens reddidit
S·L·R·I·C·Q·	siremps lex res ius caussaque omni
O·O·R·E	bus omnium rerum esto
S·L·V·S·P	suo loco vivus sua pecunia ?
S·M	sanctae memoriae
S·M	secundum mancipium
S·M	Sol Mithras
S·M	solvit merito
S·M	submedicus
S·M·D	sacrum matri Deum
S·M·V	sacra moneta Urbis
S·N	sestertii nummi
S·N·P	si non paret
SOC	socius, socii
SOC·S	sociorum servus
SOD	sodalis

SOD·AVG, AVGVST	sodalis Augustalis
SOL	solvit
SOL·L·M	solvit libens merito
S·O·P·P	sunt omnis pedaturae pedes ...
SP	semper
S·P	servus publicus *or* serva publica
SP	spectavit
SP	Spurius
S·P	stolata puella ?
S·P	sua pecunia *or* suo peculio *or* sumptu proprio *or* sumptu publico
S·P	sub praefectus
SPAER	sphaerista
S·P·B	singulares pedites Britannici ?
S·P·C·P·S	sua pecunia posuerunt
S·P·D·D	sua pecunia dono dedit
S·P·D·D·D	sua pecunia dono dedit dedicavit
SPE	spectavit
SPEC, SPECVL· SPECLAR	speculator, speculariarius
SPECTAT NVM[1]	spectator numerator
SP·F	spectabilis femina
SP·F	Spurii filius
S·P·F	sua pecunia fecit
S·P·F·C	sua pecunia faciendum curavit
S·P·FE	soror pia fecit ?
S·P·F·E·S· V·P	sua pecunia fecit et sibi vivus posuit ?
SPHAER	sphaerista
S·P·L	senatus populusque Lavininus
SPL	splendidus, splendidissimus
SPL·EQ·R	splendidus eques Romanus
S·PL·R	sacra publica Romana
S·P·M·A	senatus populusque municipii Antinatium
SPP	spectabiles
S·P·P	sua pecunia posuit
S·P·P·C	sua pecunia ponendum curavit
S·P·P·L·D· D·D	sua pecunia posuit, loco dato decreto decurionum
S·P·P·S	sacris publicis praesto sunt
S·P·P·S·F	solo publico (*or* privato ?) pecunia sua fecit
S·P·Q	senatus populusque
S·P·Q·A	senatus populusque Albensis
S·P·Q·C	senatus populusque Corsiolanus
S·P·Q·L	senatus populusque Lavininus
S·P·Q·R	senatus populusque Romanus
S·P·Q·S	sibi posterisque suis
S·P·Q·T	senatus populusque Tiburs
S·PR	sine pretio
S·P·R	sua pecunia restituerunt
SPR	subpraefectus
S·P·S·F	sibi posterisque suis fecit
S·P·S·P	sibi posterisque suis posuit

[1] *C. I. L.* XII. 5695. (See page 260.)

S·Q·H·A·P· E·S·S·A· V·D·F	si quis hanc arcam post excessum suprascriptorum aperire voluerit, dabit fisco
S·QVE·ME·F	suisque merentibus fecit
SR	Sergia (tribus)
S·R, RAT	summae rationes
SR·D·S·F·C	soror de suo faciendum curavit
S·RES·LEX·IVS· CAVSSAQVE· O·O·R·ESTO	siremps res, lex, ius caussaque omnibus omnium rerum esto
S·R·P·F· ET D	sumptibus rei publicae fecit et dedicavit
SS	sanctissimae ?
S·S	(Silvano) sancto sacrum
S·S	scripti *or* scripta sunt
S·S	semper scriptus
S·S	senatus sententia
SS	sestertius
S·S	siti sunt
SS	solverunt (ambo)
S·S	subscriptus
S·S	sumptu suo
S·S	supra scriptus, scripta
S·S	susceptum solvit
SS	sestertii, sextarii
SS·DD·NN	salvis dominis nostris (duobus)
S·S·F	sibi suisque fecit
S·SI	supra scripti
S·S·L·L·M	(votum) susceptum solvit libens laetus merito
S·S·P·Q·EOR	sibi suis posterisque eorum
S·S·Q·P·P	sibi suisque posterisque posuerunt
S·S·S	sicut supra scripti, scripta
S·S·S	summa supra scripta
S·S·S	supra scripti, scripta sunt
S·T	secutor tribuni
ST	statera
ST	Statius
ST	Stellatina (tribus)
ST	stipendia
STA	stamen
STA	Statius
STAT	statio, stationarius
STAT	statua
STAT·HER	statio hereditatium
STAT·Q· C·M	statio quadragesimae civitatis Mediomatricorum
STE, STEL, STELL, STELLA, STELLAT	Stellatina (tribus)
STI, STIP	stipendia
ST·F	stolata femina
ST·HER	statio hereditatium
STIP	stipendia
STL	Stellatina (tribus)
S·T·L	sit terra levis
STL, STLIT IVDIC	stlitibus iudicandis
S·TR	secutor tribuni
STR	strator

STRIG	striganus ?
STP	stipendiorum
STRA	strator
S·T·T·L	sit tibi terra levis
S·T·T·L·D	sit tibi terra levis dic
STVP	stupidus
S·V	senatus Vocontiorum
S·V	se vivo
S·V	spectavit victor
SVB	subheres
SVB	Suburana (tribus)
SVB A (ASC)·D	sub ascia dedicavit
SVB CVR	sub curator
SVBHE	subheredes
SVBPR, SVBPRAE, SVB- PRAEF	subpraefectus
SVBPROC	subprocurator
SVBSEQ	subsequens
SVBVIL	subvilicus
SVBVNG	subunctor
SVC	Suburana (tribus)
S·C, CV	sub cura
S·VE C	senatusve consulto
S·V·F	sibi vivus fuit
SVF	sufes
SVF	suffectus
SVF	suffragia
S·V·L·A	solvit votum libens animo
SVLP	Sulpicia (ala)
S·V·L·M	solvit votum libens merito
SVL·M	Sulevae montanae
SVM	summa
SVM	Summanus
SVMP	sumptuarius
SVM·SVM	summa summarum
SVPP	suppositicii (gladiatores)
S·V·Q	sine ulla querela
SVS·VOT	suscepto voto
S·V·T·L	sit vobis terra levis
SX	Sextus
SYR	Syriacus, Syriaca (classis)

T

T	tabula, tabularius
T	Tampiana (ala)
T	te
T	templum ?
T	tergum
T	terra
T	territorium
T	tesserarius
T	testamentum
T	tiro
T	titulus
T	Titus
T	transvecturarius
T	tribunus

T	Tripolitana
T	Tromentina (tribus)
T	tumulus
T	turma
T¹	prima
T·A	taurus auratus
TAB	tabularius
TAB	taberna
TAB	tabula, tabularius, tabulatio
TABEL, TABELL	tabellarius
TABVL	tabularius, tabularium
TAMP	Tampiana (ala)
TAVR	taurobolium
T·BAT	Transrhenanus Batavus
T·B·C	tubicen ?
T·B·Q	tu bene quiescas
T·C	titulum curavit
T·D·V·S	Telluri deae votum solvit ?
TEC	tector
TEGVL	tegularius
TEM	templum
TER	Teretina (tribus)
TER	terminus, terminalia
TER	tertius, tertia
TERET, TERETIN	Teretina (tribus)
TERM·CVR	terminandum curaverunt
TERR	territorium
TERR	terruncius
TES	tessera, tesserarius
TESM	testamentum
TESS, TESSE, TESSER	tesserarius
TEST·LEG	testamento legavit
T·F	testamentum fecit
T·F·C	testamento or titulum faciendum curavit
T·F·I	testamento or titulum fieri iussit
T·F·I·S	testamento fieri iussit sibi
T·F·R	testamento fieri rogavit
THER	thermarius
T·H·E·S	tumulo hoc (?) est sepultus
THR	Thracia, Threx
TI	Tiberius
TIB	Tiberius
TI·F	titulum fecit
TIGN	tignarius
TIR	Tirrus
TIT	titulus
TIT·DE·C· S·S	titulum dedicaverunt cum supra scriptis
TIT·P	titulum posuit
T·K	tabularium castrense
T·L	testamento legavit
T·L·H·F·C	testamento legavit; heres faciundum curavit
T·M	Threx murmillo

¹ The Ī sometimes appears on the monuments in the form of a T.

T·M·P	titulum memoriae posuit
T·M·Q·F·E·REV	tene me quia fugi et revoca
T·N·C·H·F·C [1]	testamento non cavit ; heres faciundum curavit ???
T·O·B·Q	tibi ossa bene quiescant
TOG	togatus (= advocatus)
TON	tonsor
TOP	topiarius
TORQ	torques, torquata (ala *or* cohors)
TORQ·ARMIL· PHAL	(donatus) torquibus, armillis, phaleris
TOT	Totates ? (Mars)
T·P	tanta pecunia
T·P	tertiae partis ?
T·P	testamento *or* titulum posuit
T·P	tribunicia potestate
T·P·I	testamento *or* titulum poni iussit
T·P·M	titulum posuit memoriae
T·PO·L·L·M	titulum posuit libens laetus merito
T·Q·D	totiusque domus
TR	Traianus, Traiana (legio)
TR	Transpadana
TR	Trebius
TR	Threx
TR	tribunus
TR	trierarcha
TR	trieris
TR	triumphator
TR	Tromentina (tribus)
TRA	Traianus, Traiana
TR·A	trierarcha Augusti
TRAI	Traianus, Traiana
TRAM	tramare
TRA, TRAN, TRANSPAD	Transpadana
TR·AVGG	tricliniarcha Augustorum
TRE	trecenarius
TRE	Treveri (ala)
TREB	Trebius
TREC	trecenarius
TR·ET NAV	transvectuarius et navicularius
TREV	Treveri (ala)
TR·FOR	Traiana fortis (legio)
TRI	trierarcha
TRIB	tribunus
TRIB·ET NOT	tribunus et notarius
TRIB·LAT, LATIC, LATICL	tribunus laticlavius
TRIB·MIL	tribunus militum
TRIB·MIL·A P, A POP	tribunus militum a populo
TRIB·P	tribunicia potestate
TRIB·P	tribunus plebis
TRIB·POT, PT	tribunicia potestate
TRIB·SVC	tribus Succusana
TRIPL	Tripolitana
TRIVMF, TRIVMP	triumphator, triumphatrix

TR·LAT	tribunus laticlavius
TR·M	tribunus militum
TR·M	tritici modius
TR·MIL	tribunus militum
TR·MIL·A P	tribunus militum a populo
TR·MIL·L, LEG	tribunus militum legionis
TRO	(legio) Troana (Trajana)
TRO, TROM, TROMENT, TROMENTIN	Tromentina (tribus)
T·R·P·D·S·	te rŏgo praeteriens dicas sit tibi
T·T·L	terra levis
TR·PL	tribunus plebis
TR·POT	tribunicia potestate
T·S	tatae suo [2]
T·S·F·I	testamento suo fieri iussit
T·S·T·L	terra sit tibi levis
T·T	tibi terram
T·T·L·S	tibi terra levis sit
T·V	titulo usus
T·V	ture vino
TVB	tubicen
TVB, TVBIL	tubilustrium
TVB·SAC· P·R·Q	tubicen sacrorum populi Romani Quiritium
T·V·F	titulum ? vivus fecit
T·V·F	ture vino fecerunt
TVL	Tullus
TVM	tumulus
TVN, TVNG	Tungri (cohors)
TVK	turma
TVT·AVG	Tutela Augusta
TVTEL	tutelarius
T·T	Teretina tribus
T·T·L·S	terra tibi levis sit
T·T·L·V	terra tibi levis volo ?

V

V	vale
V	Valentia (dea)
V	Valerius
V	vene = bene
V	veteranus
V	Venus
V	verna
V̄	veteranus
V	via
V	Vibius
V	vicit
V	Victoria
V	victrix (legio)
V	villa
V	vir
V	Virtus (dea)
V	urbs
V	vivus, viva, vivit, vixit

[1] Brambach, 1156.   [2] *C. I. L.* X. 1949.

V	Voltinia (tribus)
V	votum, vovit
V	utere
V	uti
V	uxor
VA	vale
V·A	vices agens
V·A	vixit annos *or* annis
VAL	Valerius, Valeria (legio)
VAL	valetudinarius, valetudinarium
V·A·L	vices agens legati
VAL·BYZ	Valeria Byzacena (provincia)
VAL·VICT	Valeria victrix (legio)
V·A·S·L·M	votum animo solvit libens merito
V·A·S·P·P	viis aedibus sacris publicis procurandis?
VB	Ubii (cohors)
V·B	vir bonus
V·B·D·R·P	vir bonus dignus re publica
V·B·M·P	voto bene merenti posuit
V·B·O·V·F	virum bonum oro vos faciatis
V·B·S	vir bonus sanctus
V·C	vir clarissimus
VC	unctor [1]
V·C·A·V·P	vir clarissimus agens vices praesidis
V·C·CONS· P·N	vir clarissimus consularis provinciae Numidiae
V·C·D·D	vir clarissimus dedit dedicavit
V·C·ET INL	vir clarissimus et inlustris
V·C·L·M	voti compos libens merito
V·C·P·P	vir clarissimus pater patrum
V·C·Q·K	vir clarissimus quaestor candidatus
V·C·R	voluntarii cives Romani
V·D	vir devotus
V·D·D	Veneri? donum dat
V·D·P·R·L·P	unde de plano recte legi possit
V·D·P·T· L·D	vir devotissimus protector lateris dominici [2]
V·D·S	vovit? de suo
VE	Velina (tribus)
VE	veteranus
VE [3]	vetus?
V·E	vir egregius
V·E·A·V·P	vir egregius agens vices praesidis
VEC	vectigal, vectura
VECT, VECTIG	vectigal
V·E·D·F [4]	vir egregius decurio factus
V·E·EQ·R	vir egregius eques Romanus
VEHIC	vehicula
VEL	velarius
VEL	veles
VEL, VELIN, VELL	Velina (tribus)

[1] Orelli, 3471.
[2] *Bullett. Comunale*, 1873, p. 51.
[3] *C. I. L.* IX. 2585.
[4] *C. I. L.* VI. 2010.

VEN	venatio, venator
VEN	Veneta (factio)
VEN	Venetia
V·E·PP	vir egregius primipilaris
VER	(Frisii) Verlutionenses (cuneus)
VER	verna
VERB	verbex
VESTIG	vestigator
VET	Voturia (tribus)
VET, VETER	veteranus
VEX, VEXI, VEXIL, VEXILL	vexillarius, vexillatio
V·F	verba fecit *or* fecerunt
V·F	Viennae fecit
V·F	vivus, viva fecit
VFEN	Oufentina (tribus)
V·F·ET L·E	vivi fecerunt et locum emerunt?
V·F·I	vivae fieri iussit?
V·F·S	verba facta sunt
V·F·S	vivus fecit sibi
V·F·S·ET S	vivus fecit sibi et suis
V·F·T	vivus fecit titulum?
V·H	vir honestissimus
V·H·A	vixit honeste? annis
VI	Vibius
VI	vineae?
V·I	vir inlustris
VI	vixit
VIAT	viator, viatorium
VIAT·TR	viator tribuni
VIAT·TR·PL	viator tribuni plebis
VI·AV	Victoria Augusta
VIB	Vibius
VIC	vicit
VIC	victimarius
VIC	victoria
VIC	vicus, vicani
VIC	victoriatus
VIC	victor, victrix (legio)
VIC·AVG	Victoria Augusta
VICE·S·C	vice sacra cognoscens
VICIM	vicimagister
VIC·LOP	vicus Lopodunensis
VIC·N	victoriati nummi
VIC·POR	Vicani Portuenses
VIC·S	vici scito
VICT	victimarius
VICT	Victorienses (collegium)?
VICT, VICTR	victrix (legio)
VIG	vigiles
VIK	vicani?
VIL	vilicus
VIL·BR	vilicus Brundisinorum
VILC	(vigesimae libertatis) vilicus
V·ILL	vir illustris
VILLA	villatici
VIL·PVB	villa publica
VIL·R·S	vilicus ripae superioris

VIN	Vinalia
VIND, VINDEL	Vindelici (cohors)
V·INL	vir inlustris
V·INL·COM	vir inlustris comes
VIN·VRB·ET OST	vinarii urbani et Ostienses
V·I·P·AN	vixit pia annos, *or* annis
VIRB	Virbialis
V·I·S	verba infra scripta
VI·S	vici scitu
V·L	(sine fraude) vel laesione ?
V·L	verna libertus ?
V·L	veteranus legionis
V·L	vir laudabilis
V·L·A·S	votum libens animo solvit
V·L·LIB·M	voto laetus libens merito
V·L·L·M·S	votum libens laetus merito solvit
V·L·M	votum libens merito
V·L·M·S	votum libens merito solvit
V·LOC·F	vivus locum fecit
V·L·P	votum libens posuit
VLP	Ulpius, Ulpia (legio)
V·L·P·M	votum libens posuit merito
V·L·R	votum libens reddidit
V·L·S	votum libens solvit *or* libentes solverunt
V·L·S·M	voto libens solvit merito
V·M·F	vene (= bene) merenti fecerunt
V·M·L·P	votum merito libens posuit
V·M·L·S	votum merito libens solvit
VN	vene = bene
VNC, VNCT	unctor
V·O	vir optimus ?
VO	Vopiscus
VOC	Vocontii (ala)
VOL	Volcanus
VOL	Voltinia (tribus)
VOL	voluntarii (cohors)
VOLC	Volcanalia
VOL·C·R	voluntarii cives Romani (cohors)
VOLT, VOLTI, VOLTIN	Voltinia (tribus)
VL, VLT	Voltinia (tribus)
VOLVNT	voluntarii (cohors)
V·O·P	viro optimo posuit (coniux)
VO·P·L·S	votum pater ? libens solvit
VOR	Vordenses (ala)
V·O·S·L·M	votum o... solvit libens merito
VOT	Voturia (tribus)
VOT·FEL·SVCC ?· LIBEN	votum feliciter susceperunt libentes
VOT·X, XX	vota decennalia, vicennalia
VOT·D	votum dedit
VOT·FEC, SOL·L·M	votum fecit, solvit libens merito
VOT·M·F	votum merito fecerunt
VOT... M·S·L	votum... merito solvit libens
VOT·RED·L	votum reddit libens
VOT·S·L·A	votum solvit libens animo
VOT·SOL·L·L	votum solvit laetus libens

V·P	vir perfectissimus
V·P	vivus posuit
V·P	votum posuit
V·P	uxori pientissimae ?
V·P·A	vixit pius annis
V·P·A·V·P	vir perfectissimus agens vices praesidis
V·P·D	vir perfectissimus dux
V·P·F	uxor piissima fecit *or* uxori piissimae fecit
V·P·L·M	votum posuit libens merito
V·P·M	votum posuit merito
V·P·P·P·H	vir perfectissimus praeses provinciae Hispaniae
V·P·P·P· MAVR· SITIF	vir perfectissimus praeses provinciae Mauretaniae Sitifensis
V·P·P·P·N	vir perfectissimus praeses provinciae Numidiae
V·P·P·P·R	vir perfectissimus praeses provinciae Raetiae
V·Q	viator quaestorius
V·Q·F	valeat qui fecit
V·QVE	(sine) ulla querella
V·Q·R·F·E·V	uti quod recte factum esse volet
V·Q·R·F·E· V·S·D·M	uti quod recte factum esse volet sine dolo malo
V·R	vir religiosus
V·R	votum reddidit
VR	urbs Roma
V·R	urbicus
VRB	urbanus, urbana (cohors)
VRBS	urbis
V·RL	vir religiosus
V·R·L·M	votum reddidit libens merito
V·S	vici scitu
V·S	votum solvit, voto soluto
V·S	vir spectabilis
V·S	Urbs sacra
V·S·A·L	votum solvit animo libens
V·S·C	vice sacra cognoscens
V·S·D·N·F· R·I·M	votum solverunt Dianae Nemorensi...
V·SE	vini sextarius ?
V·S·F	vivus *or* viva sibi fecit, vivi sibi fecerunt
V·S·F	votum solvit feliciter
V·S·I	vice sacra iudicans
V·S·L	votum solvit libens
V·S·L·A	votum solvit libens animo
V·S·L·A·D	votum solvit libens animo dat ?
V·S·L·A·F	votum solvit libens animo feliciter
V·S·L·A·P·C	votum solvit libens animo p... c...
V·S·L·A·S	votum solvit libens animo suo ?
V·S·L·H	votum solvit libens H...
V·S·L·L	votum solvit libens laetus
V·S·L·L·B· MER	votum solvit laetus libens bene merito

V·S·L·L·M	votum solvit laetus libens merito
V·S·L·P	votum solvit libens posuit
V·S·M	votum solvit merito
V·S·M·L	votum solvit merito libens
V·S·M·L·M·S	votum solvit merito libens, Mercurio sacrum ?
V·SP	vir spectabilis
V·S·P	vivus sibi posuit
V·S·P·S·S	votum susceptum pecunia sua solvit
V·SS·L·A	votum solverunt libentes animo
V·S·S·LV·M	votum susceptum solvit lubens merito
VST	ustrina
VTEI IN H·L·SC·EST	utei in hac lege scriptum est
VT·F	utere felix
VT·S·L·M	votum solvit libens merito
V·V	Valeria or Ulpia victrix (legio)
V·V	Venus victrix
VV	viri
VV	vivi or vivunt
V·V	vivus vivae
V·V	vir venerabilis ?

V·V	virgo Vestalis
V·V	uti voverant
V·V·C·C	viri clarissimi
V·V·E·E	viri egregii
V·V·F	vivus vivae fecit
VVLTIN	Voltinia (tribus)
V·V·P	vivus posuit or vivus vivo posuit
V·V·M	Virgo Vestalis Maxima
V·V·P·P	viri perfectissimi
V·V·S·FECER	vivi sibi fecerunt
V·V·S·L·M	ut voverat solvit libens merito
V·V·S·S·F	vivis supra scriptis fecit
V·V·V	vale, vale, vale !
VX	vixit, uxor
VX·DVL	uxor dulcissima
VXT	vixit

Z

Z[1]	centurio
Z	zeta = diaeta
Z·T·L	mulieris (et) Titi libertus ?

[1] *C. I. L.* VIII. 9910.

HS	sestertius
₤	sestertius
∠	dupondius
ƒ	as
II	duumvir
IIS, HS	sestertius
II SIL	duobus Silanis (consulibus)
II V, II VIR	duumvir, duumviratus
IIVIR AB AER	duumvir ab aerario
II VIR·C·P·Q	duumvir censoria potestate quinquennalis
II·VIR·I·D	duumvir iure dicundo
IIVIR Q, Q·Q, QVINQ	duumvir quinquennalis
III	tertium
III	trieris
III Ɔ·L	trium mulierum libertus, liberta
III PR, PROV	tres provinciae (Galliae)
III VIR	triumvir
III VIR·A·D·A	triumvir agris dandis adsignandis
III VIR·CAP, KA, KAP, CAPIT, KA-PIT	triumvir capitalis
III VIR MON = A·A·A·F·F	triumvir monetalis = auro argento aere flando feriundo
IIII	quadrieris
IIII	quattuorvir
IIII P·AFR	quattuor publica Africae

IIII VIR	quattuorvir, quattuorviratus
IIII VIR·I·D	quattuor vir iure dicundo
IIII VIR·PR	quattuor vir praefectus
IIII·VIR Q, Q·Q, QVINQ	quattuorvir quinquennalis
IIII VIR·V· CVR	quattuorvir viarum curandarum
V	penteris
V	quinarius
V VIR·A·D·A	quinquevir agris dandis adsignandis dis
VI	hexeris
IιιιI	sevir
IιιιI VIR	sevir, seviratus
IιιιI VIR AVG	sevir Augustalis
VI VIR EQ·R	sevir equitum Romanorum
VII VIR EPVL	septemvir epulonum
✳	denarius
X	decemvir
XVIR·A·D·A·I	decemvir agris dandis adsignandis judicandis
XVIR SACR·FAC	decemvir sacris faciundis
X V(VIR)·S (SL, STL, STLIT)· I(IVD, IVDIC, IVDIK)	decemvir stlitibus judicandis
XI PR	undecim primus
XV	quindecimvir
XV VIR·S·F	quindecimvir sacris faciundis

$\overline{\text{XVIIII}}$	decennovium (The Pomptine Marshes)
XX LIB	vigesima libertatis
XX HER, HERE, HERED, HEREDIT	vigesima hereditatium
XX P·R·M	vigesima populi Romani minus
XXXX, XL G	quadragesima Galliarum
C	centenarius
Ɔ	centesima
C	centumviri
C V	centumviri

Ɔ	centesima
Ɔ, Ɔ, ʔ, 3,), Z, Ƶ, ⟩	centurio, centuria
Ɔ	sextarius
)	conventus
CC	ducenarius
ƆƆ·L	duarum mulierum libertus
CCC	trecenarius
$\overline{\text{CCCC}}$	quadringenarius
ϴ	quingentaria (ala *or* cohors)
∽	miliaria (ala *or* cohors)

TABLE OF ABBREVIATIONS

[From *Cours d'Épigraphie Latine*, R. Cagnat, with the permission of the author.]

A

A	Adiutrix
A	aera (stipendia)
A	agitur
A	Alexandriana
A	avus
A·A·P·R	annona Augusta populi Romani
A·AVE	alter ambove
A·CV	a cubiculo, *or* a custodiis
AE	aerum
AEQ	eques
A·L·G	a legione
AM·S	amplissimus splendidissimus
AN	annualis
A·N·F·F	annum novum faustum felicem
A·P	adiutor procuratoris
AR	armorum (custos)
A·SCR	a scriniis
A·SEV	Alexandriana Severiana (legio)

B

B	bene
B	bucinator
BE·SE	beneficiarius sexmestris
BF·PR	beneficiarius praefecti, procuratoris
BF·V·C·COS	beneficiarius viri clarissimi consularis
B·M·H·T·P	bene merenti heredes testamento posuerunt
BN·R·P·N	bono rei publicae natus
BOT·RET	botum (votum) rettulit
B·P·A	beneficiarius procuratoris Augusti

C

C	cerarius
C	cultores
C	custos
ƆC	feminae duae
C·A·E	Colonia Augusta Emerita
C·B·B·V	cum bonis bene vixit
C·C	civitas convenarum
CCC·VVV	clarissimi viri tres
C·C·P·I	coloni coloniae Pacis Iuliae
C·C·R	coloni coloniae Romulae
C·E	coniux eius
C·E·C	coloni eius coloniae
C·I·F·C	cohors I Flavia Canathenorum
CIRC·N	circiter numeri
C·I·V·T	Colonia Iulia Victrix Triumphalis
CO	colonus
COL·F·C	collegae faciundum curaverunt
CONS	consecravit
CONT	contubernalis
C·O·V·F·S	coniugi optumae vivus fecit sibi
C·P	callis publicus
C·P	cohors prima
C·P·P	coniugi praeposuit
CRO, CROC	crocodes
C·SC	genas scabras (on occulist stamps)
C·S·S	cum supra scriptis
CV·AR	custos armorum

D

D	Domitiana (ala)
D·B·B·M	deo bono bene merenti
D·D	deus Dolichenus
D·D	di deae
D·D·C	deus Dolichenus Commagenus
DD·M·SS	Diis Manibus sacris
D·D·P·ET·S·S	donum dat pecunia et sumptu suo
D·D·Q	di deaeque
D·D·S	diis deabus sacrum
D·E·S	Deo Enduellico sacrum
D·F	donum fecit
D·I·M·S	deus invictus Mithras Sol
DISP·ARC·VIC	dispensatoris arcae vicarius
D·M·M	deum mater magna
D·M·N	dominicus
D·M·Q·S	dis manibus Q(uinti) sacrum *C.I.L.* II. 3382
DO	domesticus
DOLI / DOLIA	doliare (opus)
D·P	de praediis
D·Q·N·Q	de quo (qua) nihil questus (a)
D·RO·Q·TRA	dic, rogo qui transis
D·R·P	dic, rogo praeteriens
D·R·P	de re publica
D·S	dea Salus
D·S	dei sacerdos
D·S	deus Sol
D·S·L·L·D	de suo laetus libens dedit
D·S·O·M	deus sanctus optimus maximus
D·S·S	deus Sanctus Saturnus Silvanus
D·T·M·L	de tabulario marmorum Lunensium
D·TOR·AR	donatus torquibus armillis
D·V	decreto vicanorum
DV·S·C·EQ·SING	duplicarius singularis consularis equitum singularium
D·V·S	dedit voto soluto

E

E·E	exemplum epistolae
EMB	emblema
EMP	empticius
EQ·SEN	equiter seniores
E·S·L	exemplum sacrarum litterarum
EXCT	excusatus
EXPL	exploratio exploratores
EX PR	ex praecepto

F

FAB·SAG	fabrica sagittaria
F·C·ET·S·P	filiae coniugi et sibi posuit
F·C·N	figlina Caesaris nostri
FE·V·F	feliciter voto fecit
F·ET·F·V·F	filii et filiae vivi fecerunt
F·ET·M·F·C·E	funeris et memoriae faciendae curam egit
FGL	figlinae
FI	figlinae
FLV NEG	fluviatili negotiatione ?
FOD	fodinae
F·P·S·F·C	filii patri suo faciendum curaverunt
F·S·S	fit summa summarum

G

G·C	genius castrorum
G·D·A·S .	Giddabae deo Augusto sacrum (*C.I.L.* VIII. 6267)?
G·MER	genius Mercurii
GR	Graecus

H

H	hereditates
H·A·S	Herculi Augusto sacrum
HAST	hastiliarius
HEL	Helvetius
HELV	Helvetius
H·F	honorifica femina
H·P	hostes publici
H·S·F·C	heres sepulcrum faciendum curavit
H·S·H·N·L	hoc sepulcrum heredi non liceat (vendere), *C.I.L.* II. 5891
HVE	heresve
H·V·F·F	heres utriusque filius fecit

I

I·D	inferiis diis
I·D	iuveni defunctae
I·D·F	iussu dei fecit
I·H·C	imaginem honoris causa
I·O·PAR	Iuppiter Optimus Partinus
IP·S·P	ipse sibi posuit
I·S	Iuno Sima
I·S·P·P	in sua possessione posuit

K

K	carus, a
KL	calendae

L

L·A	locus adsignatus
L·A·S	Libero Augusto sacrum
L·D·D·O	locus datus decreto ordinis
LEG·S·S	legio supra scripta
LIBB	Libyae duae
L·M·IN·F·P	locus monumenti in fronte pedes
L·M·Q·P	locus monumenti quadratus pedes
L·M·Q·VP	locus monumenti quoquoversus pedes
L·P	lares publici
L·P·Q·Q·V	locus pedum quoquoversum
L·P·S	libens pecunia sua

M

M	Mithras
M	Mystae
M·A	monumentum aedificavit
MANB	manibus (*C.I.L.* VII. 575, 1336)
MAR	Marsus
M·C·D·D	municipii cultoribus dono dedit
M·D·M	monumentum diis manibus
ME	mensis
M·E·M·D·D·E	municipibus eius municipii dare damnas esto
M·F·S	mater filiis suis
M·H·H·N·S	monumentum hoc heredem non sequetur
M·I	Mithras invictus
MIN	ministrator
M·N	Marcus noster
M·N	marmora nova *or* Numidica
M·PL	minus plus
M·PR	magister primus
M·S	Mithras Sol
M·V·V·S	monitus visu votum solvit

N

N·G·V·S	numini gratus votum solvit
N·M·S·S	numerus militum Syrorum sagittariorum
N·PAL	numerus Palmyrenorum
N·R	nihilum rogatur
N·SING	numerus singularium
N·S·S	numerus supra scriptus
NT	noster, -ri
N·VOC	numerus Vocontiorum

O

O·E	olla empta
OF	officinator, officiales
OFG	opus figlinum
OM	omnibus

OSP	hospes
O·V	optimus vir

P

P·B·B·M·T·I	patri bono bene merenti testamento iussus
P·COS	pro consul
P·ET·S·S	pecunia et sumpto suo
P·F·C·C	pia fidelis constans commoda (*Limesblatt*, 1897, p. 467) (Legio VIII Aug.)
P·I	princeps inventutis
P·L	pecunia legata
P·L·V·S	posuit libens voto soluto
P·M	pecunia multaticia
PN	pronepos
POP	populus
POPIN	Popinia (tribus)
POR·COR	portus Cornelii ?
POS	posuerunt
POSV	posuerunt
P·P	pagani pagi
P·P	ponderatus pondo
P·P·A	publicum portorii Asiae
PP·FF	pii felices
P·P·S	pro pietate sua
PP·SS	pueri supra scripti
PRD, PRE	praedium
PR·P	primus pilus
PR·PR	princeps prior
PR·S	pro reditu salvo
P·S	procurator suus
P·S·C	pedites singulares consularis
P·SIG·COS	pedites singulares consularis

Q

Q·A·P	qui aerario praesunt
Q·E·R·E·T·P	quanti ea res erit tantam pecuniam
Q·E·R·F·E·D	quod eius recte factum esse dicetur
Q·F·E	quod factum est
Q·F·H·P	Quintus filius heres posuit
Q·L·A·A·R	qui locum acceperunt a re publica
Q·P·P·C·M	quinquennalis perpetuus corporis mensorum
Q·R·F·E·V	quod recte factum esse videbitur
Q·R·T·P·D·S·T·T·L	qui rogat te praeteriens dicas, sit tibi terra levis.
Q·S	quadrivis sacrum

R

R·N	Rupe natus
R·P·C	rei publicae causa
R·S	ripa superior
R·S·P	ratio sacri patrimonii
R·S·P	res summa privata

S

S	sextarius
S	signifer
S	statio
S	semis
S·A	sodalis Augustalis
S·A	Saturnus Augustus
SAC·SAT	sacerdos Saturni
SAL	salinae
S·B·A·S	Saturno Balcaranensi Augusto sacrum
S·C	strator consularis
S·C·C·C	senatus coire convocari cogi
S·C·C·E	sub cuius cura egi
SCR·CER	scriptus cerarii
S·D	Saturnus dominus
S·D·M·T·T·L	sit dis manibus tuis terra levis
S·E·S	sibi et suis
S·FR·S·C·(F)·L	sine fraude sua capere (facere) liceto
S·I·P·C	suis impensis ponendum curavit
S·P	splendidissima puella
S·P·C	statio patrimonii Caesaris
S·Q·S·S·E·Q·N·I·S·R	si quid sacri sancti est quod non iure sit rogatum
S·R	summa res
S·R·F	summa ratio fisci
S·R·P	servus rei publicae
S·S	Saluti *or* Saturno *or* Silvano sacrum
S·S·E·L·F·C	sibi suis et libertis faciendum curavit
S·S·S	Silvano Sancto (silvestri) sacrum
S·S·SIS	salve salvus sis
STIP	stipendiorum
STR, STRA	strator
S·V	soluto voto

T

TIR·LEG	tironis legendi
T·M	terra mater
T·P·C	tertiae partis conductor

V

V·A·P	vices agens praesidis
VERED	veredarii
VET·CO	vetustate corrupta
V·F	utere felix
VIK	vicarius
VIL·R·S	vilicus ripae superioris
VL	Voltinia (tribus)
VLT	Voltinia (tribus)
V·SS·LL·MM	votum solverunt libentes merito
VT·F	utere felix
V·V·S	vir venerabilis sacerdos
VV·SS·LL·MM	volentes solverunt libentes merito

ABBREVIATIONS

	OR.M.	Gold Medal
	OR.	*Aureus*
	OR.Q.	Half Aureus (*Semissis*)
	OR.T.	One third Aureus (*Tremissis*)
	AR.M.	Silver Medal
	AR.	*Denarius*
	AR.Q.	*Quinarius* and smaller div.
	POT.	Potin
	BIL.M.	Billon Medal
	BIL.	Billon
	BIL.Q.	Billon Quinarius
	BR.M.	Bronze Medal
	G.B.M.	Big Bronze Medal
	M.B.M.	Major Bronze Medal
	G.B.	Big Bronze Coin
+	G.B.	Major Bronze Coin
	M.B.	Middle Bronze Coin
+	M.B.	Smaller Middle Bronze Coin
+	P.B.	Major Size Small Bronze
	P.B.	Smaller Bronze Coin
	P.B.Q.	Small Bronze Quinarius

The names of the emperors appearing in the entries are in French, but easily recognizable. The following abbreviations, used also in the entries in the effort to determine the type of coin on which the inscription appears, are also in French, but they appear here translated into English. Those interested to check the French equivalents can check on p. 135.

Ⓑ.	British Museum
Ⓕ.	Paris, Bibliotheque Nationale
	Cabinet des Medailles
Ⓟ.	Berlin, *Munzsammlung*
Ⓣ.	Torino, *Museo Nazionale*
Ⓥ.	Wien, *Munzsammlung*
℞.	Reverse
*	Unique specimen.

TABLE DES LÉGENDES DES REVERS

I. THE MONEYERS

FROM CAESAR TO AUGUSTUS

A. ALLIENVS PRO. COS. J. César AR.
A. HIRTIVS PR. J. César OR.
A. LICIN. NERVA SILIAN. IIIVIR. A. A. A. F F. S. C. Auguste M B.
ANNIVS LAMIA SILIVS Auguste P.B.
ANNIVS SILIVS LAMIA S. C. Auguste P.B.
ANTONIO AVG. SCARPVS IMP. M. Antoine AR.
APRONIVS GALVS A. A. A. F. F. S. C. Auguste P.B.
APRONIVS GALVS IIIVIR. Auguste P.B.
APRONIVS MESSALLA A. A. A. F. F. S. C. Auguste P. B.
APRONIVS MESSALLA IIIVIR. Auguste P.B.
APRONIVS SISENNA A. A. A. F. F. S. C. Auguste P.B.
APRONIVS SISENNA IIIVIR. Auguste P.B.
BALBVS PRO. PR. Auguste OR. AR.
CAEPIO BRVTVS PROCOS. Brutus AR.
C. ANTISTI. VETVS IIIVIR. Auguste OR. (avec APOLLINI. ACTIO.) AR.
C. ANTISTIVS REGINVS IIIVIR. Auguste AR.
C. ANTISTIVS VETVS IIIVIR. Auguste AR.
C. ANTIST. REGIN. FOEDVS P. R. QVM GABINIS. Auguste OR.
C. ANTIST. VETVS FOEDVS P. R. CVM. (ou QVM) GABINIS. Auguste AR.
CASCA LONGVS. Brutus OR. AR.
C. ASINIVS C. F. GALLVS IIIVIR. A. A. A. F. F. S. C. Auguste G.B.
C. ASINIVS GALLVS IIIVIR. A. A. A. F. F. S. C. Auguste M.B.
C. CASSI. PR. COS. Cassius OR.
C. CASSIVS CELER IIIVIR. A. A. A. F. F. S. C. Auguste M.B.
C. CASSIVS C. F. CELER IIIVIR. A. A. A. F. F. S. C. Auguste G.B.
C. CENSORINVS AVG. IIIVIR. A. A. A. F. F. S. C. Auguste M.B.
C. CENSORINVS L. F. AVG. IIIVIR. A. A. A. F. F. S. C. Auguste M.B.
C. CLOVI. PRÆF. J. César M.B.
C. COSSVTIVS MARIDIANVS A. A. A. F. F. J. César AR.
C. FLAV. HEMIC. LEG. PRO PR. Brutus AR.
C. FONTEIVS CAPITO PRO. PR. M. Antoine et Octavie M.B.
C. GALLIVS C. F. LVPERCVS IIIVIR. A. A. A. F. F. S. C. Auguste G.B.
C. GALLIVS LVPERCVS IIIVIR. A. A. A. F. F. S. C. Auguste M.B.
C. MARCI. L. F. CENSORIN. AVG. IIIVIR. A. A. A. F. F. S. C. Auguste G.B.
C. MARIDIANVS J. César AR.
C. MARIVS C. F. TRO. IIIVIR. Auguste AR.
C. MARIVS TRO. IIIVIR. Auguste OR.
C. NAEVIVS CAPELLA S. C. Auguste P. B.
CN. DOMIT. AHENOBARBVS IMP. M. Antoine OR. AR.
CN. PISO CN. F. IIIVIR. A. A. A. F. F. S. C. Auguste G.B. M.B.
CN. PISO C. PLOT. RVF. L. SVRDIN. Auguste M.B.

CN. PISO FRV. F. IIIVIR. A. A. A. F. F. Auguste G.B.
CN. PISO L. SVRDIN. C. PLOT. RVF. Auguste M.B.
CN. PISO PRO. Q. — NVMA. Pompée-le-Grand AR.
C. NVMONIVS VAALA. Fulvie OR.
COSSVS CN. F. LENTVLVS. Auguste AR.
COSTA LEG. Brutus AR.
C. PLOTIVS RVFVS IIIVIR. A. A. A F. F. S. C. Auguste G.B.
C. RVBELLIVS BLANDVS. Auguste P.B.
C. SOSIVS IMP. M. Antoine P.B.
C. SOSIVS Q. M. Antoine M.B.
C. SVLPICIVS PLATORIN. Auguste AR.
C. VEIBIVS VAARVS. Lépide OR. M. Antoine OR. Octave OR.
C. VIBIVS VARVS. M. Antoine AR. Octave AR.
D. TVR. M. Antoine AR.
EPPIVS LEG. J. César GB. Sextus Pompée G.B.
GALVS APRONIVS A. A. A. F. F. S. C. Auguste P.B.
GALVS APRONIVS IIIVIR. Auguste P.B.
GALVS MESSALLA A. A. A. F. F. S. C. Auguste P.B.
GALVS MESSALLA IIIVIR. Auguste P.B.
GALVS SISENNA A. A. A. F. F. S. C. Auguste P.B.
GALVS SISENNA IIIVIR. Auguste P.B.
IMP. CAESARI SCARPVS IMP. Auguste AR.
L. AEMILIVS BVCA. J. César AR
LAMIA SILIVS ANNIVS. Auguste PB. (avec S. C.) P.B.
L. AQVILLIVS FLORVS IIIVIR. Auguste OR. AR. (avec SICIL) AR.
L. ATRATINVS AVGVR. M. Antoine M.B.
    —   —   (avec COS. DES. — HS. Δ) M. Antoine et Octavie G.B.
    —   —   (avec COS. DESIG. — B.) M Antoine et Octavie G.B. M.B.
    —   —   (avec PRAEF. CLASS. F.C. — HS. Δ.) Antoine et Octavie G.B.
L. BIBVLVS M. F. PR.. — HS. Δ. M. Antoine et Octavie BR.M.
L. BIBVLVS M. F. PRAEF. CLASS. F. C. M. Antoine M.B.
L. BIBVLVS M. F. PR. DESIG. M. Antoine MB. M. Antoine et Octavie G.B
L. BIBVLVS PRAEF. CLASS. M. Antoine et Octavie G.B.
L. BRVTVS PRIM. COS. Brutus OR.
L. BVCA J. César AR.
L. CANINIVS GALLVS IIIVIR. Auguste AR.
    —   —   (avec AVGVSTVS TR. POT.) Auguste AR.
    —   —   (avec C. C. AVGVSTI.) Auguste AR.
    —   —   (avec OB. C. S.) Auguste OR.
LENTVLVS SPINT. Brutus OR. AR. Cassius OR. AR.
L. FLAMINIVS IIIVIR. J. César AR.
L. LENTVLVS FLAMEN. MARTIALIS C-V Auguste AR.
L. LIVINEIVS REGVLVS J. César AR. Auguste AR.
L. MESCINIVS — LVD. S. — AVG. SVF. P. Auguste OR.
L. MESCINIVS RVFVS IIIVIR. — IMP. CAES. AVG. LVD SAEC. — XV. S. F. Auguste AR.
    —   —   —(avec IMP. CAES. AVGV. COMM. CONS. S. C.)   —   AR.
    —   —   —(avec S. P Q. R. V. S. PRO. S. ET RED. AVG)   —   AR.
L. MESCINIVS RVFVS. — S. P. Q. R. V. P. RED. CAES. Auguste AR.
L. MVSSIDIVS LONGVS J. César AR. Lépide OR. M. Antoine OR. Octave OR.
L. MVSSIDIVS T. F. LONGVS IIIIVIR. A. P. F. Lépide OR. M. Antoine OR. Octave OR.
L. NAEVIVS SVRDINVS IIIVIR. A. A. A. F. F. S. C. Auguste G.B M.B.
L. PLAET. CEST. Brutus OR. AR.
L. PLANC. PRAEF. VRB. Jules César OR. OR.Q.
L. PLANC. PR. VRB. Jules César OR.
L. PLANCVS IMP. ITER. M. Antoine AR.
L. PLANCVS PROCOS. M. Antoine OR. AR.
L. REGVLVS IIIIVIR. A. P. F. Lépide OR. M. Antoine OR. Octave OR.
L. SESTI. PRO. Q. Brutus AR.Q.
L. SVRDINVS IIIVIR A. A. A. F. F. S. C. Auguste M.B.

L. VALERIVS CATVLLVS S. C. Auguste P. B.
L. VINICIVS L. F. IIIVIR. — S. P. Q. R. IMP. CAE. QVOD V. M. S. EX. EA. P () IS. AD. A. DE. Auguste AR.
L. VINICIVS — S. P. Q. R. IMP. CAES. Auguste AR.
M. AGRIPPA COS. DESIG. J. César OR. César et Octave OR AR. Auguste AR
MAIANIVS GALLVS IIIVIR. A. A. A. F. F. S. C. Auguste M. B.
M. AQVINVS LEG. LIBERTAS. Cassius OR.
M. DVRMIVS IIIVIR. Auguste OR. AR. (avec HONORI.) OR. AR.
MESSALLA APRONIVS A. A. A. F. F. S. C. Auguste P. B.
MESSALLA APRONIVS IIIVIR. Auguste P.B.
MESSALLA GALVS A. A. A. F. F. S. C. Auguste P B.
MESSALLA GALVS IIIVIR. Auguste P.B.
MESSALLA SISENNA A. A. A. F. F. S. C. Auguste P.B.
MESSALLA SISENNA IIIVIR. Auguste P. B.
M. MAECILIVS TVLLVS IIIVIR. A. A. A. F. F. S. C. Auguste G.B. M.B
M. METTIVS. J. César AR.
M. MINAT. SABIN. PR. Q. Pompée-le-Grand AR.
M. MINAT. SABI. PRO. Q. Pompée-le-Grand AR.
M. OPPIVS CAPITO PRAEF. CLASS. F. C. — S M. Antoine P.B.
M. OPPIVS CAPITO PRO. PR. PRAEF. CLAS. F. C. — A. M. Antoine et Octavie P.B (avec Γ) GB. (avec HS. V) M.B.
M. OPPIVS CAPITO PRO. PR. PRAEF. CLASS. F. C. — B. M. Antoine et Octavie G.B.
M. POBLICI LEG. PRO. PR. Cn. Pompée AR.
M. SALVIVS OTHO IIIVIR. A. A. A. F. F. S. C. Auguste G.B. M.B.
M. SANQVINIVS Q. F. IIIVIR. A. A. A. F. F. S. C. Auguste G.B. M.B.
M. SERVILIVS LEG. Brutus OR. AR. Cassius OR. AR.
M. SILANVS AVG. Q. PROCOS. M. Antoine AR.
P. BETILIENVS BASSVS S. C. Auguste P.B.
P. CARISI. LEG. Auguste AR Q.
P. CARISIVS LEG. Auguste M.B.
P. CARISIVS LEG. AVGVSTI. Auguste M.B. (avec EMERITA) M.B.
P. CARISIVS LEG. PRO. PR. Auguste AR. (Avec EMERITA) (1) AR.
P. CLODIVS M. F. J. César AR. M. Antoine AR. Auguste AR.
P. CLODIVS M. F. IIIIVIR. A. P. F. M. Antoine OR. Auguste OR.
P. LICINIVS STOLO IIIVIR. A. A. A. F. F. S. C. Auguste G.B. M.B.
P. LVRIVS AGRIPPA IIIVIR. A. A. A. F. F. S. C. Auguste G.B. M.B.
P. LVRIVS AGRP. (sic.) IIIVIR A. A. A. F. F. S. C. Auguste M.B.
P. PETRON. TVRPILIAN. IIIVIR. Auguste AR.
P. PETRON. TVRPILIAN IIIVIR. FERO. Auguste AR.
P. SEPVLLIVS MACER. J. César AR. M. Antoine AR.
P. STOLO IIIVIR. Auguste AR.
P. STOLO IIIVIR. A. A. A. F. F. S. C. Auguste M.B.
P. VENTIDI. PONT. IMP. M. Antoine AR.
PVLCHER TAVRVS REGVLVS. Auguste PB. (avec S. C.) P.B
Q. AELIVS LAMIA IIIVIR. A. A. A. F. F. S. C. Auguste M.B.
Q. AELIVS L. F. LAMIA IIIVIR. A. A. A. F. F. S. C. Auguste G.B
Q. CAEP. BRVT. IMP. Brutus AR.
Q. CAEPIO BRVTVS IMP. Brutus OR. AR.
Q. CAEPIO BRVTVS PRO. COS. Brutus OR. AR.Q.
Q. LABIENVS PARTHICVS IMP. Labienus OR. AR.
Q. NASIDIV. (ou NASIDIVS) Pompée-le Grand AR.
Q. RVSTIVS FORTVNÆ Auguste OR.
Q. RVSTIVS FORTVNAE ANTIAT. Auguste AR.
Q. SALVIVS IMP. COS. DESIG. (2) Auguste AR.

(1) Variétés avec IMIRITA et IIMIIRITA.
(2) Variété avec DESG.

Q. VOCONIVS VITVLVS. J. César AR. Auguste AR.
Q. VOCONIVS VITVLVS Q. DESIGN. S. C. J. César AR. Auguste AR.
REGVLVS PVLCHER TAVRVS. Auguste P.B. (avec S. C.) P.B.
REGVLVS TAVRVS PVLCHER. Auguste P.B (avec S. C.) P.B.
SCARPVS IMP. Auguste AR. AR.Q.
SCARPVS IMP. LEG. VIII. M. Antoine AR.
SEX. NONIVS QVINCTILIAN. IIIVIR. A. A. A. F. F. S. C. Auguste M.B.
SILIVS ANNIVS LAMIA. Auguste P.B. (avec S. C.) P.B.
SISENNA APRONIVS A. A. A. F. F. S. C. Auguste P.B.
SISENNA APRONIVS IIIVIR. Auguste P.B.
SISENNA GALVS A. A. A. F. F. S. C. Auguste P.B.
SISENNA GALVS IIIVIR. Auguste P.B.
SISENNA MESSALLA A. A. A. F. F. S. C. Auguste P.B.
SISENNA MESSALLA IIIVIR. Auguste P.B.
TAVRVS REGVLVS PVLCHER. Auguste P.B. (avec S. C.) P.B.
T. CRISPINVS IIIVIR. A. A. A. F. F. S. C. Auguste M.B.
T. CRISPINVS SVLPICIAN. (ou SVLPICIANVS) IIIVIR. A. A. A. F. F. S. C. Auguste M.B
T. CRISPINVS T. F. SVLPICIAN. IIIVIR A. A. A. F. F. S. C Auguste G.B.
TI. SEMPRON. GRACCVS IIIVIR. Q. D. Auguste OR.
TI. SEMPRON. GRACCVS IIIVIR. Q. DESIG. Auguste AR.
TI. SEMPRONIVS GRACCVS IIIVIR. A. A. A. F. F. S. C. Auguste G.B M.B.
TI. SEMPRONIVS GRACCVS Q. DES. J. César AR.
TI. SEMPRONIVS GRACCVS Q. DESIG. J. César AR. (avec S. C) AR.
T. QVINCTI. CRISPIN. SVLPI. IIIVIR. A. A. A F. F. S. C. Auguste G B.
T. QVINCTIVS CRISP. IIIVIR. A. A. A. F. F. S. C. Auguste M.B.
T. QVINCTIVS CRISPIN. SVLPIC. IIIVIR. A. A. A. F. F. S. C. Auguste G.B.
T. QVINCTIVS CRISPINVS IIIVIR. A. A. A. F. F. S. C. Auguste G.B. M.B.
T. QVINCTIVS CRISPINVS SVLPIC. IIIVIR. A. A. A. F. F. S. C. Auguste G.B.
TVRPILIANVS IIIVIR. Auguste OR. AR.
TVRPILIANVS IIIVIR. FERO. Auguste OR.
TVRPILIANVS IIIVIR. FERON. Auguste OR. AR.
VARRO PROQ. Pompée-le-Grand AR.
VOLVSVS VALER. MESSAL. IIIVIR. A. A. A. F. F. S. C. Auguste M.B.
VOLVSVS VALER. MESSAL. S. C. Auguste P.B.

II. INSCRIPTIONS ON THE REVERSES OF ROMAN IMPERIAL COINS

ABVNDANT. AVG. Gallien B. Tétricus père P.B. Tétricus fils P.B. Carus P.B. Galère Maximien P.B.
ABVNDANT. AVGG. Dioclétien P.B (1). Maximien Hercule P.B.
ABVNDANTIA. Tétricus père BIL.
ABVNDANTIA AVG. Elagabale AR. Alex. Sévère AR. P.B. Mamée (hybride) AR. Trajan-Dèce OR. AR. Etruscille AR. Gallien OR.Q. B. Salonine B. Victorin B. Tétricus père P.B. Claude II. P.B. Probus P.B. Carus P.B. Carausius P.B. (avec s. c.) Gordien III. G.B. M.B.
ABVNDANTIA AVGG. Numérien OR. PB.Q. Carin P.B. Dioclétien P.B. Maximien Hercule P.B.
ABVNDANTIA AVGG. ET CAESS. NN. Maximien Hercule P.B.
ABVNDANTIA AVG. N. Probus P.B.
ABVNDANTIA AVG. S. P. Q. R. Gallien B.
ABVNDANTIA TEMPORVM. Mamée BR.M. Salonine BR.M.
ADIVTRIX AVG. Victorin OR. OR.Q. Carausius P.B.
ADLOCVT. Vérus BR.M.
ADLOCVT. AVG. COS. III. S. C. Marc-Aurèle G.B.

(1) Variété avec ABVNDAT AVGG.

ADLOCVT. AVG. S. C. Nerva G.B. Vérus G.B.
ADLOCVT. CO. S. C. Néron G.B.
ADLOCVT. COH. Caligula G.B. Néron G.B. (Avec S. C) G.B.
ADLOCVTIO. Marc-Aurèle BR.M. Vérus BR.M. Macrin BR.M. Postume BR.M.
Maxence P.B. (Avec S. C.) Galba G.B. M.B. Adrien G.B.
ADLOCVTIO AVG. Tacite BR.M. Probus OR.M. OR. BR.M. M.B. P.B. Maxence M.B.
(Avec S. C.) Philippe père G.B.
ADLOCVTIO AVGG. Philippe père BR.M. Gallien BR.M. Numérien BR.M.
ADLOCVTIO AVG. N. Constance Chlore M.B.
ADLOCVTIO AVGVSTI. Gordien III. BR.M. Gallien AR.M. (Avec S. C.) Alexandre
Sévère G.B. Gordien III. G.B.
ADLOCVTIO AVGVSTI COS. P. P. S. C. Alexandre Sévère G.B.
ADLOCVTIO AVGVSTI COS. III. P. P. Alexandre Sévère BR.M. M.B. Alexandre et
Mamée M.B.M.
ADLOCVTIO AVGVSTORVM. Philippe père et fils BR.M. Valérien AR.M. BR.M. Valé-
rien et Gallien BR.M. M.B. Gallien BR.M. Gallien et Salonin BR.M.
ADLOCVTIO COH. PRAETOR. S. C. Adrien M.B.
ADLOCVTIO MAXENTII. Maxence M.B.
ADLOCVTIO MILITVM. Probus BR.M.
ADLOCVTIO P. M. TR. P. XVII. IMP. III. COS. IIII. P. P. S. C. Caracalla G.B.
ADOPTIO PARTHIC. DIVI. TRAIAN. AVG. F. P. M. TR. P. COS. P. P. Adrien OR. AR.
ADOPTIO TRIBVNIC. POTEST. Adrien AR.
ADVENT. AVGG. Sept. Sévère OR. AR. Caracalla OR. AR.
ADVENT. AVG. GALL. PONT. MAX TR. POT. XV. COS. III. Sept. Sévère BR.M.
ADVENTV. Carausius AR.
ADVENTVI AVG. Caracalla AR. (avec S. C.) G.B.
ADVENTVI AVG. AFRICAE. Adrien OR. AR. (avec S. C.) G.B. M.B.
ADVENTVI AVG. ALEXANDRIAE. Adrien OR. (avec S. C.) G.B
ADVENTVI AVG. ARABIAE S. C. Adrien G.B. M.B.
ADVENTVI AVG. ASIAE S. C. Adrien G.B.
ADVENTVI AVG. BITHYNIAE S. C. Adrien G.B.
ADVENTVI AVG. BRITANNIAE S. C. Adrien G.B.
ADVENTVI AVG. CILICIAE S. C. Adrien G.B.
ADVENTVI AVG. FEL. Sept. Sévère AR.
ADVENTVI AVG. FELICISSIMO. Sept. Sévère OR. AR. (avec S. C.) G.B. M.B.
ADVENTVI AVG. GALLIAE S. C. Adrien G.B. M.B.
ADVENTVI AVG. HISPANIAE. Adrien AR. (avec S. C.) G.B. M.B.
ADVENTVI AVG. ITALIAE. Adrien OR. AR. (avec S. C.) G.B. M.B.
ADVENTVI AVG. IVDAEAE S. C. Adrien G.B. M.B.
ADVENTVI AVG. MACEDONIAE S. C. Adrien G.B. M.B.
ADVENTVI AVG. MAVRETANIAE S. C. Adrien G.B. M.B.
ADVENTVI AVG. MOESIAE S. C. Adrien G.B.
ADVENTVI AVG. NORICI S. C. Adrien G.B.
ADVENTVI AVG. PHRYGIAE S. C. Adrien G.B.
ADVENTVI AVG. P. M. TR. P. II. COS. II. Sept. Sévère BR.M.
ADVENTVI AVG. P. M. TR. P. II. COS. II P. P. Sept. Sévère BR.M.
ADVENTVI AVG. SICILIAE S. C. Adrien G.B.
ADVENTVI AVG. THRACIAE S. C. Adrien G.B.
ADVENTVS AVG. Adrien OR. AR. Sept. Sévère AR. Caracalla AR. Géta AR. Ela-
gabale AR. Gordien III. AR. Trajan-Dèce OR. AR. Etruscille (hybride) AR.
Hérennius AR. Hostilien AR. Tréb. Galle OR. AR. Volusien AR. Gallien OR. B.
Postume P.B. Victorin OR. B. Tétricus père OR. P.B. Claude II. BR.M. P.B.
Aurélien OR.M. P.B. Tacite BR.M. Probus OR. BR.M. P.B. PB.Q. Carin P.B. Dio-
clétien BR.M. Carausius AR. P.B. Allectus P.B. Constantin I. †P.B. P.B. Honorius OR.M. (avec S. C.) Adrien G.B. M.B. Géta M.B. Trajan-Dèce G.B. M.B. Postume G.B. M.B.
ADVENTVS AVGG. Philippe père AR. Philippe père et Otacilie BR.M. Philippe père
et fils M.B. Trébonien Galle OR. BR.M. Tréb. Galle et Volusien BR.M. M.B. Volusien BR.M. Valérien et Gallien BR.M. M.B. Gallien BR.M. M.B.M. Gallien et

Salonine M.B.M. Gallien et Salonin AR.M. BR.M. Salonin B. Dioclétien P.B.
Maximien Hercule P.B. (avec S. C.). Philippe père G.B. Maximien Hercule
BR.M.
ADVENTVS AVG. NN. Numérien OR.
ADVENTVS AVG. IMP. IIII. COS. II. P. P. S. C. Commode G.B. (1)
ADVENTVS AVG. IMP. VI. COS. III. Marc-Aurèle BR.M.
ADVENTVS AVG. N. Constantin I. OR.M. †P.B. P.B.
ADVENTVS AVG. PONT. MAX. TR. POT. COS. II. S. C. Adrien G.B. M.B.
ADVENTVS AVG. S. P. Q. R. OPT. PRINCIPI. Trajan AR.M. BR M.
ADVENTVS AVG. TR. P. III. S. C. Elagabale M.B.
ADVENTVS AVGVSTI. Adrien OR. AR. Sept. Sévère AR. Caracalla OR. AR. Géta AR.
Elagabale OR. Probus G.B. P.B. Jovien BR.M. (avec S. C.) Adrien G.B. Elaga-
bale G.B. M.B.
ADVENTVS AVGVSTI N. Constantin I. OR.M. OR. (2) P.B.
ADVENTVS AVGVSTI ROMA. Jovien BR.M.
ADVENTVS AVGVSTOR. Caracalla AR.
ADVENTVS AVGVSTORVM. Philippe père et fils BR.M. Dioclétien OR. Maximien
Hercule OR. AR.
ADVENTVS CAES. Commode OR. AR.
ADVENTVS CARAVSI. Carausius P.B.
ADVENTVS CARI AVG. Carus OR. AR.
ADVENTVS PROBI AVG. Probus OR. P.B.
ADVENTVS S. D. N. AVG. Marcien OR.M.
AED. DIVI AVG. REST. COS. IIII. Antonin AR. (avec S. C.) G.B. M.B.
AEDAE. DIVAE. FAVSTINAE. Faustine mère AR.
AEDAE. DIVI AVG. REST. COS. IIII. S. C. Antonin G.B. M.B.
AEGVPTO CAPTA. Auguste OR. AR.
AEGVPTOS Adrien OR. AR. (avec S. C.) G.B. M.B.
AELIANA PINCENSIA Adrien P.B. P.B.Q.
AEQVITAS AV. Victorin P.B.Q ?
AEQVITAS AVG. Adrien AR. Antonin AR. Sept. Sévère AR. Julie Domne AR.
Macrin OR. AR. P.B. Alexandre Sévère OR. AR. AR.Q. P.B. Maximin I. OR. AR.
Gordien III. OR. AR. Philippe père AR. Philippe fils AR. Trajan Dèce OR. AR.
Etruscille (hybride) AR. Hérennius AR. Hostilien AR. Tréb. Galle AR.M. AR.
Volusien AR. Gallien OR. OR.Q. B. Salonine B. Quiétus BILL. Posiume OR.
Victorin P.B. Marius P.B. Tétricus père OR. P.B. Tétricus fils P.B. Claude II.
OR. P.B. P.B.Q. Quintille P.B. Vabalathe P.B. Tacite BR.M. P.B. Florien P.B.
Probus P.B. Carin P.B. Maximien Hercule AR. Carausius P.B. Allectus P.B.
(avec S. C.) Domitien M.B. Adrien G.B. M.B. Macrin G.B. M.B. Alexandre
Sévère M.B. Gordien III. G.B. M.B.
AEQVITAS AVG. COS. II. Albin AR.
AEQVITAS AVGG. Sept. Sévère AR. Julie Domne AR. Caracalla AR. Philippe
père OR. AR. Philippe fils AR.M. AR. Trajan Dèce AR. Etruscille (hybride) AR.
Tréb. Galle OR. AR. Volusien OR. AR. Valérien AR.M. B. Gallien B. M.B.
Quiétus BIL. Carus P.B. Carus, Carin et Numérien BR.M. Numérien P.B.
Carin P. B. Dioclétien P.B. Maximien Hercule P.B.Q. (Avec S. C.) Philippe père
G.B. M.B. Tréb. Galle G.B. Volusien G.B.
AEQVITAS AVGG. V. Tétricus père P.B.
AEQVITAS AVG. NOSTRI. Décence AR.M.
AEQVITAS AVG. S. P. Q. R. Claude II. P.B.
AEQVITAS AVGVST. Nerva OR. AR. (avec S. C.) Vespasien M.B. Titus M.B. Domi-
tien M.B. Nerva M.B.
AEQVITAS. AVGVSTI Autonome de Galba AR.Q. Elagabale AR.M. BR.M. G.B. Alex.
Sévère AR.M. Alex. Sévère et Mamée AR M. BR.M. Maximin I. AR.M. BR.M.
Gordien III. AR.M. BR.M. Philippe père AR.M. BR M. (avee S. C.) Galba M.B.
Vitellius M.B. Vespasien M.B. Titus M.B. Alex. Sévère G.B. M.B.

---

(1) Variété avec ATVENTVS.
(2) Variétés avec AOVFNTVS et AVENTVS.

AEQVITAS AVGVSTI TR. P. COS. II. Pertinax G.B.
AEQVITAS S. C. Galba M.B.
AEQVITAS II. Sept. Sévère AR. Julie Domne AR.
AEQVITAS PVBLICA Julie Domne AR.M. Élagabale G.B. Paula AR.M. G.B. Aquilia
Sévéra G.B. Soémias AR.M. Maesa G.B. Mainée AR.M. Philippe père AR.M. Gallien BR.M. Gallien et Salonine BR.M. Salonine AR.M. BR.M. (avec S. C.) G.B.
AEQVITATI AVGG. Sept. Sévère OR. AR. Julie Domne OR.
AEQVITATI PVBLICAE Caracalla AR.M. Géta AR.M. BR.M. Paula G B. (avec S. C.)
Sept. Sévère M.B. Julie Domne G.B. Caracalla G.B. Géta G.B. M.B.
AEQVIT AVG. Gallien B.
AEQVIT. AVG. TR. P. COS. II. Pertinax OR. AR. (avec S. C.) G.B. M.B.
AEQVTAS AVG. Gallien B. Macrien jeune BIL. Quiétus BIL.
AEQVTAS AVGG. Philippe père AR. Quiétus M.B.
AERCVLI PACIF. Probus P.B.
AERES AVGVST. S. C. Titus M.B.
AESCVLAPIVS. Antonin BR.M.
AET. AVG. Gallien B.
AET. AVG. COS. V. P. P. S. P. Q. R. OPTIMO. PRINC. Trajan AR.
AET. AVG. P. M. TR. P. COS. DES. III. Adrien AR.
AET. AVG. P. M. TR. P. COS. II. (ou III). Adrien AR.
AET. AVG. S. P. Q. R. OPTIMO PRINCIPI. Trajan AR.
AETER. AVG Claude II. P.B.
AETER. AVG. P. M. TR. P. COS. III. Adrien AR.
AETERNAE MEMORIAE. Maximien Hercule M.B. Constance Chlore M.B. Galère
Maximien M.B. P.B. Romulus OR.M. AR.M. AR.Q. M.B. P.B.
AETERNAE MEMORIAE GAL. MAXIMIANI. Galère Maximien M.B. ⸶M.B.
AETERNA FELICITAS AVG. N. Maxence M.B.
AETERNA GLORIA SENAT. P. Q. R. Constance II. OR.M.
AETERNA MEMORIA. Maximien Hercule M.B. Constance Chlore M.B Galère
Maximien M.B. Romulus M.B.
AETERNA. PIETAS. Constantin I. P.B.Q.
AETERN. AVG. Gallien B.
AETERN. AVGG. Julie Domne AR.
AETERNITAS. Vespasien OR. AR. Titus AR. Domitien AR. Antonin AR. Faustine
mère OR. OR Q. AR. BR.M. Faustine jeune AR. BR.M. (avec S. C.) Faustine mère
G.B. M.B. Faustine jeune G.B.
AETERNITAS. AVG. Pesc. Niger AR. Sept. Sévère AR. Élagabale AR. Philippe fils
AR. Tréb. Galle AR. Gallien OR. B. Postume OR. Claude II. P.B. P.B.Q. Aurélien P.B. Vabalathe P.B. Tacite M.B. P.B. Florien P.B. Probus OR. P.B. (avec
S. C.) Adrien G.B. Antonin G.B.
AETERNITAS. AVGG. Philippe père AR. Tréb. Galle OR. AR. Volusien OR. Valérien OR. B. Gallien OR. Tétricus père et fils OR. Tétricus fils BR.M. Carin
P.B. Dioclétien P.B. PB.Q. Maximien Hercule P.B. Galère Maximien P.B.
(avec S. C.) Philippe père G.B. M.B. Tréb. Galle G.B.
AETERNITAS AVG. N. Maxence M.B. P.B.
AETERNITAS AVG. P. XV. Gallien B.
AETERNITAS AVGVSTI S. C. Vespasien. M.B. Adrien M.B. Gordien III. G.B.
AETERNITAS COS. V. P. P. S. P. Q. R. OPTIMO. PRINC. Trajan AR.
AETERNITAS P. R. S. C. Vespasien G.B. M.B.
AETERNITATI AVG. Gordien III. OR. OR.Q. AR. AR.Q. Gallien B. Probus P.B. (avec
S. C.) Gordien III. G.B. M.B.
AETERNITATI AVGG. Valérien B. Gallien B. Dioclétien P.B. (avec S. C.) Emilien G.B.
AETERNITATI AVGVSTA. (ou VGVSTI) S. C. Domitien M.B.
AETERNITATIBVS. Alex Sévère AR.
AETERNIT. AVG. Tétricus père P.B. Claude II. P.B. Quintille P.B. P.B.Q. Aurélien
P.B. Carin P.B. (avec S. C.) Vespasien M.B. Titus M.B.
AETERNIT. AVGG. Carin P.B. Maximien Hercule P.B.Q.
AETERNIT. IMPER. Sept. Sévère, Caracalla et Géta OR. OR.Q. AR. Philippe père
AR. Philippe fils AR.

AETERNIT. IMPERI. Septime Sévère et Caracalla AR.
— — Sept. Sévère, Caracalla et Géta AR.
— — Julie, Sept. Sévère et Caracalla OR. AR.
— — Julie, Sept. Sévère et Géta G. B.
— — Julie, Caracalla et Géta OR. AR.
— — Caracalla et Sept. Sévère OR. AR
— — Geta, Sept. Sévère et Caracalla OR. AR.
— — Carus P. B.
AETERN. MEMOR. Maximien Hercule P.B.Q.
AFRICA. Adrien OR. AR. Sept. Sévère AR. (avec S. C.) Adrien G.B. M.B. Sept. Sévère G.B. M.B.
AFRICA AVG. N. Alexandre (usurpateur) †M.B.
AFRICA COS. II. S. C. Antonin G.B. M.B.
AFRICA COS. III. P. P. Adrien BR.M.
AGRIPP. AVG. DIVI CLAVD. NERONIS CAES. MATER EX S. C. Agrippine jeune et Néron OR. AR.
AGRIPPINA DRVSILLA IVLIA S. C. Caligula G.B.
ALACRITATI. Gallien M.B.
ALAMANNIA DEVICTA. Crispus P.B. Constantin II. P.B.
ALAMANNIA GAVDIVM ROMANORVM. Constantin I. OR. OR.Q. Crispus OR. Constantin II. OR.
ALEXANDRIA. Adrien AR. (avee S. C.). G.B. M.B.
ALEXANDRIA COS. II. S. C. Antonin G.B. M.B.
ALIM. ITAL. COS. V. P. P. S. P. Q. R. OPTIMO. PRINC. Trajan OR.
ALIM. ITAL. S. P. Q. R. OPTIMO. PRINCIPI. Trajan OR. AR. (avec S. C.) G.B. M.B.
AMOR. MVTVVS AVGG. Balbin AR. Pupien AR.
ANCILIA IMPERATOR II. S. C. Antonin M.B.
AN. F. F. OPTIMO PRINCIPI S. C. Antonin M.B.
ANN. AVGG. SAECVLI FELICISSIMI S. C. Caracalla M.B.
ANN. AVG. P. M. TR. P. VIIII. IMP. VI. COS. IIII. P. P. S. C. Commode G. B.
ANN. AVG. TR. P. VI. (ou VII.) IMP. IIII. COS. III. P. P. S. C. Commode G.B. M.B.
ANN. AVG. TR. P. VIII. (ou VIIII.) IMP. VI. COS. III. P. P. S. C. Commode G.B.
ANN. DCCCLXXIIII. NAT. VRB. P. CIR. CON. Adrien OR. BR.M. (avec S. C.) G.B.
ANNONA AVG. Vespasien OR. AR. Titus OR. AR. Adrien AR. Antonin AR. Macrin OR. AR. Soémias (hybride) AR. Alex. Sévère OR. OR.Q. AR. AR.Q. P.B. Mamée (hybride) AR. Otacilie AR. Tréb. Galle AR. Gallien B. Salonine B. Postume OR. Claude II. P.B. Aurélien P.B. Dioclétien P.B. (avec S. C.) Vitellius G.B. Titus G.B. Domitien M.B. Adrien M.B. Antonin G.B. M.B. Macrin G.B. M.B. Valérien G.B.
ANNONA AVG. CERES S. C. Sept Sévère M.B.
ANNONA AVG. COS. II. P. P. S. C. Sept Sévère G.B. M.B.
ANNONA AVG. COS. II. S. C. Albin G.B.
ANNONA AVG. COS. III. S. C. Adrien M.B.
ANNONA AVG. COS. IIII. S. C. Antonin G.B. M.B.
ANNONA AVG. FELIX S. C. Antonin G.B. M.B.
ANNONA AVGG. Gordien III. AR. Philippe père OR AR. AR.Q. Philippe fils AR. Tréb. Galle OR. AR. Volusien AR. Valérien OR. B. Gallien B. Carus P.B. (avec S. C. Philippe père G.B. M.B. Gallien G.B.
ANNONA AVG. IMP. VII. COS. III. S. C. Marc Aurèle M.B.
ANNONA AVG. PONT. MAX. TR. POT. COS. DES. III. S. C. Adrien G.B. M.B.
ANNONA AVG. PONT. MAX. TR. POT. COS. II. (ou III.) S. C. Adrien G.B. M.B.
ANNONA AVG. TR. POT. COS. IIII. S. C. Antonin G.B. M.B.
ANNONA AVG. TR. POT XVII. (ou XVIIII.) COS. IIII. S. C. Antonin G.B.
ANNONA AVGVSTI Elagabale AR. Tacite P.B. (avec S. C.) Vitellius G.B. Adrien G.B. Alex Sévère G.B. M.B.
ANNONA AVGVSTI CERES COS. III. Adrien BR.M.
ANNONA AVGVSTI CERES S. C. Néron G.B. (1).

(1) Variété avec AVGSTI.

ANNONA AVGVST. S. C. Vespasien G.B. Titus G.B. Domitien G.B. Nerva G.B.
ANNONAE AVG. Sept Sévère AR. (avec S. C.) M.B.
ANNONAE AVGG. Sept Sévère AR.
ANNON. AVG. S. C. Domitien M.B.
ANN. P. M. TR. P. VIIII. (ou X.) IMP. VII. COS. IIII. P. P. Commode AR.
ANT. AVG. III. VIR. R. P. C. M. Antoine OR. AR.
ANTHE (en monogramme) Anthémius P. B.
ANTONI IMP. A. XLI. Fulvie AR.Q.
ANTON. IMP. Octave AR.
ANTONINVS ET VERVS REST. — LEG. VI M. Aurèle et Vérus AR.
ANTONIVS AVG. IMP. III. M. Antoine AR.
ANTONIVS IMP. Octave AR.
APOL. CONS. AVG. Aurélien P.B.
APOL. CONSERVAT. Emilien AR. (avec S. C.) G.B.
APOLINI. CONSERVA. Gallien B. (avec S. C.) G.B. M.B. Macrien jeune BIL.
   Quiétus BIL.
APOLINI PROPVG. Gallien B.
APOLINI PROPVGN. Valérien B.
APOLL. CONSERVAT. Emilien OR. AR. G.B.
APOLLI. CONS. Claude II. OR.
APOLLIN. Auguste AR.
APOLLINI AVG. Quintille P.B.
APOLLINI AVG. COS. II. Albin OR. AR.
APOLLINI AVGVSTO. Antonin OR. AR Sept Sévère AR. (avec S. C.) Antonin G.B.
   Sept Sévère G.B. M.B.
APOLLINI CO. AVG. Carausius P.B.
APOLLINI CONS. Claude II P.B. Quintille P.B. Aurélien OR. P.B. Carausius P.B.
APOLLINI CONS. AVG. Gallien B. Tetricus père P.B.
APOLLINI CONSERVA. Valérien OR. B. Gallien B. Macrien jeune BIL Quiétus BIL
   (avec S. C.) Valérien G.B. M.B. Gallien G.B. M.B.
APOLLINI CONSERVATORI. Gallien BR.M. Quintille BR.M.
APOLLINI PALATINO. Commode OR. AR. Sept. Sévère BR.M.
APOLLINI PAL. S. P. Q. R. Gallien B,
APOLLINI PROPVG. Valérien B. (avec S. C.) G.B.
APOLLINI SANCTO. Pesc. Niger AR.
APOLLI. PAL. S P. Q. R. Gallien B.
APOLLO CONSER. Gallien B. M.B.
APOLLO CONSERV. (ou CONSERVA) Gallien B.
APOLLO COS. AVG. Gallien OR.
APOLLO SALVTARI. S. C. Tréb. Galle G.B. M.B. Volusien G.B. M.B.
APOLL. SALVTARI Tréb. Galle OR. AR. Volusien AR. Valérien B. (avec S. C.)
   Tréb. Galle G.B.
APOL. MONETAE. P. M. TR. P. XV. IMP. VIII. COS. VI. Commode M.B (avec S. C.)
   G.B. M.B.
APOL. MONETAE. P. M. TR. P XVI. IMP. VIII. COS. VI. P. P. S. C. Commode G.B.
APOL. MONET. P. M. TR. P. XV. COS. VI. Commode AR.
APOL. PALATINO P. M. TR. P. XVI. IMP. VIII. COS. VI. P. P. Commode BR.M.
APOL. PALAT. P. M. TR. P. XVI. COS. VI. S. C. Commode G.B. M.B.
APOL. PAL. P. M. TR.. P. XVI. COS. VI. Commode AR. (avec S. C.) G.B. M.B.
APOL. SALVTARI. Volusien OR.
AQVA TRAIANA S. P. Q. R. OPTIMO PRINCIPI S. C. Trajan G.B. M.B.
ARAB. ADIAB. COS. II. P. P. Sept. Sévère OR. AR.
ARAB. ADIABENIC. Sept. Sévère AR.
ARAB. ADQ. S. P. Q. R. OPTIMO PRINCIPI. Trajan AR. (avec S. C.) G.B. M.B.
ARAB. ADQVISIT. S. P. Q. R. OPTIMO PRINCIPI S. C. Trajan G.B. M.B.
ARAB. ADQVIS. S. P. Q. R. OPTIMO PRINCIPI S. C. Trajan M.B.
ARA. PACIS S. C. Néron M.B.
ARA. PVDIC. CAES. AVG. GERMA. DAC. COS. VI. P. P. Plotine OR AR.
ARCVS. AVGG. S. C. Sept.Sévère M.B. Caracalla G.B. M.B.

ARMENIA. Vérus BR.M.
ARMENIAC. Néron AR.Q.
ARMENIA CAPTA. Auguste OR. AR.
ARMENIA ET MESOPOTAMIA IN POTESTATEM P. R REDACTAE S. C. Trajan G B
ARMENIA RECEPTA. Auguste AR.
ARMENIA TR. P. VIII. IMP. IIII. COS. III. Vérus BR.M.
ARMENIA TR. P. XVIII COS. II. Marc Aurèle. AR.
ARMEN. P. M. TR. P. XVIII. IMP. II. COS. IIII. Marc Aurèle OR. AR.
ARMEN. P. M. TR. P. XIX. IMP. II. COS. III. Marc Aurèle AR.
ARMEN. TR. P. III. IMP. II. COS. II. Vérus OR. AR.
ARMEN. TR. P. IIII. IMP. II. COS, II. Vérus. OR. AR. (avec S. C.) MB.
ARMEN. TR. P. XVIII. IMP. II. COS. III. Marc Aurèle OR.
ARNASI. Tréb. Galle BR.M.
ARNAZI. Tréb. Galle MB. Volusien G.B. M.B.
ASIA. Adrien AR.
ASIA COS. II. S. C. Antonin G.B.
ASIA RECEPTA. Auguste AR.Q.
AVCTOR PIETAT. P. M. TR P. XII. IMP. VIII. COS. V. P. P. S. C. Commode G.B.
AVCTOR PIETAT. P. M. TR. P. XIIII. IMP. VIII. COS. V. P. P. S. C. Commode G.B. M.B.
AVCT. PIET. P. M. TR. P. XII. IMP. VIII. COS. V. P. P. Commode AR.
AVENTVI AVGVSTI S. C. Tacite BR.M.
AVG. Vespasien AR. Titus AR. Domitien P.B.
AVG. EPHE. Vespasien AR. (*quelquefois avec* Φ Titus OR. AR. Domitien AR
AVG. GER. DAC. PAR. P. M. TR. P. COS. ITERO S. P. Q. R. Adrien AR.
AVG. GER. DAC. PARTHICI. P. M. TR. P. COS. VI. P. P. Plotine OR.
AVG. IMP. Galba AR.
AVG. IN PACE. Salonine B.
AVG. PATRI AVG. MATRI. Philippe fils, Philippe père et Otacilie AR.
AVG. PIVS P. M. TR. P. COS. DES. II. Antonin OR. AR.
AVG. PIVS P. M. TR. P. COS. II. Antonin OR. OR.Q. AR.
AVG. PIVS P. M. TR. P. COS. II. P. P. Antonin AR.
AVG. P. M. TR. P. COS. II. Adrien AR.Q.
AVG. PONT. DIVI F. Auguste AR.
AVG. VESPAS. (ou VESP.) LIBERI IMP. Vespasien Titus et Domitien AR
AVGVR. PON. MAX. Vespasien AR.
AVGVR. PONTIF. Auguste AR.
AVGVR. PONT. MAX. J. César AR.
AVGVR. TRI. POT. Vespasien AR. Titus AR.
AVGVST. Caïus César. AR.
AVGVSTA. Julie de Titus OR. Antonin (*hybride*) AR. Faustin mère OR. OR.Q. AR. Faustine jeune AR. (avec S. C.) Galba G.B. Antonin (*hybride*) M.B Faustine mère G.B. M.B
AVGVSTA IN PACE. Salonine B.
AVGVST. DIVI F. LVDOS SAEC. J. César OR. AR.
AVGVSTI. Autonomes de Galba AR.
AVGVSTI COS. Caracalla OR. (avec S. C.) Sept. Sévère M.B. Caracalla M.B. Géta M.B.
AVGVSTI PII FIL. Faustine jeune OR. OR.Q. AR. (avec S. C) G.B. M B.
AVGVSTI PROFECTIO. Trajan OR.
AVGVSTI. S. POR. OST. C. (ou PORT. OSTI. C.) Néron G.B.
AVGVSTO OB. C. S. Auguste OR.
AVGVSTO S. C. Marc Aurèle G.B.
AVGVSTORVM. Sept Sévère AR.M.
AVGVST. PORT. OST. S. C. Néron G.B.
AVGVST. TRIBVN. POTEST. Auguste M.B.
AVGVSTVS. Auguste OR. AR.M. AR. M.B. P.B.
AVGVSTVS AVGVSTA. Néron OR. AR
AVGVSTVS DIVI F. Auguste AR. P.B.

AVGVSTVS DIVI. F. IMP. Auguste AR.
AVGVSTVS GERMANICVS. Néron OR. AR.
AVGVSTVS O. C. S. Auguste OR.
AVGVSTVS P. R. Galba AR.
AVGVSTVS S. C. Auguste OR.
AVGVSTVS TRIBVNIC. POTEST. Auguste M.B.
AVGVSTVS TR. POT. Auguste AR.
AVRELIANVS AVG. Aurélien M.B.
AVRELIANVS AVG. CONS. Aurelien M.B.
AVSPIC. FEL Dioclétien P.B. Maximien Hercule P.B. Constance Chlore P.B
BASILICA VLPIA. Trajan OR.
BASILICA VLPIA. S. C. — S. P. Q. R. OPTIMO. PRINCIPI. Trajan G.B. (I.)
BEATA TRANQVILITAS. — VOTIS XX. Licinius fils P.B. Constantin I P.B. Crispus
   PB. Constantin II P.B.
BEATA TRANQLITAS — VOTIS XX. Constantin II P.B.
BEATITVDO PVBLICA. Magnence PB.
BEA. (OU BEAT.) TRANQVILLITAS — VOTIS XX. Constantin II PB.
BEAT. TRANQLITAS — VOTIS XX. Constantin I. P.B. Crispus P.B. Constantin II P.B
BENERI GENETRICI. Salonine B.
BONAE FORTVNAE. Valérien B. Gallien B.
BONAE SPEI. Pesc. Niger. AR. Sept. Sévère AR. Julie Domne AR.
BONA SPES. Sept. Sévère AR. Julie Domne AR. Elagabale AR.
BON. EVEN. AVG. Gallien B.
BON. EVENT. Autonomes de Galba OR. AR. Galba AR. Sept. Sévère AR.
BON. EVENT ET FELICITAS. Autonomes de Galba AR.
BONI EVENT. Sept. Sévère AR.
BONI EVENTVS. Autonomes de Galba AR. Pesc. Niger AR. Sept. Sévère AR. Julie
   Domne AR.
BONI SPES. Sept. Sévère AR.
BONO EVENTVI. Adrien BMR. (Avec S. C.) Antonin M.B.
BONO EVENTVI COS. II. S. C. Antonin M.B.
BONO GENIO IMPERATORIS. Maximin II. M.B. Constantin I. M.B.
BONO GENIO PII IMPERATORIS. Maximin II. M.B. Licinius père M.B. †M.B.
BONO REIPVBLICAE. Placidie OR. Honoria OR.
BONO REIPVBLICAE NATI. Attale PB.
BONO REIPVBLICE NATI. Victor OR.
BONVS EVENT AVG. Valérien B.
BONVS EVENTVS. Caracalla AR. Géta AR. Elagabale AR.
BONVS EVENTVS AVG. Gallien B.
BONVS EVENTVS AVGVSTI. Titus AR.
BONVS EVENTVS COS. IIII. S. C. Antonin M.B.
BRITAN IMPERATOR II. Antonin OR. (avec S. C.) M.B.
BRITANNIA COS. IIII. S. C. Antonin M.B.
BRITANNIA S. C. Adrien GB. MB. Antonin G.B.
BRITANNIA IMPERATOR II. S. C. Antonin G.B.
BRITANNIA P. M. TR. P. X. IMP. VII. COS. IIII. P. P. S. C. Commode G B.
BRITANNIA PONT. MAX. TR. POT. COS. III. S. C. Adrien M.B.
BRITTANNIA. P. M. TR. P. X. IMP. VII. COS. IIII. P. P. Commode BR.M.
BRITTANNIA S. C. Adrien M.B.
BRITT. P. M. TR. P. VIIII.' IMP. VII. COS. IIII. P. P. S. C. Commode G.B
BRVT. IMP. Brutus OR. AR.
BRVTVS. Brutus OR. AR.
BRVTVS IMP. Brutus AR.
CAESAR. J. Cesar OR. AR. Auguste AR. Constantin II AR.M.
CAESAR AVG. F. COS. CAESAR AVG. F. PR. Vespasien Titus et Domitien.
   OR. AR. (avec S. C.) M.B.
CAESAR AVG. F. COS. CAESAR AVG. TR. P. Vespasien Titus et Domitien OR.

I. Variété fautive avec PRNCIPI.

CAESAR AVG. F. COS. VI. CENS. TR. P. Vespasien Titus et Domitien AR.

CAESAR AVG. F. DES. IMP. AVG. F. COS. DES. II. S. C. Vespasien G. B.

CAESAR AVG. GALBA IMP. Galba AR.

CAESAR AVGVSTVS. Auguste OR. AR. (avec CL. V.) AR. (avec OB. CIVIS. SER.) OR. (avec O. C. S.) OR. (avec S. C.) AR. (avec S. P. Q. R.) AR. (avec S. P. Q. R. CL. V.) OR. AR.

CAESAR AVGVSTVS SIGN. RECE. Auguste AR.

CAESAR DIC. PER. AR. Octave AR.

CAESAR DIC. QVAR. J. César OR.

CAESAR DICT. J. César OR.

CAESAR DIC. TER. J. César M.B.

CAESAR DIV. F. ARMEN. CAPT. IMP. VIII (ou VIIII). Auguste AR.

CAESAR DIV. F. ARMEN. RECEP. IMP. VII. Auguste AR.

CAESAR DIVI. F. Auguste OR. AR. AR.Q.

CAESAR DIVI. F. ARME. CAPTA. Auguste AR.

CAESAR DIVI F. ARMEN. CAPT. IMP. VIII. Auguste AR.

CAESAR DIVI F. ARMENIA (ou ARMINIA) CAPTA. Auguste AR.

CAESAR DOMITIAN. COS. DES. II. S. C. Titus G.B.

CAESARES VESP. AVG. FILI. Vespasien OR.

CAESARI AVGVSTO. Auguste OR.

CAESARI AVGVSTO EX. S. C. — FOR. RE. Auguste AR.

CAESARI DIVI. F. Auguste AR.

CAESAR IIIVIR. R. P. C. Auguste AR.

CAESAR IMP. J. César AR. Auguste AR.

CAESARVM NOSTRORVM — VOT. V. Licinius fils P.B. Constantin I P.B. Crispus P.B. P.B.Q. Constantin II P.B. (avec — VOT. X.). Licinius fils P.B. Constantin I P.B. Crispus P.B. Constantin II P.B. (avec. — VOT. XX.). Crispus P.B. Constantin II P.B. (avec — VOTIS. V.). Licinius fils P.B. Crispus P.B. Contantin II P.B.

CAES. AVG. F. DESIG. IMP. AVG. F. COS. DESIG. ITE. (ou ITER.). S. C. Vespasien G.B.

CAES. AVG. F. DES. IMP. AVG. F. COS. DES. IT. (ITE. ou ITER.). S. C. Vespasien G.B.

CAES. AVG. GERMA. DAC. COS. VI. P. P. Plotine OR. AR.

CAES. DECENNALIA FEL. S. C. Trajan Dèce G.B.

CAES. DOMITIAN. COS. DES. II. S. C. Titus G.B.

CALLIOPE AVG. Probus P.B.

C. ANTONIVS M. F. PRO. COS. Caïus Antoine AR.

CAPIT. RESTIT. Domitien AR.M.

CAPPADOCIA COS. II. S. C. Antonin G. B.

CAPPADOCIA S. C. Adrien G.B. M.B.

CARITAS AVGG. Tétricus père P.B.

CARITAS MVTVA AVGG. Balbin AR. Pupien AR.

CASTOR. Géta OR. AR. ARQ. PB. Postume OR. B. Postume et Hercule B.

C. CAESAR AVG. GERMANICVS IMP. — PONT. MAXIM. TRIBVN. POTEST. COS. Caligula M.B.

C. CAESAR AVG. GERMANICVS PON. M. TR. POT. S. C. Germanicus M.B. Néron et Drusus M.B.

C. CAESAR AVGVSTVS PON. MAX. TR. POT. S. C. Germanicus M.B.

C. CAESAR COS. TER. J. César OR.

C. CAESAR DIC. TER. J. César OR.

C. CAESAR DIVI AVG. PRON. AVG. S. C. Caligula P.B.

C. CAESAR DIVI AVG. PRON. AVG. P. M. TR. P. IIII. P. P. S. C. Germanicus M.B. Néron et Drusus) M.B.

C. CAESAR IMP. COS. ITER. J. César AR.

C. CAESAR M. ANTON. M. Antoine AR.Q.

C. CAES. AVG. (ou AVGVS.) F. Auguste OR. AR.M. AR.

C. CAES. DIC. TER. J. César G.B.

C. CASSEI. IMP. Cassius AR.

C. CASSI. IMP. Cassius OR. AR.

C. CASSI. IMP. LEIBERTAS. Cassius OR AR

C. CLODI. MACRI LIBERA. S. C. Cl. Macer AR.
CENS. P. P. P. Domitien AR.
CERER. AVG. Julie Domne AR.
CERERE. AVG. (OU AVGVS.) Julie Domne AR.
CEREREM S. C. Julie Domne M.B.
CERER. FRVG. (OU FRVGIF). Pesc. Niger AR. Sept. Sévère AR.
CERER. FRVGIFER. Sept. Sévère AR.
CERERI AVG. Salonine B.
CERERI FRVFER. Pesc. Niger AR.
CERERI FRVG. Pesc. Niger AR. Sept. Sévère AR.
CERERI FRVGIF. Julie Domne AR. P.B.
CERERI FRVGIS. Caracalla AR.
CERES. Antonin AR. Faustine mère OR. AR. Faustine jeune AR. Lucille BR.M.
  Crispine OR. AR. BR.M. Julie Domne BR.M. (avec S. C.) Tibère G.B. Faustine
  mère G.B. M.B. Faustine jeune G.B. M.B. Lucille G.B. M.B. Crispine M.B.
  Julie Domne G.B. M.B.
CERES AVG. Othon AR. Claude II P.B. (avec S. C.) Vitellius G.B. M.B.
CERES AVGVST. Vespasien OR. AR. Titus OR. AR. Domitien OR. AR. (avec S. C.)
  Vespasien M.B. Titus M.B. Julie de Titus M.B. Domitien M.B.
CERES AVGVSTA S. C. Claude I M.B. Galba M.B.
CERES EGETIAE. (OU SEGESTAE). Salonine B.
CER. QVINQ. ROMAE CON. S. C. Néron P.B.
CER. QVINQ. ROM. CO. S. C. Néron † M.B. P.B.
CER. QVINQ. ROM. CON. S. C. Tibère (hybride) P.B. Néron † M.B. P.B.
CER. QVINQ. RO. S. C. Néron † M.B.
CERTAMEN QVINQ. ROM. CON. Néron P.B.
CERTA. QVINQ. ROM. CO. (OU CON.) S. C. Néron P.B.
CERT. QVINQ. ROM. CO. (OU CON.) S. C. Néron P.B.
CHORS. TERTIA PRAETORIA. Gallien OR.M.
CHORTIS SPECVLATORVM. M. Antoine AR.
CHORTIVM PRAETORIARVM. M. Antoine OR. AR.
CIVIB. ET SIGN. MILIT. A. PART. RECVP. Auguste OR. AR.
CIVIB. ET SIGN. MILIT. A. PART. RECVPER. Auguste AR.
CIVITATIBVS ASIAE RESTITVTIS S. C. Tibère G.B. Restitution de Titus G.B.
CLARITAS AVG. Postume et Hercule OR. B. Galère Maximien AR.
CLARITAS AVGG. Dioclétien P.B. Maximien Hercule P.B. Constance Chlore P B.
  Galère Maximien P.B.
CLARITAS REIPVB. Constantin II P.B.
CLARITAS REIPVBLICAE. Constantin I OR. P.B. Crispus P.B. Constantin II OR. P.B.
C. L. CAESARES AVGVSTI F. COS. DESIG. PRINC. IVVENT. Auguste OR. AR.
CLEMENTIA AVG. Antonin AR. (avec S. C.) Adrien G.B.
CLEMENTIA AVG. COS. II. Albin AR.
CLEMENTIA AVG. COS. III. Adrien AR.
CLEMENTIA AVG. COS. III. P. P. Adrien OR.Q. AR. (avec S. C.) G.B. M.B.
CLEMENTIA AVG. IMP. VI. COS. III. S. C. Marc Aurèle G.B.
CLEMENTIA AVG. P. P. COS. III. Adrien AR. (avec S. C.) G.B. M.B.
CLEMENTIA AVG. TR. P. XXX. IMP. VIII. COS. III. S. C. Marc Aurèle G.B.
CLEMENTIAE CAESARIS. J. César AR.
CLEMENTIAE S. C. Tibère M.B.
CLEMENTIA IMP. GERMAN. Vitellius OR. AR. (avec S. C.) M.B.
CLEMENTIA IMP. GERMANICI. Vitellius OR.
CLEMENTIA TEMP. Gallien OR.Q. B. Tacite P.B. P.B. Florien P.B. Probus P.B.
  Carus P.B. Numérien P.B. Carin P.B. Dioclétien P.B. Maximien Hercule P.B.
CLEMENT. TEMP. Maximien Hercule P.B.
CLEM. P. M. TR. P. COS. III. Adrien AR.
CLEM. TR. POT. III. COS. II. Marc Aurèle OR. AR. (avec S. C.) G.B. M.B.
CLEM. TR. POT. IIII. COS. II. Marc Aurèle AR.
CLEM. TR. POT. VI. COS. II. Marc Aurèle OR. AR.
CLEM. TR. POT. XII. COS. IIII. Antonin AR.

CLE. TR. POT. III. COS. II. S. C. Marc Aurèle G.B.
CLODI. MACRI S. C. Cl. Macer AR.
CN. MAG. IMP. Cn. Pompée G.B.
CN. MAGNVS IMP. Cn. Pompée AR.
COCLES. Antonin BR.M.
COHH. PRAET. VI. (ou VII.) P. VI. F. Gallien B.
COHORT. PRAETO. S. C. Adrien G.B.
COHORT. PRAET. PRINCIPI SVO. Gallien G.B.
COH. PRAETOR. S. C. Adrien G.B. M.B.
COHR. PRAET. Carausius P.B.
COL. L. AN. COM. P. M. TR. P. XV. IMP. VIII. COS. VI. S. C. Commode G.B. M.B.
COM. ASI. — ROM. ET. AVG. Claude I AR.M. Nerva AR.M.
COM. ASIAE — ROM. ET. AVGVST. Auguste AR.M.
COM. BIT. Adrien AR.M.
COM. BIT. ROM. S. P. AVG. Adrien AR.M.
COM. BIT. S. P. R. ROM. S. P. AVG. Adrien AR.M.
COMES AVG. Victorin OR. B. Tétricus père OR. BIL. P.B. Tétricus fils BIL. P.B.
    Probus P.B. Dioclétien P.B. Carausius P.B. Allectus OR. Constance Chlore P B.
COMES AVGG. Tétricus fils P.B. Dioclétien P.B. Maximien Hercule P.B. Constance
    Chlore P.B. Galère Maximien OR. P.B.
COMES AVGGG. Carausius P.B.
COMES. AVG. N. Tétricus père P.B.
COM. IMP. AVG. Tétricus fils P.B.
COMIS AVGGG. Maximien Hercule P.B.
COMITATVS AVGG. Dioclétien OR. Maximien Hercule OR. Constance Chlore OR.
    Galère Maximien OR.
COMIT. AVG. Tétricus père P.B.
COMITES AVGG. ET. CAESS NNNN. Constance Chlore OR.
COMITI AAVVGG. Maximin II † P.B. P.B. Licinius père † M.B. P.B. Constantin I P.B.
COMITI AVG Postume et Hercule OR. Tétricus père P.B.
COMITI AVGG. NN. Maximien Hercule OR. Constantin I † M.B. ⁀ P.B. P.B.
COMITI PROBI AVG. Probus P.B (1).
COMOB. (sans autre légende) Placidie OR.T. Valentinien III OR.T. Honoria OR.T
    Avitus P.B.Q. Majorien OR.T. AR Anthemius OR. OR.T. Olybrius OR.T. Glycère
    OR.T. AR. Népos OR. OR.T. Augustule OR.T.
COM. OLVTETIO. Tétricus fils P.B.
CONC. COMMODI P. M. TR. P. XVI. IMP. VIII. COS. VI. S. C. Commode G.B.
CONC. COM. P. M. TR. P. XVI. COS. VI. Commode OR. AR.
CONCDIAE. Sabine AR.
CONC. EXER. Auréhen P.B.
CONC. EXERC. Quintille P.B.
CONC. MIL. P. M. TR. P. X. IMP. VII. COS. IIII. P. P. Commode AR. (avec S. C.) M.B.
CONC. MIL. P. M. TR. P. XI. IMP. VII. COS. IIII. P. P. S. C. Commode G.B. M.B.
CONC. MIL. P. M. TR. P. XI. IMP. VII. COS. V. P. P. Commode OR. AR.
CONCOBDIA. Crispine et Commode BR.M. Mamée AR.
CONCO. EXER. Claude II P.B. Quintille P.B. Aurélien P.B.
CONCOR. AVG. Gallien B. Salonin B. Claude II P.B. Aurélien M.B. (avec S. C.)
    Vespasien G B.
CONCOR COMMODI. P. M. TR. P. XVI. COS. VI. S. C. Commode G.B. M.B.
CONCORD. AEQVIT. Postume OR. B.
CONCORD. AET. Salonine B.
CONCORD. AVG. Tétricus père P.B. Probus P.B. (avec S. C.) Galba G.B. Titus M.B.
CONCORD. AVG. COS. II. Vérus AR.
CONCORD. AVG. ET. CAES. Sévère II OR.
CONCORD. AVG. TR. P. COS. II. Vérus AR (avec S. C.) G. B.
CONCORD. AVG. TR. P. XV. (ou XVI) COS. III. Marc Aurèle AR.
CONCORD. AVG. TR. P. XVII (ou XVIII) COS. III. Marc Aurèle OR. AR.

1. Variété avec PRIBI. pour PROBI.

CONCORD. AVG. TR. P....... S. C. COS. III. Marc Aurèle G.B.
CONCORD. AVGVST. S. C. Vespasien M.B.
CONCORD. AVGVSTOR. COS. II. Vérus OR. (avec S. C.) G.B.
CONCORD. AVGVSTOR. TR. P. COS. II. S. C. Vérus G.B. M.B.
CONCORD. AVGVSTOR. TR. P. II. COS. II. S. C. Vérus G.B. M.B.
CONCORD. AVGVSTOR. TR. P. XV. (ou XVI.) COS. III. S. C. Marc Aurèle G.B. M.B.
CONCORD. COS. IIII. S. C. Antonin M.B.
CONCORD. DIVI NER. NEP. P. M. TR. P. COS. Adrien OR.
CONCORD. EQVIT. Gallien B. Postume B. Victorin P.B. Tétricus père P.B.
CONCORD. EQVITVM. Postume B.
CONCORD. EXER. Claude II P.B. Quintille OR. P.B.
CONCORD. EXERC. Quintille P.B.
CONCORD. EXERC. IMP. VII. COS. III. S. C. Marc Aurèle M.B.
CONCORDIA. Autonomes de Galba OR. AR. Adrien AR. Aelius AR. Faustine mère OR. Marc Aurèle AR. Faustine jeune OR. OR.Q. AR. Lucille OR. AR. Crispine AR. Crispine et Commode BR.M. Pesc. Niger OR. Sept. Sévère AR. Julie Domne AR. P.B. Géta (*hybride*) AR. Paula OR. AR. AR.Q. Aquilia Sévéra AR. M.B. Annia Faustine AR. Alex. Sévère AR. P.B. Quintille P.B. (avec S. C.) Faustine mère G.B. Marc Aurèle M.B. Faustine jeune G.B. M.B. Lucille G.B. M.B. Crispine G.B. M.B. Albin G.B. Paula G.B. M.B. Aquilia Sévéra G.B. M.B. Annia Faustine G.B. M.B.
CONCORDIA AETERNA. Paula OR (avec S. C.) G.B. M.B.
CONCORDIA AGV. Théodose II M.B.
CONCORDIA AV. Carausius P.B.
CONCORDIA AVG. Vespasien OR. AR. Titus OR. AR. Domitien AR Sabine OR. OR.Q. AR. Antonin OR. AR. Faustine mère OR. AR. Faustine jeune OR. Gordien d'Afrique père AR. Gordien III OR. AR. Philippe père AR. Gallien OR.M. OR. Salonine B. Tétricus père P.B. Claude II P.B. Quintille AR? P.B. Aurélien OR. G.B. M.B. P.B. Sévérine P.B. Probus P.B. Carin OR. (avec S.C.) Vitellius G.B. M.B. Vespasien M.B. Titus M.B. Julie de Titus M.B. Domitien M.B. Adrien M.B. Sabine G.B. M.B. Faustine mere G.B. M.B. Caracalla M.B. Gordien III G.B. Etruscille G.B. Emilien G.B.
CONCORDIA AVG. COS. II. Aelius BR.M.
CONCORDIA AVGG. Plautille OR. AR. P.B. Paula AR. Orbiane AR. AR.Q. Gordien d'Afrique fils AR. Balbin AR. Pupien AR. Tranquilline AR. AR.Q. Philippe père OR. AR. Philippe père et Otacilie BR.M. G.B. Otacilie OR. AR. Philippe fils AR. Trajan Dèce et Etruscille BR.M. Trajan Dèce, Etruscille, Hérennius et Hostilien AR. Etruscille AR. Hérennius AR. Hostilien AR. Tréb. Galle OR. AR. Volusien OR. AR. Emilien AR. Cornélia Supéra AR. Valérien B. Gallien B. Gallien et Salonine OR. AR.M. BR.M. Salonine B. Régalien AR. Tétricus père P.B. Aurélien P.B. Sévérine P.B. Magnia Urbica OR. Dioclétien OR. P.B. Maximien Hercule OR. M.B. P.B. Constance Chlore P.B. Galère Maximien P.B. Licinius père AR.M. Gratien OR. P.B. Théodose I AR.M. AR. Honorius OR. (I) P.B. (avec S. C.) Plautille M.B. Balbin G.B. M.B. Pupien G.B. M.B. Tranquilline M.B. Otacilie G.B. M.B. Etruscille G.B. Trajan Dèce, Herennius et Hostilien G.B. Tréb. Galle G.B. M.B. Volusien G B. M.B. Valérien G.B. Gallien G.B. M.B.
CONCORDIA AVGG. ET CAESS. Maximien Hercule OR.M. Constance Chlore OR.M. OR.
CONCORDIA AVGG. ET CAESS. NN. Sévère II OR.
CONCORDIA AVGG. ET. CAESS. NNNN. Dioclétien OR. Maximien Hercule OR.
CONCORDIA AVGGG. (2) Gratien OR. AR. P.B. Valentinien II OR. P.B. Théodose I OR. AR.M. AR. P.B. Magnus Maximus OR. AR. Honorius OR. P.B. (avec VOT. V. MVL. X.) Théodose I OR. (avec VOT. X. MVLT. XV.) Valentinien II OR. Théodose I OR. (avec VOT. X. MVLT. XX.) Valentinien II OR. Théodose I OR. (avec VOT. XV. MVLT. XX.) Valentinien II OR.

---

(1) La légende est suivie, à partir du règne d'Honorius, d'une des lettres numérales grecques : A. B. Γ. Δ. E. ς. Z. H. Θ. I. ou Λ sur l'or.

(2) Cette légende est presque toujours suivie d'une des lettres : A. B. Γ. Δ. E. ς. Z. H. Θ. I. K. Λ. ou N, sur l'or.

CONCORDIA AVGGGG. (1) Gratien OR. Valentinien II OR. Théodose I OR.
CONCORDIA AVGG. NN. Maximien Hercule OR. Licinius père OR. Licinius fils
P.B. Constantin I OR. Crispus OR.
CONCORDIA AVGG. NOSTR. Constance Chlore OR.
CONCORDIA AVGVST. Domitille AR. Domitia OR. AR. (avec S. C.) Vespasien M.B.
Titus M.B. Julie de Titus M.B. Domitien M.B.
CONCORDIA AVGVSTA. Néron OR. AR.
CONCORDIA AVGVSTI. Vespasien AR. Titus AR. Julie de Titus AR. (avec S. C.)
Vitellius M.B. Vespasien G.B. M.B. Titus M.B.
CONCORDIA AVGVSTOR. Aurélien P.B.
CONCORDIA AVGVSTOR. TR. POT. XV. COS. III. S. C. Marc Aurèle G.B.
CONCORDIA AVGVSTORVM. Septime Sévère OR. Alex. Sévère BR.M. Alex. Sévère
et Orbiane BR.M. M.B.M. Orbiane OR. Philippe fils, Philippe père et Otacilie
AR.M. M.B. Valérien Gallien et Salonine BR.M. Valérien, Salonin, Gallien et
Salonin AR.M. Salonine BR.M. (avec S. C.) Géta G.B. Alex. Sévère G.B. Orbiane
G.B (2) M.B. Tranquilline G.B. M.B.
CONCORDIA CAES. AVGG. NN. Dioclétien BR.M.
CONCORDIA CAESS. NOSTR. Sévère II OR.
CONCORDIA COS. II. Adrien BR.M. (avec S. C.) Marc Aurèle M.B.
CONCORDIA DACICO (ou DAC.) PARTHICO P. M. TR. P. COS. III. P. P. S. C. Adrien
G.B. M.B.
CONCORDIAE. Antonin AR. Faustine mère AR. Julie Domne AR. Plautille OR.
AR. (avec S. C.) Antonin G.B. Faustine mère G.B.
CONCORDIAE AETERNAE. Caracalla, Sept. Sévère et Julie Domne OR. AR. Ca-
racalla OR. Plautille OR. AR. P.B. (avec S. C.) Géta G. B.
CONCORDIAE AVG. Gallien B.
CONCORDIAE AVGG. Caracalla BR.M. Géta OR. Valérien B. Dioclétien P.B. Maximien
Hercule P.B. Constance Chlore P.B. Galère Maximien P.B. (avec S. C.) Sept.
Sévère G.B. Caracalla G.B. M.B. Géta G.B.
CONCORDIAE AVGG. NN. Dioclétien OR. AR. Constance Chlore OR.
CONCORDIAE AVGVSTOR. Vérus OR.
CONCORDIAE AVGVSTOR. TR. P. COS. II. Vérus OR. AR.
CONCORDIAE AVGVSTOR. TR. P. II. COS. II. Vérus OR.
CONCORDIAE AVGVSTOR. TR. P. XV. (ou XVI.) COS. III. Marc Aurèle OR.
CONCORDIAE AVGVSTORVM. Alex. Sévère et Orbiane BR.M.
CONCORDIAE AVGVSTORVM COS. II. Vérus OR.
CONCORDIAE COMMODI AVG. Commode OR. AR.
CONCORDIAE EXERCITI. Valérien B.
CONCORDIAE MILITVM. Sept. Sévère OR. AR. Gallien B. Marius B. Sévérine OR.
P.B. Maximien Hercule OR. P.B.
CONCORDIA EQVIT. Postume B.
CONCORDIA EXERC. Gallien B.
CONCORDIA EXERCI. Florien P.B. Probus P.B.
CONCORDIA EXERCIT. Valérien B. Gallien OR. B. (avec S. C.) Valérien G.B. M.B.
Gallien G.B. M.B.
CONCORDIA EXERCITI. Valérien B.
CONCORDIA EXERCITVVM. Vespasien AR. Nerva OR. AR. (avec S. C.) Nerva G.B. M.B.
Adrien G.B. Antonin G.B. M.B.
CONCORDIA EXERCITVVM. COS. III. S. C. Marc Aurèle G.B.
CONCORDIA EXERCITVVM. TR. P. COS. S. C. Antonin M.B.
CONCORDIA F. AVGG. Constance Chlore P.B.
CONCORDIA FELIX. Lucille BR.M. Julie Domne AR. Caracalla OR. AR. Plautille AR.
CONCORDIA FELIX. DD. NN. Maximien Hercule M.B. Galère Maximien M.B. Cons-
tantin I M.B.
CONCORDIA IMPERII. Sévère II M.B. Maximin II M.B. Constantin I M.B.
CONCORDIA LEGI. Aurelien P.B.

---

(1) Quelquefois suivi de S sous Gratien, et de A. B. ou Γ sous Théodose 1.
(2) Variété avec AVGVSTIRVM.

CONCORDIA M. (OU MIL.). Carausius P.B.
CONCORDIA MILI. Aurélien OR. P.B.
CONCORDIA MILIT. Sept. Sévère OR. Caracalla AR. Elagabale AR. Gordien III AR.
AR.Q. Valérien B. Gallien OR. B. Marius B. Aurelien P.B. Probus P.B. Carausius
AR. P.B. (avec S. C.) Géta G.B. M.B. Gordien III G.B. M.B.
CONCORDIA MILITVM. Dide Julien OR. Géta BR.M. Gordien III AR. Pacatien AR.
Marius OR. B. Aurélien M.B. P.B. Tacite P.B. Florien P.B. Probus P.B. Dioclétien
OR. P.B. Maximien Hercule M.B. P.B. Carausius OR. AR. P.B. Constance Chlore
P.B. Galère Maximien P.B. Sévère II P.B. Maximin II P.B. Constantin I P.B.
Constance II M.B. Vétranion M.B. Constance Galle M.B.
CONCORDIA PERPET. DD. NN. Maximien Hercule M.B. Constantin I M.B.
CONCORDIA PERP. DD. NN. Constantin I M.B.
CONCORDIA PONT. MAX. TR. POT. COS. S. C. Adrien G.B.
CONCORDIA PONT. MAX. TR. POT. COS. DES. II. S. C. Adrien M.B.
CONCORDIA PONT. MAX. TR. POT. COS. II. S. C. Adrien G.B. M.B.
CONCORDIA P. R. Vitellius OR. AR.
CONCORDIA PRAETORIANORVM. Autonomes de Galba AR. Vitellius AR.
CONCORDIA PROVINCIA. Galba AR.
CONCORDIA PROVINCIARVM. Autonomes de Galba AR. Galba OR. AR. P.B.
CONCORDIA SENATV. S. C. Vespasien G.B.
CONCORDIA TR. POT. COS. II. S. C. Adrien M.B. Aelius G.B.
CONCORDIA TR. POT. III. COS. II. Marc Aurèle OR.
CONCORDI. LEGI. Aurélien OR. P.B.
CONCORDI. MILIT. Aurélien P.B.
CONCORD. IMPERII. Galère Maximien M.B. Maximin II M.B.
CONCORD. LEGI. Claude II P.B. Aurélien OR. P.B.
CONCORD. MI. Carausius P.B.
CONCORD. MILI. Probus P.B (1).
CONCORD. MILIT. Dide Julien OR. AR. Marius B. Aurélien P.B. Sévérine P.B
Tacite P.B. Florien OR. P.B. Probus P.B. Carausius AR. P.B. Constantin I M.B·
P.B. (avec S. C.) Dide Julien G.B. M.B. Aurélien G.B.
CONCORD. MILIT. FELIC. ROMANOR. Maximien Hercule OR.
CONCORD. MILITV. Probus P.B.
CONCORD. PARTH. F. DIVI. NER. NEP. P. M. TR. P. COS. Adrien AR.
CONCORD. PARTHIC. DIVI. TRAIAN. AVG. F. P. M. TR. P. COS. P. P. Adrien OR. AR.
CONCORD. P. M. TR. P. COS. DES. II. Adrien AR.
CONCORD. P. M. TR. P. COS. II. Adrien OR. AR.
CONCORD. P. M. TR. P. COS. DES. III. Adrien AR.
CONCORD. P. M. TR. P. COS. III. Adrien AR.
CONCORD. PONT. MAX. TR. POT. COS. S. C. Adrien G.B.
CONCORD. TRIB. POT. COS. Antonin OR. (avec S. C.) G.B.
CONCORD. TRIB. POT. COS. DES. II. Antonin OR.
CONCORD. TRIB. POT. COS. II. Aelius OR. AR.
CORCORD. TRI. POT. COS. DES. II. Antonin OR.
CONCORD. TR. POT. COS. II. Aelius OR. OR.Q. AR. (avec S. C.) G.B. M.B.
CONCOR. EXER. Claude II PB. Quintille P.B.
CONCOR. EXERC. Valérien B. Claude II OR.
CONCOR. EXERCI. Claude II P.B.
CONCOR. LEGG. Valérien B.
CONCOR. MIL. Valérien B. Gallien B.
CONCOR. MILIT. Carausius PB.
CONCORPIA. AVGG. NN. Crispus OR.
CONG. AVG. TR. POT. XX. IMP. II. COS. IIII. S. C. Antonin G.B.
CONG. AVG. III. TR. P. XX. IMP. III. COS. III. S. C. Marc Aurèle M.B.
CONG. AVG. III. TR. POT. XX. IMP. III. COS. III. S. C. Marc Aurèle G.B.
CONG. AVG. IIII. TR. P. VII. IMP. IIII. COS. III. Vérus OR.
CONG. AVG. IIII. TR. P. XXI. IMP. IIII. COS. III. S. C. Marc Aurèle OR.

(1) Variété avec NILI pour MILI.

CONG. AVG. IIII. TR. POT. XXI. IMP. II. COS. IIII. S. C. Antonin G B.
CONG. AVG. VIII. COS. IIII. Antonin AR. (avec S. C.) G.B. M.B.
CONGIAR. PR. S. C. Nerva G.B.
CONGIAR. PRIMVM P. R. DAT. S. C. Titus G.B.
CONGIARIVM TERTIVM S. C. Trajan G.B.
CONG. POP. R. S. C. Néron G.B.
CONG. I. DAT. POP. S. C. Néron G.B.
CONG. II. COS. II. S. C. Domitien G.B.
CONG. II. DAT. POP. R. Néron G.B. (avec S. C.) G.B.
CONG. II. DAT. POP. S. C. Néron G.B.
CONG. II. POP. R. D. S. C. Septime Sévère BR.M.
CONG..... DAT. POPVLO. S. C. Néron G.B.
CONOB. (*sans autre légende*). Théodose I OR.T. Valentinien III OR.T. Avitus OR.
   OR.T. Majorien OR.T. Sévère III OR.Q. OR T. Anthémius OR T. Népos OR.T.
CONSACRATIO. Sept. Sévère AR. Salonin B. Valérien jeune B. Victorin P.B. Té-
tricus père P.B. Claude II P.B.
CONSAECRATIO. Claude II P.B.
CONSECR. Tétricus père P.B.
CONSECRATIO. Auguste (*Restitution de Gallien*)(1) BIL. Vespasien (*Restitution
de Gallien*) BIL. Titus (*Pestitution de Gallien*) BIL. Domitien AR. (*hybride*).
Nerva (*Restitution de Gallien*) BIL. Trajan (*Restitution de Gallien*) BIL. Plotine OR. AR.Q. Marciane OR. OR.Q. AR. Matidie OR. AR. Adrien OR. AR. (*Restitution de Gallien*) BIL. Sabine OR. AR. Antonin OR. AR. BR.M. (*Restitution de
Gallien*) BIL. Faustine mère OR. OR.Q. AR. BR.M. Marc Aurèle OR. AR. *Restitution de Gallien*) BIL. Faustine jeune AR. Vérus AR. Commode AR. (*Restitution de Gallien*) BIL. Pertinax OR. AR. Sept. Sévère OR. AR. P.B. (*Restitution
de Gallien*) BIL. Julie Domne AR. Caracalla AR. Maesa AR. Alex. Sévère (*Restitution de Gallien*) BIL. Pauline AR. Mariniane OR. B. B.Q. Gallien B. M.B. Salonin OR. OR.Q. B.M. BIL (2). B.Q. BR.M. M.B. Victorin B. B.Q. Tétricus père P.B.
Tétricus fils P.B. Claude II BR.M. G.B. P.B. P.B.Q. Quintille P.B.Q. Aurélien P.B.
Carus OR. P.B. Numérien P.B. Nigrinien OR. P.B. Constance Chlore OR. M.B.
(avec S. C.) Marciane G.B. Sabine G.B. Antonin G.B. M.B. Fausine mère G.B. M.B.
Marc Aurèle G.B. M.B. Faustine jeune G.B. M.B. Vérus G.B. Commode G.B. Cris-
pine G.B. Pertinax G.B. M.B. Sept. Sévère G.B. Julie Domne G.B. Caracalle G.B.
Maesa G.B. Pauline G.B. Mariniane G.B. M.B. Salonin G.B. M.B.
CONSECRATIO AV. Tétricus père P.B.
CONSECRATIO AVG. Carus P.B.
CONSECR. AVG. Claude II P.B.
CONSEN. EXERCIT. Vespasien OR. AR.
CONSENSV. SENAT. ET EQ. ORDIN. P. Q. R. Auguste M.B.
CONSENSVS EXERCIT. Vespasien AR.
CONSENSVS EXERCITVVM. Vitellius OR. AR. (avec S. C.) M.B.
CONSENSVS HISPANIARVM S. C. Vitellius M.B.
CONSER. AV. Carausius AR.
CONSER. AVG. Claude II P.B.
CONSERVA. AVG. Probus P.B.
CONSERVAT. AVG. Tétricus père P.B. Claude II P.B. Aurélien P.B. Probus OR.
M.B. P.B. Dioclétien P.B. Carausius OR. P.B.
CONSERVAT. AVGG. Valérien B. Gallien B.
CONSERVAT. AVGGG. Dioclétien P.B.
CONSERVAT. MILIT. Tacite P.B.
CONSERVATOR AFRICAE SVAE. Maximien Hercule M.B. Maxence M.B. Constan-
tin I. M.B.
CONSERVATOR AVG. Elagabale OR. AR. Uranius OR. Gallien B. Aurélien P.B.
Tacite OR. Florien OR.
CONSERVATOR AVGG. Dioclétien P.B. Maximien Hercule P.B.
CONSERVATOR AVGGG. Numérien OR

---

(1) Toutes ces restitutions attribuées à Gallien appartiennent certainement au règne
de Philippe. Ces monnaies ont dû être frappées à l'occasion des fêtes de l'an mille.

(2) Variété avec CINCECRATIO.

CONSERVATOR AVGVSTI COS. IIII. Elagabale BR.M.
CONSERVATORES AVG. Postume OR. B. Claude II P.B.
CONSERVATORES AVGG. Dioclétien et Maximien Hercule M.B.
CONSERVATORES KART. SVAE. Maximien Hercule M.B. Maxenee M.B. Constantin I M.B.
CONSERVATORES VRB. SVAE. Maximien Hercule M.B. Maxence M.B. Constantin I M.B.
CONSERVATOR EXERC. Gallien B.
CONSERVATORI AVG. Postume OR.
CONSERVATORI AVGGG. Carausius OR.
CONSERVATORI AVG. N. Maxence M.B.
CONSERVATORI PATRIS PATRIAE. Trajan OR. AR. (avec S. C.) G.B.
CONSERVATORI VRBIS SVAE. Constantin I P.B.
CONSERVATORI VRB. SVAE. Maxence OR.
CONSERVATOR KART. SVAE. Constantin I AR.
CONSERVATOR MILITVM Tacite P.B.
CONSERVATOR VRBIS SVAE. Maxence OR. AR.
CONSERVAT. PIETAT. Gallien B (1) Claude II P.B.
CONSERVATRICI. AVGG. Macrien jeune OR.
CONSERVAT. VRBIS SVAE. Maxence P.B.
CONSERVT. AVGG. Valérien B. Gallien B.
CONSER. VRB. SVAE. Maxence AR. M.B.P.B.Q.
CONSERV. VRB. SVAE. Maximien Hercule AR. M.B. Maxence M.B. P.B.P.B.Q. Constantin I M.B.
CONS. PRINC. AVG. Aurélien P.B.
CONSTANS AVG. Constant AR.
CONSTANS AYG. (sic). Constant AR.
CONSTANS CAESAR. Constant AR.M. AR.
CONSTANS NOB. CAESAR. Constant P.B.
CONSTANS P. F. AVG. Constant AR.M.
CONSTANTIAE AVGVSTI. Antonia OR. AR. Claude I OR. AR. (avec S. C.) G.B. M.B.
CONSTANTI AVG. Constance Chlore OR.
CONSTANTINIANA DAFNE. Constantin I OR. AR. P.B.
CONSTANTINI. — AVG. — VOTIS. XX. Constantin I P.B. Crispus PB. (avec — VOTIS. XXX.) Constantin I OR.M.
CONSTANTINI AVGVSTI — VOTIS XX. Constantin I P.B.
CONSTANTINI CAES. — VOT. X. Constantin II OR.M. (avec — VOTIS X.) Constantin II OR.M. OR.
CONSTANTINI M. AVG. — VOT. X. Constantin I P.B.
CONSTANTINI MAX. C. — VOT. XX. Constantin I P.B.
CONSTANTINO P. AVG. B. R. P. NAT. Constantin I M.B.
CONSTANTINOPOLI. (ou CONSTANTINOPOLIS). Autonomes de Constantin I G.B. M.B. P.B. P.B.Q. Constantin II G.B.M.
CONSTANTINVS AVG. Constantin I OR.M. AR.M. AR. P.B. Constantin II OR. AR. P.B.
CONSTANTINVS AVGVSTVS. Constantin I AR. Constantin II AR.
CONSTANTINVS AYG. (sic). Constantin II AR.
CONSTANTINVS CAES. Constantin II OR. AR. P.B. P.B.Q.
CONSTANTINVS CAESAR. Constantin II OR. AR.M. AR. P.B. P.B Q.
CONSTANTINVS IVN. N. C. Constantin II P.B.
CONSTANTINVS IVN. NOB. C. Constantin II P.B.
CONSTANTINVS MAX. AVG. Constantin I AR.M.
CONSTANTIVS AVG. Constance II AR.M. AR.
CONSTANTIVS AVGVSTVS. Constance II AR.
CONSTANTIVS CAES. Constance II P.B.
CONSTANTIVS CAESAR. Constance II OR. AR.M. AR. P.P.
CONSTANTIVS NOB. CAES. Constance II P.B.
CONSTANTIVS P. F. AVG. Constance II AR.M.

---

1) Variété avec CONSERVAT. PETAT.

CONZTANTINVZ (*sic*) AVG. Constantin I OR.M.
CONSVL. AVGG. NN. Maximien Hercule OR. Constance Chlore OR.
CONSVL. CAESS. Constance Chlore OR. Galère Maximien OR.
CONSVL. DD. NN. Licinius père OR. Constantin I OR.
CONSVL. P. P. PROCOS. Licinius père OR.
CONSVL. P. P. PROCONSVL. Maximien Hercule OR. Maximin II OR. Licinius père OR. Constantin I OR.
CONSVL II. Élagabale AR.
CONSVL II. P. P. Elagabale OR. AR.
CONSVL II. P. P. PROCONSVL. Maxence P.B.Q.
CONSVL III. P. P. PRO COS. Maximien Hercule OR.
CONSVL IIII. P. P. PRO COS. Dioclétien OR. AR. Maximien Hercule OR. AR.
CONSVL V. P. P. PRO COS. Dioclétien OR. Maximien Hercule OR. Constance Chlore OR.
CONSVL VI. P. P. PRO COS. Dioclétien OR.M. OR. Maximien Hercule OR.
CONSVL VII. P. P. PRO COS. Dioclétien OR. Maximien Hercule OR. Maximin II OR.
CONSVL VIII. P. P. PRO COS. Dioclétien OR. Maximien Hercule OR.
COR. AVG. Carausius P.B.
COS. Géta OR. AR. AR.Q. BR.M.
COS. DESIG. III. TR. POT. Vespasien OR.
COS. DES. II. Marc Aurèle OR. AR.
COS. DES. IT. PON. M. TR. P. IMP. S. C. Claude II P.B.
COS. DES. PRINC. IVVENT. Néron AR.M.
COS. DES. III. PON. M. TR. P. III. P. P. — R. CC. Caligula P.B.
COS. ITER. ET TER. (ou TERT.) DESIG. Auguste AR.
COS. ITER. ET TER. DESIG. DIVO. IVL. Auguste OR. AR.
COS. ITER. FORT. RED. Vespasien OR. AR. (avec S. C.) M.B.
COS. ITER. TR. POT. Vespasien OR. AR. (avec S. C.) M.B.
COS. ITER. TR. POTESTAE. Vespasien OR.
COS. ITERVM TRIBVN. POT. ROMA ET AVGVSTVS S. C. Vespasien G.B.
COS. LVDOS SAECVL. FEC. Caracalla OR. AR. (avec S. C.) M.B.
COS. LVD. SAEC. FEC. S. C. Caracalla OR. AR.
COS. P. P. Commode OR.Q. AR.
COS. QVAT. PON. M. TR. P. IIII. P. P. S. C. Caligula P.B.
COS. QVINQ. J. César. OR.
COS. TERT. DICT. ITER. J. César. AR.
COS. TERT. PON. M. TR. P. III. (ou IIII.) P. P. — R. CC. Caligula P.B.
COS. II. Trajan AR.M. Marc Aurèle OR. OR.Q. AR. Vérus AR. Albin OR.Q. AR. Sept. Sévère AR.Q. Caracalla OR. AR. AR.Q. Géta AR. Macrin OR.Q. Victorin OR. Maximien Hercule OR. (avec S. C.) Antonin G.B. Marc Aurèle M.B. Vérus G.B. M.B. Pertinax G.B. Albin G.B. M.B. Caracalla M.B.
COS. II. DES. III. P. P. S. C. Trajan M.B.
COS. II. DESIGN. III. P. P. Nerva AR.
COS. II. DIANA. PERG. Trajan AR.M.
COS. II. P. P. Sept. Sévère OR.Q. AR. AR.Q. P.B. Philippe père AR.
COS. II. P. P. CONG. PR. S. C. Trajan G.B.
COS. III. Vespasien AR. Titus AR. Domitien OR. Nerva AR.M. Adrien OR. OR.Q. AR.M. AR. AR.Q. BR.M. Sabine AR.M. Antonin OR. AR. BR.M. Autonomes d'Antonin P.B. Marc Aurèle AR. BR.M. M.B. Vérus BR.M. Caracalla AR. Elagabale OR.Q. Postume B. Tétricus père P.B. Claude II P.B. Dioclétien OR. Maximien Hercule OR. Carausius P.B. (avec S. C.) Adrien G.B. M.B. † M.B. P.B. Antonin G.B. Marc Aurèle G.B. M.B. P.B. Vérus G.B.
COS. III. DES. IIII. Antonin AR.
COS. III. DES. IIII. P. P. S. C. Trajan G.B. M.B.
COS. III. DIANA PERG. Nerva AR.M.
COS. III. FORT. RED. Vespasien OR. AR. Adrien BR.M.
COS. III. LVDOS SAECVL. FEC. Sept. Sévère OR. AR. (avec S. C.) M.B.
COS. III. LVD. SAEC. FEC. S. C. Sept. Sévère G.B. M.B.
COS. III. PATER PATRIAE. Nerva OR. AR. Plotine (*hybride*) AR.

COS. III. P. P. Nerva AR. Adrien OR. BR.M. Marc Aurèle OR. OR.Q. AR. Sept. Sévère AR. AR.Q. P.B. Caracalla OR.Q. AR.Q. Elagabale AR. (avec S. C.) Adrien G.B. M.B. † M.B. P.B.

COS. III. P. P. CLEMENTIA AVG. S. C. Trajan M.B. Adrien G.B. M.B.

COS. III. P. P. INDVLGFNTIA AVG. S. C. Adrien G.B.

COS. III. P. P. IVSTITIA AVG. S. C. Adrien M.B.

COS. III. P. P. OB. ALIM. Sept. Sévère M.B.

COS. III. SARD. Adrien AR.M.

COS. III. TR. POT. Vespasien OR. Antonin OR.

COS. IIII. Vespasien AR. Titus OR. AR. Domitien OR. AR. Nerva AR.M. Antonin OR. OR.Q. AR. BR.M. Autonomes d'Antonin P.B. Marc Aurèle OR. Faustine mère (hybride) OR. Postume B. Dioclétien OR. (avec S. C.) Autonomes de Trajan P.B. Antonin G.B. M.B. Autonomes d'Antonin P.B.

COS. IIII. POT. S. C. Antonin G.B.

COS. IIII. P. P. Caracalla OR.Q. AR.Q. Gallien B.

COS. V. Vespasien OR. AR. Titus OR. AR. Domitien OR. AR. Postume B.

COS. V. CONGIAR. SECVND. S. C. Trajan G.B.

COS. V. P. P. S. P. Q. R. OPTIMO PRINC. Trajan OR. OR.Q. AR. AR.Q.

COS. V. PRINCEPS IVVENT. S. C. Domitien M.B.

COS. VI. Vespasien OR. AR. Titus OR. AR. Commode BR.M.

COS. VI. P. P. Commode OR.Q. AR.Q. BR.M.

COS. VI. P. P. S. P. Q. R. Trajan OR. AR. AR.Q.

COS. VI. P. P. S. P. Q. R. OPTIMO PRINC. Trajan AR.

COS. VII. Vespasien OR. AR. Titus AR. Domitien AR.

COS. VII. DES. VIII. Domitien AR.

COS. VII. DES. VIII. P. P. Domitien OR. AR.

COS. VII. P. P. Commode OR. (avec S. C.) M.B.

COS. VIII. Vespasien OR. AR. Titus AR.

COS. VIIII. Vespasien OR. Domitien OR.

COS. XIII. Domitien OR.

COS. XIIII. Domitien OR.

COS. XIIII. LVD. SAEC. A. POP. FRVG. AC. S. C. Domitien G.B.

COS. XIIII. LVD. SAEC. FEC. Domitien OR. AR. AR.Q. (avec S. C.) G.B. M.B.

COS. XIIII. LVD. SAEC. FECIT. S. C. Domitien G.B. M.B.

COS. XVI. Domitien M.B.

COS. XVII. CENS. P. P. P. Domitien AR.M.

CRISPVS CAESAR. Crispus OR. P.B.

CRISPVS NOB. CAES. Crispus OR.

ƆVAXA (sic). Bonose BIL.

DA. CAP. COS. V. P. P. S. P. Q. R. OPTIMO. PRINC. Trajan AR.

DA. CAP. S. P. Q. R. OPTIMO. PRINCIPI. Trajan M.B.

DACIA. Trajan Dèce OR. AR. AR.Q. Trajan Dèce et Etruscille BR.M. Gallien B. (avec S. C.) Adrien G.B. M.B. Trajan Dèce G.B. M.B.

DACIA AVGVST. PROVINCIA S. C. Trajan G.B. M.B.

DACIA COS. II. S. C. Antonin G.B.

DACIA FELIX. Trajan Dèce OR. AR. Claude II P.B. Aurélier P.B. P.B.Q. (avec S. C.) Trajan Dèce G.B. M.B.

DACICVS COS. IIII. P. P. Trajan OR. AR.

DACICVS COS. V. P. P. Trajan OR. OR.Q. AR.Q.

DAC. PARTHICO P. M. TR. P. COS. P. P. S. C. Adrien G.B. M.B.

DAC. PARTHICO P. M. TR. P. COS. P. P. I. S. C. Adrien G.B.

DAC. PARTHICO P. M. TR. POT. XX. COS. VI. P. P. S. C Trajan P.B.

DANVBIVS — SALVS REIP. Constantin I BR.M.

DANVVIVS COS. V. P. P. S. P. Q. R. OPTIMO. PRINC. Trajan AR.

DARDANICI. Trajan P.B. Autonomes d'Adrien P.B.

DEAE SANC. CERERI. Autonomes d'Hélène II P.B.

DEAE SEGETIAE. Salonine OR. B.

DEA ISIS FARIA. Autonomes d'Hélène II. P.B.Q.

DEBELLATOR HOSTIVM. Constance II BR.M.

DEBELLATORI GENTIVM BARBARARVM. Constantin I OR.M. avec GOTHIA TR. Constantin I OR.

DEBELLATORI GENTT. BARBARR. Constantin II BR.M. Constant l BR.M. Constance II BR.M.

DE BRITANN. (ou BRITANNI). Claude I OR. AR.

DE BRITANNIS. Claude I AR.M. AR.

DECVRSIO. Néron G.B. (avec s. c.) G.B.

DEDICATIO AEDIS. Faustine mère AR. (avec s. c.) G.B.

DEFENSOR ORBIS. Victorin AR. B.

DE GERM. Néron Drusus OR. AR. Claude I OR. AR.

DE GERMA. IMP. VIII. COS. III. P. P. S. C. Marc Aurèle G.B.

DE GERMANIS. Néron Drusus OR. AR. Claude I OR. AR. Commode OR. AR (avec s. c.) Commode M.B.

DE GERMANIS IMP. VIII. COS. III. P. P. S. C. Marc Aurèle G.B.

DE GERMANIS TR. P. II. COS. P. P. S. C. Commode G.B.

DE GERM. IMP. VIII. COS. III. P. P. S. C. Marc Aurèle M.B.

DE GERM. TR. P. II. COS. S. C. Commode G.B.

DE GERM. TR. P. II. COS. P. P. Commode OR. (avec s. c.) G.B. M.B.

DE GERM. TR. POT. COS. II. Commode OR.

DE GERM. TR. POT. II. COS. P. P. Commode OR.

DE GERM. TR. POT. II. COS. S. C. Commode G.B.

DE GERM. TR. P. XXX. (ou XXXI.) IMP. VIII. COS. III. P. P. Marc Aurèle OR. AR.

DE ISIDI. Autonome d'Hélène II P.B.

DE IVDAEIS. Vespasien OR. AR.

DELMATIVS CAESAR. Delmace OR. AR.

DEO CABIRO. Claude II P.B.

DEO MARTI. Gallien B. M.B. Salonin B.

DEO SANCTO NILO. Autonomes de Julien II P.B. P.B.Q.

DEO SANCTO SARAPIDI. Autonomes de Julien II P.B.

DEO SARAPIDI. Autonomes de Julien II P.B. P.B.Q. de Julien II et Hélène † M.B. P.B. d'Hélène P.B.

DEO SARARIDI. Autonomes de Julien II P.B.

DEO SERAPIDI. Autonomes de Julien II M.B. P.B. P.B.Q. de Julien II et Hélène † M.B. P.B. d'Hélène II P.B.Q.

DEO VOLKANO. Gallien B. Salonin B. Valérien jeune OR. B.

DE PARTHIS. Auguste AR.

DE PIA MATRE PIVS FILIVS. Philippe père Otacilie et Philippe fils AR.

DE SARMATIS. Commode OR. AR. (avec s. c.) M.B.

DE SARMATIS IMP. VIII. COS. III. P. P. S. C. Marc Aurèle G.B.

DE SARMATIS TR. P. II. COS. P. P. S. C. Commode G.B.

DE SARM. IMP. VIII. COS. III. P. P. S. C. Marc Aurèle G.B. M.B.

DE SARM. TR. P. II. COS. P. P. Commode OR (avec s. c.) G.B. M B.

DE SARM. TR. P. II. COS. S. C. Commode G.B.

DE SARM. TR. POT. II. COS. Commode OR.

DE SARM. TR. P. XXX. IMP. VIII. COS. III. P. P. Marc Aurèle OR. AR.

DE SARM. TR. P. XXXI. IMP. VIII. COS. III. P. P. Marc Aurèle AR.

DES. II. S. C. Marc Aurèle G.B.

DES. IIII. S. C. Antonin G.B. M.B.

DESTINATO IMPERAT (ou IMPERATORE). Caracalla AR.

DEVICTA IVDAE S. C. Vespasien G.B.

DEVS SARA. Autonomes de Julien II et Hélène P.B.

DIANA CONS. Carausius P.B.

DIANA CONS. AVG. Gallien B.

DIANAE CONS. AVG. Gallien B. Salonine B. Claude II P B.

DIANAE LVCIFERAE. Postume B. M.B.

DIANAE LVCIFERE. Postume B.

DIANA EPHESIA. Agrippine et Claude AR.M. Adrien AR.M

DIANA EPHESIA COS. III. P. P. Adrien AR.M.

DIANAE REDVCI. Postume B.

DIANAE VICTR. Claude II P.B.
DIANAE VICTRI. Emilien OR. AR.
DIANA FELIX. Gallien OR. B. G.B.
DIANA LVCIF. Faustine jeune OR. AR. Claude II OR. P.B. Quintille P.B. (avec s.
C.) Faustine jeune G.B. M.B.
DIANA LVCIFERA. Lucille AR. Julie Domne OR. AR. P.B. Plautille AR. Alex. Sévère
AR. Gordien III OR. AR. Valérien B. Gallien B. Salonine B. (avec s. c.) Faus-
tine jeune G.B. M.B. Lucille G.B. Crispine G.B. M.B. Julie Domne G.B. M.B.
Plauti le G.B.
DIANA EPHE. Claude I AR.M.
DII NVTRITORES. Salonin B.
DINA DINA PIA AVGVSTA S. C. Commode M.B.
DI PATRII. Caracalla OR (avec s. c.) Sept. Sévère G.B. Caracalla M.B. Géta G.B. M.B.
DIS AVSPICIB. TR. P. II. COS. II. P. P. Sept. Sévère OR. AR. (avec s. c.) G.B. M.B.
DIS AVSPICIBVS P. M. TR. P. III. Sept. Sévère BR.M.
DISCIPLINA AVG. Adrien OR (avec s. c.) G.B. Antonin G.B.
DISCIPVLINA AVG. S. C. Adrien G.B. M.B.
DIS CONIVGALIBVS. Crispine OR.
DIS CVSTODIBVS. Pertinax AR. (avec s C.) G.B.
DIS GENITALIBVS. Crispine AR.
DIS GENITORIBVS S. C. Pertinax G.B.
DIVA AVGVSTA. Auguste M.B. Galba OR. AR.
DIVAE .VLIAE AVG. DIVI TITI F. S. P. Q. R. Julie de Titus G.B.
DIVAE MATIDIAE SOCRVI S. C. Adrien BR.M.
DIVI AVG. PRON. AVGVST. GERMANICVS PON. MAX. TR. POTEST. COS. Caligula M.B.
DIVI CAESARIS MATER. S. C Domitia G.B. M.B.
DIVI CAESAR MATRI. S. C. Domitia G.B.
DIV. CAES. MATER. S. C. Domitia M.B.
DIVI F. Octave AR.Q.
DIVI M. PII F. P. M. TR. P. III. COS. II. P. P. Sept. Sévère OR (avec s.C.) G.B. M.B.
DIVI M. PII F. P. M. TR. P. IIII. COS. II. P. P. Sept. Sévère BR.M.
DIVIS PARENTIBVS. Adrien Trajan et Plotine OR.
DIVI TITI FILIA. Julie de Titus OR. AR.
DIVO AVG. PARENTI. Marc Aurèle M.B.
DIVO AVG. S. C. Caligula G.B.
DIVO AVG. T. DIVI VESP. F. VESPASIAN. S. C. Titus G.B.
DIVO AVG. T. DIVI VESP. F. VESPASIANO. Domitien G.B.
DIVO AVG. VESP. (ou VESPAS.) Titus G.B.
DIVO AVGVSTO S. P. Q. R. Tibère G.B. (avec OB CIVES (ou CIVIS) SER. G.B.
DIVO PIO. Antonin AR. (avec s. c.) G.B. M B.
DIVOS IVLIVS. J. César et Auguste G.B.
DIVO VESP. Domitien AR.M.
DIVVS AVGVSTVS PATER. Tibère G.B. Titus G.B.
DIVVS AVGVSTVS S. C. Nerva G.B.
DIVVS AVGVSTVS VESP. (ou VESPASIAN). Titus G.B.
DIVVS CAESAR IMP. DOMITIANI F. Domitien AR. Domitia OR. AR.
DIVVS IVLIVS. J. César et Auguste AR.
DIVVS PATER TRAIAN. Trajan AR.
DIVVS PATER TRAIANVS. Adrien AR. Gordien d'Afrique fils OR.
DIVVS TRAIAN. AVG. PARTH. PATER S. C. Adrien G.B.
DIVVS VESPASIAN. Titus OR.
D. N. CONSTANTINI AVG. — VOT. XX. Constantin I P.B.
D. N. CONSTANTI AVG. — VOT. XX. Constantin I P.B.
D. N. CONSTANTINI M. AVG. — VOT. X. Constantin I P.B.
D. N. CONSTANTINI MAX. AVG. Constantin I P.B. Constantin II P.B. (avec — VOT
X.) Constantin II P.B. (avec — VOT. XX) Constantin I P.B. Crispus P.B. Cons-
tantin II P.B. (avec — VOT. XXX.) Constantin I P.B.
D. N. CONSTANTINI MAX. INV. AVG. — VOT. XX. Constantin I P.B.
D. N. CONSTANTINVS M. AVG. — VOT. XX. Constantin I P.B.
N. CONSTANTINVS MAX. AVG. — VOT. XXX. Constantin I P.B.

D. N. CONSTANTINVS MAX. TRIVMF. AVG. Constantin I AR.M.
D. N. CONSTANTIVS VICTOR SEMPER AVG. Constance II OR.M.
D. N. IVLIANVS CAES. Julien II AR.M.
D. N. IVLIANVS NOB. CAES. Julien II AR.M.
D. N. LICINI AVG. — VOT. XX. Licinius père P.B.
D. N. LICINI AVGVSTI. — VOT. XX. Licinius père P.B.
D. N. LICINI INVICT. (OU INVICTI) AVG. — VOT. XX. Licinius père P.B.
D. N. LICINI MAX. AVG. — VOT. XX. Licinius père P.B.
D. N. LIC. LICINI AVGVSTI. — VOT. XX. Licinius père P.B.
D. N. VALENS VICTOR SEMPER AVG. Valens OR.M.
DOMINI N. LICINI AVG. — VOT. XX. Licinius père P.B.
DOMINOR. NOSTROR. CAESS. — VOT. V. Crispus P.B. Constantin II P.B. (avec —·
    VOT. X.) Constantin I P.B. Crispus P.B. Constantin II P.B. (avec — VOT. XX.)
    Cons·antin II P.B.
DOMINORVM NOSTRORVM CAESS. — VOT. V. Licinius fils P.B. Constantin II P.B.
    (avec — VOT. X.) Crispus P.B.
DOMINORVM NOSTRORVM CAES. — VOT. V. Licinius fils P.B.
DOMIT. COS. II. Domitien P.B.
DOMITIANVS COS. II. Domitien M.B.
DOMITILLAE IMP. CAES. VES. AVG. S. P. Q. R. Domitille G.B.
DONA AVG. Gallien B.
DRVSVS CAESAR TI. AVG. F. DIVI AVG. N. PONT. TR. POT. II. S. C. Drusus G.B.
DRVSVS CAESAR TI. AVGVSTI F. TR. POT. ITER. S. C. Livie M.B.
ECVITAS MVNDI. Carausius P.B.
EID. MAR. Brutus AR.
ENTTLOICKCSS (1). Philippe père OR.M.
EQVESTER ORDO PRINCIPI IVVENT. Claude I AR. Néron OR. AR. (avec S. C.) Com-
    mode M.B.
EQVIS ROMANVS. Constantin I OR.M.
ERCVLI PACIF. (OU PACIFERO). Probus P.B.
ERCVL. VICTORI. Emilien OR. AR. (avec S. C.) G.B.
ETERNITAS AVGG. S. C. Tréb. Galle G.B.
ETIAII (2). Sept. Sévère AR.
EXER. CAPPADOCICVS S. C. Adrien G.B.
EXERC. AVGVSTORVM. Licinius fils BR.M.
EXERC. BRITAN. (OU BRITANNICVS) S. C. Adrien G.B.
EXERC. DACICVS S. C. Adrien G.B.
EXERC. GERMA. S. C. Adrien G.B.
EXERC. HISPANICVS S. C. Adrien M.B.
EXERC. HISPAN. S. C. Adrien G.B.
EXERCITVS AVG. S. C. Postume G.B. M.B.
EXERCITVS DACICVS S. C. Adrien G.B.
EXERCITVS GERMANICVS S. C. Adrien G.B.
EXERCITVS INLYRICVS S. C. Trajan Dèce G.B. M.B.
EXERCITVS MAVRETANICVS S. C. Adrien G.B.
EXERCITVS PARTHICVS. Adrien BR.M.
EXERCITVS PERS. Probus BR.M.
EXERCITVS RAETICVS S. C. Adrien G.B.
EXERCITVS SYRIACVS S. C. Adrien G.B.
EXERCITVS VAC. (OU YSC) S. C. Postume G.B.
EXERC. NORICVS S. C. Adrien G.B.
EXERC. SYRIAC. (OU SYRIACVS) S. C. Adrien G.B.
BXER. MOESIACVS S. C. Adrien G.B.
EX ORACVLO APOLLINIS. Philippe père, Otacilie et Philippe fils BR.M.
EXPECTA. Carausius P.B.
EXPECTATE VENI. Carausius AR. P.B.

(1) Légende barbare et indéchiffrable.
(2) pour VESTA.

EXPED. AVG. COS. III. S. C. Adrien G.B.

EXPED. AVG. P. M. TR. P. COS. III. S. C. Adrien G.B.

EXPICTA. Carausius P.B.

EXP. VENI. Carausius P.B.

EX S. C. Claude I OR. AR. Vespasien OR. AR Faustine mère OR. AR. (avec S. C.) G.B.

EX S. C. OB CIVES SER. Galba G.B.

EX S. C. OB CIVES SERVATOS. Claude I OR. AR. Galba G.B.

EX S. C. P. P. OB CIVES SERVATOS. Claude I G.B.

EX SENATVS CONSVLTO. Marciane AR. Faustine mère OR (avec S. C.) Marciane G.B.

EXVPERATOR OMNIVM GENTIVM. Constantin I BR.M.

F. ADVENT. AVGG. NN. Dioclétien AR. Maximien Hercule AR. Constance Chlore AR Galère Maximien AR.

FATIS VICTRICIBVS. Dioclétien OR. Maximien Hercule OR. (avec S. C.) Dioclétien OR.

FECV....... Tétricus père P.B.

FECVND. AVGVSTAE. Faustine jeune OR. AR. Alex. Sévère (hybride) AR. Mamée AR. AR.Q. (avec S. C). Faustine jeune G.B. M.B.

FECVNDITAS. Faustine jeune AR. Lucille OR. AR. Julie Domne OR. AR. Elagabale AR. Maesa AR. (avec S. C.) Faustine mère G.B. Faustine jeune G.B. M.B. Lucille G.B. M.B. Crispine G.B. M.B. Julie Domne G.B. M.B.

FECVNDITAS AVG. Maesa AR. AR.Q P.B. Uranius OR. Etruscille OR. AR. Gallien B. Salonine OR.Q. B. G.B. M.B. Claude II M.B. (?) P.B. (avec S. C.) Etruscille G.B. M.B.

FECVNDITAS AVGG. Etruscille AR.

FECVNDITAS AVGVST. Faustine jeune AR.

FECVNDITAS AVGVSTA. Lucille AR.

FECVNDITAS AVGVSTAE. Lucille BR.M. (avec S. C.) Maesa G.B. M.B. Mamée G.B. M.B.

FECVNDITAS TEMPORVM Orbiane BR.M. Otacilie AR.

FECVNDITATI AVG Julie Domne BR.M.

FECVNDITATI AVGVSTAE. Faustine jeune OR. BR.M.

FEL. ADVENT. AVGG. NN. Dioclétien AR. Maximien Hercule AR. Constance Chlore AR.

FEL. AVG. COS. II. Albin AR.

FEL. AVG. P. M. TR. P. COS. II. Adrien OR. AR.

FEL. AVG. P. M. TR. P. COS. DES. III. Adrien OR. AR.

FEL. AVG. P. M. TR. P. COS. III. Adrien AR.

FEL. AVG. P. M. TR. P. X. IMP. VII. COS. IIII. P. P. Commode AR.

FEL. AVG. P. M. TR. P. XI. IMP. VII. COS. IIII. P. P. Commode OR. AR.

FEL. AVG. P. M. TR. P. XI. IMP. VII. COS. V. P. P. Commode OR. AR. (avec S. C.) G.B

FEL. AVG. TR. P. VI. (OU VII.) IMP. IIII. COS. III. P. P. S. C. Commode G.B. M.B.

FELIC. AVG. Claude II P.B.

FELIC. AVG. P. M. TR. P. COS. III. Adrien AR.

FELIC. AVG. TR. P. III. COS. II. Vérus M.B.M. (avec S. C.) G.B. M.B.

FELICIA DECENNALIA. — VOT. X. MVLT. XX. Constant I OR.M.

FELICI. AET. Gallien B.

FELICIA TEMPORA. Caracalla OR. AR. Géta AR. Probus P.B.Q. Dioclétien P.B.Q. Licinius fils OR.M. OR. Constantin I OR.

FELICI. AVG. Gallien B.

FELICIBVS AVGG. Valérien et Gallien AR.M.

FELICI PVBLICA. Carin P.B.

FELICITA AV. Carausius AR.

FELICITA REDVCIS S. C. Vespasien M.B.

FELICITAS. Julie Domne AR. Postume G.B. M.B. Carausius AR. (avec S. C.) Faustine jeune M.B. Julie Domne G.B. M.B.

FELICITAS AVG. Trajan AR. Adrien AR. Aelius OR. AR. Elagabale AR. Alex. Sévère AR. P.B. Postume OR.M. OR. B. G.B. M.B. Victorin B. Marius B. Tétricus père P.B. Tétricus fils P.B. Claude II OR. P.B. Quintille P.B. Tacite

P.B. Florien P.B. Probus P.B. Dioclétien P.B. Maximien Hercule P.B. Carausius
P.B. (avec S. C.) Adrien G.B. M.B. Aelius G.B. M.B. Antonin G.B. M.B. Mamée
G.B M.B. Gordien III, G.B. M.B. Postume G.B. M B

FELICITAS AVG. COS. II. Albin AR. (avec S. C.) Antonin G.B.

FELICITAS AVG. COS. III. Marc Aurèle OR. AR.

FELICITAS AVG. COS. III. P. P. Adrien AR.

FFLICITAS AVG. COS. IIII. Marc Aurèle AR. (avec S. C.) Antonin M.B.

FELICITAS AVGG. Sept. Sévère AR. P.B. Julie Domne AR. Caracalla OR. AR. P.B.
Géta AR. Pupien AR. Philippe fils AR. Tréb. Galle AR. B. Valérien OR.B. Gallien
OR.B. Salonine B. M.B. Salonin OR.Q. B. Numérien P.B. Maximien Hercule P.B.
(avec S. C.) Valérien G.B. M.B. Gallien G.B. M.B.

FELICITAS AVGG. NN. Constantin I † P.B.

FELICITAS AVGG. NOSTR. Maximien Hercule OR. Constance Chlore OR.

FELICITAS AVG. IMP. VI. COS III. S. C. Marc Aurèle M.B.

FELICITAS AVG. IMP. VIIII. (ou X.) COS. III. P. P. S. C. Marc Aurèle G.B.

FELICITAS AVG. N. Probus P.B.

FELICITAS AVG. NOSTR. Constance Chlore OR.

FELICITAS AVGVSTA. Hélène I. BR.M.

FFLICITAS AVGVSTI COS. II. C. S. Antonin M.B.

FELICITAS AVGVSTI S. C. Adrien G.B. M.B. Antonin M.B.

FELICITAS AVGVSTI. — VICT. GORDIANI. Gordien III BR.M.

FELICITAS AVGVST. S. C. Trajan G.B. M.B.

FELICITAS CAESS. NOSTR. Sévère II OR.

FELICITAS COS. II. Albin AR. (avec S. C.) G.B. M.B.

FELICITAS COS. IIII. S. C. Antonin M.B.

FELICITAS IMPP. Philippe père AR. Philippe fils AR.

FELICITAS PERPETVA. Mamée BR.M. M.B.M. Constant I OR.T. AR. Constance II OR.Q.
AR. Magnence OR.T. AR.

FELICITAS PERPETVA AVG. Alex. Sévère et Mamée M.B.M.

FELICITAS PERPETVA AVGEAT REM. DD. NN. Constantin I OR M.

FELICITAS PERPETVA AVG. ET CAESS. NN. Constantin II OR.M.

FELICITAS PERPETVA AVGG. ET CAESS. NN. Constantin I OR.M.

FELICITAS PERPETVA SAECVLI. Constantin I OR.

FELICITAS PERPETVA. — VOT. V. Constant I OR.M. OR. AR.M. (avec — VOT. X.
MVLT. XX.) Constance II OR. (avec — VOT. XX. MVLT. XXX.) Constance II. AR.M.

FELICITAS POPVLI ROM. Philippe père BR.M.

FELICITAS POSTVMI AVG. Postume BR.M.

FELICITAS P. R. Adrien OR. AR. (avec S. C.) G.B. M.B.

FELICITAS PVBL. Pacatien AR. Tréb. Galle AR. Volusien AR. Maximien Hercule P.B.

FELICITAS PVBLIC. Maximien Hercule P.B.

FELICITAS PVBLICA. Sept. Sévère AR. Sept. Sévère, Julie Domne, Caracalla et Géta
OR. Julie Domne AR. Caracalla AR. Géta OR. AR. P.B. Maesa AR. Mamée OR.
AR. AR.Q. P.B. Maximin I. AR. Gordien III AR. Tréb. Galle OR. AR. AR.Q. Volu-
sien OR. AR.M. Salonine OR.B. Postume G.B. (1) M.B. Tétricus père OR. Tétri-
cus père et fils OR. Tacite P.B. Carus P.B.Q. Carausius P.B. Constance Chlore
P.B. Maxence M.B. Hannibalien AR. (avec S. C.) Galba M.B. Vespasien M.B. Titus
M.B. Domitien M.B. Géta M B. Mamée G.B. M.B. Tréb. Galle G.B. Volusien G.B.
M.B. Postume G.B.

FELICITAS REIPVBLICAE. Carus P.B. Carin P.B. Constantin I. OR. Gratien M.B.
(avec — VOT. XV. MVLT. XX.) Constance II OR.

FELICITAS REIPVBLICE. Magnence AR.M. M.B (2). (avec — VOT. XV. MVLT. XX.)
Constance II AR. (avec — VOT. XX. MVLT. XXX.) Constance II. AR. (avec — VOTIS
XV MVLTIS. XXX.) Constance II. AR. (avec — VOTIS. XX. MVLTIS. XXX.) Constan-
tin II OR.

_____

(1) Variété avec PVBLICAT.

(2) Variétés fautives avec REIPVBILCE et REIPVILICE.

FELICITAS ROMANORVM. Constantin I AR.M. AR. Constance II AR.M. Constance Galle AR.M. Gratien P.B. (avec — VOT. XXXV. MVLT. XXXX.) Constance II OR. (Avec — VOTIS. XV. MVLTIS XX) Constance II. OR.
FELICITAS SAE. Probus P.B.
FELICITAS SAEC. Maximien Hercule P.B.
FELICITAS SAECV. Probus P.B.
FELICITAS SAECVL. Claude II P.B.
FELICITAS SAECVLI. Sept. Sévère, Julie Domne, Caracalla et Géta OR. AR. Caracalla OR. Gallien OR.B. Aurélien P.B. Tacite P.B. Florien P.B. Probus P.B. Allectus P.B. Constantin II. BR.M. (avec S. C.) Vérus BR.M. Sept. Sévère G.B. M.B. Caracalla M.B. Géta M.B. Trajan Dèce BR.M. G.B. M.B. Valérien G.B.
FELICITAS SAECVLI AVGG. NN. — VIC. AVGG. Maximien Hercule OR. Sévère II OR.
FELICITAS SAECVLI CAESS. NN. — VIC. CAESS. Sévère II OR. Maximin II OR.
FELICITAS SEC. Probus P.B.
FELICITAS TEMP. Elagabale AR. Philippe père AR. Postume OR.B. Tacite P.B. Florien P.B. Probus P.B. (avec S. C.) Mamée M.B. Philippe père G.B M.B.
FELICITAS TEMPOR. Pesc. Niger AR. Sept. Sévère AR. Julie Domne AR. Caracalla AR. Géta OR. AR. P.B. (avec S. C.) G.B.
FELICITAS TEMPORVM. Pesc. Niger AR. Caracalla AR. Macrin OR. AR. Alex. Sévère AR. Alex. Sévère et Mamée OR.M. BR.M. M.B.M. Gordien III OR. AR. Otacilie BR.M. Julien (usurpateur) P.B. (avec S. C.) Macrin G.B. M.B. Gordien III G.B. Tranquilline G.B.
FELICITAS TEMPORVM IIII. ET III. COS. Valérien BR.M.
FELICITATEM ITALICAM Caracalla AR.
FELICITA TEMP. S. C. Gordien III M.B.
FELICITATEM PVBLICAM. Caracalla AR.
FELICITATI AVG. Adrien AR.
FELICITATI AVG. COS. III. P. P. Adrien AR. (avec S. C.) G.B M.B.
FELICITATI AVG. COS. IIII. Antonin AR. (avec S. C.) G.B.
FELICITATI AVG. P. P. COS. III. S. C. Adrien G.B. M.B. Marc Aurèle M.B.
FELICITATI AVG. P. P. IMP. VIII. COS. III. S. C. Marc Aurèle M.B.
FELICITATI AVGVSTI. Adrien AR. Gallien OR.
FELICITATI AVGVSTI S. C. COS. III. P. P. Adrien G.B.
FELICITATI CAES. S. C. Marc Aurèle M.B. Commode M.B.
FELICITATI PERPETVAE. AVG. COS. V. P. P. S. C. Commode G.B.
FELICITATI POPVLI ROMANI. Alex. Sévère BR.M.
FELICIT. AVG. Gallien OR.B. B.Q. Tétricus père P.B.
FELICIT. AVGVSTORVM S. C. Valérien G.B.
FELICIT. AVGVST. S. C. Galba M.B.
FELICIT. DEORVM. Mariniane B. Gallien B.
FELICIT. ERPETVI. Constantin I OR.T.
FELICIT. PERP. Victorin B. Maximien Hercule P.B.
FELICIT. PVB. Gallien B.
FELICIT. PVBL. Gallien B. Salonine B. Dioclétien P.B. Maximien Hercule P.B Carausius P.B.
FELICIT. PVBLIC. S. C. Titus G.B.
FELICIT. PVBLICA. Carin OR.Q. P.B.
FELICIT. SAECVL..... Crispus BR.M.
FELICIT. TEM. Tacite P.B.
FELICIT. TEMP. Gordien III OR. AR. Aurelien P.B. Tacite P.B. Florien P.B Probus P.B (1). Carausius P.B.
FELICIT. TEMPO. Sept. Sévère AR.
FELICIT. TEMPOR. Pesc. Niger AR. Sept. Sévère AR. Paula AR. Gordien III AR. Philippe père AR. (avec S. C.) Gordien III G.B. M.B.
FELIC. PERPETVAE AVG. Commode AR.
FELIC. PERPETVAE AVG. COS. VI. P. P. S. C. Commode G.B.
FELIC. PVBL. Volusien AR.

(1) Variété avec FELICT. TEMP.

FELIC. SAEC. COS. IIII. Antonin AR.
FELIC. SAECVLI. Aurélien P.B.
FELIC. T. C. V. P. Victorin P.B.Q.
FELIC. TEMP. Tacite OR. P.B.
FELIC. TEMPO. Claude II P.B.(1).
FELIX ADVENT. AVGG. NN. Dioclétien OR. M.B.Maximien Hercule M.B. Constance Chlore M.B. Galère Maximien M.B.
FELIX ADVENTVS AVGGG. Valentinien I OR.M. Valens OR.M.
FELIX ADVENTVS AVG. N. Constantin I OR.M. Constance II OR.M. Valentinien OR.M. Valentinien II OR.M.
FELIX CARTHAGO. Maximien Hercule OR.
FELIX INGRESSVS SEN. AVG. — VOT. XXX. Maximien Hercule OR.
FELIX KARTHAGO. Maxence OR.
FELIX PROCESS. CONSVLAT. AVG. N. Maxence OR. AR.
FELIX PROCESSVS COS. II. (ou III.). Crispus OR.
FELIX PROCESSVS COS II. AVG. Constantin II OR.
FELIX PROCESSVS COS. IIII. AVG. N. Constantin I OR.
FELIX PROCESSVS COS. VI. Constantin I OR.
FELIX PROCESSVS COS. VI. AVG. N. Constantin I OR.
FELIX PROGENIES CONSTANTINI AVG. Crispus OR.M.
FELIX ROMA. Adrien BR.M.
FEL. P. M. TR. P. VIIII. (ou X.) IMP. VII. COS. IIII. P. P. Commode AR.
FEL. PROCES. CONS. III. AVG. N. Maxence M.B.
FEL. PROCESS. CONS. III. A. N. Maxence M.B.
FEL. PROCESS. CONS. III. AVG. N. Maxence M.B.
FEL. P. R. P. M. TR. P. COS. III. Adrien AR. Albin AR.
FEL. PVBLICA P. M. TR. P. XI. IMP. VII. COS. V. P. P. S. C. Commode G.B.
FEL. PVBLICA P. M. TR. P. XII. IMP. VIII. COS. V. P. P. S C. Commode G.B.
FEL. TEM. COS. II. S. C. Vérus G.B.
FEL. TEMPORVM. Carausius P.B.
FEL. TEMP. REPARATIO. Autonomes de Constantinople G.B.M. Constant I M.B. † M.B. † P.B. P.B. Contance II BR.M. M.B. †M.B. P.B. Vétranion(?) P.B. Magnence M.B. P.B.Q. Constance Galte M.B. P.B. Julien II OR. P.B. Gratien M.B. (avec — LXXII.) Constance II P.B. Constance Galle P.B. (avec. — VOT. XX.) Constant I AR. Constance II AR.
FEL. TEMP. TR. P. XV. COS. III. Marc-Aurèle AR. (avec S. C.) G.B. M.B.
FIDEI AVG. Caracalla AR.
FIDEI COHORTIVM. AVG. Commode AR.
FIDEI COH. P. M. TR. P. XII. COS. V. S. C. Commode G.B.
FIDEI COH. P. M. TR. P. XV. COS. VI. Commode AR.
FIDEI COH. P. M. TR. P. XVI. COS. VI. Commode AR. (avec S. C.) G.B. M.B.
FIDEI COH. P. M. TR. P. XVII. COS. VI. Commode AR.
FIDEI EQVITVM. Gallien OR.
FIDEI EXERCITVI. — VIC. AVG. Pesc. Niger AR.
FIDEI EXERCITVS. Caracalla AR.
FIDEI EXER. — VIC. AVG. Pesc. Niger AR.
FIDEI LEG. Gallien B.
FIDEI LEG. TR. P. COS. Sept. Sévère OR. AR. (avec S. C.) G.B. M.B.
FIDEI LEG. TR. P. COS II. Sept. Sévère AR.
FIDEI MILIT. P. M. TR. P. II. (ou III.) COS. II. P. P. Sept. Sévère BR.M
FIDEI MILITVM. Caracalla AR.
FIDEI PRAET. Gallien OR. B. G.B.
FIDEI PVBLICAE. S. C. Domitien M.B.
FIDE. MILI. Carausius P.B.
FIDEM MILITV. Carausius AR.
FIDEM MILITVM. Carausius P.B.
FIDES. Autonomes de Galba AR.

(2) Variété avec TENPO.

FIDES AEQVIT. Postume OR.B.
FIDES AVG. Claude II P.B.
FIDES AVG. COS. II. Albin AR.
FIDES AVGG. ET CAESS. NN. Maximien Hercule M.B.
FIDES AVG. P. XV. Gallien B.
FIDES AVGVST. S. C. Plotine G.B.
FIDES EQVIT. Postume OR.B.
FIDES EQVITVM. Postume B.
FIDES EXER. Quintille P.B.
FIDES EXERC. COS. IIII. S. C. Antonin G.B. M.B.
FIDES EXERC. S. C. Postume M.B.
FIDES EXERC. VIII. Gallien B.
FIDES EXERCI. Tétricus père P.B. Claude II P.B.
FIDES EXERCIT. Quintille P.B. Allectus P.B. (avec S. C.) Domitien G.B. Trajan G.B. Emilien G.B.
FIDES EXERCITAS. Postume B.
FIDES EXERCIT. AVGG. Numérien P.B.
FIDES EXERCITI. Postume B. Aurélien P.B.
FIDES EXERCIT. P. M. TR. P. XI. IMP. VII. COS. V. P. P. Commode BR.M.
FIDES EXERCITVS Caracalla AR. Elagabale OR. AR. Alex. Sévère AR. P.B. Gordien III AR. BR.M. Philippe père AR. Philippe fils AR. Gallien AR.M. Postume OR. B. M.B. Victorin OR. Constantin I OR. (avec S. C.) Elagabale G.B. M.B. Philippe père G.B. M.B.
FIDES EXERCITVVM. Autonomes de Galba AR. Vitellius OR. AR. (avec S. C.) Vitellius G.B. M.B. Vespasien G.B.
FIDES EXERCITVVM. COS. III. S. C. Marc Aurèle G.B. M.B.
FIDES EXERCITVVM. IMP. VIII. COS. III. P. P. S. C. Marc Aurèle M.B.
FIDES FORTVNA S. C. Vespasien M.B.
FIDES LEG. Gallien B.
FIDES LEG. (OU LEGION) COS. II. Albin AR.
FIDES MAXIMA. Probus BR.M.
FIDES MIL. Gallien OR.B. Salonine (hybride) B. Carausius P.B.
FIDES MILI. Aurélien OR.
FIDES MILIT. Philippe père OR Q. AR. Gallien OR. B. Claude II P.B. Quintille OR. P.B. Aurélien OR. P.B. Tacite P.B. Florien P.B. Probus P.B. Carus P.B. Carin P.B. Dioclétien P.B. Maximien Hercule P.B. Carausius P.B. Constance Chlore P.B. Galère Maximien P.B
FIDES MILITAS. Victorin B.
FIDES MILITVM. Galba AR. Caracalla AR. Macrin OR. AR. Diaduménien OR. AR. Elagabale OR. AR. Alex. Sévère AR. BR.M. P.B. Alex. Sévère et Mamée BR.M. M.B.M. Mamée (hybride) AR. Maximin I AR. AR.Q. Gordien III OR. AR. Philippe père OR. AR. Pacatien AR. Valérien OR. BIL.M. B. Gallien OR.M. OR. OR.Q. B. B.Q. M.B. Salonine (hybride) B. Salonin B. Macrien jeune BIL. Postume B. B.Q. G.B. M.B. Lélien B. Victorin OR. B. Marius OR. Tétricus père BIL.Q. P.B. P.B.Q. Tétricus fils P.B. Claude II OR. B. M.B. (?). P.B. Quintille OR. P.B. Aurélien OR. P.B. Tacite M.B. P.B. Florien P.B. Probus OR.M. M.B. P.B. P.B.Q. Carus P.B. Carin OR. P.B. Magnia Urbica P.B. Dioclétien P.B. Maximien Hercule M.B. P.B. Carausius P.B. Allectus P.B. Constance Chlore OR. M.B. Sévère II M.B. Maxence OR. M.B. (avec S. C.) Macrin G.B. M.B. Alex. Sévère G.B. M.B. Maximin I G.B. M.B. Gordien III G.B. M.B. Philippe père G.B. M.B. Valérien G.B. Gallien G.B. M.B.
FIDES MILITVM AVGG. ET CAESS. NN. Maximien Hercule M.B. Constanee Chlore M.B. Sévère II M.B.
FIDES MILITVM AVGG. NN. Maxence M.B
FIDES MILITVM AVG. N. Maxence M.B. P.B.
FIDES MIL. P. M. TR. P. Macrin AR.
FIDES MVTVA. Pupien AR.
FIDES MVTVA. AVGG. Balbin AR.
FIDES PRAETORIANORVM. Autonomes de Galba AR. Vitellius AR.
FIDES PVBL. Vespasien AR. Titus AR. (avec S. C.) Balbin G.B.

FIDES PVBLI. Domitien AR.
FIDES PVBLICA. Adrien AR. Caracalla AR. Macrin AR. Elagabale AR. (avec S. C.)
    Vespasien G.B. M.B. Titus M B. Adrien G.B. M.B.
FIDES VICTOR. Probus P.B.
FID. EXERC. S. C. Macrin G.B.
F.D. EXERCIT. S. C. Phlippe père G.B.
FID. EXERCIT. P. M. TR. P. XI. IMP. VII. COS. V. P. P. S. C. Commode G.B.
FID. EXERC. P. M. TR. P. X. IMP. VII. COS. IIII. P. P. Commode OR. AR.
FID. EXERC. P. M. TR. P. XI. (ou XII.) IMP. VII. COS. V. P. P. Commode AR.
FID. EXERC. TR. P. III. COS. II. Géta AR.
FID. MILITVM. Gallien OR. B. Claude II P.B.
FID. MIL. S. C. Commode G.B.
FID. PRAET. Gallien B.
FILICITA. AVG. Postume G.B.
FISCI IVDAICI CALVMNIA SVBLATA S. C. Nerva G B.
FL. HELENA AVGVSTA. Hélène I P.B.
FL. IVL. CONSTANS P. F. AVG. Constant AR.
FL. IVL. CONSTANS P. F. AVGG. (sic. Constant AR.
FLORENTE FORTVNA P. R. Autonomes de Galba AR.
FOR. FEL. P. M. TR. P.XIIII. COS. V. DES. VI. Commode AR.
FOR. IIIL. SAL. Probus P.B.
FOR. RED. P. M. TR. P. X IMP. VII. COS. IIII. P. P. Commode AR. (avec S. C)
    G.B.
FOR. RED. P. M. TR. P. XI. IMP. VII. COS. V. P. P. Commode AR. (avec S. C.) M.B.
FOR. RED. P. M. TR. P. XII. IMP. VIII. COS. V. P. P. Commode AR.
FOR. RED. P. M. TR. P. XIII. IMP. VIII. COS. V. P. P. S. C. Commode G.B M.B
FORTA REDVC. Sept. Sévère AR.
FORT. DVCI. TR. P. XXX. IMP. VIII. COS. III. Marc Aurèle AR.
FORT. FELI. P. M. TR. P. XIII. IMP. VII. COS V. P. P. Commode BR.M.
FORT. FELI. P. M. TR. P. XIIII. IMP. VIII. COS. V. P. P. Commode OR.M. BR.M.(avec
    S. C.) G.B. M.B.
FORT. FELI. P. M. TR. P. XIIII. IMP. VIII. COS. V. DES. VI. S. C. Commode G.B.
FORT. FEL. P. M. TR. P. XIIII. COS. V. P. P. Commode AR.
FORTI. FORTVNAE. Galère Maximien † M.B.
FORTITVDO AVG. INVICTA. Albin AR.
FORT. MANENT P. M. TR. P. XIIII. COS. V. P. P. S. C. Commode M.B.
FORT. MANENT. TR. P. XIIII. IMP. Commode AR.
FORT. R. AVG. Julie Domne AR.
FORT. RE. Albin AR.
FORT. RED. CAES. AVG. S. P. Q. R. Auguste OR. AR.M. AR.
FORT. RED. COS. ITER. Vespasien AR.
FORT. RED. COS. III. Adrien AR. BR.M. Marc Aurèle AR. (avec S. C.) Adrien G.B.
    M.B. Marc Aurèle M.B.
FORT. RED. COS. III. P. P. Adrien AR. (avec S. C) G.B. M.B.
FORT. RED. COS. VI. P. P. S. P. Q. R. Trajan OR. AR.
FORT. RED. DAC. PARTHICO. P. M. TR. P. COS. P. P. S. C. Adrien G.B.
FORT. RED. DIVI. NER. NEP. P. M. TR. P. COS. Adrien OR. AR.
FORT. RED. IMP. IIII. COS. II. P. P. S. C. Commode G.B.
FORT. RED. PARTH. F. DIVI. NER. P. M. TR. P. COS. Adrien AR.
FORT. RED. PARTHIC. DIVI. TRAIAN. F. P. M. TR. P. COS. P. P. Adrien AR.
FORT. RED. PARTHICO. P. M. TR. P. COS. VI. P. P. S. P. Q. R. Trajan AR.
FORT. RED. P. M. TR. P. COS. DES. II. Adrien AR.
FORT. RED. P. M. TR. P. COS. II. Adrien OR. AR.
FORT. RED. P. M. TR. P. COS. III. Adrien AR. (avec S. C.) M.B.
FORT. RED. P. M. TR. P. COS. VI. P. P. S. P. Q. R. Trajan OR. AR.
FORT. RED. P. M. TR. P. XIIII. COS. III. P. P. Caracalla AR. (avec S. C.) G.B. M.B.
FORT. RED. P. M. TR. P. XIX. COS. III. P. P. Sept. Sévère AR. (avec S. C.) M.B.
FORT. RED. PONT. MAX. TR. POT. COS. S. C. Adrien G.B. M.B.
FORT. RED. PONT. MAX. TR. POT. COS. DES. II. S. C. Adrien G.B. M.B.
FORT. RED. PONT. MAX. TR. POT. COS. II. (ou III.) S. C. Adrien G.B. M.B.

FORT. RED. S. C. SENATVS POPVLVSQVE ROMANVS. Trajan G.B. M.B.
FORT. RED. S. P. Q. R. OPTIMO PRINCIPI. Trajan OR. AR.
FORT. RED. .... TR. POT. COS. S. C. Trajan G.B.
FORT. RED. TR. P. III. COS. II. Julie Domne (*hybride*) AR. Géta AR. (avec s. c.) G.B. M.B.
FORT. RED. TR. P. III. COS. II. P. P. Géta OR. AR. (avec s. c.) M.B.
FORT. RED. TR. P. V. IMP. II. COS. II. S. C. Vérus M.B.
FORT. RED. TR. P. VIII. IMP. V. COS. III. Vérus. OR. AR.
FORT. RED. TR. P. XIIII. COS. III. Caracalla AR.
FORT. RED. TR. P. XXII. (ou XXIII.) IMP. V. COS. III. Marc-Aurèle OR. AR.
FORT. RED. TR. P. XXX. IMP. VIII. COS. III. Marc Aurèle AR.
FORT. RED. TR. POT. II. COS. II. Vérus OR. (avec s. c.) G.B.
FORT. RED. TR. POT. III. COS. II. S. C. Vérus G.B. M.B.
FORT. RED. TR. POT. VIII. (ou VIIII.) IMP. V. COS. III. S. C. Vérus G.B. M.B.
FORT. RED. TR. POT. XXII. (ou XXIII.) IMP. V. COS. III. S. C. Marc Aurèle G B M.B
FORT. REDVC. Sept. Sévère AR. (1).
FORT. REDVCI. Adrien AR.
FORT. REDVCI. COS. II. Albin BR.M. (avec s. c.) G.B. M B.
FORT. REDVCI TR. POT. COS. II. S. C. Albin G.B.
FORT. REDVX. Julie Domne AR. Gordien III OR. AR Gallien B. Macrien jeune BIL. Quiétus BIL. Victorin B. Carausius P.B.
FORTVNA. Carausius P.B.
FORTVNA AVG. Galba OR. AR. Adrien OR. AR. Elagabale AR. Paula AR. Postume B. Tetricus père P.B. Claude II P.B. Carus OR. P.B. Carausius AR. P.B. (avec s. c.) Adrien G.B. M.B. Antonin G.B. M.B. Postume M.B.
FORTVNA AVG. COS. II. Albin AR. (avec s. c.) Antonin G.B. M.B.
FORTVNA AVGG. Carin P.B.
FORTVNA AVG. S. P. Q. R. Gallien B.
FORTVNA AVGVST. Vespasien OR. AR. Domitille AR. Titus OR. AR. Domitien AR Nerva OR. AR. (avec s. c.) Domitien M B. Nerva G.B. M.B.
FORTVNA AVGVSTI. Vespasien OR. (avec s. c.) Domitien M.B. Trajan M B.
FORTVNA AVGVSTI COS. II. S. C. Antonin M.B.
FORTVNA COS. IIII. Antonin AR
FORTVNAE. Carausius P.B.
FORTVNAE AVG. Elagabale AR. (avec s. c)Vespasien G.B.
FORTVNAE AVG. COS. II. Albin OR.
FORTVNAE AVGG. Sept. Sévère OR. AR.
FORTVNAE AVGVSTI S. C. Domitien M.B.
FORTVNAE DVCI C. V. P. P. Commode BR.M.
FORTVNAE FELICI. Didia Clara AR. Julie Domne OR. AR. BR.M. P.B. Alex. Sévère P.B. (avec s. c.) Julie Domne G.B. M.B.
FORTVNAE MANENTI COS. V. P. P. S. C. Commode G.B.
FORTVNAE MANENTI C. V. P. P. Commode AR.
FORTVNAE MVLIEBRI. Faustine jeune AR.
FORTVNAE EPHESIA. Adrien AR.M.
FORTVNAE RE. Pesc. Niger AR.
FORTVNAE RED. Pesc. Niger AR. Claude II P.B. (2). Quintille P.B.
FORTVNAE REDV. Pesc. Niger AR.
FORTVNAE REDVC. Pesc. Niger AR. (avec s. c.) Lucile G.B.
FORTVNAE REDVCA S. C. Adrien M.B.
FORTVNAE REDVCI. Adrien AR. Pesc. Niger AR. Sept. Sévère OR. AR. Julie Domne AR. Elagabale AR. AR.Q. Maesa AR. Alex. Sévère AR. Tréb. Galle BR.M. Tréb. Galle et Volusien BR.M. Volusien BR.M. Gallien B. Claude II P.B. (avee s. c.) Vespasien G.B. M.B. Titus G.B. Trajan G.B. M.B. Adrien G.B. M.B. Sept. Sévère G.B. M.B. Elagabale G.B M.B
FORTVNAE REDVCI AVGG. ET CAESS. Maximien Hercule P.B.
FORTVNAE REDVCI AVGG. ET CAESS. NN. Constance Chlore M.B.

(1) Variétés fautives avec RDEVC et REDVG.
(2) Variété avec FOVTVNAE RED.

FORTVNAE REDVCI AVGG. NN. D'oclétien M.B. Maximien Hercule M.B. Constance Chlore M.B. Galère Maximien M.B.

FORTVNAE REDVCI CAESS. NN. Dioclétien M.B. Maximien Hercule M.B. Constance Chlore M.B. Galère Maximien M.B.

FORTVNAE REDVCI COS. II. Albin BR.M.

FORTVNAE REDVCI C. V. P. P. Commode BR.M.

FORTVNA OBSEQVENS COS. IIII. Antonin OR. AR. (avec S. C.) G.B. M.B

FORTVNA P. R. Nerva OR. AR. (avec S. C.) G.B. M.B.

FORTVNA RED. Gallien B. Claude II P.B. Carin P.B. Dioclétien P.B. Carausius P.B.

FORTVNA REDV. Carausius P.B.

FORTVNA REDVCI. Sept. Sévère AR

FORTVNA REDVX. Sept. Sévère OR. AR. AR.Q. Caracalla AR. Elagabale AR. Mamée AR. Gordien III AR. Philippe père OR. AR. Pacatien AR. Valérien B. Gallien OR. OR.Q. B. BR.M. Salonine B. Postume B. Tétricus père P.B. Claude II P.B. Quintille P.B. Aurélien OR. P.B. Florien P.B Carin P.B. Dioclétien P.B. Carausius P.B. (avec S. C.) Septime Sévère M.B. Gordien III G.B. M.B. Philippe père G.B. M.B.

FORTVNA REDVX S. P. Q. R. Claude II P.B.

FORTVNA REDVX VIIC. Gallien B.

FORTVNA SPES. Adrien OR.

FORTVNE AVG. Sept. Sévère AR.

FORTVN FELIC. Paula AR.

FORTVN. REDVC. Sept. Sévère AR. Julie Domne AR

FORTVN. REDV. CAESARI AVG. S P. Q. R. Auguste OR. AR.

FOATVN. REDVC. CAESARI AVGVS. S. P. Q. R. Auguste OR. AR.

FORTVN. REDVCI. Julie Domne AR.

FORTV. REDVC. Sept. Sévère AR.

FORVM TRAIAN. Trajan OR.

FORVM TRAIANI S. P. Q. R. OPTIMO PRINCIPI S. C. Trajan G.B.

FRANC. ET ALAM. — GAVDIVM ROMANORVM. Constantin I OR.

FRANCIA. — GAVDIVM ROMANORVM. Constantin I OR OR.Q. Crispus OR.Q.

FR FR. FRVG. Pesc. Niger AR.

FVNDATOR PACIS. Sept. Sévère OR. AR. P.B. Julie Domne (hybride) AR. Caracalla AR. Géta AR.

FVNDAT. PACIS. Sept. Sévère AR. Licinius père P.B.Q. Constantin I P.B.Q.

FVRTVNAE FELICI. Sept. Sévère AR.

GALBA IMP. Galba AR.

GALLIA. Autonomes de Galba AR. Galba AR

GALLIA HISPANIA. Galba AR.

GALLIENVS AVG. Gallien B.

GALLIENVS CVM. EXERC. SVO. — IOVI VICTORI. Valérien B.

GAVDETE ROMANI. — SIC XX. SIC XXX. Maximien Hercule OR.Q.

GAVDIVM AVGVSTI NOSTRI. Constantin I. OR.M.

GAVDIVM POPVLI ROMANI. Constant I OR.M. (avec — SIC V. SIC X.) Constant I OR.M. OR. OR.Q. AR.M. AR. BR.M. (avec — SIC X. SIC XX.) AR.M. Constance II OR.M. OR. AR.M (avec — SIC XX. SIC. XXX.) Constantin I OR. AR. Constance II AR.M. (avec — VOTIS XX. MVLTIS XXX.) OR.M. (avec — VOT. V. MVLT. X.) Constant I OR.

GAVDIVM REIPVBLICAE. Constantin I OR. OR.Q.

GAVDIVM ROMANORVM (1). Maximien Hercule OR. Constantin I OR. Constantin II OR.T. Constance II OR.M. Jovien OR.M. (avec — VOT. X. MVLT. XV.)Constant I AR.M. (avec — VOT. X. MVLT. XX.) AR.M. (avec — VOT. XX.) BR.M. Constance II BR.M. (avec — VOT. XX. MVLT. XXX) AR.M.

GEN. AVG. FELIC. COS. V. (ou VI.)Commode OR. AR.

GEN. AVG. FELIC. P. M. TR. P. XV. IMP. VIII. COS. VI. S. C. Commode G.B.

---

(1) Voir cette légende avec ALAMANNIA. — FRANC. ET ALAM. — FRANCIA. — SARMATIA.

GEN. CIVIT. NICOM. Autonomes d'Hélène II P.B. P.B.Q.
GEN. ILLYRICI. Trajan Dèce AR. (avec S. C.) G.B.
GENIO AVG. Gallien B.
GENIO AV. GENIO CC. Maximin II P.B.
GENIO AVGG. ET CAESARVM NN Constance Chlore M.B. (1). Galère Maximien M.B Sévère II M.B. Maximin II M.B. Constantin I M.B.
GENIO AVGVST. Licinius père †.M.B. P.B.
GENIO AVGVSTI. Maximien Hercule AR.M. M B. Galère Maximien M.B. †.M.B. P.B. Maximin II M.B. †.M.B. ✝.P.B. Licinius père M.B. †.M.B. P.B Q. Constantin I M.B. †.M.B. P.B. (avec S. C.) Néron M.B. P.B.
GENIO AVGVSTI. CMII. (en monogramme) Galère Maximien M.B. Maximin II MB Licinius père M.B. †.P.B. Constantin I †.M.B.
GENIO AVGVSTI D. N. (2). Licinius père M.B.
GENIO AVGVSTI PII Maximin II M.B.
GENIO CAESARIS. Maximien Hercule M.B. Maximin II M.B. †.M.B. Licinius père M.B. Constantin I M.B. (avec CMII.) Maximin II M.B. Constantin I M.B. (avec N.) Maximin II M.B.
GENIO EXERCITVS. Galère Maximien M.B. Maximin II M.B. †.M.B. Licinius †.M.B. Licinius père M.B.
GENIO FEL. (ou FIL.) AVGG. Constantin I. P.B.
GENIO IMPERATORIS. Maximien Hercule M.B. Galère Maximien M.B. Maximin II M.B. †.M.B. Licinius père M.B. Constantin I M.B.
GENIO POP. ROM. Dioclétien M.B Maximien Hercule M.B. P.B. Galère Maximien M.B. Maximin II M.B. †.M.B. P.B. Licinius père M.B. †.P.B. P.B. Constanin I M.B. †.M.B. P.B.
GENIO POPVLI ROM. Maximin II M.B Constantin I M.B.
GENIO POPVLI ROMANI. Dioclétien M.B. Dioclétien et Maximien Hercule M.B. Maximien Hercule M.B. P.B. Maximien Hercule et Dioclétien M B. Domitius Domitien M.B. Constance Chlore AR.M. M.B. P.B. Constance Chlore et Maximien Hercule M.B. Constance Chlore et Galère Maximien M.B. Galère Maximien AR.M. M.B. †.M.B. Sévère II AR.M. M.B. PB. P.B.Q. Sévère II et Maximin II M.B. Maximin II M.B. P.B. P.B.Q. Licinius père †.M.B. P.B. Constantin I M.B. †.M.B. P.B.
GENIO P. R. Autonomes de Galba AR. Adrien OR. (avec S. C.) Titus M.B.
GENIO SENATVS. Antonin AR. Caracalla AR. (avec S. C.) Antonin G.B. M.B.
GENI. P. R. S. C. Titus M.B.
GENIVM P. R. Vespasien AR.
GENIVS AVG. Gallien B. Tétricus père P.B. Claude II P.B. Quintille P.B. (avec S. C.) Gallien G.B. M.B.
GENIVS AVGVSTI. Maximin II P.B.
GENIVS EXER. Gallien P.B.
GENIVS EXERC. Carin P.B.
GENIVS EXERCI. Claude II M.B. P.B. (3).
GENIVS EXERC. ILLYRICIANI. Trajan Dèce OR. AR. AR.Q. Hérennius AR. (avec S. C.) Trajan Dèce G.B. M.B.
GENIVS EXERCITI Aurélien P.B. Carin P.B.
GENIVS EXERCITVS ILLYRICIANI. Trajan Dèce OR. AR. (avec S. C.) G B. M.B.
GENIVS EXER. ILLYRICIANI S. C. Trajan Dèce G.B.
GENIVS ILL. (ou ILLY.). Aurélien P.B.
GENIVS ILLYR. Aurélien OR. P.B.
GENIVS ILLYRICI. Trajan Dèce OR.
GENIVS L. Tétricus père P.B.
GENIVS POP. ROMANI Antonin OR. AR. (avec S. C.) M.B.
GENIVS POPVLI. Claude II P.B.
GENIVS POPVLI ROMANI. Adrien BR.M. Antonin OR.
GENIVS P. R. Autonomes de Galba OR. AR. Sept. Sévère AR.

(1) Variété avec CAESAVM.
(2) Ou plutôt CMH.
(3) Variété avec EXRCI.

GEN. LVG. COS. II. Albin OR. AR.

GEN. P. R. Autonomes de Galba AR.

GEN. P. R. P. M. TR. P. COS. III. Adrien OR. AR.

GERMANIA Adrien AR.

GERMANIA CAPTA. S. C. Domitien G.B.

GERMANIA SVBACTA IMP. VI. COS. III. Marc Aurèle BR.M. (avec S. C.) G.B M.B.

GERMANICO AVG. IMP. VI. COS. III. S. C. Marc Aurèle G.B.

GERMANICVS. Domitien OR.

GERMANICVS ARTAXIAS. Germanicus AR.

GERMANICVS CAESAR. Germanicus M.B.

GERMANICVS COS. X. Domitien OR.

GERMANICVS COS. XIIII (ou XV.). Domitien OR. AR.

GERMANICVS COS. XVI. Domitien OR. M.B.

GERMANICVS COS. XVII. Domitien OR.

GERMANICVS MAXIMVS Gallien B.

GERMANICVS MAX. TER. Valérien B. Gallien B.

GERMANICVS MAX. V. Gallien B(1). B.Q. Postume B. G.B. M.B.

GERMAN. MAX. TR. P. Gallien B.

GERM MAX. CARPICI MAX. III. ET. II. COS. Philippe père, Otacilie et Philippe fils BR.M.

GERM. (OU GER.) P. M. TR. P. IMP. P. P. S. C. Néron P.B.

GER. P. M. TR. P. P. P. S. C. Néron P.B.

GER. PONT. MAX. TR. P. IMP. P. P. S. C. Néron P.B.

GLORIA AVGG. Constantin I OR.M.

GLORIA CONSTANTINI AVG. Constantin I OR M. (avec — VOT. V.) Crispus et Constantin II OR.M

GLORIA ET REPARATIO TEMPORVM. Magnence OR.

GLORIA EXERCIT. Procope P.B.

GLORIA EXERCITVS. Constantin I OR.M. P.B. P.B.Q. Autonomes de Constantinople P.B. de Rome P.B. Delmace P.B. P.B.Q. Constantin II AR.M. P.B. P B.Q. Constant I P.B. P.B.Q. Constance II AR.M. P B. P.B.Q. Constance Galle AR.M.

GLORIA EXERCITVS. GALL. Constantin I OR.Q.

GLORIA EXERCITVS KART. Alexandre (usurpateur) †.M.B.

GLORIA NOVI SAECLI. Gratien AR.

GLORIA NOVI SAECVLI. Gratien OR. P.B.

GLORIA NVVI SAECVLI. Gratien AR.

GLORIA ORBIS COS. IIII. Probus BR.M.

GLORIA ORBIS COS. V. Probus AR.M. BR.M.

GLORIA PERPET. Licinius père P.B.Q. Constantin I P.B.

GLORIA PERPETVA AVG. N. Constantin I OR.M.

GLORIA REIPVB. Honorius P.B.Q.

GLORIA REIPVBLICAE. Constant I OR.M. Constance II OR.M. OR. Constance Galle OR. OR.Q. Julien II OR. Valens OR. Valentinien II P.B.Q. Valentinien III P.B.Q. (avec — VOT. V.) Jovien OR. (avec — VOT. V MVLT X.) Constance Galle OR. Julien II OR. Valentinien I OR.M. (avec — VOT. XX. MVLT. XXX.) Constant I OR. Constance II, OR. (avec — VOT. XXX. MVLT. XXXX.) Constance II, OR.M. OR. AR. (avec — VOT. XXXV. MVLT. XXXX.) OR. (avec — VOT. XXXX.) OR. (avec — VOTIS V.) Constance Galle OR. (avec — VOTIS V. MVLTIS X.) Julien II OR.

GLORIA REIPVBLICE. Thèodose I P.B. P.B.Q.

GLORIA ROMANOR. Magnence M.B.

GLORIA ROMANORVM. Constantin I OR.M. OR. BR.M. P.B. Crispus OR. Constantin II OR.M. AR.M. Constant I OR.M. BR.M. M.B. Constance II OR.M. BR.M. M.B. P.B. Népotien M.B. Vétranion P.B. Magnence BR.M. M.B. P.B. Décence OR.M. M.B. Constance Galle OR.M. BR.M. M.B. Julien II OR.M. Jovien AR.M. Valentinien I OR.M. OR. AR.M. M.B. P.B. Valens OR.M. OR. AR.M. M.B. P.B Procope M.B P.B.Q. Gratien OR.M. OR. AR.M. AR M.B. P.B. Valentinien II OR.M. AR.M. G.B. M.B. P.B. Thèodose I AR.M. AR. M.B. P.B. P.B.Q. Eugène OR.M. AR.M. Honorius

riété avec GERMACVS.

OR.M. OR.Q. AR M. AR. AR.Q. M.B. P.B. P.B.Q. Attale P.B. Valentinien III OR.
AR. (avec — VOT. V. MVLT. X.) Constance II BR.M. Constance Galle BR.M.
(avec — VOT. X MVLT. XX.) Valentinien I OR. Valens OR. (avec — VOT. XX.)
Constance II BR M. Julien II OR.Q(1). (avec — VOT. XXX. MVLT. XXXX.) Constant I BR.M. Constance II AR.M.

GLORIA SAECVLI VIRTVS CAES. Constantin I OR AR.

GLORIA SAECVLI VIRTVS CAESARIS (ou CAESS.). Constantin I BR.M.

G. P. R Autonomes de Galba OR.

G. P. R. TR. POT. COS. II. S. C. Antonin M.B.

HADRIANVS AVG. P. P. Adrien AR.M.

HAEC VOTA MVLT. ANN. Constantin I AR.

HERC. COMITI. Tétricus fils P.B.

HERC. COMMODIANO P. M. TR. P. XVI. IMP. VIII. COS. VI. P. P. Commode BR.M.
(avec S. C.) G.B. M.B.

HERC. COM. P. M. TR. P. XVI. COS. VI. Commode OR.

HERC. DEVSONIENSI. Postume OR. B. G.B. M.B (avec S. C.) G.B.

HERC. DEVSONIENSI AVG. Postume G.B.

HERC. GADIT. P. M. TR. P. COS. III. Adrien OR.

HERC. PACIFERI. Postume B.(2).

HERC. PACIFERO. Postume B (3). G.B. M.B. Maximien Hercule P.B. (avec S. C.)
Postume G B. M.B.

HERC. PAC. TR. P. IIII. IMP. II. COS. II. Vérus OR.

HERC. ROM. COND. COS. VII. P. P. Commode OR.

HERC. ROM. CONDITORI COS. VII. P. P. C. S. Commode M.B.

HERC ROM. CONDITORI P. M. TR. P. XVIII. COS. VII. P. P. Commode BR M. (avec
S. C.) G.B.

HERCVLES ADSERTOR. Autonomes de Galba AR.

HERCVLI ARCADIO. Postume B.

HERCVLI ARGIVO. Postume B.

HERCVLI AVG. Postume OR.

HERCVLI AVGG. Maixmien Hercule AR.Q. P.B.

HERCVLI COMITI AVG. Maximien Hercule OR.

HERCVLI COMITI AVG. COS. III. Postume BR.M.

HERCVLI COMITI AVGG. ET CAES. N. Maxence OR.

HERCVLI COMITI AVGG. ET CAESS. NN. Maximien Hercule OR. Constance Chlore
OR. Maxence OR Constantin I OR.

HERCVLI COMITI AVGG. NN. Maxence OR. Constantin I OR.

HERCVLI COMITI AVGG. NOST. Maximien Hercule OR.

HERCVLI COMITI AVG. N. Maxence OR. P.B.

HERCVLI COMITI CAESS. NOSTR. Sévère II OR. Maximin II OR.

HERCVLI COMITI S. C. Commode M.B.

HERCVLI COMMODO AVG. Commode AR.

HERCVLI CONS. AVG. Gallien B.

HERCVLI CONS. AVGG. Maximien Hercule OR.

HERCVLI CONS. CAES. Constance Chlore OR.M. OR.

HERCVLI CONSER. AVGG. ET CAESS. NN. Maximien Hercule OR. Constance Chlore
OR. Sévère II OR.

HERCVLI CONSERVAT. Dioclétien P.B. Maximien Hercule OR. P.B.

HERCVLI CONSERVAT CAES. Constantin I P.B.

HERCVLI CONSERVATORI. Maximien Hercule OR. AR.M. M.B. Constance Chlore OR.

HERCVLI CONSERVATORI AVGG. Maximien Hercule OR.M.

HERCVLI CONSERVATORI CAES. Constantin I P.B.

HERCVLI CRETENSI. Postume OR.

HERCVLI DEBELLAT. Dioclétien OR. Maximien Hercule OR.

HERCVLI DEBELLATORI. Maximien Hercule AR. G.B.M.

(1) Variété avec GLORIA ROMAMORVM.
(2) Variété avec PACIFECI.
(3) Variété avec PVCIFERO.

HERCVLI DEFENS. Sept. Sévère OR. AR.M. AR.
HERCVLI DEVSONIENSI. Postume OR. B. G.B. M.B.
HERCVLI ERVMANTINO. Postume B. Probus OR.
HERCVLI GADITANO. Postume B.
HERCVLI IMMORTALI. Postume B. Probus OR. Maximien Hercule OR.
HERCVLI INVICT. Carausius P.B.
HERCVLI INVICTO. Postume OR. B. G.B. Postume B.
HERCVLI INVICTO AVGG. Dioclétien P.B. Maximien Hercule OR. P.B.
HERCVLI LIBYCO. Postume OR.
HERCVLI MAGVSANO. Postume B. G B.
HERCVLI NEMAEO. Postume OR. B.
HERCVL. INVICTO. Postume M.B.
HERCVLIO MAXIMIANO AVG. Dioclétien BR.M.
HERCVLI PACIF. Probus P.B. Maximien Hercule P.B. Carausius P.B.
HERCVLI PACIFERO. Postume OR. Probus P.B. Dioclétien P.B. Maximien Hercule
OR. M.B P.B.
HERCVLI PISAEO. Postume B.
HERCVLI ROMANO AVG. Commode OR. AR. M.B.M. Postume B. Probus QR. (avec S.C.)
Commode G.B. M.B.
HERCVLI ROMANO AVG. P. M. TR. P. XVIII. COS. VII. P. P. Commode BR.M.
HERCVLI ROMANO AVGV. Commode BR.M. (avec S. C.) G.B.
HERCVLI ROMANO AVGV. COS. VII. P. P. Commode BR.M.
HERCVLI ROMANO AVGVSTO S. C. Commode G.B.
HERCVLI THRACIO. Postume OR. B.
HERCVLI VICTORI. Maximien Hercule QR. M.B. P.B. Constance Chlore OR. M.B.
Galère Maximien †.M.B. Sévère II OR. M.B. Maximin II AR. M.B. †.M.B. Li-
cinius père M B. †.M.B. Constantin I M.B. †.P.B. (avec NK.) Sévèrell OR.
HERCVLI VICTORI VOT. X. Maximien Hercule BR.M.
HERCVLO CONS. AVG. Gallien B.
HERCVL. ROMAN AVGV. Commode OR. AR. (avec S. C.) M.B
HERCVL. ROMANO AVGV. S. C. Commode G.B
HER. DEVSONIENS. Postume M.B.
HER. DEVSONIENS. (OU DEVSONIENSI) AVG. Postume G.B.
HILAR. AVG. P. M. TR. P. XII. IMP. VIII. COS. V. P. P. Commode OR. AR. (avec S.
C.) G.B.
HILAR. AVG P. M. TR. P. XIII. IMP. VIII. COS. V. P. P. S. C. Commode G.B.
HILARI AVGG. Tétricus fils P.B.
HILARITAS. Marc Aurèle OR. Faustine jeune OR. AR. Lucille AR. Commode OR.
AR. Crispine AR. Julie Domne OR. AR. AR.Q Plautille AR. Tétricus père P.B.
(avec S. C.) Antonin G.B. Marc Aurèle G.B. M.B. Faustine jeune G.B. M.B. Vérus
G.B Lucille G.B. M.B Commode G.B. MB. Crispine G.B. M.B. Julie Domne
G.B. M.B.
HILARITAS AVG. Caracalla AR. Elagabale AR. P.B. Postume B Tétricus père P.B.
Carausius P.B. Allectus P.B.
HILARITAS AVGG. Tétricus père OR. BIL. BR.M. P.B. Tétricus père et fils OR. Té-
tricus fils OR. P.B. Claude II (hybride) P.B.
HILARITAS AVGGG. Carausius P.B.
HILARITAS AVG. TR. P. VIII. IMP. V. (OU VI.) COS. IIII. P. P. S. C. Commode G.B
HILARITAS P. R. COS. III. S. C. Adrien G.B M.B.
HILARITAS P. R. S. C. Aelius G.B.
HILARITAS P. P. COS. III. S. C. Antonin (hybride) G.B.
HILARIT. AVG. P. M. TR. P. XII. (OU XIII.) IMP. VIII. COS. V. P. P. S. C. Com-
mode G.B.
HILAR. P. R. P. M. TR. P. COS. III. Adrien AR.
HILAR. TEMPOR. Didia Clara OR. AR. (avec S. C.) G.B. M.B.
HISPANIA. Auguste OR. Autonomes de Galba AR. Galba OR. AR. Vespasien OR.
Adrien OR. AR. (avec S. C.) Galba AR. Adrien G.B. M.B. Aelius G.B.
HISPANIA CLVNIA SVL. S. C. Galba G B.

HISPANIA COS. II. S. C. Antonin G.B.
HOC SIGNO VICTOR ERIS. Constance II. M.B. Vétranion M.B. Constance Galle OR.
M.B. P.B.
HONORI AVG. COS. IIII. S. C. Antonin G.B. M.B.
HONOS. Marc Aurèle OR. AR. (avec S. C.) G.B. M.B.
HONOS ET VIRTVS S. C. Galba(1) G.B. Vitellius G.B. Vespasien G.B.
HONOS TR. POT. II. COS II. S. C. Marc Aurèle M.B.
HONOS TR. POT. III COS. II. S. C. Marc Aurèle G.B.
HONOS TR. POT. IIII. COS. II. S. C. Marc Aurèle M.B.
HONOS TR. POT. VI. COS. II. S. C. Marc Aurèle G.B. M.B.
HORIENS AVGG. S. C. Gallien G.B.
HVMANITAS AVGG. Probus P.B.
IAN. CLV. Auguste AR.
IANO CONSERVAT. Pertinax AR.
IANO PATRI. Gallien OR.
IANVM CLVSIT PACE P. R. TERRA MARIQ. PARTA. Néron OR.
IANVM CLVSIT PACE P. R. VBIQ. PARTA. Néron OR.
IIII. LIBERALITAS AVG. Sept. Sévère AR. Caracalla AR. (avec S. C.) Sept. Sé-
vère M.B.
IIIVIR. A. A. A. F. F. Auguste P.B. (avec S. C.) P.B.
IIIVIR. ITER. COS. ITER. ET TER. DESIG. Auguste AR.
IIIVIR. R. P. C. M. Antoine AR. AR.Q. M. Antoine et Octavie AR.M Auguste AR.Q.
IIIVIR R. P. C. COS DESIG. ITER. ET TER. M. Antoine OR. AR.
IIIVIR. R. P. C. COS. DESIG. ITER. ET TERT. M. Antoine OR.
IIT. (ou LII.). J. César OR. AR. AR.Q.
IL. S. VI. AV. Carausius AR.
IMP. Auguste AR. Galba OR. AR.
IMP. AVG. Galba OR.
IMP. CAES. Domitien AR.
IMP. CAESAR. Auguste OR. AR. AR.Q. Domitien AR.
IMP. CAESAR AVG. COS. XI. Aguste AR.
IMP. CAESAR DIVI F. Auguste AR.
IMP. CAESAR DIVI F. IIIVIR ITER. Auguste AR.
IMP. CAESAR DIVI F. IIIVIR R. P. C. Auguste AR.
IMP. CAESAR TRA. HADRIAN. Adrien P B.Q.
IMP. CAESAR TRAIAN. AVG. GERM. Trajan P.B.
IMP. CAESAR TRAIAN. HADRIANVS AVG. Adrien P.B.
IMP. CAES. DIVI. VESP. F. DOMIT. AVG. P. M. TR. P. P. P S. C. Titus G.B.
IMP. CAES. DOMIT. AVG. GERM. COS. XV. (ou XVI.) CENS. PER. P. P. S. C. Julie de
Titus G B.
IMP. CAES. TRAIAN. AVG. GER. DAC. P. P. REST. (2). Pompée le Grand AR. J. César
OR. AR. Brutus AR. Auguste OR. AR. Auguste et Agrippa AR. Tibère OR.
Claude I OR. Autonomes de Galba OR. Galba OR. Vespasien OR. Titus OR.
Nerva OR.
IMP. CAES. TRAIAN. AVG. GERM. Trajan P.B. P.B.Q.
IMP. CAES. VES. AVG. Vespasien P.B.
IMP. CAES. VESPASIAN. AVG. Vespasien P.B.
IMP. CAES. VESPASIAN. COS. IIII. Vespasien P.B.
IMP. CAES. VESP. AVG. COS. VII. (ou VIII.). Vespasien P.B.
IMP. CAE. TRAIAN. HADRIANVS AVG. Adrien P.B.
IMP. D. AVG. REST. S. C. Agrippa M.B.
— (Avec — PROVIDENT.) Auguste M.B.
IMP. D. CAES. AVG. REST. S. C. Claude I G.B. M.B.

(1) Variété avec HONOS. TE. VIRTVS.
(2) Et au revers des Familles . Aemilia AR. Caecilia AR. Carisia AR. Cassia AR. Claud a
AR. Cornélia AR. Cornulicia AR. Decia AR. Didia AR. Eppia AR. Horatia AR. Livineia AR.
Lucretia AR. Mamilia AR Marcia AR. Maria AR. Memmia AR. Minucia AR. Norbana AR.
Numonia AR. Porcia AR. Quinctia AR. Rubria AR. Scribonia AR. Servilia AR. Sulpicia AR.
Titia AR. Tullia AR. Valeria AR. Incertaine AR. Campanienne AR.

IMP. D. CAES. AVG. RESTITVIT S. C. Auguste M.B.

IMP. D. CAES. DIVI. VESP. F AVG. REST. S. C. Tibère M.B. Drusus jeune M B. Germanicus M.B.

IMP. DIOCLETIANO III ET MAXIMIANO COSS. Dioclétien et Maximien Hercule OR.M. BR.M.

IMP. DOMIT. AVG. GERM. Domitien P.B. (avec S. C.) P.B.

IMP. DOMIT. AVG. GERM. COS. XI. (XII. XIIII. XV. ou XVI.). Domitien P.B.

IMP. DOMITIAN. AVG. GERM. Domitien P.B

IMP. D. VESP. AVG. REST. S. C. Julie de Titus M.B. (avec S. P. Q. R). Auguste M.B.

IMPE. C. L. SEP. SEVERVS P. AVG. Sept. Sévère AR.M.

IMPER. Vespasien AR. Titus AR.

IMPERATOR. Antonin AR.

IMPERATOR II. Antonin OR. OR.Q. AR. Autonomes d'Antonin P.B. Faustine mère (hybride) AR. (avec S. C.) Antonin G.B. M.B.

IMPERATOR VII. Trajan OR.

IMPERATOR. VIII. Trajan OR. (avec S. C.) G.B.

IMPERATOR VIIII. S. C. Trajan G B.

IMPERATOR PONT. MAX. AVG. TR. POT Caligula AR.

IMPERII FELICITAS. Marc Aurèle AR Sept. Sévère et Géta OR. Caracalla AR

IMPER. RECEPT. Claude I OR. AR.

IMP. ET CAESAR AVG. FILI COS. Caracalla AR. Géta AR.

IMP. HADRIAN. DIVI NER. TRAIAN. OPT. FIL. REST. Trajan AR.

IMP. — LVDOS SAECVL Auguste OR.

IMP. INVICTI PII AVG. Sept. Sévère et Caracalla OR. AR.

IMP. NERVA CAESAR AVGVSTVS REST. S. C. Auguste G.B.

IMP. NERVA CAES. AVG. Nerva P.B.

IMP. NERVA CAES. AVG. P. M. TR. P. COS. III. P. P. — REST. S. C. Agrippine mère G.B.

IMP. NERVA CAES. AVG. REST. Auguste AR. (avec S. C.) M.B.

IMP. NERVA TRAIAN AVG. GER. Trajan P.B. P.B.Q.

IMP. PROBVS AVG. CONS. II. Probus G.B.M.

IMP. PROBVS CONS. II. Probus BR.M. G.B.M.

IMP. T. CAESAR DIVI VESP. AVG. P. M. TR. P. P. P. COS. VIII. REST. S. C. Auguste G.B.

IMP. T. CAES. AVG. F. DES. IMP. DOMITIAN AVG. F. COS. DESIG. II. S. C. Vespasien G.B.

IMP. T. CAES. AVG. P. M. TR. P. P. P. COS. VIII. S. C. Titus G.B.

IMP. T. CAES. AVG. REST. S C. — PROVIDENT. Auguste M.B.

IMP. T. CAES. DIVI VESP. F. AVG. P. M. TR. P. P. P. COS. VIII. S. C. Auguste G.B. Vespasien G.B. Domitille G.B.

IMP. T. CAES. DIVI VESP. F. AVG. P. M. TR. P. P. P. COS. VIII REST. S. C. Auguste G.B. Tibère G.B. Drusus l'Ancien G.B. Agrippine mère G.B. Galba G B.

IMP. T. CAES. DIVI VESP. F. AVG. P. M. — TR. P. P. P. COS. VIII. RESTITV. S. C. Livie G.B. Drusus jeune M.B. Germanicus M.B.

IMP. T. CAES. DIVI VESP. F. AVG. P. M. — TR. P. P. P. COS. VIII. RESTITVIT S C. Tibère G.B. Germanicus M.B.

IMP. T CAES. DIVI VESP. F. AVG. P. M. TR. P. P. P. COS. VIIII. S. C Domitille G.B.

IMP. T. CAES. DIVI VESP. F. AVG. REST. S. C. Tibère M.B. Drusus jeune M.B Germanicus M.B. Galba M.B.

IMP. T. CAES. DIVI VESP. F. AVG. RESTIT. S. C. Livie M.B.

IMP. T. CAES. DIVI VESP. F. AVG. RESTITVIT S. C. Tibère M.B.

IMP. T. CAES. VESP. AVG. RESTITVIT S. C. — PROVIDENT. Auguste M.B.

IMP. TER. M. Antoine AR.

IMP. TERTIO IIIVIR R. P. C. M. Antoine AR.

IMP. TITVS. Titus P.B.

IMP. TITVS VESP. REST. S C. Claude I M.B.

IMP. TR. POT. XX. COS IIII. S. C. Antonin G.B.

IMP. T. VESP. AVG. COS. VIII. Titus P B.
IMP. T. VESP. AVG. REST. S. C. Auguste M.B. Agrippa M.B. Claude I G.B. M B
Galba M.B. Titus M.B.
IMP. T. VESP. AVG. RESTITVIT. S. C. Auguste M.B.
IMP. T. VESP. AVG. REST. S. C. — PROVIDENT. Auguste M.B.
IMP. VESPASIAN AVG. Vespasien P.B.
IMP. II. Autonomes d'Antonin P.B.
IMP. II. COS. P. P. Commode BR.M.
IMP. II. COS. II. P. P. Commode BR.M. (avec S. C.) G B. M.B.
IMP. II. COS. III. DES. (ou DESIGN.) II.I. P. P. Nerva AR.
IMP. II. COS. IIII. P. P. Nerva OR. AR. AR.Q. Caracalla BR.M. (avec S. C.) Nerva
G.B. M. B.
IMP. II. TR. POT. COS. III. S. C. Antonin G.B.
IMP. III. Autonomes de Trajan P.B.
IMP. III. C S. II. P. P. Commode BR.M. (avec S. C.) G.B. M.B.
IMP. III. COS. VI. P. P. Commode BR.M.
IMP. IIII. COS. IIII. DES. V. P. P. S. C. Trajan G.B. M.B.
IMP. V. COS. II. DESIG. III. S. C. Vespasien M.B.
IMP. V. P. P. COS. II. DESIG. III. Vespasien OR.
IMP. VI. COS. III. Marc Aurèle OR. AR. (avec S. C.) G.B. M.B.
IMP. VI. COS. III. VIC. GER. Marc Aurèle OR. AR. (avec S. C.). G.B. M.B. Faustine
jeune (hybride) M.B.
IMP. VII. COS. III. Marc Aurèle AR. BR.M. (avec S. C.) G.B. M.B.
IMP. VII. COS. III. VIC. AVG. Marc Aurèle BR.M.
IMP. VIII. Titus OR. AR.
IMP. VIII. COS. III. Marc Aurèle AR. BR.M.
IMP. VIII. COS. III. CLEMENTIA AVG. S. C. Marc Aurèle G.B.
IMP. VIII. COS. III. PAX AETERNA AVG. S. C. Marc Aurèle G.B. M.B.
IMP. VIII. COS. III. P. P. Marc Aurèle BR.M.
IMP. VIII. COS. III. P. P. PAX AETERNA AVG. S. C. Marc Aurèle M.B.
IMP. VIII. COS. XI. CENS. POTES. P. P. Domitien AR.
IMP. VIII. COS. XI. CENS. POT. P. P. Domitien AR.M.
IMP. VIIII. COS. III. P. P. Marc Aurèle BR.M. (avec S. C.) G.B. M.B.
IMP. VIIII. COS. XI. CENSORIA POTESTAT P. P. Domitien OR. AR.
IMP. VIIII. COS. XI. CENSOR. POT. P. P. Domitien OR.
IMP. VIIII. COS. XI. CENS. POT. P. P. Domitien OR. AR.M. AR..
IMP. X. Auguste OR. AR.
IMP. X. ACT. Auguste OR. AR.
IMP. X. COS. III. P. P. Marc Aurèle BR.M. (avec S. C.) M.B.
IMP. X. COS. V. Postume B. Victorin (hybride) B
IMP. X. SICIL. Auguste OR. AR.
IMP. XI. Auguste AR.
IMP. XI. ACT. Auguste OR. AR.
IMP. XI. COS. XI. CENS. P. P. P. Domitien AR.
IMP. XI. COS. XII. CENS. POT. P. P. Domitien OR.
IMP. XI. COS. XII. CENS. P. P. P. Domitien OR. AR. AR.Q.
IMP. XI. SICIL. Auguste OR.
IMP. XII. Auguste OR. OR.Q. AR.
IMP. XII. ACT. Auguste OR. AR.
IMP. XII. COS. XII. CENS. P. P. P. Domitien OR. AR. AR.Q.
IMP. XII. SICIL. Auguste OR. AR.
IMP. XIII. Vespasien AR. Titus AR.
IMP. XIII. COS. XII. CENS. P. P. P. Domitien AR.
IMP. XIIII. Auguste OR. AR Vespasien OR.
IMP. XIIII. COS. XII. CENS. P. P. P. Domitien OR. AR.
IMP. XIIII. COS. XIII. CENSOR PERPETVVS. S. C. Domitien M.B.
IMP. XIIII. COS. XIII. CENS. P. P. P. Domitien OR. AR. AR.Q.
IMP. XIIII. COS. XIIII. CENS. P. P. P. Domitien OR.M. OR. OR.Q. AR. AR.Q

IMP. XV. COS. XIIII. CENS P. P. P. Domitien AR.
IMP. XV. SICIL. Auguste OR.M.
IMP. XVI. (XVII. ou XVIII.) COS. XIIII. CENS. P. P. P. Domitien AR.
IMP. XIX. Vespasien AR.
IMP. XIX. COS. XIIII. CENS. P. P. P. Domitien AR.
IMP. XXI. COS. XIIII. (ou XV.) CENS. P. P. P. Domitien AR.
IMP. XXI. COS. XVI. CENS. P. P. P. Domitien AR.M. AR. AR.Q. M.B.
IMP. XXII. COS. XVI. (ou XVII.) CENS. P. P. P. Domitien AR.
IMP. XXIII. COS. XVI. CENS. P. P. P. Domitien M.B.
IMP. XXXXII. COS. XVII. P. P. Placidie OR. Valentinien III OR.
IMVISTO IMPER. Pesc. Niger AR.
INDVLG. AVG. Gallien OR. B.
INDVLGENT. AVG. Gallien OR.Q. B. B.Q. Salonine B. (avec S. C.) Gallien M.B.
INDVLGENTIA AVG. Vérus G.B. Sept. Sévère AR. Alex. Sévère OR. AR. Maximin I
     AR. Gallien B. B.Q. Victorin OR. Florien P.B. Probus P.B. (avec S. C.) Faus-
     tine jeune G.B. Alex. Sévère G.B. M.B. Maximin I G.B. M.B.
INDVLGENTIA AVG. COS. III. Adrien AR.
INDVLGENTIA AVG. COS. III. P. P. Adrien AR. (avec S. C.) G.B. M.B.
INDVLGENTIA AVG. COS. IIII. S. C. Antonin G.B. M.B.
INDVLGENTIA AVG. P. P. COS III. Adrien AR. Sabine (*hybride*) AR (avec S. C.)
     Adrien G.B. M.B.
INDVLGENTIA AVGG. IN CART. Caracalla OR. AR.
INDVLGENTIA AVGG. IN CARTH. Septime Sévère OR. AR. Julie Domne (*hybride*)
     AR. Caracalla OR. (avec S. C.) Septime Sévère G.B. M.B. Caracalla G.B. M.B.
INDVLGENTIA AVGG. IN ITALIAM. Sept. Sévère AR. Caracalla AR.
INDVLGENTIAE AVG. Caracalla AR. Macrien jeune BIL (1). Quiétus BIL.(2).
INDVLG. FECVNDAE. Caracalla AR.
INDVLG. PIA POSTVMI AVG. Postume OR.M. OR.
INT. VRB. S. C. Gallien G.B. M.B.
INVICTA ROMA AETERNA. Attale OR. OR.T. AR.M. AR.
INVICTA ROMA FELIX KARTHAGO. Alexandre (*usurpateur*) †.M.B.
INVICTA ROMA FEL. KARTHAGO. Alexandre (*usurpateur*) OR. AR.
INVICTA VIRTVS. Sept. Sévère AR. Caracalla OR. AR.
INVICT. IMPERAT. Pesc. Niger AR.
INVICT. IMP. TROPAE. Pesc. Niger AR. Sept. Sévère AR.
INVICTO AVG. Gallien B. Postume OR. AR.
INVICTO IMP. Pesc Niger AR. Sept. Sévère AR.
INVICTO IMPER. (ou IMPERAT.). Pesc. Niger AR.
INVICTO IMP. TA. Pesc. Niger AR.
INVICTO IMP. TROPAE. Sept. Sévère AR.
INVICTO IMP. TROPAEA. Pesc. Niger AR. Sept. Sévère AR.
INVICTO IMP. TROPAEI. Sept. Sévère AR.
INVICTO IMP. TROPHAEA. Pesc. Niger AR.
INVICTO IMPERAI. Pesc. Niger AR.
INVICTV. AVG. Postume B.
INVICTVS. Gallien B. Victorin OR. B. M.B. Tétricus père P.B. Tétricus fils P.B.
     Quintille P.B.
INVICTVS AVG. Victorin OR. Claude II P.B. Carausius P.B.
INVICTVS SACERDOS AVG. Elagabale OR. AR. (avec S. C.) G.B. M.B.
INVITA ROMA FEL. KARTHAGO. Alexandre (*usurpateur*) OR.
IO. CANTAB. Gallien B.
I. O. M. Commode BR M.
I. O. MAX. CAPITOLINVS. Autonomes de Galba AR. Vitellius AR.
I. O. M. CAPITOLINVS. Autonomes de Galba AR.
I. O. M. ET FORT. CONSER. DD. NN. AVG. ET CAES. Licinius père et fils †.M.B.
I. O. M. ET VICT. CONSER. DD. NN. AVG. ET CAES. Licinius père et fils †.M.B.
I. O. M. ET VIRTVTI DD. NN. AVG. ET CAES. Licinius père et fils † M.B.

(1) Variété avec AVE pour AVG.
(2) Variété avec INDVLGNTIAE AVG.

I. O. M. SPONSORI SAECVLI AVG. Postume M.B.

I. O. M. SPONSOR. SEC. AVG. Commode AR.

I. O. M. SPONSOR. SEC. AVG. COS. VI. P. P. S. C. Commode G.B.

I. O. M. S. P. Q. R. V. S. PR. S. IMP. CAE. QVOD. PER. EV. R. P. IN. AMP. ATQ. TRAN. S. E. Auguste (Mescinia) AR.

IOV. ET HERCV. CONSER. AVGG. Dioclétien P.B. Maximien Hercule P.B.

IOV. EXSVP. P. M. TR. P. XI. (ou XII.) IMP. VIII. COS. V. P. P. Commode AR.

IOVI AVG. Carausius P.B.

IOVI AVGG. Dioclétien P.B. Maximien Hercule P.B Constance Chlore P.B.

IOVI AVG. IMPERATOR II S. C. Antonin M.B.

IOVI CONS. AVG. Gallien B. Probus P.B. Galère Maximien P.B.

IOVI CONS. AVGG. Dioclétien P.B.

IOVI CONS. CAES. Dioclétien M.B. Maximien Hercule M.B. Galère Maximien OR M.B. Maximin II OR.

IOVI CONSER. Aurélien B. P.B. P.B.Q. Carin P.B. Allectus P.B.

IOVI CONSER. AVGG. Dioclétien OR. P.B.

IOVI CONSER. IOVII. CONS. Dioclétien M.B.

IOVI CONSERV. Aurélien OR. Carausius P.B.

IOVI CONSERVA. Valérien OR. B. Gallien OR. B. Probus P.B. Carausius P.B. (avec S. C.) Valérien G.B. Gallien G.B.

IOVI CONSERVAT. Adrien AR. Philippe fils AR. Emilien AR. Valérien B. (1) B.Q. Gallien B. Postume B. Florien P.B. Probus P.B. Julien (*usurpateur*) P.B. Dioclétien OR. P.B. P.B.Q. Maximien Hercule OR. M.B. P.B. Constance Chlore M.B. Constantin I M.B. (avec S. C.) Domitien M.B. Emilien G.B. Gallien G B.

IOVI CONSERVAT. AVG. Dioclétien OR. P.B. Maximien Hercule OR. AR.Q. P.B.

IOVI CONSERVAT. AVGG. Dioclétien OR. OR.Q. AR.Q. M.B. P.B. P.B.Q. Maximien Hercule OR.M. OR. OR.Q. P.B. P.B.Q. Constance Chlore OR.Q. P.B.

IOVI CONSERVAT. AVGG. ET CAESS. NN. Dioclétien OR. Maximien Hercule OR. Constance Chlore OR. Galère Maximien OR.

IOVI CONSERVATO. Probus P.B.

IOVI CONSERVATOR. Maximin II M.B.

IOVI CONSERVATORI. Adrien BR.M. Commode BR.M. Pesc. Niger. OR. AR. Sept. Sévère OR. AR. Caracalla AR. Macrin OR. AR. Elagabale AR. Alex. Sévère OR. AR. Alex Sévère et Mamée BR.M. Balbin AR. Pupien AR. Gordien III OR. AR. Philippe fils AR. Valérien OR. B. B.Q. Gallien OR. B. B.Q. Macrien jeune BIL. Quiétus BIL. Postume B. Victorin B. (2) Tétricus père OR. Claude II P.B. Quintille P.B. Aurélien P.B. Dioclétien OR.M. OR. BR.M. P.B.P.B.Q. Maximien Hercule OR. M.B. P.B. Allectus P.B. Constance Chlore OR. M.B. †.M.B. Galère Maximien OR. BR.M. †.M.B. Maximin II OR. M.B. †.M.B. P.B. Alexandre (*usurpateur*) M.B. Licinius père OR. AR.M. G.B.M. M.B. †.M.B. P.B. Licinius fils OR.M. OR. P.B. Valens (*usurpateur*) †.M.B. Martinien P.B. Constantin I OR. AR. M.B. †.M.B. †.P.B. P.B. Crispus P.B. Constantin II P.B. Autonomes de Julien II P.B.Q. (avec S. C.) Domitien M.B. Adrien G.B. Commode G.B. Macrin G.B. M B. Alex. Sévère G.B. Balbin M.B. Pupien M.B. Gordien III G.B. M.B. Emilien G.B Valérien G.B. M.B. Gallien G.B.

IOVI CONSERVATORI AVG. Dioclétien OR. OR.Q. P.B. Maximien Hercule P.B. Constance Chlore OR. M B. Maximin II M.B. Licinius père OR. BIL. M.B. †.M.B. P.B. Constantin I OR. P.B.

IOVI CONSERVATORI AVGG. Dioclétien OR P.B. Maximien Hercule P.B. Maximin II OR. M.B †M.B. Licinius père OR. OR.Q. M.B. †.M.B. P.B. P.B.Q. Constantin I OR. OR.Q. M.B. † M.B. P.B. Crispus P.B. Constantin II P.B.

IOVI CONSERVATORI AVGG. ET CAESS. NN. Maximien Hercule OR. Maximin II OR.

IOVI CONSERVATORI AVGG. NN. Maximien Hercule OR. Constance Chlore OR. Maximin II †.M.B. P.B. Licinius père M.B. †.M.B. P B. Constantin I M.B. †.M.B. †.P.B. P.B.

---

(1) Variété avec IOVI CONSRVAT

(2) Variété avec CONSERVATOBI.

IOVI CONSERVATORI AVG. — IOVIVS AVG. Dioclétien BR.M. Maximien Hercule BR.M.
IOVI CONSERVATORI AVG. N. Maxence M.B.
IOVI CONSERVATORI CAES. — SIC V. SIC X. Licinius fils OR.
IOVI CONSERVATORI CAESS. Licinius fils P.B. Crispus P.B. Constantin II P.B.
IOVI CONSERVATORI CAESS. NN. Galère Maximien OR. Sévère II OR. Maximin
  II OR.
IOVI CONSERVATORI NK. Maximien Hercule OR. (avec NK. LYKC.) OR.
IOVI CONSERVATORI ORBIS. Valérien B. Dioclétien OR.
IOVI CONSERVATORI P. XV. Gallien B.
IOVI CONSERVAT. P. XV. Gallien B.
IOVI CONSERV. AVG. Claude II P.B.
IOVI CONS. LICINI AVG. — SIC X. SIC XX. Licinius père OR.
IOVI CONS. PROBI. AVG. Probus P.B.
IOVI CRESCENTI. Gallien B. Salonin OR.B.
IOVI CVSTODI. S.C. Adrien G.B.
IOVI DEFENS. SALVTIS AVG. Commode AR.
IOVI DEFENS. SALVTIS AVG. COS. VI. P. P. S. C. Commode G.B.
IOVI DEO S. C. Auguste M.B.
IOVI ET HERCV. CONSER. AVGG. Dioclétien P.B.
IOVI ET HERCVLI CONS. AVGG. Dioclétien P.B.
IOVI ET HERCVLI CONS. CAES. Constance Chlore P.B. Galère Maximien P.B.
IOVI EXORIENTI. Salonin G.B.
IOVI EXSVPER. P. M. TR. P. XI. IMP. VIII. COS. V. P. P. S. C. Commode G.B. M.B.
IOVI EXSVPER. P. M. TR. P. XII. IMP. VIII. COS. V. P. P. Commode OR. (avec S.
  C.) M.B.
IOVI EXSVPER. P. M. TR. P. XIIII. COS. V. P. P. S. C. Commode G B.
IOVI EXSVPER. P. M. TR. P. XIIII. IMP. VIII. COS. V. P. P. S. C. Commode M.B.
IOVI FVLGERAT. Claude II P.B.
IOVI FVLGERATORI. Dioclétien M.B. P.B. Maximien Hercule OR. M.B. P.B P.B.Q.
  Constance Chlore OR.
IOVI INVICTO. Sept. Sévère AR.
IOVI IVVENI P. M. TR. P. XII. IMP. VIII. COS. V. P. P. S. C. Commode G.B.
IOVI IVVENI P. M. TR P. XIII. IMP. VIII. COS. V. P. P. Commode BR.M.
IOVI IVVENI P. M. TR. P. XIIII. IMP. VIII. COS. V. P. P. Commode BR.M. (avec S. C.)
  G.B. M.B.
IOVI IVVENI P. M. TR. P. XIIII. IMP. VIII. COS. V. DES. VI. S. C. Commode G.B.
IOVIO CONSERVATORI CAESS. Licinius fils OR.
IOVIO ET HERCVLIO. Dioclétien et Maximien Hercule OR.M.
IOVI OLY. (ou OLYM). Auguste AR.
IOVIO PROPAGAT. ORBIS TERRARVM. Maximin II †.M.B.
IOVI OPTIMO MAXIMO S. P. Q. R. Adrien BR.M.
IOVI PATRI. Gallien B.
IOVI PRAE. ORBIS Pesc. Niger AR. Sept. Sévère OR. AR.
IOVI PROPVGNAT. Gallien B. Postume B. Dioclétien P.B. Maximien Hercule P.B
IOVI PROPVGNATOR. Gallien OR.
IOVI PROPVGNATORI. Sept. Sévère AR. P.B. Alex. Sévère OR. AR. Gallien B. Po-
  stume B. G.B. M.B. (avec S. C.) Alex. Sévère G.B. M.B.
IOVIS CONSERVATOR. Maximien Hercule OR. Sévère II OR.
IOVIS CONSERVATOR AVGG. Galère Maximien OR.M.
IOVIS CVSTOS. Vespasien AR. Titus AR.
IOVIS CVSTOS C. V. S. C. Caracalla G.B.
IOVIS OLYMPIVS. Adrien AR.M.
IOVI SOSPITATORI. Sept. Sévère AR. Caracalla AR. Géta AR. (avec S. C.) Cara-
  calla G.B. M.B. Géta G.B.
IOVI SOSPITATORI AVG. S. C. Sept. Sévère BR.M.
IOVIS PROPVGNATOR. Alex. Sévère AR. (avec S. C.) G.B.
IOVIS STATOR. Gordien III AR. AR.Q. Gallien OR. B. (avec S. C.) Gordien III
  G.B. M.B.
IOVIS STATORI. Gallien OR.

IOVI STATORI. Antonin OR. Alex. Sévère AR. P.B. Gordien III OR. AR. Philippe père AR. Tréb. Galle AR. Gallien OR. OR.Q. B. M. B. Postume OR. B. Victorin B. Tétricus père P.B. Tétricus fils P.B.Claude II OR. P.B. Aurélien P.B. Vabalathe P.B. Tacite P.B. Florien P.B. Probus P.B. Carausius P.B. (avec S. C.) Antonin G.B. Gordien III G.B. M.B.

IOVIS TONANT. Auguste OR. AR.

IOVIS TONANTIS. Auguste OR.

IOVIS VICTORIAE COS. II. Albin AR.

IOVIS VIRTVTI S. C. Domitien G.B.

IOVI TVTATORI AVGG. Dioclétien P.B. Maximien Hercule P.B.

IOVI VIC. Carausius P.B.

IOVI VIC. P. M. TR. P. XV. COS. III. P. P. Caracalla OR.

IOVI VICT. Sept. Sévère AR.

IOVI VICTORI. Adrien OR. Albin AR. Sept. Sévère OR. Elagabale AR. Régalien AR. Postume B. Tétricus père OR. P.B. Tétricus père et fils OR. Claude II OR. G.B. M.B. P.B. Quintille P.B. Aurélien P.B. Florien OR. Probus P.B. Carus P.B. Numérien P.B. Carin P.B. Dioclétien OR. P.B. (avec S. C.) Domitien G.B.

IOVI VICTORI COS. II. Albin OR.

IOVI VICTORI. — IMP. C. E. S. Gallien B.

IOVI VICTORI IMP. III. COS. II. (ou III.) P. P. S. C. Commode G.B.

IOVI VICTORI P. M. TR. P. XV. COS III. P. P. Sept. Sévère AR.M.

IOVI VICT. P. M. TR. P. XV. COS. III. P. P. Sept. Sévère AR.

IOVI VIRTVTI S. C. Domitien G.B.

IOVI VLTORI. Commode OR. Alex. Sévère OR. AR. AR.Q. BR.M. Gallien OR. B. Salonine (hybride) B. Dioclétien OR. (avec S. C.) Alex. Sévère G.B. M.B. Gallien G.B. M.B.

IOVI VLTORI P. M. TR. P. III. COS. P. P. Alex. Sévère BR.M. M.B. (avec S. C.) G.B.

IOVI VOT. SVSC. PRO SAL. CAES. AVG. S. P. Q. R. Auguste AR.

IOV. IVVEN. P. M. TR. P. XIIII. COS. V. P. P. Commode AR.

IOV. IVVEN. P. M. TR. P. XIIII. COS. V. DES. VI. Commode AR.

IOV. PROPVGNAT. Galère Maximien P.B.

IOV. TON. Auguste OR. AR.

IRTS AVG. (1). Claude II P.B.

ISIS FARIA. Julien II P.B. Autonomes d'Hélène II P.B.(2). P.B.Q.

ITALIA. Adrien AR. Antonin AR. (avec S. C.) G.B.

ITALIA FELIX. Adrien AR.

ITALIA P. M. TR. P. VIIII. IMP. VII. COS. IIII. P. P. S. C. Commode G.B.

ITALIA P. M. TR. P. X. IMP. VII. COS. IIII. P. P. S. C. Commode G.B. M.B.

ITALIA REST. S. P. Q. R. OPTIMO PRINCIPI S. C. Trajan M.B.

ITALIA TR. POT. COS. II. S. C. Antonin M.B.

ITALIA TR. POT. COS. III. Antonin OR. AR. BR.M. (avec S. C.) G.B.

ITALIA TR. POT. COS. IIII. S. C. Antonin G.B.

ITOVIA S. C. Faustine mère M.B.

ITER. J. César OR.

IVBENTVS AVG. VII. C. Gallien B.

IVCVNDITATI AVG. Alexandre Sévère AR.

IVDAEA. Vespasien OR. AR. Adrien BR.M. (avec S. C.) G.B.

IVDAEA CAPTA S. C. Vespasien G.B. M.B. Titus G.B. M.B. Domitien G.B.

IVDAEA DEVICTA. Vespasien OR. AR.

IVDAEA DEVICTA. — IMP. T. CAES. Titus OR.

IVD. CAP. S. C. Vespasien † .M.B. Titus G.B. P.B.

IVDEA CAPTA S. C. Vespasien M.B.

IVENTVS AVG. Vabalathe P.B.

IVLIAE AVGVST. Live G.B.

IVNO. Faustine mère OR.Q. AR. Faustine jeune OR. AR. Crispine AR. Julie Domne OR.Q. AR. AR.Q. Maesa OR. AR. Mamée AR. (avec S. C.) Faustine mère

---

(1) Pour VIRTVS AVG.

(2) Variété fautive avec AIRA. ISISF.

G.B. M.B. Faustine jeune G.B. M.B. Vérus (*hybride*) M.B. Lucille G.B. M.B. Crispine M.B. Julie Domne G.B. M.B. Maesa G.B. M.B.

IVNO AVG. Salonine B.

IVNO AVGVSTAE. Mamée AR. (avec S. C.) G.B. M.B.

IVNO CONSERVAT. Otacilie AR. Philippe fils AR. Gallien (*hybride*) B.

IVNO CONSERVATRIX. Julie Domne AR. Paula AR. Maesa AR. Mamée OR. AR. AR. Q. P.B. Otacilie AR. (avec S.C.) Mamée G.B. M.B. Otacilie G.B.

IVNO LVCINA. Otacilie AR. (avec S. C.) Crispine M.B.

IVNO MARTIALIS. Tréb. Galle AR. AR Q. Volusien AR.

IVNONEM. Julie Domne AR.Q (avec S. C.) G.B. M.B.

IVNONI AVG. Cornélia Supéra AR.

IVNONI CONS. AVG. Gallien B. Salonine B.

IVNONI LVCINAE. Faustine jeune OR. Lucille AR. (avec S. C.) Faustine jeune G.B. M.B. Lucille G.B. M.B. Julie Domne G.B. M.B.

IVNONI MARTIALI. Auguste (*Restitution de Gallien*) BIL. Hostilien AR. Tréb. Galle AR.M. AR. BR.M. Tréb. Galle et Volusien BR.M. Volusien OR. AR. (avec S. C.) Tréb. Galle G.B. M.B. Volusien G.B. M.B.

IVNONI REDINE. Dryantille AR.

IVNONI REGINAE. Adrien (*hybride*) AR. Sabine OR. AR. AR.Q. Faustine mère OR. AR. Faustine jeune AR. Salonine AR.M. (avec S. C.) Sabine G.B. M.B. Faustine mère G.B. M.B. Faustine jeune G.B. M.B. Crispine G.B.

IVNONI SISPITAE S. C. Antonin G.B.

IVNONI SISPITAE TR. P. II. IMP. II. COS. P. P. Commode AR. (avec S. C.) G.B.

IVNO REGI. Maesa AR.

IVNO REGINA. Lucille AR. Manlia Scantilla OR. AR. Julie Domne OR. AR. Soaemias AR. Maesa AR. Etruscille AR. Cornélia Supéra AR. Gallien B. Salonine OR. AR.M. M.B. P.B.Q. Claude II P.B. Sévérine M.B. P.B. Magnia Urbica P.B. (avec S. C.) Faustine jeune M.B. Lucille G.B. M.B. Commode M.B. Crispine M.B. Manlia Scantilla G.B. M.B. Julie Domne G.B. M.B. Salonine G.B. M.B.

IVNO VICTRIX. Salonine B.

IVPPITER CONSERVATOR. Autonomes de Galba AR. Domitien OR. AR.

IVPPITER CONSERVATOR. TR. P. V. IMP. IIII. COS. II. P. P. S. C. Commode G.B.

IVPPITER CONSERVATOR. TR. P. VI. (ou VII.) IMP. IIII. COS. III. P. P. S. C. Commode G.B.

IVPPITER CVSTOS. Néron OR. AR. Autonomes de Galba AR. (avec S. C. Domitien G.B.

IVPPITER LIBERATOR. Néron OR. Autonomes de Galba AR.

IVPPITER VICTOR. Vitellius OR. AR.

IVSSV RICHIARI REGES. Honorius AR.

IVSTI. AVG. Pesc. Niger AR.

IVSTITIA. Sept. Sévère AR. Caracalla AR. Paula AR.

IVSTITIA AVG. Adrien OR. Pesc. Niger AR. (avec S. C.) Adrien G.B. M.B.

IVSTITIA AVG. COS. III. Adrien AR.

IVSTITIA AVG. COS. III. P. P. Adrien AR. (avec S. C.) G.B. M.B.

IVSTITIA AVG. P. P. COS. III. Adrien AR. (avec S. C.) G.B. M.B.

IVSTITIA AVG. TR. P. XXXIII. IMP. X. COS. III. P. P. Marc Aurèle AR.

IVSTITIA AVGVST. Nerva OR. AR. (avec S.C.) M.B.

IVSTITIA AVGVSTI. Pesc. Niger OR. AR. (avec S. C.) Alex. Sévère G.B.

IVSTITIA PARTH. F. DIVI NER. NEP. P. M. TR P. COS. Adrien AR.

IVSTITIA PARTHIC. DIVI TRAIAN. AVG. P. M. TR. P. COS. P. P. Adrien AR.

IVSTITIA P. M. TR. P. COS. DES. II. Adrien AR.

IVSTITIA P. M. TR. P. COS. II. Adrien AR.

IVSTITIA TR. POT. XIIII. COS. IIII. S. C. Antonin M.B.

IVST. VENERAB. Constantin I P.B.Q.

IVST. VEN. MEM. Constantin I P.B.Q.

IVVENT. Tétricus fils P.B.

IVVENTA IMPERII. Caracalla OR. AR.

IVVENTAS. Marc Aurèle OR. OR.Q. AR. (avec S. C.) G.B. M.B.

VVENTAS TR. POT. III. COS. II. S. C. Marc Aurèle M.B.

IVVENTVS. Crispus BR.M. (avec S. C.) Marc Aurèle M.B.

VVENTVS AVG. Claude II P.B.
IVVENTVS COS. II. S. C. Marc Aurèle M.B.
IXPICTATIA MIL. Carausius AR.
K. Autonomes de Constantinople P.B. Fausta AR.Q.
LAET. AVG. P. M. TR. P. XII. IMP. VIII. COS. V. P. P. Commode AR.
LAET. FVNDATA. Philippe père OR. AR. (avec S. C.) G.B. M.B.
LAETI. Postume M.B.
LAETIA. AVGG. Gallien OR.
LAETIS AVG. Tétricus père P.B.
LAETITA. Carausius P.B.
LAETIT. AVG. Tétricus père P.B.Q. Carausius P.B. Allectus P.B.
LAETIT. FVNDAT Philippe père OR. AR.
LAETITIA. Faustine jeune OR. AR. Lucille AR. Julie Domne OR. AR. Postume G.B
  Carausius P.B. (avec S.C.) Faustine jeune G.B(1). M.B. Commode G.B. Crispine
  G.B. M.B. Aquilia Sévéra G.B. M.B.
LAETITIA AVG. Gallien OR. B. Salonine B. Postume OR. B. G.B.(2) M.B. Victorin
  OR. B. Tétricus père P.B(3). Tétricus fils P.B(4). Claude II P.B. Quintille P.B.
  Aurélien P.B. Sévérine P.B. Tacite P.B. Probus P.B. Carausius P.B. Allectus
  P.B. (avec S. C.) Gallien G.B. M.B. Postume G.B. M.B.
LAETITIA AVGG. Sept. Sévère AR. Valérien OR. B. Gallien OR. B. Tétricus père
  P.B. Tétricus fils P.B. Constance Chlore P.B. Galère Maximien P.B.
LAETITIA AVGGG Dioclétien P.B. Carausius P.B.
LAETITIA AVG. N. Gordien III OR. AR. Philippe père AR. Tétricus père OR. P.B.
  Tétricus fils P.B. Claude II P.B. (avec S. C.) Gordien III G.B. M.B.
LAETITIA AVG. VII. C. Gallien B.
LAETITIA AVGVSTI. Tétricus fils P.B.Q. Probus P.B. Allectus P.B.
LAETITIA COS. IIII. Antonin OR.
LAETITIAE AVG. Commode AR.
LAETITIAE PVBLICAE. Faustine jeune OR. AR. (avec S. C.) G.B. M.B.
LAETITIA FVND. Gallien B. Tacite P.B. Florien P.B. Probus P.B Carin P.B. Dio-
  clétien P.B. Carausius P.B.
LAETITIA PVB. Faustine jeune AR.
LAETITIA PVBL. Elagabale AR. Maesa AR.
LAETITIA TEMPOR. COS. II. Pertinax OR AR.
LAETITIA TEMPORVM Sept. Sévère OR. AR. Caracalla OR. AR. Géta AR
LAETITIA TEMPORVM COS. II. S. C. Pertinax G.B. M.B.
LAETITI. AVG. Allectus P.B.
LAETIT. TEMP. Gallien B.
LAHTITIA AVG. N Gordien III AR.M.
LARGITIO. Constance II BR.M. Magnence BR.M.
L. CLODI MACRI. Cl Macer AR. (avec S. C.) AR.
L. CLODI MACRI CARTHAGO S. C. Cl. Macer AR.
L. CLODI MACRI LIBERA S. C. Cl. Macer AR.
L. CLOD. (ou CLODI) MACRI LIBERATRIX. S. C. Cl. Macer AR.
L. C. MACRI CARTHAGO S. C. Cl. Macer AR.
LEP. (ou LEPID.) IMP. Lépide AR.Q.
LEG. XVI. Auguste (5) AR.Q

LEG. PRI.	M. Antoine	AR.
LEG. II.	—	AR.
LEG. III.	—	AR.
LEG. IIII.	—	AR.
LEG. IV.	—	OR. AR.
LEG. V.	—	AR.
LEG. VI.	—	OR. AR

(1) Variété avec LAETITAS.
(2) Variété avec LAITITIA AVG.
(3) Variété avec LAETITAS AVG.
(4) Variété avec LATITIA AVG.
(5) Les monnaies légionnaires sont classées par règnes.

LEG. VII.	M. Antoine	AR.
LEG. VIII.	—	AR.
LEG. VIIII.	—	AR.
LEG. IX.	—	AR.
LEG. X.	—	AR.
LEG. XI.	—	AR.
LEG. XII.	—	AR.
LEG. XII. ANTIQVAE.	—	AR.
LEG. XIII.	—	AR.
LEG. XIIII.	—	AR.
LEG. XIV.	—	OR. AR.
LEG. XV.	—	AR.
LEG. XVI.	—	AR.
LEG. XVII.	—	AR.
LEG. XVII. CLASSICAE.	—	AR.
LEG. XVIII.	—	AR.
LEG. XVIII. LIBYCAE.	—	AR.
LEG. XIIX.	—	AR.
LEG. XVIIII.	—	AR.
LEG. XIX.	—	OR. AR.
LEG. XX.	—	AR.
LEG. XXI.	—	AR.
LEG. XXII.	—	AR.
LEG. XXIII.	—	AR.
LEG. XXIV.	—	AR.
LEG. XXV.	—	AR.
LEG. XXVII.	—	AR.
LEG. XXIX.	—	AR.
LEG. XXX.	—	AR.
LEG. I. LIB. MACRIANA.	Clodius Macer	AR.
LEG. I. MAC.	—	AR.
LEG. III. LIB. AVG.	—	AR.
LEG. I. ADIVT. TR. P. COS.	Septime Sévère	AR.
LFG. I. ITALICA TR. P. COS.	—	AR.
LEG. I. ITAL. TR. P. COS	—	AR.
LEG. I. MIN. TR. P. COS.	—	OR. AR.
LEG. II. ADIVT. TR. P. COS.	—	AR
LEG. II. ITAL TR. P. COS..	—	AR.
LEG. III. ITAL. TR. P. COS.	—	AR.
LEG. III. IT. AV. TR. P. COS.	—	AR.
LEG. IIII. FL. TR. P. COS.	—	AR.
LEG. V. MAC. TR. P. COS.	—	AR.
LEG VII. CL. TR. P. COS.	—	AR.
LEG. VIII. AVG. TR. P. COS.	—	AR.
LEG. XI. CL. TR. P. COS.	—	AR.
LEG. XIII. GEM. TR. P. COS.	—	AR.
LEG. XIIII. GEM. TR. P. COS.	—	AR.
LEG. XIIII. GEM. M. V. TR. P. COS.	—	OR. AR.
LEG. XIIII. GEM. M. V. TR. P. COS. S. C.	—	G.B.
LEG. XXII. TR. P. COS	—	AR.
LEG. XXII. PRI. TR. P. COS.	—	AR.
LEG. XXX. VLP. TR. P. COS.	—	AR.
LEG. XXX. VL. TR. P. COS.	—	AR.
LEG. I. ADI. V. P. V. F.	Gallien	B.
LEG. I. ADI. VI. P. VI. F(1).	—	B.
LEG. I. ADI. VII. P. VII. F.	—	B.
LEG. I. AVG. VI. P. VI. F.	—	B.
LEG. I. ITAL. VI. P. VI. F.	—	B.

(1) Variété avec LEG. I. ADI. VI. P. VI. E.

LEG. I. ITAL. VII. P. VII. F.	Gallien	
LEG. I. MIN. VI. P. VI. F.	—	B
LEG. I. MIN. VII. P. VII. F.	—	B.
LEG. II. ADI. VI. P. VI. F.	—	B.
LEG. II. AD. VII. P. VII. F.	—	B.
LEG. II. CL. AD. VI. P. VI. F.	—	B.
LEG. II. ITAL. VI. P. VI. F.	—	B.
LEG. II. ITAL. VII. P. VII. F.	—	B.
LEG. II. PART. V. P. V. F.	—	B.
LEG. II. PART. VI. P. VI. F.	—	B.
LEG. II. PART. VII. P. VII. F.	—	B.
LEG. III. ITAL. VI. P. VI. F.	—	B.
LEG. III. ITAL. VII. P. VII. F.	—	B.
LEG. IIII. FL. VI. P. VI. F.	—	B.
LEG. IIII. FL. VII. P. VII. F.	—	B.
LEG. V. MAC. VI. P. VI. F.	—	B.
LEG. V. MAC. VII. P. VII. F.	—	B.
LEG. VI. CL. VI. P. VI. F.	—	B.
LEG. VII. CLA. VI. P. VI. F.	—	B.
LEG. VII. CL. VI. P. VI. F.	—	B.
LEG. VII. CL. VII. P. VII. F.	—	B.
LEG. VIII. AVG. V. P. V. F.	—	B.
LEG. VIII. AVG. VI. P. VI. F.	—	B.
LEG. VIII. AVG. VII. P. VII. F.	—	B.
LEG. X. GEM. VI. P. VI. F.	—	B.
LEG. X. GEM. VII. P. VII. F.	—	B.
LEG. XI. CL. VI. P. VI. F.	—	B.
LEG. XIII. GEM. VI. P. VI. F.	—	B.
LEG. XIIII. GEM. VI. P. VI. F.	—	B.
LEG. IIXX. VI. P. VI. F.	—	B.
LEG. IIXX. VII. P. VII. F.	—	B.
LEG. XX. VI. P. VI. F.	—	B.
LEG. XXII. VI. P. VI. F.	—	B.
LEG. XXX. VLP. VI. P. VI. F.	—	B.
LEG. XXX. VLP. VII. P. VII. F.	—	B.
LEG. PRIMA MINERVINA P. F.	Victorin	OR.
LEG. II. TRAIANA P. F.	—	OR.
LEG. IIII. FLAVIA P. F.	—	OR.
LEG. V. MACIDONICA P. F.	—	OR.
LEG. X. FRETENSIS P. F.	—	OR.
LEG. XIII. GEMINA P. F.	—	OR.
LEG. XIIII. GEMINA P. F.	—	P.B.
LEG. XX. VAL. VICTRIX P. F.	—	OR.
LEG. XXII. P. F.	—	OR.
LEG. XXII. PRIMIGENIE	—	P.B.
LEG. XXX. VLP. VICT. P. F.	—	OR. AR.
LEG. I. MIN.	Carausius	P.B.
LEG. II. AVG.	—	P.B.
LEG. II. PARTH.	—	P.B.
LEG. III.	—	P.B.
LEG. III. SIPC.	—	AR.
LEG. IIII. FL.	—	OR. AR. P.B.
LEG. IIII. FLAVIA. P. F.	—	P.B.
LEG. VII. CL.	—	P.B.
LEG VIII. AVG.	—	P.B.
LEG. IIXX. PRIMIG.	—	P.B.
LEG. XXI. VLPIA.	—	P.B.
LEG. XXI. VLPIA VI.	—	P.B.
LEG. XXV. V.	—	P.B.
LEG. XXX. VLPIA.	—	P.B.

LEG. II.   'Allectus **P.B.**
LEIBERTAS. Brutus AR. AR.Q. Néron OR.
LETITIA AVG. Tétricus pére P.B. Carausius P.B.
LETITIA AVGVSTI. Tétricus père P.B.
LETITIA TEMP. Tacite P.B.
LIB. IIII. Antonin OR. AR.
LIB. IIII. P. M. TR. POT. COS. IIII. S. C. Antonin G.B. M.B.
LIB. IIII. TR. POT. COS. IIII. Antonii. OR.Q. AR.
LIB. V. COS. IIII. Antonin OR.
LIB. VI. COS. IIII. Antonin OR.Q. AR.
LIB. VII. P. M. TR. POT. COS. IIII. S. C. Antonin G.B.
LIB. VIII. P. M. TR. POT. XXI. COS. IIII. S. C. Antonin G.B. M.B.
LIB. VIII. TR. POT. XXI. COS.IIII. Antonin AR.
LIB. AVG. Gallien OR. B.
LIB. AVG. LEG. III. Clodius Macer AR.
LIB. AVG. P. M. TR. P. COS. II. S. C. Pertinax G.P. M.B.
LIB. AVG. P. M. TR. P. XI. IMP. VII. COS. V. P. P. Commode AR. (avec s. c.) G.B.
LIB. AVG. P.M. TR. P. XV. COS. VI. Commode OR. AR. (avec s. c.) M.B.
LIB. AVG. P.M. TR. P. XV. IMP. VIII. COS. VI. S. C. Commode G.B..
LIB. AVG. P.M. TR. P. XVI. COS. VI. Commode AR.
LIB. AVG. P.M. TR. P. XVII. COS. VII. P.P. Commode OR. AR. (avec s. c.) G.B.
LIB. AVG. P.M. TR. P. XVII. IMP. VIII. COS. VII. S. C. Commode G.B.
LIB. AVG. P.M. TR. P. XX. COS. III. Marc Aurèle AR.
LIB. AVG. R. XL. S. C. Galba M.B.
LIB. AVG. TR. P. COS. II. S. C. Pertinax G.B. M.B.
LIB. AVG. TR. P. V. IMP. IIII. COS. II. P.P. Commode OR. AR. (avec s. c.) M.B.
LIB. AVGVSTOR. TR. P. COS. II. Vérus OR. (avec s. c.) G.B.
LIB. AVGVSTOR. TR. P. XV. COS. III. Marc Aurèle OR. (avec s. c.) G.B. M.B.
LIB. AVGVSTOR. TR. POT. XX. COS. III. S. C. Marc Aurèle C.B.
LIB. AVG. II. Caracalla OR. AR.
LIB. AVG. II. COS. II. P.P. Elagabale OR.
LIB. AVG. II. P.M. TR. P. II. COS. II. P.P. Elagabale OR.
LIB. AVG. II. TR. P. XV. COS. IIII. Marc Aurèle AR.
LIB. AVG. III. S. C. Alex. Sévère M.B.
LIB. AVG. III. P.M. TR. P. X. COS. III. P.P. Sept. Sévère AR.
LIB. AVG. III. PONTIF. MAX. TR. P. V. COS. II. P.P. Alex. Sévère et Mamée AR. M.
(avec s. c.) Alex. Sévère M.B. Alex. Sévère et Mamée M.B.
LIB. AVG. III. TR. P. VI. COS. II Vérus AR.
LIB. AVG. III. TR. P. XX. COS III. Marc Aurèle AR.
LIB. AVG. IIII. TR. P. VI. IMP. IIII. COS. III. P.P. Commode AR. (avec s. c.) G.B.
LIB. AVG. V. TR. P. VII IMP. IIII. COS. III. P.P. Commode AR.
LIB. AVG. VI. P.M. TR. P. XI. IMP. VII. COS. V. P.P. Commode AR.
LIB. AVG. VIII. P.M. TR. P. XVII. COS. VII. P.P. Commode OR. AR. (avec s. c.) M.B.
LIB. AVG. VIIII. P.M. TR. P. XVII. COS. VII. P.P. Commode AR.
LIB. AVG. VIIII. P.M. TR. P. XVII. IMP. III. COS. IIII. P.P. S. C. Caracalla G.B.
LIB. AVGG. VI. ET V. Caracalla OR. AR. Géta OR. (avec s. c.) Caracalla G.B.
LIBERA. AVG. Sept. Sévère AR.
LIBERAL. AVG. Sept. Sévère AR. I. Domne AR. Gallien OR. B. B.Q. Claude II. P.B.
LIBERAL. AVG. COS. Sept. Sévère OR. AR.
LIBERAL. AVG. P M. TR P. X. IMP. VII. COS. III. S. C. Commode G.B.
LIBERAL. AVG. P.M. TR. P. XII. IMP. VIII. COS. V. P.P. S. C. Commode M.B.
LIBERAL AVG. TR. P. COS. S. C. Sept. Sévère G.B.
LIBERAL AVG. TR. P. COS. II. S. C. Sept. Sévère G.B.
LIBERAL AVG. TR. P. V. IMP. II. COS. II. S. C. Vérus M.B.
LIBERAL AVG. TR. P. XIX. IMP. II. COS. III. S. C. Marc Aurèle M.B.
LIBERAL AVGVSTOR. IMP. VIII. COS. III. P.P. S. C. Marc Aurèle G.B.
LIBERAL. AVG. II. P.M. TR. P. COS. II. P.P. S. C. Elagabale M.B.
LIBERAL. AVG. II. P.M. TR. P. II. COS. II. P.P. S. C. Elagabale G.B.
LIBERAL. AVG. III. P.M. TR. P. COS. III. Adrien AR.
L

LIBERAL. AVG. V. COS. III. Marc Aurèle AR.
LIBERAL. AVG. V. COS. IIII. Antonin AR.
LIBERAL. AVG. VI. IMP. VII. COS. III. Marc Aurèle OR. AR.
LIBERAL. AVG. VI. P.M. TR. P. XI. IMP. VII. COS. V. P.P. S. C. Commode G.B. M.B.
LIBERAL. AVG. VII. P.M. TR. P. XV. IMP. VIII. COS. VI. S. C. Commode G.B.
LIBERAL. AVG. VIIII. Caracalla OR. AR.
LIBERALIT. Carausius P.B.
LIBERALITAS AVG. Commode OR. AR. Caracalla AR. Macrin OR. AR. Elagabale
AR. Alex. Sévère OR. AR. P.B. Maximin I OR. AR. Gordien III AR. Etruscille
(hybride) AR. Postume OR. B. Tétricus père P.B. Claude II P.B. Quintille P.B.
Carausius P.B. (avec S. C.) Commode G.B. M.B. Macrin G.B. Maximin I. G.B.
M.B. Trajan Dèce BR. M. G.B. M.B.
LIBERALITAS AVG. COS. S. C. Alex. Sévère M.B.
LIBERALITAS AVG. COS. III. Adrien AR.
LIBERALITAS AVG. COS. III. P. P. Adrien AR. (avec S. C.) G.B. M.P.
LIBERALITAS AVGG. Sept. Sévère AR. Caracalla AR. Philippe père AR Philippe
père et Otacilie BR.M. Tréb. Galle AR. Volusien AR. Valérien OR. B. Gal-
lien B. Gallien et Salonine BR.M. Salonin B. Régalien AR. Tétricus père P.B.
Carin OR. (avec S. C.) Philippe père G.B M.B. Tréb. Galle G.B. M.B Volu--
sien G.B. M.B. Valérien G.B. M.B. Gallien G.B. M.B.
LIBERALITAS AVGG. COS. II. S. C. Caracalla M.B.
LIBERALITAS AVG. IMP. II. COS. P. P. S. C. Commode M.B.
LIBERALITAS AVG. P.M. TR. POT. COS. II. S. C. Antonin G.B.
LIBERALITAS AVG. PONT. MAX. TR. POT. COS. II. (ou III.) S. C. Adrien G.B.
LIBERALITAS AVG. P. P. COS. III. Adrien AP. (avec S. C.) G.B.
LIBERALITAS AVG. TR. P. II. (ou V.) COS. S. C. Commode G.B.
LIBERALITAS AVG. TR. P. V. IMP. IIII. COS. II. P. P. S. C. Commode G.B. M.B.
LIBERALITAS AVGVS. Caracalla AR.
LIBERALITAS AVGVSTI Alex. Sévère OR. Maximin I BR.M. (avec S. C.) Macrin
G.B. Alex. Sévère G.B. M.B. Maximin I G.B
LIBERALITAS AVGVSTI II. S. C. Alex. Sévère M.B.
LIBERALITAS AVGVSTOR. Valérien et Gallien P.B.
LIBERALITAS AVGVSTORVM Géta AR. Balbin AR. Pupien AR. BR.M. Gallien et
Salonine BR.M. (avec S. C.) Géta G.B. Balbin G.B. M.B. Pupien G.B. M.B.
Gordien III G.B.
LIBERALITAS AVG. II. Antonin OR. Sept. Sévère OR. AR. Caracalla AR. Elaga-
bale AR. AR Q. Alex. Sévère OR. AR. Gordien III OR. AR. Philippe père et fils
AR. (avec S. C.) Gordien III G.B. M.B.
LIBERALITAS AVG. II. P. M. TR. P. COS. II. P. P. S. C. Elagabale G.B.
LIBERALITAS AVG II. TR. P. II. COS. S. C. Commode G.B.
LIBERALITAS AVG. II. TR. P. III. COS. IMP. S. C. Commode G.B.
LIBERALITAS AVG. III. Antonin OR. AR. Caracalla AR. Elagabale AR. P.B. Alex.
Sévère AR. Gordien III AR. (avec S. C.) Adrien G.B. Antonin G.B. Gordien III
G.B. M.B. Philippe fils G.B. Gallien G.B. M.B.
LIBERALITAS AVG. III. COS. III. S. C. Adrien G.B.
LIBERALITAS AVG. IIII. Caracalla AR. Elagabale AR. Alexandre Sévère OR. AR
AR.Q. P.B. Gordien III AR. (avec S. C.) G.B. M.B.
LIBERALITAS AVG. IIII. COS. III. S. C. Adrien G.B.
LIBERALITAS AVG. IIII. COS. IIII. S. C. Antonin G.B.
LIBERALITAS AVG. V. Caracalla AR. Géta AR. Alex. Sévère OR. AR. (avec S. C.)
Antonin G.B. M.B.
LIBERALITAS AVG. VI. Adrien OR. AR. Caracalla AR. Géta AR. (avec S. C.) Adrien
G.B. M.B.
LIBERALITAS AVG. VI. IMP. VII. COS. III. S. C. Marc Aurèle G.B. M.B.
LIBERALITAS AVG. VII. Adrien OR. AR. Commode OR. AR. Caracalla AR. (avec
S. C.) Adrien G.B
LIBERALITAS AVG. VII. COS. IIII. Antonin AR.
LIBERALITAS AVG. VII. IMP. VIII. COS. III. P. P. S. C. Marc Aurèle G.B.
LIBERALITAS AVG. VIII. Caracalla AR. (avec S. C.) G.B.

LIBERALITAS AVG. VIIII. COS. IIII. Antonin OR. AR. (avec S. C.) G.B.
LIBERALITAS AVGG. I. Valerien et Gallien M.B.
LIBERALITAS AVGG. II. Philippe père OR. AR. Philippe fils AR. Valérien B. (avec
S. C.) Philippe père G.B. M.B. Philippe fils G.B. Valérien G.B. Gallien M.B.
LIBERALITAS AVGG. III. Philippe père AR. Philippe fils AR. Tréb. Galle AR. Valé-
rien OR. B. Gallien OR. B. (avec S. C.) Philippe père G.B. M.B. Philippe fils
G.B. Valérien G.B. M.B. Valérien et Gallien M.B.
LIBERALITAS AVGG. IIII. Sept. Sévère AR. Philippe fils AR. (avec S. C.) Sept.
Sévère M. B. Caracalla M.B. Philippe fils G.B.
LIBERALITAS AVGG. V. Sept. Sévère OR. AR. Caracalla AR. Alex. Sévère AR.
LIBERALITAS AVGG. VI. Sept. Sévère OR. AR. F.D. Caracalla OR.
LIBERALITAS AVGG. VI. ET V. S. C Géta G.B. M.B.
LIBERALITAS AVGVSTI II. Alex. Sévère M.B. Gordien III BR.M. (avec S. C.) Elaga-
bale G.B. M.B. Alex. Sévère G.B M.B. Gordien III M.B.
LIBERALITAS AVGVSTI III. S. C. Alex. Sévère G.B. M.B. Philippe père G.B.
LIBERALITAS AVGVST. IIII. S. C. Alex. Sévère G B. M.B. Gordien III G.B. M.B.
LIBERALITAS AVGVSTI V. S. C. Alex. Sévère G.B. Gordien III G.B.
LIBERALITAS COS. IIII. S. C.-VI. Antonin G.B.
LIBERALITAS P.M. TR. P. COS. II. S. C. Antonin G.B.
LIBERALITAS IIII. S. C. Antonin M.B.
LIBERALITAS V. COS. IIII. Antonin OR.
LIBERALITAS VII. COS. IIII. Antonin OR. AR. (avec S. C.) G.B.
LIBERALITAS XI. IMP. IIII. COS. P. P. Constantin I OR.
LIBERALIT AVG. Gallien B.
LIBERAL. V. TR. P. VII. IMP. IIII. COS. III. P. P. Commode OR. (avec S. C.) G.B.
LIBERATIS CIVIBVS. Pertinax AR. (avec S. C.) G.B.
LIBERATORI VRBIS SVAE Constantin I M.B. † M.B.
LIBERATOR ORBIS Licinius père † M.B. P.B. Constantin I P.B.
LIBERATOR REIPVBLICAE Magnence OR.M.
LIBER. AVG. Septime Sévère AR.
LIBERI IMP. AVG. VESPAS. Vespasien AR.
LIBERI IMP. GERMAN. Vitellius OR. AR.
LIBERI IMP. GERMANICI. Vitellius OR.
LIBERI IMP. GERM. AVG. Vitellius OR. AR.
LIBERI IMP. VESPAS. Vespasien AR.
LIBERIS IMP. GERMANICI. Vitellius OR.
LIBERITAS Quintille P.B.
LIBERITAS AVG. Alex. Sévère AR. Gallien B. Claude II P.B. Aurélien P.B.
LIBERLAS AVGG. Régalien AR.
LIBERO CONS. AVG. Claude II P.B.
LIBERO PATRI Sept. Sévère OR. AR. Caracalla AR.
LIBERO P. CONS. AVG. Gallien B.
LIBERTAS Brutus AR. Autonomes de Galoa AR. Nerva AR. Gallien B. Quin-
tille P.B.
LIBERTAS AVG. Sept Sévère AR. Caracalla AR. Elagabale OR. AR. AR.Q. Alex.
Sévère AR. P.B. Mamée (hybride) AR. Volusien AR. Gallien B. Postume B.
Claude II P.B. Quintille P.B. Aurélien P.B. Tacite P.B. (avec S. C.) Caracalla
G.B. Elagabale M B. Gordien III G.R. M.B. Volusien G.B.
LIBERTAS AVGG. Sept. Sévère AR. Trajan Dèce AR. Tréb. Galle OR. OR.Q. AR.
Volusien OR. AR. Gallien OR. (avec S. C.) Tréb. Galle G.B. M.B. Valérien P.B.
LIBERTAS AVG. IMP. II. COS. P. P. S. C. Commode G.B. M.B.
LIBERTAS AVG. IMP. II. COS. II. P. P. S. C. Commode M.B.
LIBERTAS AVG. TR. P. VI. IMP. IIII. COS. III. P. P. S. C. Commode G.B. M.B.
LIBERTAS. AVG. TR. P. XI. IMP. VII. COS. V. P. P. S. C. Commode G.B.
LIBERTAS AVGVS. S. C. Galba M.B.
LIBERTAS AVGVSTA. Caracalla AR. (avec S. C.) Caligula (hybride) M.B. Claude
M.B. Galba G.B.
LIBERTAS AVGVSTI. Elagabale AR. (avec S. C.) Vitellius M.B. Vespasien G.B. Ela-
gabale G.B. M.B. Alex. Sévère G.B. M.B.

LIBERTAS AVGVST R. XL. S. C. Galba G.B. M.B.
LIBERTAS. COS. HII. S. C. Antonin G.B. M.B.
LIBERTAS P. R. Autonomes de Galba AR. Galba AR.
LIBERTAS PVBLICA. Galba OR. AR. Vespasien AR. Nerva OR. AR. Tréb. Galle AR.
Volusien AR. Alexandre (*usurpateur*) OR. Constantin I P.B. (avec S. C.) Galba
G.B. M.B. Vespasien G.B. M.B. Nerva G.B. M.B. Adrien G.B. M.B. Antonin M.B.
Géta G.B.
LIBERTAS PVBLICA COS. II. S. C. Antonin G.B. M.B.
LIBERTAS RESTITVIA. Vespasien AR.
LIBERTAS RESTITVTA. Autonomes de Galba OR. AR. Galba OR. AR. Vitellius OR.
AR. (avec S. C.) Galba G.B. Vitellius M.B. Vespasien G.B.
LIBERTAS RESTITVTA PONT. MAX. TR. POT. COS. III. S. C. Adrien G.B.
LIBERTAS SAECVLI Conastntin II P.B.
LIBERTAS XL. R. S. C. Galba M B.
LIBERTATI. Autonomes de Galba AR.
LIBERT. AVG. Sept. Sévère AR. Gallien B. Claude II P.B. Quintille P.B Auré-
lien P.B. (avec S. C.) Galba G.B. M.B.
LIBERT. AVG. P. M. TR. P. XI. IMP. VII. COS. V. P. P. Commode OR. AR.
LIBERT. AVG. P. M. TR. P. XIIII. IMP. VIII. COS. V. P. P. S. C. Commode G.B.
LIBERT. AVG. R. XL. S. C. Galba G.B.
LIBERT. IMPERATOR II. S. C. Antonin M.B.
LIBERT. P. M. TR. P. XIII. IMP. VIII. COS. V. P. P. Commode OR.
LIB. LEG. I. MACRIANA. Clodius Macer AR.
LIB. PVB. P M. TR. P. COS. III. Adrien OR. AR.
LICINI AVG. — VOTIS XX. Licinius père P.B. Constantin I P.B.
LICINI AVGVSTI. — VOTIS XX. Licinius père P.B.
LIT. AV (ou AVG.) Carausius P.B.
LITI AVG. Crrausius P.B.
LIITIT. AV. (ou AVG.) Carausius P.B.
LIITITI AV. Carausius P.B.
LOCVPLETATORI ORBIS TERRARVM S. C. Adrien G.B.
LVBENTVS AVG. VII. C. Gallien B.
LVDI SAECVL. Auguste AR.
LVNA LVCIFERA. Julie Domne OR. AR. P.B. Diaduménien AR. Gallien B. (avec S. C.)
Julie Domne G.B. M.B.
LVNA LVCIF. P. XV. Gallien B.
L. VITELL. CENSOR. II. S. C. Vitellius G.B.
L. VITELLIVS COS. III. CENSOR. Vitellius OR. AR.
MAC. AVG S. C. Néron M.B.
MACRIANA LIB. LEG. I. Clodius Macer AR.
MAGNIFICENTIAE AVG. COS. VII. P. P. Commode AR. (avec S. C.) M B.
MAGN. PIVS IMP. F. Sex. Pompée G.B.
MAGN. PROCOS. Pompée le Grand AR.
MAGNVS. Pompée le Grand AR.
MAG. PIVS. IMP. ITER. Sex. Pompée AR.
MAISAI (*sic*) AVG. Alex. Sévère AR.
M. ANT. IMP. Lépide et M. Antoine AR.Q.
M. ANT. IMP. COS. DESIG. ITER. ET TER. IIIVIR R. P. C. M. Antoine et Octavie M. B.
M. ANT. IMP. IIIVIR R. P. C. M. Antoine AR.
M. ANTO. COS. III. IMP. IIII. M. Antoine AR.
M. ANTON. C. CAESAR. M. Antoine AR.Q.
M. ANTON. COS. IMP. Lépide et M. Antoine AR.
M. ANTON. IMP. Lépide et M. Antoine AR. AR.Q.
M. ANTON. IMP. AVG. IIIVIR. R. P. C. Lépide et M. Antoine OR. AR.
M. ANTONIO COS. III. IMP. IIII. Lépide et M. Antoine OR. M. Antoine AR.
M. ANTONIVS IIIVIR R. P. C. M. Antoine OR. AR.
M. ANTONIVS M. F. M. N. AVG. IMP. ITE. M. Antoine OR.
M. ANTONIVS M. F. M. N. AVGVS. IMP. TER. M. Antoine OR. AR.
MAR.......AVG. Tétricus père P.B.Q.

MARES VLTORI. (sic). Autonomes de Galba AR.
MARINIANO XX. COS. Gallien BR.M.
MAR. PROP. Hérennius AR. Hostilien AR.
MARS ADSERTOR. Autonomes de Galba AR.
MARS AVG. S. P. Q. R. Gallien B.
MARS CONSERV. Vespasien AR.
MARS INVICTVS. Aurélien P.B. (1).
MARS PACATOR. Sept. Sévère AR.
MARS PATER. Sept. Sévère AR. BR.M. (avec S. C.) G.B. M.B.
MARS PATER COS. II Albin AR.
MARS PROPVG. Gordien III AR. Hostilien AR.
MARS PROPVGNAT. Gordien III AR. (avec S. C.) G.B. M.B.
MARS PROPVGNATOR. Constance Chlore OR.
MARS VICTO. Carausius P.B.
MARS VICTOR. Caracalla AR. Elagabale OR. AR. P.B. Gallien B. Postume B. Victo-
rin B. Tétricus père P.B. Tétricus fils P.B. Claude II M.B. P.B. Tacite OR.
P.B. Probus OR. P.B. Numérien P.B. Carin P.B. Dioclétien OR. P.B(2.) Maximien
Hercule M.B. †.M.B. Carausius P.B. Constantin I †.M.B. (avec S. C.) Galba
G.B. Vitellius G.B. Vespasien G.B. Elagabale G.B. M.B.
MARS VLTOR. Autonomes de Galba OR. AR. Vespasien OR. AR. Caracalla AR. Alex.
Sévère OR. AR. P.B. Gallien B. Claude II G.B. M.B. P.B. Quintille P.B. Tacite
M.B. Probus OR.Q. P.B.Q. Carus OR. Carin OR. Carausius P.B. (avec S. C.)
Alex. Sévère G.B. M.B.
MARTEM PROPVGNATOREM. Gordien III OR. AR. Tréb. Galle AR. Volusien AR.
(avec S. C.) Gordien III G.B.
MARTI. Adrien AR.
MARTI AVG. Carausius P.B.
MARTI AVGVSTO. Pesc. Niger AR.
MARTI COMITI VICTORI AVG. N. Maxence OR.
MARTI CONSER. Gallien B.
MARTI CONSERV. Constantin I P.B.
MARTI CONSERVAT. AVG. N. Maxence M.B.
MARTI CONSERVATORI. Maximin II † M.B. Licinius père OR. P.B. Constantin I
M.B. †.M.B. †.P.B. P.B.
MARTI CONSERVATORI AVGG. ET CAESS. NN. Maximien Hercule OR.
MARTI CONSERVATOR: AVG. N. Maxence †.M.B.
MARTI CONSERV. AVGG. ET CAESS. Maxence OR.
MARTI CONSERV. AVGG. ET CAESS. NN. Maxence OR.
MARTI INVICTO. Pesc. Niger AR. Aurélien P.B.
MARTI PAC. (ou PACAT). Quintille P.B.
MARTI PACATORI. Caracalla AR.
MARTI PACI. Quintille P.B. Aurélien P.B.
MARTI PACIF. Emilien OR. AR. Gallien B. Claude II P.B. Quintille P.B. Auré-
lien P.B. Tacite P.B. Florien P.B. Probus P.B. Dioclétien P.B. Carausius P.B.
Constantin I †.M.B. (avec S. C.) Valérien G.B. Gallien G.B.
MARTI PACIFE. Gallien B. Carausius P.B.
MARTI PACIFER. Gallien B.
MARTI PACIFERO. Sept. Sévère AR. P.B. Alex. Sévère OR. AR. AR.Q. P.B. Maximin I
OR. Gordien III AR. Tréb. Galle AR. Volusien AR. Gallien OR. OR.Q. B. B.Q.
Postume B. Claude II G.B. M. M.B. P.P. Florien P.B. Probus P.B. Dioclétien OR.
(avec S.C.) Alex. Sévère G.B. Maximin I G.B. M.B. Tréb. Galle G.B. Gallien M.B.
MARTI PACIFERO P. M. TR. P. V. COS. II. P. P. S. C. Sept. Sévère G.B.
MARTI PACIL. Quintille P.B.
MARTI PATRI. Sévère II OR.
MARTI PATRI CONSERVATORI. Maxence M.B. Constantin I M.B. P.B.
MARTI PATRI NK. Sévère II OR. Constantin I OR.
MARTI PATRI NK. LV. XC. Constantin I OR.

(1) Variété avec INVCTVS
(2) Variété avec NICTOR.

MARTI PATRI PROPVG. (OU PROPVGNATORI). Constantin I M.B ✝.M.B.
MARTI PATR. SEMP. VICTORI. Maximien Hercule M.B. Constantin I M.B.
MARTI PROPAG. IMP. AVG. N. Maxence AR.
MARTI PROPVGNAT. Gallien OR. B.
MARTI PROPVGNATORI. Caracalla AR. P.B. Macrien AR. Hérennius AR. Hostilien
  OR. AR. Gallien B. Macrien père BIL. Macrien jeune BIL. Quiétus BIL.
  Constance Chlore OR. Galère Maximien OR. Constantin I M.B.
MARTI PROPVGT. Emilien AR.
MARTI PROPVGNATORI. Gallien OR.
MARTIS. Tétricus père P.B.
MARTIS VLTORIS. Auguste OR. AR.
MARTI VICTOR. Pesc. Niger AR.
MARTI VICTORI. Pesc. Niger. AR. Sept. Sévère AR. Géta AR. Alex. Sévère AR.
  Claude II P.B Florien OR.
MARTI VICTORI AVG. Gallien B. Probus P.B. Maxence M.B.
MARTI VICTORI AVG. N. Maxenee. M.B.
MARTI VICTORI COMITI AVG. N. Maxence OR.
MARTI VICTORI IMP VI. (OU VII.) COS. III. S. C. Marc Aurèle M.B.
MARTI VLT. IMPERATOR II. Antonin OR.
MARTI VLTORI. Autonomes de Galba AR Caracalla AR. Dioclétien OR. (avec S.
  C.) Antonin G.B. Caracalla G.B. M.B.
MARTI VLTORI AVG. Commode AR.
MARTI VLTORI AVG. COS. VI. P. P. S. C. Commode G.B. M.B.
MARTI VLTORI IMP. VI. COS. III. Marc Aurèle BR.M.
MART. PACAT. P. M. TR. P. XIIII. IMP. VIII. COS. V. P. P. S. C. Commode G.B.
MART. PACAT. P. M. TR. P. XIIII. IMP. VIII. COS. V. DES. VI. S. C. Commode G.B.
MART. PAC. P. M. TR. P. XIIII. COS V. P. P. Commode OR. AR.
MART. PAC. P. M. TR. P. XIIII. COS. V. DES. VI. Commode AR.
MART. VICT. (VICTO OU VICTOR.). Sept. Sévère AR.
MART. VLT. Auguste OR. AR.
MART. VLT. IMPERATOR II. Antonin OR.
MART. VLTO. Auguste OR. AR.M.
MAR. VLT. Auguste OR. AR.
MAR. VLT. COS. II. Albin AR.
MAT. AVGG. MAT. SEN. MAT. PATR. Julie Domne AR.
MAT. AVGG. MAT. SEN. M. PATR. Julie Domne OR. AR. (avec S. C.) G.B. M.B
MATER AVG. ET CASTRORVM. Mamée BR.M.
MATER AVGG. Julie Domne OR. AR. (avec S. C.) G.B. M.B.
MATER AVGVSTI ET CASTRORVM. Mamée BR.M.
MATER CASTRORVM. Julie Domne AR. Mamée BR.M. (avec S. C.) Julie Domne M.B.
MATER DEVM. Julie Domne OR. AR. (avec S. C.) G.B. M.B. Soémias G.B. M.B.
MATIDIA AVG F. — CAES. AVG. GERMA. DAC. COS. VI. P. P. Marciane OR. AR.
MATRI AVGVSTORVM ET CASTRORVM. Julie Domne BR.M.
MATRI CASTR. Julie Domne AR.M.
MATRI CASTRORVM. Faustine jeune OR. AR. Julie Domne OR. AR. (avec S C.)
  Faustine jeune G.B. M.B. Julie Domne G.B. M.B. Mamée M.B.
MATRI DEV. CONSERV. AVG. Commode AR.
MATRI DEVM. Julie Domne AR.
MATRI DEVM CONSERV. AVG. COS. VI. P. P. S. C. Commode G.B.
MATRI DEVM SALVTARI S. C. Faustine ère G.B.
MATRI MAGNAE. Faustine jeune OR. AR. (avec S. C.) G.B. M.B. Lucille G.B. Julie
  Domne G.B.
MAVRETANIA S. C. Adrien G.B. M.B. Commode G.B.
MAVRETANIA COS II. S. C. Antonin G.B.
MAXIMINVS NOBILISSIMVS CAESAR. Maximin II M.B.
MAX. TRIB. POT. IMP. P. P. S. C. Néron P.B.
MAX. TRIB. POT. P. P. S. C. Néron P.B.
MAX. TRIVMF. AVG. D. N. CONSTANTINVS. Constantin I OR.M.
MEM. DIVI CONSTANTI. Constance Chlore M.B.

MEM. DIVI MAXIMIANI. Maximien Hercule M.B.
MEMORIA DIVI CONSTANTI. Constance Chlore BR.M. M.B.
MEMORIA DIVI CONSTANTI AVG. Constance Chlore M.B.
MEMORIA AETERNAE. Claude II OR. P.B.Q. Maximien Hercule P.B.Q. Constance Chlore P.B.Q.
MEMORIAE GAL. MAXIMIANI. Galère Maximien † M.B.
MEMORIA FELIX. Constance Chlore M.B. † M.B. P.B.
MENTI LAVDANDAE. Pertinax AR.
MERCVRIO. CONS. AVG. Gallien B.
MERCVRIO FELICI. Postume B.
MERCVRIO PACIFERO S. C. Postume G.B.
METAL. AVRELIANIS. Autonomes d'Adrien P.B.
METAL. DELM. Autonomes d'Adrien P.B.
METALLI PANNONICI. Trajan P.B.
METALLI VLPIANI. Trajan P.B.
METALLI VLPIANI DELM. Trajan P.B.
METALL. VLPIANI PANN. Trajan P.B.
MET. NOR. Adrien P.B.
MILLIARIVM. SAECVLVM. COS III. S. C. Philippe père G.B. M.B. Philippe fils (hybride) M.B.
MILLIARIVM SAECVLVM S. C. Otacilie G.B. M.B.
MILITVM FIDES. Probus P.B.
MIN. AVG. P. M. TR. P. XVI. COS. VI. Commode OR. AR
MINER. AVG. P. M. TR. P. XVI. Commode OR.
MINER. AVG. P. M. TR. P. XVI. COS. VI. S. C. Commode G.B M.B
MINER. AVG. P. M. TR. P. XVI IMP. VIII. COS. VI. P. P. Commode BR.M.
MINER. FAVTR. Postume OR. AR.
MINER. PAC. COS. II. Albin AR.
MINER. PACIF. S. C. Albin G.B.
MINER. PACIF. COS II. Albin AR. (avec S. C) G.B.
MINERVA. Géta AR. (avec S. C.) M.B.
MINERVA. AVG. Gallien B. Postume M.B. Tétricus fils P.B. Aurélien P.B.
MINERVA. AVG. S. P. Q. R. Gallien B Claude II P.B.
MINERVA AVG. VII. C. Gallien B.
MINERVAE VICTRICI. Géta AR.
MINERVA PACIFERA COS. Géta AR.
MINERVA SANCT. Sept. Sévère AR.
MINERVA VICTRIX. Orbiane AR. Uranius OR.
MINERV. FAVTR. Postume G.B. M.B.
MINER. VICT. Pesc. Niger AR. Sept. Sévère AR.
MINER. VICT. P. M. TR. P. XIIII IMP. VIII. COS. V. P. P. Commode BR.M. (avec S. C.) G.B. M.B.
MINER. VICT. P. M. TR. P. XIIII. IMP. VIII. COS. V. DES. VI. S. C. Commode G.B. M.B.
MINER. VICTRIC. Sept. Sévère AR.
MINER. VICTRIS. Pesc. Niger AR.
MINER. VICTRIX. Julie Domne (hybride) AR. Caracalla OR. AR. P.B. Géta OR. AR. (avec S. C.) Caracalla M.B.
MINER. VICTR. P. M. TR. P. XV. IMP. VIII. COS. VI. P. P. S. C. Commode M.B.
MINERV. SANCT. Géta OR. AR.
MIN. PAC. COS. II. Albin AR.
MIN. VICT. P. M. TR. P. XIIII. COS. V. P. P. Commode OR. AR.
MIN. VICT. P. M. TR. P. XIIII. COS. V. DES. VI. Commode AR.
M. LEP. COS. IMP. Lépide AR. AR.Q.
M. LEPID. COS. IMP. Lépide AR.
M. LEPID. IMP. Lépide AR.
M. LEP. IMP. Lépide AR. AR.Q.
MLETHRM. PROPVGNATOREN PII. Gordien III OR.M.
MNES. Constant I OR.
MODERATIONI. S. C. Tibère M.B.

MON. Tétricus père P.B.

MON. AVG. P. M. TR. P. XII. IMP. VIII. COS. V. P. P. S. C. Commode G.B.

MON. AVG. P. M. TR. P. XIII. IMP. VIII. COS. V. P. P. Commode BR.M.

MON. AVG. TR. POT. XIIII. COS. IIII. S. C. Antonin G.B. M.B.

MONETA. Autonomes de Galba AR. Tétricus fils P.B.

MONETA AVG. Adrien OR.Q. AR. Sabine AR. Antonin AR. Faustine mère AR. Pesc. Niger AR. Sept. Sévère AR. Julie Domne AR. Caracalla AR. Alexandre Sévère AR. Trajan Dèce BR.M. Gallien OR.M. AR.M. B. BR M. G.B. Gallien et Salonine BR.M. Postume B. M.B. Tétricus père P.B. Claude II BR.M. G.B.M. P.B. Florien BR.M. G.B.M. Probus. BR.M. G.B.MF Dioclétien BR.M. G.B. Maximien Hercule AR M. Carausius AR. P.B. Allectus P.B. Constance II G.B.M. Julien II BR.M. Jovien BR.M. G.B. (avec S. C.) Adrien G.B. M B. Antonin G.B. Pertinax G.B.

MONETA AVGG. Sept. Sévère OR. AR. Caracalla AR. Tréb. Galle AR.M. Volusien OR. AR.M. BR.M. Valérien AR.M. Valérien et Gallien AR.M. Gallien AR.M. BR.M. G.B. Salonine AR.M. Salonin AR.M. BR.M. Carus BR.M. G.B.M. Numérien BR.M. G.B.M. Carin BR.M. G.B.M. Dioclétien BR.M. G.B.M. Dioclétien et Maximien Hercule G.B.M. Maximien Hercule BR.M. G.B.M. Carausius P.B. Constance Chlore AR.M. BR.M. G.B.M. Galère Maximien BR.M. G.B.M. P.B. Maximin II G.B.M. Constantin I BR.M. Valens M.B.

MONETA AVGG. ET CAESS. NN. Maximien Hercule M.B. Maximin II BR.M.

MONETA AVGGG. Carausius P.B. Valentinien I G.B. Valens G.B..

MONETA AVG. N. Maxence BR.M.

MONETA AVGVST. S. C. Domitien M.B.

MONETA AVGVSTI. Nerva AR. Adrien BR.M. Alex. Sévère AR. Gordien III AR.M. Tacite BR.M. (avec S. C.) Domitien M.B. Adrien G.B. M.B. Alex. Sévère G.B.

MONETA AVGVSTI COS. II. S. C. Antonin G.B. M.B.

MONETA AVGVSTORVM. Constantin I BR.M.

MONETA CAESARVM. Crispus BR.M.

MONETA COS. Pesc. Niger AR.

MONETAE AVG. Pesc. Niger AR. Sept. Sévère AR.

MONETAE AVG. II. COS. Julie Domne AR.

MONETA II. AVG. Sept. Sevère AR.

MONETA IOVI ET HERCVLI AVGG. Dioclétien BR.M. G.B.M. Dioclétien et Maximien Hercule BR.M. Maximien Hercule BR.M. G.B M.

MONETA SACRA AVGG. ET CAESS. NN. Dioclétien M.B. Maximien Hercule M.B. Constance Chlore M.B. Galère Maximien M.B.

MONETA SACRA AVGG. ET CAESS. NOSTR. Dioclétien M.B.

MONETA S. AVGG. ET CAESS. NN. Dioclétien M.B. Maximien Hercule M.B. Constance Chlore M.B. Galère Maximien M.B.

MONET. AVG. Sept. Sévère AR. Julie Domne AR.

MONET. AVG. COS. II. Albin AR.

MONET. AVG. COS. II. P. P. S. C. Sept. Sévère G.B.

MONETA VRBIS VESTRAE Crispus BR.M. Constantin II G.B M.

MONETE AVG. Pesc. Niger AR.

MONITA AVG. Postume M.B. Carausius P.B.

MON. RESTITVTA S C. Alex. Sévère M.B.

M. SACRA AVGG. ET CAESS. NN. Dioclétien M.B. Maximien Hercule M.B. Constance Chlore M.B. Galère Maximien M.B.

MT. ES. Constance II OR.

MVLTIS X. Galère Maximien P.B.Q.

MVNIFICENTIA. Antonin BR.M.

MVNIFICENTIA AVG. Sept. Sévère AR. (avec S. C.) G.B. Elagabale M.B.

MVNIFICENTIA AVG. COS. IIII. S. C. Antonin M.B.

MVNIFICENTIA AVG. TR. P. VIII. (ou VIIII.) IMP. VI. COS. IIII. P. P S. C. Commode M.B.

MVNIFICENTIA GORDIANI AVG. Gordien III BR.M.

NAVIVS. Antonin BR.M.

NEPOS (en monogramme). Népos P.B. P.B.Q.

NEP. RED. Vespasien OR. AR. Titus OR. AR.

NEP. RED. COS. III. S. C. Adrien G.B.

NEPT. COMITI. Postume OR.

NEPTVN. AVG. Claude II P.B. (1).

NEPTVNO CONS. AVG. Gallien B. Tétricus père P.B.

NEPTVNO REDVCI. Postume B. M.B.

NERO CLA. CAE. (ou CAES.) AVG. GER. Néron P.B.Q.

NERO CLAV CAE. AVG. Néron P.B.Q.

NFRO CLAV. CAE. AVG. GER. Néron P.B. P.B.Q.

NERO CLAVD. CAESAR AVG. Néron P.B.

NERO CLAVDIVS CAES. AVG. GERM. Néron P.B.

NERO CLAVDIVS DRVSVS GERMAN. IMP. S. C. Néron Drusus G.B.

NERO CL. CAE. AVG Néron P.B Q.

NERO CL. CAE. AVG. GER. Néron P.B.Q.

NERO ET DRVSVS CAESARES. Néron et Drusus M. B.

NERONI CLAVD. DIVI F. CAES. AVG. GERM. IMP. P. M. TR. P. — EX S. C. Agrippine jeune et Néron OR. AR.

NILVS. Adrien OR. AR. (avec S. C.) G.B. M.B.

NOB. CAESS. Constantin I Crispus et Constantin II M.B.

NOBILITAS. Sept. Sévère AR (2). AR.Q. Julie Domne AR. Caracalla AR.Q. Géta OR. AR. AR.Q. P.B. Élagabale AR. Alex. Sévère AR. (avec S. C) Géta G.B. M.B.

NOBILITAS AVGG. Philippe père AR. Tétricus père OR. P.B. Tétricus fils P.B. (avec S. C.) Philippe père G.B. M.B.

NOBILITAS AVG. P. M. TR. P. XI. (ou XII.) IMP. VIII. COS. V. P. P. S. C. Commode G.B.

NOBILIT. AVG. P. M. TR. P. XI. IMP. VIII. COS. V. P. P. Commode AR. (avec S. C.) M.B.

NOBILIT. AVG. P. M. TR. P. XII. IMP. VIII. COS V. P. P. Commode OR. AR. (avec S. C.) M.B.

OB CI. SERVATOS. Autonomes de Galba AR.

OB CIVES SERVATOS. Vespasien AR.

OB CIVIS SERVATOS. Auguste OR. AR. G.B. Autonomes de Galba AR.

OB CIVIS SERVATOS S. P. Q. R. CL. V. Auguste OR. AR.

OB CONSERVATIONEM PATRIAE. Gallien AR.M.

OB CONSERVATIONEM SALVTIS. Gallien AR.M. M.B.

OB CONSERVATIONEM SALVTIS AVGG. Gallien M.B.

OB CONSERVAT SALVT. Gallien OR.

OB LIBERTATEM RECEPTAM. Gallien AR.M. M.B.

OB LIBERTAT. REC. Gallien OR.

OB REDDIT. LIBERT. Gallien AR. B. M.B.

OB VICTORIAM TRIVMFALEM — VOT. X. MVLT. XV. Constant I OR. Constance II OR. (avec — VOT. X. MVLT. XX.) Constant I OR.

OB VICTORIAM TRIVMPHALEM. — VOT. X. MVLT. XV. Constant I OR. avec — VOT. X. MVLT. XX.) Constance II OR.M. (avec VOT. — XV.) OR.

OOOOO. Carausius P.B.

OPI AVG. Antonin AR. (avec S. C.) G.B.

OPI DIVINAE TR. P. COS. II. Pertinax AR.

OP, DIVIN. TR. P. COS. II. Pertinax OR. AR. (avec S. C.) G.B. M.B.

OPTIME MAXIME COS. V. P. P. S. C. Commode M.B.

OPTIME MAXIME C. V. P. P. Commode AR. (avec S. C.) M.B.

ORIE. AVG. Postume OR. Carausius P.B.

ORIEN. AVG. Tétricus père P.B. Carausius P.B.

ORIENS. Salonin B. (avec S. C.) Postume G.B.

ORIENS A. Carausius P.B.

ORIENS AVG. Gordien III AR. Valérien B. Gallien OR. OR.Q. B. Régalien AR. Postume P.B. Victorin B. Tétricus père P.B. Tetricus fils P.B. Claude II P.B.

---

(1) Variété avec NEPTVS. AVG.

(2) Ce mot est écrit NCBILITAS. sur la monnaie d'argent de Septime Sévère.

Aurélien OR. P.B. P.B.Q. Probus OR. P.B. P.B.Q. Carin OR. P.B. Dioclétien OR.
P.B. Carausius AR. P.B. Allectus OR. P.B. Constance Chlore OR. Galère Maxi-
mien OR. (avec S. C.) Gallien G.B.
ORIENS AVGG. Valérien OR.Q. B. B.Q. Gallien OR. OR.Q. B. Salonin B. Valérien
jeune OR.B. Tétricus père P.B. Numérien OR. P.B. Carin P.B. Dioclétien P.B.
Maximien Hercule P.B. Constance Chlore P.B. Galère Maximien P.B. Maxi-
min II OR. avec S. C.) Valérien G.B. M.B. Gallien G.B. M.B.
ORIENS AVGVSTI. Probus OR.
ORIENS AVGVSTOR Galère Maximien OR.
ORIENS DIVI NER. NEP. P. M. TR. P. COS. Adrien OR.
ORIENS P. M. TR. P. COS. DES. II. Adrien OR.
ORIENS P. M. TR. P. COS. II. Adrien OR.
ORIGINI. AVG. Probus P.B.
ORIVNA AVG.(I). Carausius AR.
P. Autonomes de Rome (Constantin I) AR.Q.
PACATORES GENTIVM. Maximien Hercule OR. Constance Chlore OR.
PACATORI ORBIS. Valérien B. Gallien B.
PACATOR ORBIS. Sept. Sévère OR. AR. Caracalla OR. AR. Postume B. Aurélien P.B.
Florien P.B. Probus OR. Numérien P.B. Carausius P.B.
PACATOR ORIENTIS. Aurélien P.B.
PACE FVNDATA. Phlippe père AR.
PACE P. R. TERRA MARIQ. PARTA IANVM. CLVSIT. S. C. Néron G.B. M.B.
PACE P. R. VBIQ. PARTA IANVM CLVSIT. S. C. Néron M.B.
PACI AETERNAE. Sept. Sévère AR. Caracalla OR.
PACI AETERNAE COS. V. P. P. S. C. Commode G.B.
PACI AETERNAE C. V. P. P. Commode AR.
PACI AETERNAE TR. P..... IMP. VIII. COS. V. P. P. S. C. Commode G.B.
PACI AETERN. P. M. TR. P. XI. IMP. VIII. COS. V. P. P. S. C. Commode M.B.
PACI AETER P. M. TR. P. XIII. IMP. VIII. COS. V. P. P. Commode BR.M.
PACI AETER. P. M. TR. P. XIIII. COS. V. P. P. S. C. Commode M.B.
PACI AETER. P. M. TR. P. XIIII. IMP. VIII. COS. V. P. P. Commode OR.M.
PACI AET. P. M. TR. P. VI. COS. II. S. C. Sept. Sévère G.B.
PACI AVG. Volusien AR. Emilien AR. (avec S. C.) G.B. M.B.
PACI AVG. COS. IIII. Antonin AR.
PACI AVG. TR. P. VI. IMP. III. COS. II. S. C. Vérus G.B.
PACI AVGVSTAE. Claude I OR. AR. Autonomes de Galba AR. Vespasien AR.
PACI AVGVSTAE EPE. Vespasien AR. Domitien AR.
PACI AVGVSTAE EPHE. Titus AR.
PACI AVGVSTAE Φ. Vespasien AR.
PACI AVGVSTI. Vespasien OR. AR. Sept. Sévère AR.
PACI AVGVST. S. C. Domitien G.B.
PACI ORB. TERR. AVG. Vespasien OR. AR.
PACI ORB. TERR. AVG. EPE. Titus AR.
PACI ORB. TERR. AVG. EPHE. Vespasien AR. Domitien AR.
PACI ORB. TERR. AVG. Φ. Vespasien AR.
PACI PERP. Auguste AR. Antonia M.B.
PACI PERPET. Constantin I P.B. P.B.Q.
PACI P. R. Autonomes de Galba AR.
PACIS EVENT. Vespasien AR.
PACIS FVND. Constantin I P.B.Q.
PACIS S. C. Domitien M.B.
PACTR. ORBIS. Tétricus père P.B.Q.
PANNONIAE. Traian Dèce OR. AR Hérennius AR. Hostilien AR. Quintille P.B.
Aurélien P.B. (avec S. C.) Trajan Dèce G.B. M.B.
PANNONIAE AVG. Julien (usurpateur) P.B.
PANNONIA TR. POT. COS. II. S. C. Aelius G.B. M.B.
PAR. AR. AD. Sept. Sévère AR.
PAR. AR. ADIAB. COS. II. P. P. Sept. Sévère AR.

(1) Leçon fautive. Il faut lire : FORTVNA AVG.

PAR. AR. AD. TR. P. VI. COS. II. P. P. Sept. Sévère AR.
PAR. ARAB. PONT. ADIAB. COS. II. P. P. Sept. Sévère OR. AR. (avec S. C.) G.B. M.B.
PART. ARAB. TR. P. VI. COS. II. P. P. Sept. Sévère AR.
PARTHIA CAPTA P. M. TR. P. COS. VI. P. P. S. P. Q. R. Trajan OR. AR.
PARTHIA COS. II. S. C. Antonin G.B.
PARTHIC. DIVI NER. NEP. P. M. TR. P. Adrien AR.
PARTHIC. DIVI TRAIAN. AVG. F. P. M. TR. P. COS. P. P. Adrien OR. AR.
PARTHICO P. M. TR. P. COS. VI. P. P. S. P. Q. R. Trajan OR. OR.Q. AR. AR.Q.
PART. MAX. P. M. TR. P. VIIII. (ou X.). Sept. Sévère AR. Caracalla (*hybride*) AR.
PART. MAX. P. M. TR. P. X. COS. III. P. P. Sept. Sévère AR.
PART. MAX. PON. TR. P. V. COS. Caracalla AR.
PART. MAX. PONT. TR. P. IIII. Sept. Sévère AR. Caracalla AR.
PART. MAX. PONT. TR. P. IIII. COS. Caracalla OR. AR.
PART. MAX. PONT. TR. P. V. Caracalla AR.
PART. MAX. PONT. TR. P. V. COS. Caracalla AR.
PART. MAX. TR. P. VIIII. Sept. Sévère P.B.
PATER SENAT. P. M. TR. P. XII. IMP. VIII. COS. V. P. P. Commode OR. AR.
PATER SENATVS P. M. TR. P. XII. IMP. VIII. COS. V. P. P. S. C. Commode G.B. M.B.
PATIENTIA AVGVSTI COS. III. Adrien AR.
PAT. P. M. TR. P. COS. II Adrien AR.
PATRES SENATVS. Balbin AR. Pupien OR. AR.
PAT. SENAT. P. M. TR. P. XII. IMP. VIII. COS. V. P. P. Commode AR.
PAX. Auguste AR.M. AR. Autonomes de Galba AR. Vespasien OR. Constance
Galle AR.
PAX AET. Carausius P.B.
PAX. AETERN. Philippe père. AR. Trajan Dèce AR. Dioclétien OR.M. P.B (1). Maxi-
mien Hercule P.B.
PAX AETERNA Sept. Sévère AR. Gordien III AR. BR.M. Philippe père OR. AR.
Philippe fils OR. AR. AR.Q. Pacatien AR. Trajan Dèce AR. Tréb. Galle AR.
Volusien AR. Gallien B. Tétricus père OR. BIL. Claude II P.B. Tacite P.B.
Florien M.B. P.B. Probus OR. Carus OR. M.B. Carin OR. P.B.Q. Maximien
Hercule P.B. (avec S. C.) Gordien III G.B. M B. Philippe père G.B. M.B. Phi-
lippe fils G.B. M.B. Florien M.B.
PAX AETERNA AVG. Maesa AR.Q. Alexandre Sévère OR. AR. AR.Q. Mamée AR.Q.
Gallien G.B. M.B (avec S. C.) Alex. Sévère G.B.
PAX AETERNA AVG. S. P. Q. R. Claude II P.B.
PAX AETERNA AVG. N. Maxence OR. Constantin I OR.
PAX AETERNA S. P. Q. R. Claude II P.B.
PAX AGG. Tétricus fils P.B.(2).
PAX AVG. Galba OR. Vespasien OR. AR. Titus OR. Domitien OR. Antonin AR.
Alex. Sévère OR. AR. P.B. Volusion AR. Gallien OR. OR.Q. AR.M. B. Salonine
B. Postume B. B.Q. G.B. M.B. Laelien B. Victorin OR. B. (3). Tétricus père
P.B. P.B.Q. Tétricus fils P.B. (4). P.B.Q. Claude II P.B. Tacite P.B. Probus P.B.
Bonose BIL. Carus OR. P.B. Carus et Carin P.B. Numérien P.B. Dioclétien M.B.
P.B. Carausius AR. P.B. Allectus OR. P.B. (avec S. C.) Galba G.B. M.B. Vespa-
sien G.B. M.B. Titus M.B. Domitien M.B. Nerva G.B. Adrien G.B. M.B.
Antonin G.B. M.B. Alex. Sévère G.B. Gallien OR.M. G.B. M.B. Pos tume M.B.
PAX AVG. COS. II. Albin AR.
PAX AVG. COS. IIII. S. C. Antonin G.B.
PAX AVGG. Tréb. Galle AR. Volusien OR. AR. Valérien OR. B. Gallien OR. B.
Salonin B. Valérien jeune B. Tétri us père P.B. P.B.Q. Tétricus père et fils
P.B. Tétricus fils P.B. Carus P.B. Carus et Carin P.B. Numérien M.B. P.B.
P.B Q. Carin P.B. P.B.Q. Dioclétien P.B. Maximien Hercule AR.Q. P.B. P.B.Q.
Carausius P.B. Constance Chlore P.B. Galère Maximien P.B. (avec S. C.)
Tréb. Galle G.B. M.B. Volusien G.B. M.B. Gallien G B. M.B.

PAX AVGGG. Dioclétien P.B. Maximien Hercule P.B. Carausius P.B. Carausius, Dioclétien et Maximien Hercule P.B.

PAX AVG. — MVLT. X. Carausius OR.

PAX AVG. TR. POT. COS. II. S. C. Antonin C.B.

PAX AVG. TR. P. VI. COS. II. Vérus OR. AR.

PAX. AVG. TR. P. XX. COS III. Marc Aurèle AR

PAX. AVG. TR. P. XXX. IMP. VIII. COS. III Marc Aurèle AR.

PAX AVG. TR. P. XXXI. IMP. VIII. COS. III. P. P. Marc Aurèle AR.

PAX AVGVS. Tréb. Galle AR. Volusien AR. (avec S. C.) AR.

PAX AVGVST. Vespasien OR. Titus OR. AR. Nerva AR. Gordien III AR. (avec S. C.) Galba G.B. M.B. Vespasien G.B. .MB. Titus G.B. M.B. Domitien G.B. M.B. Gordien III G B. M.B.

PAX AVGVSTA. Tibère M.B. (avec S. C.) Galba M.B. Vespasien M.B.

PAX AVGVSTI. Nerva AR. Elagabale AR. Maximin I OR. AR. AR.Q. P.B Gordien III OR. AR. (1) Philippe père AR. Trajan Dèce AR. Valérien B. Gallien B. Postume B. Claude II P B. Quintille P.B. Aurélien P.B. Tacite P.B. Florien P.B. Probus P.B. Carus P.B. Carin P B. Carausius P.B. Maximin II P.B. (avec S. C.) Vitellius G.B. M.B. Vespasien G.B. M.B. Titus G.B. Elagabale G.B. M.B. Alexandre Sévère G.B. Maximin I G.B. M.B. Trajan Dèce G.B.

PAX AVGVSTORVM. Carus M.B. Carin M.B. P.B. Constantin I AR. Constance II AR.

PAX. COS. V. P. P. S. P. Q. R. OPTIMO PRINC. Trajan AR.

PAX EQVITVM. Postume B.

PAX ETERNA Maesa AR.

PAX ET LIBERTAS. Autonomes de Galba AR.

PAX EXERC. Claude II OR.

PAX EXERCI. Claude II P.B.

PAX EXERCITI. Carus P.B.

PAX FVNDATA Gallien B.

PAX FVNDATA CVM PERSIS. Philippe père AR.

PAX GER. S. C. Vitellius G.B.

PAX ORBIS TERRARVM. Othon OR. AR.

PAX PARTH. F. DIVI NER. NEP. P. M. TR. P. COS. Adrien AR.

PAX PARTPIC. DIVI TRAIAN. (ou TRAIANI.) AVG. F. P. M. TR. P. COS. P. P. Adrien AR.

PAX PERPETVA. Tacite OR. Licinius fils P.B. Crispus P.B Valentinien I OR.Q. Valens OR.T. — (avec VOT. V. MVLT. X.) Valentinien I OR.T.

PAX PERPETVA AVGG. NN. Constantin I P.B.

PAX P. M. TR. P. COS. DES. II. Adrien AR.

PAX P. M. TR. P. COS. II. Adrien AR.

PAX P. M. TR. P. VI. IMP. IIII. COS. II. S. C. Faustine mère G.B.

PAX PONT. MAX. TR. POT. COS. S. C. Antonin G.B.

PAX P. R. Auguste OR. Autonomes de Galba AR.

PAX P. ROMANI S. C. Vespasien G.B.

PAX PVBLICA. Balbin AR. Pupien AR. Gallien OR. B. Salonine B. Tacite OR. P.B. Hélène 1 P.B.Q. Théodora P.B.Q. Autonomes de Constantinople (Constantin I) P.B. P.B.Q. (avec S. C.) Maximin I G.B. Balbin G.B. Pupien G.B. Gallien G.B M.B.

PAXS AVG. Emilien AR.

PAXS AVGVSTI S. C. Galba M.B. Vespasien M.B.

PAX S. P. Q. R. OPTIMO PRINCIPI. Trajan AR.

PAX TRIB. POT. COS. II. S. C. Antonin G.B.

PAX TR. P. VI. IMP. IIII. COS. II. Vérus AR. (avec S. C.) Faustine mère (hybride) G B. Vérus G.B.

PAX TR. P. XX. IMP. III. (ou IIII.) COS. III. Marc Aurèle AR.

PAX TR. P. XXXI. IMP. VIIII. COS. III. Marc Aurèle AR.

PAX TR. POT. COS. II. S. C. Antonin G.B M.B.

PAX TR. POT. XIIII. COS. IIII. Antonin OR. AR.

PAX. TR. POT. XV. COS. IIII. Antonin OR.

(1) Variété avec PAX AVGSTI.

P. D. Commode M.B.
P. D. S. P. Q. R. LAETITIAE C. V. Commode M.B.
PERPETVA CONCORDIA. Sept. Sévère, Julie Domne, Caracalla et Géta OR.
PERPETVA FELICITAS. Constantin I OR.
PERPETVA VIRTVS. Constantin I M.B. P.B.
PERPETVA VIRTVS AVG. Licinius père OR.
PERPETVETAS. Gratien AR. Valentinien II AR. Théodose I AR.
PERPETVITA AVG. Florien P.B.
PERPETVITAS AVG. Constantin I M.B.
PERPETVITAS AVGG. Sévère II M.B. Maxtmien II M.B. Constantin I M.B.
PERPETVITAS IMP. AVG. Alex. Sévère BR.M
PERPETVITATE AVG. Florien OR. P.B. Probus P.B. Carus P.B.
PERPETVITATI AVG. Alex. Sévère AR. P.B. Gallien B. (avec S. C.) Alex. Sévère G.B.
PERPETVIT. AVG. Florien P.B. Probus P.B.
PHOENICE COS. II. S. C. Antonin G.B.
PIAETAS AVG. Probus P.B. Carausius P.B.
PIAETAS AVGVSTI. Carausius P.B.
PIE. AVG. PONT. MAX. TR. POT. COS. III. S. C. Adrien M.B.
PIETA. AVG. Tétricus père P.B. Tétricus fils P.B.
PIETAS. Pompée le Grand AR. Aelius AR. Lucille OR. OR.Q. AR. BR.M. Caracalla
AR. Géta AR. Claude II P.B. Constantin I P B.Q. (avec S. C.) Sabine G.B. M.B.
Faustine jeune G.B. M.B. Lucille G.B. M.B. Julie Domne G.B.
PIETAS AVG. Matidie AR. Adrien AR. Sabine AR. Antonin OR. Fausine mère
OR. AR. Marc Aurèle OR. AR. Commode AR. P.B. Elagabale AR. Annia Faus-
tine AR. Maesa AR. P.B. Alex. Sévère AR. Maxime OR. AR. P.B. Gordien
d'Afrique fils AR. Gordien III AR. Tranquilline AR. Otacilie OR. AR. Hostilien
OR. Gallien OR. B. Salonine B. Salonin OR.M. OR.Q. B. Quiétus BIL. Postume
OR. B. Victorin B. Tétricus père P.B. Claude II P.B. Quintille P B. Aurélien
P.B. Probus P.B. Numérien P.B. P.B.Q. Carin P.B. Maximien Hercule P.B.
Carausius P.B. Allectus P.B. (avec S. C.) Adrien G.B. M.B. Sabine G.B. M.B.
Antonin M.B. Faustine mère G.B. M.B. Marc Aurèle BR.M. G.B. M.B. Commode
G.B. M.B. Maesa G.B. M.B Alex. Sévère G.B. Maxime G.B. M.B. Gordien III G.B.
M.B. Otacilie G.B M.B. Salonine M.B. Salonin M. B.
PIETAS AVG. COS. III. P. P. Adrien AR.
PIETAS AVGG. Julie Domne OR. OR.Q. AR. AR.Q. P.B. Plautille OR. AR. Otacilie
AR. Philippe père, Otacilie et Philippe fils BR.M. Philippe fils OR. Trajan
Dèce AR. Hérennius OR. AR. Hostilien OR. AR. Tréb. Galle OR. AR. Volusien
OR. OR.Q. AR Valérien B. Gallien B. B.Q. Salonine AR.M. B (I). B.Q. Sa-
lonin OR. OR.Q. B. M.B. Tétricus père P.B. Tétricus fils BIL. P.B. Zénobie
P.B. Numérien OR. P.B. P.B.Q. Carin P.B. P.B.Q. Maximien Hercule OR. P.B.
Constance Chlore OR. P.B. Galère Maximien P.B. (avec S. C.) Julie Domne
G.B. M.B. Plautille G.B. M.B. Gordien III G.B. Otacilie G.B. M.B. Philippe fils
M.B. Trajan Dèce G.B. Hérennius G.B. M.B. Hostilien G.B. Tréb. Galle G.B.
M.B. Volusien G.B. M.B. Salonine G.B. M.B. Salonin M.B.
PIETAS AVGG. ET CAESS. NN. Dioclétien QR. Maximien Hercule OR. Constance
Chlore OR. Galère Maximien OR.
PIETAS AVG. IMP. VIII. COS. III. P. P. S. C. Marc Aurèle G.B.
PIETAS AVG. N. Otacilie AR.
PIETAS AVG. TR. P. III. Tétricus père P.B.
PIETAS AVG. TR. P. VI. COS. II. Vérus AR.
PIETAS AVG. TR. P. XX. COS. III. Marc Aurèle AR.
PIETAS AVG VII C. Gallien B.
PIETAS AVGVS. Tétricus fils P.B.
PIETAS AVGVST. Domitille AR. Julie de Titus AR. Matidie OR. AR. Salonine B.
(avec S. C.) Titus G.B. Matidie G.B Adrien G.B. M.B. Hostilien M.B.
PIETAS AVGVSTA. Domitille AR. Hélène I BR.M. (avec S. C.) Titus G.B.

---

(1) **Variété** avec PIETAS AGG.

PIETAS AVGVSTAE. Mamée AR. P.B. Otacilie OR. AR(I). BR.M. Fausta OR.M. BR.M. (avec S C.) Otacilie G.B. M.B.
PIETAS AVGVST. FEL. Hélène I BR.M.
PIETAS AVGVSTI. Adrien AR. Gordien III OR. AR. (avec s. c.) Galba G.B. Adrien G.B. M.B.
PIETAS AVGVSTI N. Constantin I OR.M.
PIETAS AVGVSTI NOSTRI. Constantin I OR.M.OR. Constance II OR.M.
PIETAS AVGVSTO. Tétricus père P.B. Tétricus fils P.B (2).
PIETAS AVGVSTOR. Philippe fils AR. Tétricus fils BIL. P.B.
PIETAS AVGVSTORVM Hérennius AR. Hostilien AR. Valérien et Gallien AR.M. BR.M. Valérien père et Salonin AR.M. (avec s. c.) Hérennius G.B. M B. Hostilien G.B. Salonin G.B.
PIETAS COS. M. Antoine OR. AR.
PIETAS DDD. NNN. AVGVSTORVM. Valens OR.M.
PIETAS FALERI. Gallien et Salonine AR.M.
PIETAS MILITVM. Alex. Sévère AR.
PIETAS MVTVA AVGG. Balbin Pupien AR.
PIETAS PARTH. F. DIVI NER. NEP. P. M. TR. P. COS. Adrien AR.
PIETAS PARTHIC. DIVI TRAIAN. AVG F. P. M. TR. P. COS. P. P. Adrien AR.
PIETAS P. M. TR. P. COS. DES. II. Adrien AR.
PIETAS P. M. TR. P. COS II. Adrien AR.
PIETAS PVBLICA. Manlia Scantilla AR. Julie Domne AR. Géta AR.
PIETAS ROMANA. Hélène I P.B. Théodora AR. P.B.Q.
PIETAS SAECVLI. Gallien B. Salonin B.
PIETAS TRIB. POT. COS. Antonin OR. AR. (avec s. c.) OR. G.B. M.B.
PIETAS TRIB. POT. COS. DES. II. S. C. Antonin G.B. M.B.
PIETAS TRIB. POT. COS. II. Aelius OR.
PIETAS TR. POT. COS. II. Aelius OR. AR. (avec s. c.) G.B. M B.
PIETAS TR. POT. III. COS. II. Marc Aurèle OR. (avec s. c.) G.B. M.B.
PIETAS TR. POT. XIIII. COS. IIII. Antonin AR. (avec s. c.) G.B.
PIETAS TR. POT. XV. COS. IIII. Antonin AR.
PIETAT. AVG. Sept. Sévère AR.
PIETATI. Julie Domne OR.
PIETATI AVG. Sabine AR. Pescennius Niger AR.
PIETATI AVG. COS. III. P. P. Adrien AR.
PIETATI AVG. COS. IIII. Antonin OR. AR. BR.M. (avec s. c.) G.B. M.B. Commede (hybride) M.B.
PIETATI AVGG. Valérien B. Gallien B.
PIETATI AVG. TR. POT. XIIII. COS. IIII. S. C. Antonin M.B.
PIETATI AVGVSTAE S. C. Julie Domne G.B. M.B.
PIETATI SENATVS COS. V. P. P. S. C. Commode G.B.
PIETATI SENATVS C. V. P. P. Commode OR. AR.
PIET. AVG. TR. P. XXXI. IMP. VIIII. COS. III. P. P. Marc Aurèle AR.
PIET. AVG. S. C. Faustine mère M.B.
PIET. COS. V. P. P. S. P. Q. R. OPTIMO PRINC. Trajan. A R.
PIETIS AVG. Tétricus père P.B.
PIET. SAECVLI. Gallien B.
PIET. SENAT. P. M. TR. P. XIIII. COS. V. P. P. S. C. Commode M.B.
PIET. S. P. Q. R. OPTIMO PRINCIPI. Trajan AR.
PIO IMP. OMNIA FELICITA P. M. TR. P. XV. IMP. VIII. COS. V. P. P. Commode BR.M.
PIVS IMP. Pompée le Grand G.B
PLEBEI VRBANAE FRVMENTI CONSTITVTO S. C. Nerva G.B.
PLVR. NATAL. FEL. Maximien Hercule P.B.Q. Constantin I AR.Q. P.B.Q.
P. M. AVGVR. COS. III. Claude I AR.
P. MAX. TR. P. III. Caracalla OR. AR.

(1) Variété avec PIETAS AVGVSTE.
(2) Variété avec PIETAS AVSTO.

P. MAX. TR. P. IIII. COS. Caracalla AR.
P. MAX. TR. P. VIII. COS. II. P. P. Sept. Sévère AR.
P. M. G. M. TR. P. COS. III. P. P. Postume OR.
P. M. TB. P. VII. COS. II. P. P. Aurélien OR.
P. M. T. P. P. P. COS. IIII. S. C. Vespasien P.B.
P. M. TR. COS. II. P. — COS. Victorin B.
P. M. TRIB. P. COS. IIII. P. P. PRO. COS. Constantin I OR.
P. M. TRIB. P. COS. IIII. S. C. Vespasien P.B.
P. M. TRIB. P. COS. VI. P. P. PRO. CQS. Constantin I OR.
P. M. TRI. COS. III. P. P. Probus P.B.
P. M. TRI. P. CON. P. P. Gordien III AR.
P. M. TRI. P. COS. P. P Carin OR. Maximien Hercule BR.M.
P. M. TRI. P. COS. II. P. P. Probus P.B.
P. M. TRI. P. COS. III. Probus OR. P.B.
P. M. TRI P. X. P. P. COS. V. Gallien BR.M.
P. M. TR. P. CONSVL. Tacite OR.
P. M. TR. P. COS. Dide Julien OR. AR. Alex. Sévère AR. Postume G.B. Aurélien
OR. (avec S. C.) Dide Julien G.B. M.B.
P. M. TR. P. COS. DES. II. Trajan AR. Adrien AR.
P. M. TR. P. COS. P. P. Macrin AR. Elagabale AR. P.B. Alex. Sévère OR. AR. P.B
Gordien d'Afrique père AR. Philippe père BR.M. Postume OR. B. Tétricus
père OR. P.B. Quintille P.B. Aurélien OR. Probus P.B. Numérien P.B. (avec
S. C.) Elagabale G.B. M.B. Alex. Sévère G.B. M.B. Gordien d'Afrique père G.B.
Gordien d'Afrique fils G.B. Carin G.B.M.
P. M. TR. P. COS. I P. P. Postume B. (1).
P. M. TR. P. COS. II. Adrien OR.Q. AR.Q. P.B. (avec S. C.) G.B. M.B. Antonin
G.B. M.B.
P. M. TR. P. COS. II. P.P. Trajan OR. AR. Sept. Sévère AR. Balbin AR. Pupien OR.
AR. Postume OR. B. B.Q. G.B. M.B. Victorin B. Constantin I P.B. (avec S. C.)
Sept. Sévère G.B. Balbin G.B. M.B. Pupien G.B. B.M. Postume G.B. M.B.
P. M. TR. P. COS. III. Adrien OR. OR.Q. AR. M. AR.Q. BR.M. P.B. Probus P.B. (avec
S. C.) Adrien G.B. M.B. P.B. Antonin G.B.
P. M. TR. P. COS. III. P. P. Nerva (hybride) AR. Trajan OR. AR. AR.Q. Marc
Aurèle AR. Postume OR.Q. B. M.B. (avec S. C.) G.B. M.B.
P. M. TR. P. COSS. III. S. C. Adrien M.B.
P. M. TR. P. COS. IIII. P. P. Trajan OR. AR. AR.Q. M. B. Postume OR.B. Postume
OR. (avec S. C.) Postume G.B.
P. M. TR. P. COS. V. Postume G.B.
P. M. TR. P. COS. V P. P. Trajan OR. AR.
P. M. TR. P. COS. VI. P. P. S. P. Q. R. Trajan OR. OR.Q. AR. AR.Q.
P. M. TR. P. IMP. P. P. S. C. Néron P.B. P.B.Q.
P. M. TR. P. IMP. V. COS. III. P. P. Postume OR.
P. M. TR. P. IMP. VI. COS. V. P. P. Gallien OR.M.
P. M. TR. POT COS. Caligula OR.Q. (avec S. C.) Antonin G.B.
P. M. TR. POT. COS. DES. II. Tacite OR (avec S. C.) Antonin G.B. M.B.
P. M. TR. POT. COS. P. P. Tréb. Galle AR.
P. M. TR. POT. COS. II. Antonin BR.M. (avec S. C) G.B. M.B.
P. M. TR. POT. COS. III. S. C. Antonin G.B.
P. M. TR. POTES. COS. III Adrien AR.
P. M. TR. POT. ITER. Caligula OR.Q.
P. M. TR. POT. P. P. S. C. Vespasien P.B.
P. M. TR. POT. S. C. Emilien G.B. M.B.
P. M. TR. P. P. P. Maximin I OR. AR. AR.Q. Maximien Hercule OR. (avec S. C.)
Néron P.B. Maximin I G.B. M.B.
P. M. TR. P. P. P. COS. Aurélien P.B.
P. M. TR. P. P. P. COS. III. S. C. Vespasien P.B.
P. M. TR. P. P. P. COS. IIII. S. C. Vespasien P.B.

---

(1) Variété avec V. M. TR. P. COS. I. P. P.

P. M. TR. P. P. P. COS. V. S. C. Vespasien P.B.
P. M. TR. P. P. P. COS. VI. S. C. Vespasien P.B.
P. M. TR. P. P. P. COS. VIII. S. C. Vespasien P.B.
P. M. TR. P. P. P. PROCOS. Maximin II OR.
P. M. TR. P. T. P. P. COS. Aurélien P.B.
P. M. TR. P. I. P. P. Emilien AR. (avec S. C.) G.B.
P. M. TR. P. I. P. P. C. Emilien AR.
P. M. TR. P. II. COS. P. P. Macrin OR. AR. P.B. Alex. Sévère OR. AR. AR.Q. P B. Maximin I AR. BR.M. Gordien III OR. AR. AR.Q. Philippe père OR. AR. Philippe fils AR. Valérien OR. B. Gallien B. Victorin B. Tétricus péré OR. Claude II BR.M. P.B. (avec S. C.) Macrin G.B. M.B. Alex. Sévère G.B. M.B. Maximin I G.B. M.B. Gordien III G B. M.B. Philippe père G B. M.B.
P. M. TR. P... II. D. S. C. Maximin I OR.
P. M. TR. P. II. COS. II. P. P. Sept. Sévère OR. AR. Caracalla AR. Elagabale OR. AR. Valérien B. Gallien B. (avec S. C.) Géta G.B. Elagabale G.B.
P. M. TR. P. III. COS. Gallien OR.
P. M. TR. P. III. COS. P. P. Alex. Sévère OR. OR.Q. AR. P.B. Gordien III OR.M. OR. AR. AR.Q. Philippe père AR. BR.M. Philippe père, Otacilie et Philippe fils BR.M. Tétricus père OR. (avec S. C.) Maximin I G.B. M.B. Gordien III G.B. M.B. Philippe père G.B. M.B.
P. M. TR. P. III. COS. II. P. P. Sept. Sévère AR. Gordien III AR. AR.Q. Philippe père AR. Valérien OR. Victorin OR. B. Tétricus père OR. (avec S. C.) Sept. Sévère G.B. M.B. Gordien III G.B. M.B.
P. M. TR. P. III. COS. III. P. P. Elagabale OR. AR. BR.M. P.B. Valérien OR. B. Gallien B. Postume OR. B. Victorin B. (avec S. C.) Elagabale G.B. M.B.
P. M. TR. P. IIII. COS. P. P. Alex. Sévère OR.M. OR. OR.Q. AR. P.B. Maximin I AR. Maximin I et Maxime BR.M. Philippe père AR. Philippe fils AR. (avec S. C.) Alex. Sévère G.B. M B. Maximin I G.B. M.B.
P. M. TR. P. IIII. COS. II. Tréb. Galle OR. AR Volusien OR. AR.M. AR. (avec S. C.) Philippe père G.B.
P. M. TR. P. IIII. COS. II. P. P. Sept. Sévère OR. AR. Gordien III OR. AR. Philippe père AR. Philippe fils AR. (avec S. C.) Sept. Sévère G.B. M.B. Gordien III G.B. M.B. Philippe père G.B. M.B. Philippe fils G.B. M.B. Tréb. Galle G.B. Volusien G.B. Emilien (hybride) G.B.
P. M. TR. P. IIII. COS. III. Gallien B.
P. M. TR. P. IIII. COS. III. P. P. Adrien BR.M. Elagabale OR. AR. AR.Q. P.B. Philippe père AR. Valérien B. Gallien B. Postume OR. B. Aurélien OR. (avec S. C.) Elagabale G.B M.B. Postume G.B. M.B.
P. M. TR. P. IIII. COS. III. DES. IIII. S. C. Elagabale G.B.
P. M. TR. P. V. COS. II. P. P. Sept. Sévère OR. AR. Alex. Sévère OR. AR. P.B. Gordien III OR. AR. BR.M. (avec S. C.) Sept. Sévère G.B. Alex. Sévère G.B. M.B. Alex. Sévère et Mamée M.B. Gordien III G.B. M.B.
P. M. TR. P. V. COS. III. Gallien B.
P. M. TR. P. V. COS. III. P P. Philippe père AR. Valérien B. Gallien OR.M. B. M.B. (avec S. C.) Philippe père G.B. M.B. Gallien G.B.
P. M. TR. P. V. COS. IIII. P. P Elagabale OR. AR. Valérien B. Gallien B. Salonin (hybride) B. (avec S. C.) Elagabale G.B. M.B. Valérien G.B. M.B.
P. M. TR. P. V COS. V. P. P. Postume B.
P. M. TR. P. VI. AVG. IMP. Trajan AR.
P. M. TR. P. VI. COS. Gallien B.
P. M. TR. P. VI. COS. P. P. Philippe père AR. Philippe fils AR.
P. M. TR. P. VI. COS. II. P. P. Sept. Sévère AR. Alex. Sévère OR. OR.Q. AR. AR.Q. P.B. Gordien III OR.M. OR. AR. BR.M. Aurélien OR. (avec S. C.) Sept Sévère G.B. M.B. Alex. Sévère G.B. M.B. Gordien III G.B. M.B.
P. M. TR. P. VI. COS. III. P. P. Postume OR.
P. M. TR. P. VI. COS. V. P. P. Probus P.B.Q.
P. M TR. P. VII. COS. Gallien B.
P. M. TR. P. VII. COS. P. P. Gallien OR. B.
P. M. TR. P. VII. COS. II. P. P. Sept. Sévère OR. AR. Alex. Sévère OR. AR. AR. Q.

BR.M. P.B. Gordien III AR. BR.M. (avec S. C.) Alex. Sévère G.B. M.B. Gordien III G.B.

P. M. TR. P. VII. COS. III. P. P. Alex. Sévère AR. Gallien B. Postume OR.

P. M. TR. P. VII. COS. IIII. P. P. Gallien B.

P. M. TR. P. VII. IMP. V. COS. IIII. Commode BR.M.

P. M. TR. P. VIII. COS. II. P. P. Sept. Sévère OR. AR. Julie Domne (*hybride*) AR.

P. M. TR. P. VIII. COS. III. P. P. Alex. Sévère AR. BR.M. M.B. (avec S. C.) Antonin M.B. Alex. Sévère G.B. M.B.

P. M. TR. P. VIII. COS. IIII. P. P. Dioclétien P.B. Maximien Hercule P.B.

P. M. TR. P. VIII. IMP. VI. COS. III. P. P. Commode BR.M.

P. M. TR. P. VIII. IMP. VI COS. IIII. P. P. Commode OR.Q. BR.M. (avec S. C.) M.B.

P. M. TR. P. VIIII. COS. II. P. P. Sept. Sévère AR.

P. M. TR. P. VIIII. COS. III. P. P. Alex. Sévère OR. AR. P.B. (avec S. C.) G.B. M.B.

P. M. TR. P. VIIII. COS. III. P. P. — VOT. X. Alex. Sévère OR.M. BR.M. Alex. Sévère et Mamée BR.M. (avec S. C.) Alex. Sévère G.B. M.B.

P. M. TR. P. VIIII. COS. IIII. P. P. Gallien OR.M. OR. B. Postume B.

P. M. TR. P. VIIII. IMP. VI. COS. IIII. P. P. Commode OR. OR.Q. AR. AR.Q. BR.M. (avec S. C) G.B. M.B.

P. M. TR. P. VIIII. IMP. VII. COS. IIII. P. P. Commode AR. AR.Q. (avec S. C.) G.B.

P. M. TR. P. VIIII. IMP. VII. COS. IIII. P. P. — D. P. R. C. Commode AR.

P. M. TR. P. VIIII. OS. II. P. P. Alex. Sévère AR.

P. M. TR. P. X. COS. III. P. P. Sept. Sévère OR. Alex. Sévère AR. (avec S. C.) G.B. M.B.

P. M. TR. P. X. COS. III. P. P. VIC. PAR. Sept. Sévère OR.

P. M. TR. P. X. COS. IIII. P. P. Gallien OR. B.

P. M. TR. P. X. COS. V. P. P. Postume B.

P. M. TR. P. X. COS. V. P. P. — VO. XX Postume B.

P. M. TR. P. X. COS. V. P. P. — VOT. XX. Postume OR.

P. M. TR. P. X. IMP. VII. COS. IIII. P. P. Commode OR.Q. AR. AR.Q. BR.M. (avec S. C.) G.B. M.B.

P. M. TR. P. X. IMP. VII. COS. IIII. P. P. — VICT. BRIT. Commode BR.M.

P. M. TR. P. XI. COS. III. P. P. Sept. Sévère OR. AR. AR.Q. Alex. Sévère OR. AR. AR.Q. (avec S. C.) G.B. M.B.

P. M. TR. P. XI. IMP. VII. COS. V. P. P. Commode OR. AR. AR.Q. BR.M. (avec S. C.) G.B. M.B.

P. M. TR. P. XI. IMP. VIII. COS. V. P. P. Commode AR.

P. M. TR. P. XII. COS. III. P. P. Sept. Sévère AR. Alex. Sévère OR. AR. BR.M. (avec S. C.) Sept. Sévère G.B. Alex. Sévère G.B. M.B.

P. M. TR. P. XII. COS. V. P. P. Gallien B.

P. M. TR. P. XII. COS. VI. P. P. Gallien B. M.B.

P. M. TR. P. XII. IMP. VIII. COS. V. P. P. Commode OR. AR. AR.Q. BR.M. (avec S. C.) G.B. M.B.

P. M. TR. P. XIII. COS. III. P. P. Sept. Sévère OR. AR. Julie Domne (*hybride*) AR. Caracalla AR. Alex. Sévère OR. AR. (avec S. C.) Sept. Sévère M.B. Alex. Sévère G.B. M.B.

P. M. TR. P. XIII. C VI. P. P. Gallien B.

P. M. TR. P. XIII IMP. VIII. COS. V. P. P. Commode OR. AR. AR.Q. BR.M. (avec S. C.) G.B. M.B.

P. M. TR. P. XIIII. COS. III. P. P. Sept. Sévère OR. AR. P.B. Caracalla AR. AR.Q. Alex. Sévère AR. Alex. Sévère et Mamée BR.M. (avec S. C.) Sept. Sévère G.B. M.B. Caracalla G.B. Alex. Sévère G.B. M.B.

P. M. TR. P. XIIII. IMP. VIII. COS. V. P. P. Commode OR.Q. AR. AR.Q.

P. M. TR. P. XV. COS. III. P. P. Sept. Sévère OR. AR. AR.Q. P.B. Caracalla AR. AR.Q. (avec S. C.) Sept. Sévère G.B. M.B. Caracalla G.B. M.B.

P. M. TR. P. XV. COS. VII. Gallien B.

P. M. TR. P. XV. IMP. VIII. COS. VI. P. P. Commode OR.Q. AR. AR.Q. BR.M. (avec S. C.) G.B. M.B.

P. M. TR. P. XV. P. P. Gallien B.

P. M. TR. P. XVI. COS. III. P. P. Sept. Sévère OR. OR.Q. AR. AR.Q. BR.M. Julie
Domne (*hybride*) AR. Caracalla P.B. (avec s. c.) Sept. Sévère G.B. M.B.
P. M. TR. P. XVI. COS. IIII. P. P. Caracalla OR. AR. (avec s. c.) G.B. M.B.
P. M. TR. P. XVI. COS. VI. Commode AR.Q.
P. M. TR. P. XVI. COS. VII. Gallien B.
P. M. TR. P. XVI. IMP. II. COS. IIII. P. P. Caracalla OR. (avec s. c.) G.B. M.B.
P. M. TR. P. XVI. IMP. VIII. COS. VI P. P. Commode AR.Q. BR.M. (avec s. c.) M.B.
P. M. TR. P. XVII. COS. III. P. P. Sept. Sévère AR. P. B. Caracalla AR. (avec s. c.)
Sept Sévère G.B. M.B.

P. M. TR. P. XVII. COS. IIII. P. P. Caracalla OR. AR. P.B.
P. M. TR. P. XVII. IMP. III. COS. III. P. P. S. C. Caracalla G.B.
P. M. TR. P. XVII. IMP. III. COS. IIII. P. P. Caracalla OR. (avec s. c.) G.B. M.B.
P. M. TR. P. XVII. IMP. III. COS. IIII. (sic) P. P. Caracalla G.B.
P. M. TR. P. XVII. IMP. VIII. COS. VII. P. P. Commode OR. AR. BR.M. M.B.M. Com-
mode et Marcia BR.M. (avec s. c.) Commode G.B. M.B.
P. M. TR. P. XVIII. COS. P. P. S. C. Caracalla M.B.
P. M. TR. P. XVIII. COS. III. P. P. Sept. Sévère OR. AR. P.B. (avec s. c.) G.B. M.B.
P. M. TR. P. XVIII. COS. IIII. P. P. Caracalla OR.M OR. AR. P.B. (avec s. c.) M.B.
P. M. TR. P. XVIII. IMP. II. COS. Marc Aurèle OR.
P. M. TR. P. XVIII. IMP. III. COS. III. Marc Aurèle AR. Vérus (*hybride*) AR.
P. M. TR. P. XVIII. IMP. III. COS. IIII. P. P. S. C. Caracalla G.B.
P. M. TR. P. XVIII. IMP. VIII. COS. VII. P. P. Commode AR.
P. M. TR. P. XIX. COS. III. P. P. Sept. Sévère AR. (avec s. c.) M.B.
P. M. TR. P. XVIIII. COS. IIII. P. P. Caracalla OR.M. OR. AR. P.B. (avec s. c.) M.B.
P. M. TR. P. XIX. IMP. II. COS. III. Marc Aurèle OR. AR.
P. M. TR. P. XIX. IMP. III. COS. III. Marc Aurèle AR. Vérus (*hybride*) AR.
P. M. TR. P. XX. COS. IIII. P. P. Caracalla OR. AR. (avec s. c). G.B. M.B.
P. M. TR. P. XX. COS. IIII. P. P. VICT. PART. — VOT. XX. Caracalla OR.
P. M. TR. P. XX. COS. IIII. P. P. — VO. XX. S. C. Caracalla G.B.
P. M. TR. P. XX. IMP. III. COS. III. Marc Aurèle OR. AR.
P. M. TR. P. XX. IMP. III. COS. IIII. P. P. S. C. Caracalla G.B. M.B.
P. M. TR. POT. III. Caligula OR.Q.
P. M. TR. POT. III. COS. II. P. P. Philippe père, Otacilie et Philippe fils BR.M.
P. M. TR. POT. III. IMP. V. COS. X. P. P. Domitien OR. AR. AR.Q.
P. M. TR. POT. III. IMP. VI. COS. X. P. P. Domitien OR. AR.
P. M. TR. POT. IIII. IMP. VIII. COS XI. P. P. Domitien OR. AR. AR.Q.
P. M. TR. POT. XX. COS. VI. P. P. S. C. Trajan P.B.
P. M. TR. POTES. COS. III. Adrien AR.
PON. MA. TR. P. IMP. P. P. Néron P.B. (avec s. c.) P.B.
PON. MA. TR. P. IMP. S. C. Néron P.B.
PON. MAX. Vespasien AR.
PON. MAX. TR. P. COS. II. Vespasien AR.
PON. MAX. TR. P. COS. III. Vespasien AR.
PON. MAX. TR. P. COS. IIII. Domitien AR.
PON. MAX. TR. P. COS. V. Vespasien AR.
PON. MAX. TR. P. COS. VI. Vespasien OR. AR. Titus AR.
PON. MAX. TR. P. COS. VII. Vespasien AR.
PON. MAX. TR. P. POT. P. P. COS. V. CENS. Vespasien M.B. Titus M.B. (avec s. c.
Vespasien M.B.
PON. MAX. TR. P. S. C. Néron P.B.
PON. M. TR. P. COS. II. S. C. Pertinax M.B.
PON. M. TR. P. IMP. COS. DES. IT. — P. N. R. Claude I P.B.
PON. M. TR. P. IMP. COS. DES. IT. S. C. Claude I P.B.
PON. M. TR. P. IMP. COS. II. — P. N. R. Claude I P.B.
PON. M. TR. P. IMP. P. P. COS. II. (ou III.) S. C. Claude I P.B.
PON. M. TR. P. IMP. P. P. S. C. Néron P.B.
PON. M. TR. P. P. P. COS. III. S. C. Vespasien P.B.
PONTIF. Commode M.B.M.
PONTIF. COS. Géta AR. (avec s. c.) M.B.

PONTIF. COS. II. Géta OR. AR. BR.M. (avec S. C.) G.B. M.B.

PONTIFEX. Caïus Antoine AR.

PONTIFEX COS. Géta AR. (avec S. C.) M.B. Alex. Sévère G.B. M.B.

PONTIFEX MAX. TR. P. II. COS. II. Gordien III BR.M.

PONTIFEX MAX. TR. P. III. COS. P. P. Gordien III BR.M. (avec S. C.) G.B. M.B.

PONTIFEX MAX. TR. P. IIII. COS. II. P. P. Gordien III BR.M. M.B. Philippe père BR.M. Philippe père, Otacilie et Philippe fils BR.M. Philippe père et fils BR.M.

PONTIFEX MAX. TR. P. IIII. COS. II. — VICTOR. AVGG. Philippe fils BR.M.

PONTIFEX MAX. TR. P. V. COS. III. P. P. Philippe père OR.M.

PONTIFEX MAX. TR. P. V. COS. III. — VICTORIA AVGG. Philippe fils BR.M.

PONTIFEX TRIBVN. POTESTATE XII. S. C. Tibère M.B.

PONTIFEX TR. P. II. (ou III.) Caracalla OR. AR.

PONTIFEX TR. P. X. COS. II. Caracalla OR. (avec VOT. X.) BR.M.

PONTIF. MAX. Tibère M.B.

PONTIF. MAXIM. Auguste OR. AR. Tibère OR. AR. Vespasien AR. Titus AR. (avec S. C.) Vespasien M.B.

PONTIF. MAXIM. TRIBVN. POTEST. XVII. (XXIII. ou XXIIII.) S. C. Tibère M.B.

PONTIF. MAXIM. TRIBVN. POTEST. XXIX. (XXX. ou XXXI.) S. C. Auguste M.B.

PONTIF. MAXIM. TRIBVN. POTEST. XXXIIII. S. C. Auguste M.B. Tibère M.B.

PONTIF. MAXIM. TRIBVN. POTEST. XXXVI. (XXXVII. ou XXXIIX.) S. C. Tibère M.B.

PONTIF. MAX. TRIBVNIC. POTEST. XXXVIII. S. C. Tibère M.B.

PONTIF. MAX. TRIBVN. POTEST. XXXVI. (XXXVII. ou XXXIIX.) S. C. Tibère M.B.

PONTIF. MAX. TRI. P. P. P. Valérien BR.M.

PONTIF. MAX. TR. P. Elagabale OR. AR. P.B. (avec S. C.) G B. M.B

PONTIF. MAX. TR. P. COS. P. P. Macrin OR. AR. (avec S. C.) G B.

PONTIF. MAX TR. P. COS. VII. CENS. Vespasien P.B.

PONTIF. MAX. TR. P. EX S. C. Néron OR.

PONTIF. MAX. TR. P. IMP. P. P. Néron M.B. (avec S. C.) Tibère (hybride) P.B. Néron M.B. P.B.

PONTIF. MAX. TR. POT. IMP. P. P. Néron M.B. (avec S. C.) M.B. P.B.

PONTIF. MAX. TR. POT. P. P. COS. VIIII. CENS. S. C. Vespasien M.B.

PONTIF. MAX. TR. P. P. P. Macrin AR. (avec S. C.) Néron P.B. Macrin G.B. M.B.

PONTIF. MAX. TR. P. II. COS. P. P. Macrin AR. BR.M (?). Alex. Sévère P.B. (avec S. C.) Macrin G.B. M B. Alex. Sévère G.B. M.B.

PONTIF. MAX. TR. P. II. COS. II. ET COS. Tréb. Galle et Volusien BR.M.

PONTIF. MAX. TR. P. II. COS. II. P. P. Macrin OR. AR. Elagabale OR. Alex. Sévère AR. (avec S. C.) Macrin G.B. M.B. Elagabale G.B. M.B.

PONTIF. MAX. TR. P. II. COS. II. S. C. Tréb. Galle M.B.

PONTIF. MAX. TR. P. II. P. P. EX S. C. Néron OR. AR.

PONTIF. MAX. TR. P. III. COS. P. P. s. C. Alex. Sévère G.B. M.B.

PONTIF. MAX. TR. P. III. P. P. EX. S. C. Néron OR. AR.

PONTIF. MAX. TR. P. IIII. COS. P. P. S. C. Alex. Sévère G.B.

PONTIF. MAX. TR. P. IIII. COS. II. P. P. — VICTORIA AVGG. Philippe père BR.M.

PONTIF. MAX. TR. P. IIII. P. P. EX S. C. Néron OR. AR.

PONTIF. MAX. TR. P. V. COS. II. P. P. Alex. Sévère BR.M. Alex. Sévère et Mamée BR.M. (avec S. C.) Alex. Sévère G.B. M.B.

PONTIF. MAX. TR. P. V. P. P. EX S. C. Néron AR.

PONTIF. MAX. TR. P. VI. COS. IIII. P. P. EX S. C. Néron OR. AR.

PONTIF. MAX. TR. P. VI. P. P. EX S. C. Néron AR.

PONTIF. MAX. TR. P. VII. COS. II. P. P. Alex. Sévère BR.M. P.B.

PONFIF. MAX. TR. P. VII. (VIII., VIIII. ou X.) COS. IIII. P. P. EX S. C. Néron OR. AR.

PONTIF. M. TR. POT. IMP. P. P. S. C. Néron M.B.

PONTIF. TRIBVNIT. POTESTA. ITERO S. C. Drusus M.B.

PONTIF. TRIBVN. POTEST. ITER S. C. Drusus M.B.

PONTIF. TRI. POT. Titus OR. AR.

PONTIF. TR. P. COS. II. Géta AR. (avec S. C.) M.B.

PONTIF. TR. P. COS. III. Vespasien AR. Titus AR.

PONTIF. TR. P. COS. IIII. Vespasien AR. Titus OR. AR

PONTIF. TR. P. COS. V. Titus AR.

PONTIF. TR. POT. Titus OR. AR.
PONTIF. TR. P. II. COS. II. Géta OR. AR. (avec S. C.) G.B. M.B.
PONTIF. TR. P. II. S C. Caracalla M.B.
PONTIF. TR. P. III. Sept. Sévère AR. Caracalla AR. (avec S. C.) G.B.
PONTIF. TR. P. III. COS. II. Géta OR. AR. (avec S. C.) G.B. M.B.
PONTIF. TR. P. III. COS. III. P. P. S. C. Elagabale G.B. M.B.
PONTIF. TR. P. III. P. P. Géta AR.
PONTIF. TR. P. VI. COS. Caracalla AR
PONTIF. TR. P. VII. COS. Caracalla OR.
PONTIF. TR. P. VIII. COS. II. Sept. Sévère AR. Caracalla OR. AR. (avec S C.) M.B.
PONTIF. TR. P. VIIII. COS. II. Caracalla AR. P.B. (avec S. C.) G.B. M.B.
PONTIF. TR. P. X. COS. II. Caracalla OR. AR. AR.Q. (avec S. C.) G.B. M.B.
PONTIF. TR. P. X. COS. III. Sept. Sévère AR.Q.
PONTIF. TR P. XI. COS. III. Sept. Sévère AR.Q. Caracalla OR. AR. AR.Q. (avec S. C.) G.B. M.B.
PONTIF. TR. P. XI. COS. III. PROF. Caracalla AR.
PONTIF. TR. P. XII. COS. III. Caracalla OR. AR. P.B. (avec S. C.) G.B. M.B.
PONTIF. TR. P. XIII. COS. III. Caracalla OR. AR. (avec S. C.) G.B. M.B.
PONTIF. TR. P. XIIII. COS. III. Caracalla AR. (avec S. C.) G.B.
PONT. MAX. Othon OR. AR. Vespasien OR. AR. Titus AR. Antonin BR.M.
PONT. MAXIM. Vitellius OR. AR.
PONT. MAXIM. COS. III. IMP. VII. TR. POT. XXII. Tibère M.B. †.M.B.
PONT. MAX. TRIB. POT. Vespasien OR.
PONT. MAX. TRIB. POT. II. LIBERALITAS AVG. Adrien BR.M.
PONT. MAX. TRIB. P. P. P. PRO. COS. Constantin I OR.Q.
PONT. MAX. TR. P. COS. P. P. S. C. Macrin G.B. M.B.
PONT. MAX. TR. P. COS. II. DESIG. III. S. C. Vespasien M.B.
PONT. MAX. TR. P. COS. VII. P. P. Vespasien OR.
PONT. MAX. TR. P. S. C. Tibère (hybride) †.M.B.
PONT. MAX. TR. P. POT. COS. Antonin OR. AR. (avec S. C.) G.B. M.B.
PONT. MAX. TR. POT. COS. II. Trajan OR. OR.Q. AR. AR.Q. Antonin BR.M. (avec S. C.) Adrien M.B.
PONT. MAX. TR. POT. COS. II. DESIG. III. S. C. Vespasien M.B.
PONT. MAX. TR. POT. COS. III. Adrien AR.M. (avec S. C.) G.B. M.B.
PONT. MAX. TR. POT. IMP. S. C. Claude I P.B.
PONT. MAX. TR. P. II. COS. II. Elagabale AR.
PON. TR. POT. S. C. Titus P.B.
PONT. TR. P. II. Caracalla OR. AR.
PONT. TR. P. VI. COS. Caracalla OR. AR.
POP. ROMANVS. Autonomes de Constantin I P.B.Q.
POPVL. IVSSV. Auguste AR.
PORT (ou PORTV.) AVG. S. C. Néron G.B.
PORTVM TRAIANI S. C. Trajan G.B.
POTESTAS PERPETV. S. C. Alex. Sévère G.B.
P. P. COS. III. Sept. Sévère OR.
P. P. COS. VII. DES. VIII. Domitien AR.
P. P. OB CIVES SERVATOS. Claude I AR.M.
P. P. TR. P. (ou POT.) COS. III. S. C. Antonin G.B
P. R. Autonomes de Galba AR. de Constantinople P.B. de Rome (Constantin).P.B.
PRAEF. CLAS. ET ORAE. MARIT. EX S. C. Pompée le Grand AR. Sextus Pompée AR.
PRAEF. ORAE MARIT. ET CLAS. EX S. C. Pompée le Grand AR.
PRAEF. ORAE MARIT. ET CLAS. S. C. Pompée le Grand AR. Sextus Pompée AR.
PRAESIDIA REIPVBLIC. Constance Chlore P.B.
PRAETOR. RECEPT. Claude I OR. AR.
PRIM. DECE. S. C. Caracalla P.B.
PRIMI DECEN. COS. IIII. Antonin OR. OR.Q. AR.
PRIMI DECENNALES COS. II. S. C. Pertinax (hybride) M.B.

PRIMI DECENNALES COS. III. Marc Aurèle OR. AR. Faustine jeune (*hybride*) AR. (avec S.C.) Marc Aurèle G.B. M.B. Faustine mère (*hybride*) M.B. Faustine jeune (*hybride*) G.B.
PRIMI DECENNALES COS. IIII. Antonin AR. (avec S.C.) G.B. M.B.
PRIMI DECENN P. M. TR. P. X. IMP. VII. COS. IIII. P. P. S. C. Commode M.B.
PRIMIS X. MVLTIS XX. Dioclétien P.B. Max. Hercule P.B. (avec — VOTA.) Maximien Hercule P.B. (avec — VOT. X.) Dioclétien P.B. MaximienHercule P.B. (avec — VOT. X. ET XX.) Dioclétien P.B. (avec — VOT. X. FEL.) Dioclétien OR. P.B. (avec — VOT. XX.) Maximien Hercule P.B.
PRIMI XX. IOVI AVGVSTI. Dioclétien OR.
PRIMO AVSP. Galère Maximien P.B.Q.
PRINCEPS IVVENTVT. Vespasien AR. Domitien OR. AR. P.B.
PRINCEPS IVVENTVTIS. Titus AR. Domitien OR. AR. (avec S. C.) M.B.
PRINCIPIA IVVENTVTIS. Crispus P.B.
PRINCIPIA IVVENTVTIS SARMATIA. Constantin II OR.M. OR.
PRINCIPI IMPERII ROMANI. Maxence OR.
PRINCIPI IVBENTVTIS. Salonin OR. B.
PRINCIPI IVVENT. Maxime AR. Gordien III AR. Philippe fils OR. AR. AR.Q. Gallien B. Salonin B. M.B. Florien P.B. Probus P.B. Numérien OR. P.B. Carin M.B. P.B. Carausius AR. Constance Chlore P.B.Q. Galère Maximien P.B.Q. Crispus P.B.Q. (avec S. C.) Philippe fils G.B. M.B. Volusien G.B. Salonin G.B. M.B.
PRINCIPI IVVENT. B. R. P. NAT. Constantin I M.B.
PRINCIPI IVVENTVS. Constance Chlore P.B.
PRINCIPI IVVENTVT. Probus P.B. Carus P.B. Numérien P.B. Carin P.B Dioclétien P.B. Galère Maximien OR.Q. P.B. P.B.Q. Constance Chlore P.B. P.B.Q. Maximin II OR. P.B. Constantin I OR. P.B.Q.
PRINCIPI IVVENTVTI. Carin P.B. Constance Chlore M.B.
PRINCIPI IVVENTVTIS. Caracalla OR. AR Diaduménien AR. Philippe fils OR. AR. BR.M. Hérennius OR. AR. AR.Q. Hostilien OR. AR. BR.M. Volusien OR. OR.Q. AR. Salonin OR. B. B.Q. BR.M. G.B. M.B. Dioclétien M.B. Carausius P.B. Constance Chlore OR.M. OR. M.B. †.M.B. P.B. Galère Maximien OR. M.B. P.B.Q. Sévère II OR. P.B.Q. Maximin II OR. M.B. Maxence M.B. Licinius père OR. Licinius fils OR.Q. P.B.Q. Constantin I OR.M. OR. OR.Q. AR.M. AR. M.B. †.M.B. †.P.B. P.B. P.B.Q. Crispus OR. OR.Q OR.T. BR M. P.B. Delmace OR. Constantin II OR.M. OR. OR.Q. G.B.M. P.B. Constant I OR. OR.T AR. Constance II OR.M. OR. OR.Q. AR. P.B.Q. Décence AR.M. (avec S. C.) Commode M.B. Caracalla G.B. Maxime G.B. M.B. Philippe fils G.B. M.B. Hérennius G.B. M.B. Hostilien G.B. M.B. Tréb. Galle M.B. Volusien G.B. Salonin M.B.
PRINCIPI IVVENTVTIS FORT. REDVCI Commode OR. AR.
PRINCIPI IVVENTVTIS. — VOT. V. Julien II P.B.
PRINCIPIS IVVENTVTI. Probus OR. Carin OR.
PRINCIPIS PROVIDENTISSIMI. — SAPIENTIA. Licinius père OR.Q. Constantin I OR.
PRINCIPIVM IVVENTVTIS. Gratien OR.
PRINCIP. IVVENT. Vespasien AR. Salonin M.B. (avec S. C) Vespasien M.B. Domitien M.B.
PRINCIP. IVVENTVTIS. Titus AR.M.
PRINCIPS IVVENTVT. Domitien P.B.
PRINCITI IVVENTVTIS. Décence AR.M.
PRINC. IVVENT. Domitien AR.M. Commode OR. AR. P.B. Caracalla AR. Géta OR. AR. BR.M. P.B. Hérennius OR. AR. Salonin B. Tétricus père P.B. Tétricus fils P.B. (avec S. C.) Commode G.B. M.B. Hostilien G.B. Tréb. Galle G.B.
PRINC. IVVENT. COS Sept. Sévère AR. Géta OR. AR. (avec S. C.) G.B. M.B.
PRINC. IVVENTVT. Géta AR. Tétricus fils P.B.
PRINC. IVVENTVTIS. Caracalla AR. Géta AR. Diaduménien OR. AR. AR.Q. Maxime AR. P.B. Philippe fils OR. Hérennius AR. Hostilien OR. Salonin OR. B. M.B. (avec S. C.) Diaduménien G.B. M.B. Alex. Sévère M.B. Hérennius G.B. M.B.
PRIN. IVVENT. Tétricus père P.B.
PRO. AVG Tétricus père P.B.

PRO. AVG. P. M. TR. P. COS. III. Adrien AR.

PRO. AVG. P. M. TR. P. COS. VI. P. P. S. P. Q. R. Trajan OR. AR.

PROBVS P. F. AVG. COS. IIII. Probus BR.M.

PROCOS. Pompée le Grand OR.

PROF. AVGG. FEL. Sept. Sévère AR.

PROF. AVGG. P. M. TR. P. XVI. Sept. Sévère AR.

PROF. AVGG. P. M. TR. P. XVI. S. C. Sept. Sévère G.B. M.B.

PROF. AVGG. PONTIF. TR. P. XI. COS. III. S. C. Caracalla G.B.

PROF. AVGG. PONTIF. TR. P. XII. COS. III. S. C. Caracalla M.B.

PROF. AVGG PONTIF. TR. P. XII. S. C. Caracalla G.B.

PROF. AVG. PONTIF. MAX. TR. P. X. COS. III. P. P. Alex. Sévère BR.M. M.B. Alex. Sévère et Mamée M.B.M.

PROF. AVG. PONTIF. TR. P. XI. COS. III. S. C. Caracalla M.B.

PROF. AVG. PONTIF. TR. P. VII. (ou XI.) S. C. Caracalla G.B.

PROF. AVG. PONT. M. TR. P. XIX. S. C. Caracalla G.B.

PROFECTIO AVG. Trajan OR. Sept. Sévère OR. AR. Caracalla AR. Alex. Sévère AR. Gordien III BR.M. (avec S. C.) Trajan G.B Sept. Sévère G.B. M.B.

PROFECTIO AVG. COS. III. Marc Aurèle BR.M. (avec S. C.) G.B.

PROFECTIO AVGG. Licinius père OR.

PROFECTIO AVG. IMP. III. COS. II. P. P. S. C. Commode G.B.

PROFECTIO AVG. P. M. TR. P. VI. COS. II. S. C. Sept. Sévère M.B.

PROFECTIO AVG. TR. P. II. COS. II. Vérus OR. AR. (avec S. C.) G.B.

PROFECTIO AVG. TR. P. III. COS. II. S. C. Vérus M.B.

PROFECTIO AVGVSTI. Alex. Sévère BR.M. Alex Sévère et Mamée BR.M. (avec S. C.) Alex. Sévère G.B. M.B. Postume G.B.

PROF. PONTIF. TR. P. XI. COS. III. Caracalla AR. (avec S. C.) M.B.

PROPAGO IMPERI. Caracalla OR. Plautille OR. AR. Orbiane (?) AR.

PROPRAE AFRICAE. Claudius Macer AR.

PROPR. AFRCAE Claudius Macer AR.

PROPVGNATORI IMP. VIII. COS. III. P. P. S. C. Marc Aurèle G.B.

PRO VALETVDINE CAESARIS S P. Q. R. Auguste OR.

PROV. AVG. COS. II. Albin AR.

PROV. AVG. TR. P. VIII. IMP. VI. COS. IIII. P. P. S. C. Commode G.B. M.B.

PROVDENTIA AVG. Carausius P.B.

PROV. DEOR. TR. P. COS. II. Antonin AR. Marc Aurèle OR. AR. Vérus AR. (avec S. C.) Marc Aurèle G.B. M.B. Vérus G.B.

PROV. DEOR. TR. P. II. (ou III.) COS. II. Vérus AR.

PROV. DEOR. TR. P. V. IMP. IIII. COS. II. P. P. .S C. Commode G.B. M.B.

PROV. DEOR. TR. P. VI. (ou VII.) IMP. IIII.COS. III. P. P. S. C. Commode G.B. M.B.

PROV. DEOR. TR. P. VIII. IMP. VI. COS. I!II. P. P. S. C. Commode G.B.

PROV. DEOR. TR. P. XV. COS. III. Marc Aurèle OR. AR. (avec S. C.) G.B. M.B.

PROV. DEOR. TR. P. XVI. COS. III. Marc Aurèle AR. (avec S. C) G.B.

PROV. DEOR. TR. P. XVII. (ou XVIII.) COS. III. Marc Aurèle AR.

PROVDNTIA. Tétricus père P.B.Q.

PROVDNTIA AV. Carausius P.B.

PROVENTI. AVG. Claude II P.B.

PROVI. AV. Carausius P.B.

PROVI. AVG. Gallien B. Claude II P.B.

PROVID. AVG. Sept. Sévère AR. Gordien III OR. Philippe père AR. Gallien OR. B. B.Q.Salonine B. Victorin B. Tétricus père P.B. Tétricus fils P.B. Claude II P.B. Quintille P.B. Tacite P.B. Carausius P.B. Allectus P.B.

PROVID. AVG. COS. Albin OR. AR. (avec S. C.) G.B.

PROVID. AVGG. Sept. Sévère AR. P.B. Julie Domne AR. Volusien AR. Valérien B. Gallien B. Carausius P.B.

PROVID. AVGGG. Carausius P.B.

PROVID. AVG. P. M. TR. P. XI. IMP. VIII. COS V. P. P. S. C. Commode G.B.

PROVID. AVG. P. M. TR. P. XII. IMP. VIII. COS V. P. P. Commode BR.M. (avec S. C.) M.B.

PROVID. COS. VI. P. P. S. P. Q. R. Trajan AR.

PROVID. D. AVG. Tacite P.B
PROVID. DEOR. Victorin B. Tacite P.B.
PROVID. DEOR. COS. II Pertinax OR. AR.
PROVID. DEOR. COS. III. Postume OR.Q.
PROVID. DEORVM. Caracalla AR. Géta AR. Elagabale AR. Alex. Sévère AR. P.B(I).
PROVID. DEORVM COS. II. S. C. Pertinax G.B.
PROVID. DEORVM QVIES AVGG. Dioclétien OR. Maximien Hercule OR.
PROVIDE. AVG. Tacite P.B. Florien P.B. Probus P.B. Carausius P.B. Allectus P.B.
PROVIDE. AVGG. Carin P.B.Q.
PROVIDEN. AVG. Gallien OR.Q. B. Claude II P.B. Quintille P.B. Aurélien P.B. P.B.Q. Tacite P.B. Florien P.B. Probus P.B. Carausius P.B.
PROVIDEN AVG. COS. II. Albin AR.
PROVIDEN. AVGGG. Carausius P.B.
PROVIDEN. DEOR. Aurélien P.B. Sévérine P.B. Tacite P.B. Florien P.B. Probus P.B.
PROVIDEN. DEORVM. COS. II. S. C. Pertinax G.B.
PROVIDEN. S. C. Agrippa M.B.
PROVIDENT. Carausius P.B. (avec S. C.) Auguste M.B. Néron M.B. Galba M.B. Vitellius M.B. Vespasien M.B. Titus G.B. M.B. Domitien M.B.
PROVIDENT. AVG. Gordien III AR. Tréb. Galle AR. Volusien AR. Gallien B. Claude II M.B. P.B. Quintille P.B. P.B.Q. Aurélien P.B. P.B.Q. Tacite P.B.Q. Probus P.B. Carus OR. P.B. P.B.Q. Numérien P.B. Dioclétien P.B. Carausius P.B.
PROVIDENT. AVGG. Carus P.B. Numérien P.B. Carin P.B.
PROVIDENT AVGVS. (ou AVGVST.) S. C. Titus M.B.
PROVIDENT. DEOR. Tacite P.B. Dioclétien P.B. Maximien Hercule P.B. Constance Chlore P.B. Galère Maximien P.B.
PROVIDENT. DEOR. QVIES AVGG. Dioclétien M.B. Maximien Hercule M.B.
PROVIDENTI. Carausius P.B.
PROVIDENTIA. Commode BR.M. Sept. Sévère OR. AR. Caracalla AR. Tétricus père P.B.
PROVIDENTIA AVG. Adrien AR. Sept. Sévère AR. Alex. Sévère OR. AR. P.B. Maximin I OR. AR. AR.Q. P.B. Gordien III OR. AR. Philippe père AR. Tréb. Galle OR. AR. Gallien OR. OR.Q. B. Salonine B. Valérien jeune B. Postume OR. OR.Q. AR.Q. B. M.B. Victorin OR. B. Tétricus père P.B(2). Tétricus fils P.B. Claude II P.B. Tacite P.B. P.B.Q. Florien P.B. Probus P.B. Carus P.B. Carin P.B. Dioclétien AR. P.B. Carausius P.B. Allectus P.B. (avec S. C.) Adrien G.B. M.B. Alex. Sévère G.B. M.B. Maximin I G.B. M.B. Gordien d'Afrique père G.B. Gordien II. G.B. M.B. Hostilien G.B.
PROVIDENTIA AVGG. Gordien d'Afrique père OR. AR. Gordien d'Afrique fils AR. Tréb. Galle AR. Volusien AR. Valérien B. Gallien OR. AR. B. Régalien AR. Tétricus fils P.B. Dioclétien OR. AR. Maximien Hercule OR. AR. Constance Chlore OR. AR. Galère Maximien OR. AR. (ave S. C.) Gordien d'Afrique père G.B. Gordien d'Afrique fils G.B.
PROVIDENTIA AVG. IMP. VI. COS. III. S. C. Marc Aurèle G.B.
PROVIDENTIA AVG. N. Probus P.B.
PROVIDENTIA AVGVSTI. Probus P.B.
PROVIDENTIA AVGVSTI COS. III. Adrien M.B.
PROVIDENTIA AVGVSTI S. P. Q. R. S. C. Trajan G.B. M.B(3).
PROVIDENTIA DEOR. Galère Maximien P.B. (avec S. C.) Postume G.B.
PROVIDENTIA DEORVM. Antonin AR. Sept. Sévère AR. Géta AR. Macrin AR. Balbin AR. Pupien AR. Sévérine P.B. Tacite OR. P.B. Dioclétien M.B. P.B. Maximien Hercule P.B. Constance Chlore P.B. (avec S. C.) Adrien G.B. M.B. Macrin G.B. M.B. Alex. Sévère G.B. M.B. Balbin G.B. M.B. Pupien G.B. M.B.
PROVIDENTIA DEORVM COS. II. Pertinax OR. AR. (avec S. C.) G.B. M.B.

(1) Variété avec PROVAD. DEORVM.
(2) Variété avec PROVIDEMTA AVG.
(3) Variété fautive : PROVIDNTIA AVGVSTI S. P. C. O. R. S. C.

PROVIDENTIA DEORVM QVIES AVGG. Dioclétien M.B. Maximien Hercule M.B.
PROVIDENTIAE AVG. Commode OR. AR. Probus P.B. (avec S. C.) Commode G.B.
PROVIDENTIAE AVGG. Dioclétien AR. Constance Chlore P.B. Hélène I P.B. Licinius père P.B. Constantin I P.B. Crispus (hybride) P.B. Constantin II P.B. Constance II P.B.
PROVIDENTIAE CAES. Constantin II P.B. Constance II P.B.
PROVIDENTIAE CAESS. Licinius père P.B. Licinius fils P.B. Constantin I P.B. Crispus P.B. Constantin II P.B. Constance II P.B.
PROVIDENTIAE CΔS. Constantin II P.B.
PROVIDENTIAE DEORVM. Antonin OR. AR. Caracalla OR. AR. (avec S. C.) Antonin G.B. M.B. Caracalla G.B. M.B.
PROVIDENTIAE DEORVM COS. II. S. C. Pertinax G.B. M.B.
PROVIDENTIA SENATVS S. C. Nerva G.B.
PROVIDENTI. AVG. Dioclétien P.B. Carausius P.B.
PROVID. PARTHICO P. M. TR. P. COS. VI. P. P. S. P. Q. R. Trajan AR.
PROVID. P. M. TR. P. COS. VI. P. P. S. P. Q. R. Trajan OR. AR.
PROVID. TR. P. COS. II. P. P. Trajan OR. AR.
PROVIT. AVG. Allectus P.B.
PROV. PROBI AVG. NOSTRI. Probus P.B.
P. R. RESTITVTA. Autonomes de Galba AR.
PVBLICA FEL. P. M. TR. P. XII. IMP. VIII. COS. V. P. P. S. C. Commode G.B.
PVBLICA LIBERTAS S. C. Galba M.B.
PVBLIC. FEL. P. M. TR. P. XII. IMP. VIII. COS. V. P. P. Commode AR.
PVDICITIA. Sabine AR. Faustine jeune AR. Lucille OR. AR. P.B. Crispine OR. Sept. Sévère AR. Julie Domne AR. AR.Q. Soémias AR. Maesa OR. AR. AR.Q. P.B. Alex. Sévère (hybride) P.B. Orbiane AR. Mamée AR. P.B. Gallien B. Salonine B. B.Q. (avec S. C.) Sabine G.B. M.B. Faustine jeune G.B. MB. Lucille M.B. Crispine G.B. Julie Domne G.B. M.B. Maesa G.B. M.B. Salonine G.B. M.B.
PVBICITIA AVG. Paula AR. Gordien III AR. Otacilie OR. AR.M. AR. BR.M. Trajan Dèce AR. Etruscille OR. AR. Hérennius AR. Hostilien AR. Tréb. Galle AR. Salonine AR.M. B. Magnia Urbica OR. BR.M. (avec S. C.) Tranquilline(?) G.B. Otacilie G.B. M.B. Etruscille BR.M. G.B. M.B. Salonine G.B.
PVDICITIA AVGG. Volusien AR. Salonine B.
PVDICITIAE AVGVSTAE. Mamée BR.M. Etruscille BR.M. M.B. Salonine AR.M.
PVDIC. P. M. TR. P. COS. III. Adrien AR.
PVELLAE FAVSTINIANAE. Faustine mère OR. AR. (avec S. C.) G.B.
PX GA. Bonose BIL.
QVADRAGENS REMISSAE S. C. Galba M.B.
QVADRAGENSVMA REMISSA S. C. Galba M.B.
QVATERNIO. Valérien et Gallien AR.M.
QVIES AVG. Maximien Hercule M.B. P.B.Q.
QVIES AVGG. Dioclétien M.B.
QVIES AVGVSTORVM. Dioclétien M.B.
QVINQVENNALES AVG. Q. Postume OR.Q.
QVINQVENNALES AVG. V. X. Postume OR.Q.
QVINQVENNALES POSTVMI AVG. VOT. X. Postume OR.
QVINQVENNALES POSTVMI AVG. X. Postume OR. P.B.
QVINTO FELIX S. C. Hostilien G.B.
QVOD VIAE MVN. SVNT. Auguste OR. AR.
RECTORI ORBIS. Caracalla AR.
RECTOR. ORBIS. Dide Julien OR. AR. Sept. Sévère AR. Caracalla OR. AR. Elagabale OR. AR. (avec S. C.) Dide Julien G.B. M.B. Caracalla G.B. M.B.
RECTOR. TOTIVS ORBIS. Constantin I OR.
RECVPERATOR VRBIS SVAE. Constantin I P.B.
REDITVS AVG. Florien P.B.
REDVCI FORTVNAE S. C. Vespasien M.B.
REDVCIS FELICITA. S. C. Vespasien M.B.
REGI ARTIS. Claude II P.B.
REGNA ADSIGNATA. Trajan OR. (avec S. C.) G.B.

RELIG. AVG. IMP. VI. COS. III. Marc Aurèle AR.
RELIG. AVG. IMP. VII. COS. III. Marc Aurèle AR. (avec S. C.) G.B. M.B.
RELIGIO AVGG. Valérien B.
RELIQVA VETERA HS. NOVIES MILL. ABOLITA S. C. Adrien G.B.
RENOBATIO VRBIS ROME. Magnence M.B.
RENOVATIO VRBIS ROME. Décence M.B.
RENOVAT. ROMA. Carausius AR. P.B.
RENOVAT. ROMANO. Carausius AR.
REPARATIO FEL. TEMP. Procope OR. G.B. M.B. P.B.
REPARATIO PVBLICA. Procope P.B.
REPARATIO REIPVB. Gratien AR.M. M.B. Valentinien II M.B. Théodose I M.B. Magr.us Maximus M.B. Honorius M.B.
REPARATIO REIPVBLICAE. Gratien M.B.
REPARATIO TEMPORVM. Gratien M.B.
REQVIES CONSTANTIO PIO PRINC. Constance Chlore P.B.
REQVIES OPTIMOR. MERIT. Claude II P.B. P.B.Q. Maximien Hercule P.B. P.B.Q. Constance Chlore P.B. P.B.Q.
REQVIES OPTIMORVM MERITOR. Constance Chlore P.B.Q.
REQVIES OPTIMORVM MERITORVM. Claude II P.B. Maximien Hercule P.B.Q. Constance Chlore P.B.Q.
REQVIES OPT. MER. Claude II P.B.Q. Maximien Hercule P.B.Q. Constance Chlore P.B.Q.
REST. GALLIAR Postume B.
REST. ITAL. COS. V. P. P. S. P. Q. R. OPTIMO PRINC. Trajan OR.
REST. ITALIA S. P. Q. R. OPTIMO PRINCIPI S. C. Trajan G.B.
RESTIT. GALLIAR. Gallien B.
RESTIT. GALLIARVM. Postume B.
RESTIT. ILYRICI. Probus P.B.
RESTIT. PIETATIS. Claude II P.B.
RESTITOR GALLIAE. Postume B.
RESTITOR. GALLIAP. Postume B. M.B.
RESTITOR. GALLIAR. Postume M.B.
RESTITOR. REIP. Valens AR.
RESTIT. SAECVLI. Aurélien P.B. Carausius P.B.
RESTITVTA. Autonomes de Galba AR.
RESTITVTA LIBERTAS S. C. Vitellius M.B.
RESTITVT. GALLIAR. Gallien B.
RESTITVT. GENER. HVMANI. Valérien B. Gallien B.
RESTITVTI. GENER. HVMANI. Valérien B.
RESTITVTIO REIP. Attale OR.
RESTITVT. MON. S. C. Alex. Sévère G.B.
RESTITVT. ORBIS. Aurélien P.B. Probus P.B. Carus P.B. Carin P.B. Valens AR.
RESTITVTORES VRBIS. Sept. Sévère AR.
RESTITVTOR EXERCITI. Aurélien P.B. Probus P.B.
RESTITVTOR GALLIAR. Gallien B. Salonin G.B. Postume B. G.B. (avec S. C.) G.B.
RESTITVTOR GALLIARVM. Gallien B.
RESTITVTORI ACHAIAE. Adrien OR. AR. (avec S. C.) G.B. M.B.
RESTITVTORI AFRICAE. Adrien OR. AR. (avec S. C.) G.B. M.B.
RESTITVTORI ARABIAE. S. C. Adrien G.B.
RESTITVTORI ASIAE. S. C. Adrien G.B.
RESTITVTORI BITHYNIAE S. C. Adrien G.B. M.B.
RESTITVT. ORIEN. (OU ORIENT.). Aurélien P.B.
RESTITVT. ORIENTIS. Valérien B. Gallien B. Aurélien P.B(1).
RESTITVTORI GALLIAE. Adrien AR. (avec S. C.) G.B. M.B.
RESTITVTORI GALLIARVM VOTIS PVBLICIS. Victorin BR.M.
RESTITVTORI HISPANIAE. Adrien OR. AR. (avec S. C.) G.B. M.B.
RESTITVTORI ITALIAE. Adrien OR. (avec S. C.) G.B. M.B.

(1) Variété avec ORIGENTIS.

RESTITVTORI ITALIAE IMP. VI. COS. III. S. C. Marc Aurèle G.B.
RESTITVTORI LIBERTATIS. Constantin I OR.
RESTITVTORI LIBYAE S. C. Adrien G.B.
RESTITVTORI MACEDONIAE S. C. Adrien G.B. M.B.
RESTITVTORI NICOMEDIAE S. C. Adrien G.B. M.B.
RESTITVTORI ORBIS. Aurélien P.B.
RESTITVTORI ORBIS TERRARVM S. C. Adrien G.B.
RESTITVTORI PHRYGIAE S. C. Adrien G.B. M.B.
RESTITVTORI SICILIAE S. C. Adrien G.B. M.B.
RESTITVTORI VRBIS. Sept. Sévère OR. AR. Géta AR.
RESTITVTOR. LIBERTATIS. Magnence OR.
RESTITVTOR. MON. S. C. Alex. Sévère M.B.
RESTITVTOR. ORBIS. Gordien III (hybride) AR. Valérien OR. B. B.Q. Gallien OR.
B. Postume B. Claude II P.B. Aurélien P.B. Tacite P.B. Probus P.B. (avec S.
C.) Valérien G.B. Gallien G.B.
RESTITVTOR ORIENTIS. Aurélien OR.
RESTITVTOR REIP. Autonomes de Constantinople (Constantin) G.B.M. Vétra-
nion AR. Jovien AR.M. Valentinien I AR.M. AR. P.B. Valens AR.M. AR. P.B.
RESTITVTOR. REIPV. Valens AR.
RESTITVTOR REIPVBLICAE. Valentinien I OR. AR.M. AR. G.B. Valens OR.M. OR.
AR.M. AR. G.B.M. G.B. Gratien OR. Valentinien II OR.M. Théodose I OR.M.
Magnus Maximus OR. AR.M. Constantin III OR.
RESTITVTOR ROM. Jovin AR.
RESTITVTOR SAEC. (SAECVL. ou SAECVLI). Probus P.B.
RESTITVTOR SAECVLI VOT. X. Florien BR.M.
RESTITVTOR S. AVG. Probus P.B.
RESTITVTOR SECVL. Probus P.B.
RESTITVTOR VRBIS. Sept. Sévère OR. AR. P.B. Caracalla OR. AR. Géta AR. Macrin
AR. (avec S. C.) Sept. Sévère G.B. M.B. Caracalla G.B. M.B. Géta M.B.
RESTITVT. REIPVBLICAE. Tacite G.B.M.
RESTITVT. SAEC. (ou SAECVLI). Probus P.B (1).
RESTITVTORI LIBERTATIS. Constantin II OR.
REST. ORBIS. Postume OR. B.
REX ARMEN. DAT. TR. P. IIII. IMP. II. COS. II. Vérus OR. (avec S. C.) Marc Aurèle
(hybride) G.B. Vérus G.B. M.B.
REX ARMENIIS DATVS IMP. II. TR. P. IIII. COS. II. Vérus OR. (avec S. C.) G.B
REX ARMENIIS DATVS S. C. Antonin G.B.
REX PARTHIS DATVS S. C. Trajan G.B.
REX PARTHVS. Trajan OR. (avec S. C.) G.B.
REX QVADIS DATVS S. C. Antonin G.B.
RMA (sic). Autonomes de Galba AR.
ROMA. Néron OR. AR. P.B. Autonomes de Galba AR. Vespasien OR. Autonomes
d'Adrien P.B. Marc Aurèle BR.M. Autonomes de Rome (Constantin I) P.B.
(avec S. C.) Néron G.B. M.B. Clodius Macer AR. Galba G.B. M.B. Vespasien
G.B. M.B. Titus G.B. M.B. Domitien G.B. M.B. Adrien G.B. M.B.
ROMA AET. Aurélien M.B.
ROMA AETER. (ou AETERN.). Probus P.B.
ROMA AETERNA. Adrien OR. Caracalla OR. Probus OR. (avec S. C.) Adrien G.B.
Antonin G.B. Emilien M.B.
ROMA BEATA. Constant II BR.M. Constance II BR.M.
ROMA COS. IIII. Antonin AR. (avec S. C.) M.B.
ROMAE AETER. Aurélien OR. M.B. P.B. Tacite P.B. Probus P.B. Maximien Her-
cule M.B. Carausius P.B. Constantin I M B.
ROMAE AETER. AN. MILL. ET PRIMO. Pacatien AR.
ROMAE AETER. AVGG. Constantin I P.B.
ROMAE AETERN. Pesc. Niger AR. Emilien AR. Numérien P.B. Dioclétien P.B.
Allectus P.B. Constance Chlore P.B. (avec S. C.) Emilien G.B.

(1) Variété avec RESTITVT. SEC.

ROMAE AETERNAE. Adrien OR. AR. Pesc. Niger OR. AR. Albin AR. Sept. Sévère AR. Géta AR. Alex. Sévère OR. BR.M. Alex. Sévère et Mamée BR.M. M.B.M. Gordien d'Afrique père OR. AR. Gordien d'Afrique fils AR. Gordien III AR. AR.Q. Philippe père OR. AR. Otacilie AR. Philippe fils OR. AR. Trajan Dèce AR. Hostilien AR. Tréb. Galle AR. Volusien AR. Valérien OR. B. Gallien OR. B. Salonine OR. B. Macrien jeune OR. BIL. Quiétus BIL. Postume OR. B. Victorin OR. Tétricus père OR. Claude II OR. P.B. Aurélien P.B. P.B.Q. Tacite OR. P.B. Florien OR. Probus OR. G.B. P.B. Carus OR. Carin OR. Dioclétien OR. Carausius P.B. Constance Chlore BR.M. M.B. P.B. Alexandre (usurpateur) AR.(?) †.M.B. Constant I BR.M. (avec S. C.) Antonin G.B. M.B. Crispine G.B. Sept. Sévère G.B. M.B. Alex. Sévère G.B. M.B. Gordien d'Afrique père G.B. Gordien d'Afrique fils G.B. Gordien III G.B. M.B. Hostilien G.B. M.B. Tréb. Galle G.B. Valérien M.B. Tacite OR.

ROMAE AETERNAE AVG. Étruscille AR. Hostilien OR. AR. Tréb. Galle AR. Volusien AR.

ROMAE AETERNAE AVG. N. Alexandre (usurpateur) †M.B.

ROMAE AETERNAE COS. V. P. P. S. C. Commode G.B.

ROMAE AETERNAE C. V. P. P. Commode AR.

ROMAE AETERNAE P. P. Julie Domne OR.

ROMAE AETERNAE. — X. Licinius père P.B. Licinius fils P.B. (avec — XV.) Licinius père P.B. Licinius fils P.B. Constantin I P.B. Crispus P.B. Constantin II P.B. (avec — XX.) Licinius père P.B. Constantin I P.B.

ROMAE AETERNE. Aurélien P.B.

ROMAE FELICI. Commode AR.

ROMAE FELICI COS. VI. Commode AR.

ROMAE RESTITVTAE. Constantin I M.B. P.B.

ROM. AETERNAE AVG. Hostilien AR.

ROM. AETER. P. M. TR. P. VIIII. IMP. VII. COS. IIII. P. P. Commode AR. (avec S. C.) M.B.

ROMA FELIX. Adrien AR.

ROMA FELIX COS. III. Adrien AR.

ROMA FELIX COS. III. P. P. Adrien AR.

ROMANO RENOV. Carausius AR.

ROMANO RENOVA. Carausius OR.

ROMA PERPETVA. Vespasien AR.

ROMA P. M. TR. P. X. IMP. VII. COS. IIII. P. P. Commode AR.

ROMA RENASC. Autonomes de Galba AR. Galba OR. AR.

ROMA RENASCENS. Galba OR. AR. (avec S. C.) Vitellius M.B. Nerva G.B.

ROMA RENASCES. Autonomes de Galba AR. Galba OR. AR.

ROMA RESTI. S. C. Galba G.B.

ROMA RESVRGENS. Vespasien AR.

ROMA RESVRGES S. C. Vespasien G.B.

ROMA R. XL. S. C. Galba G.B.

ROMA S. VRB. Sept. Sévère AR.M.

ROMA TR. POT. XIIII. COS. IIII. S. C. Antonin G.B. M.B.

ROMA VICTRIX. Galba OR. AR. (avec S. C.) Vespasien G.B. M.B. Titus M.B.

ROME HERC. Carausius AR.

ROM. ET AVG. Auguste BR.M. G.B. M.B. P.B. Tibère G.B. M.B. P.B. Claude I M.B. P.B. Néron M.B. Domitien AR.M.

ROM. FEL. P. M. TR. P. XI. COS. V. Commode AR.

ROM. FEL. P. M. TR. P. XVI. COS. VI. Commode OR. AR. (avec S. C.) G.B. M.B.

ROM. P. M. TR. P. VIIII. IMP. VII. COS. IIII. P. P. Commode AR.

ROMVLO AVGVSTO S. C. Antonin G.B. M.B.

ROMVLO CONDITOR. Commode AR.

ROMVLO CONDITORI. Adrien OR. AR. BR.M. (avec S. C.) G.B.

SABINAE. Constance II BR.M.

SACERD. COOPT. IN OMN. CONL. SVPRA NVM. EX. S. C. Néron OR. AR.

SACERD. DEI SOLIS ELAGAB. Elagabale AR.Q.

SACERD. DEI SOLIS ELAGABAL. S. C. Elagabale M.B.

SACERDOS DEI SOLIS ELAGAB. Elagabale AR. AR.Q. P.B. (avec S. C.) G.B. M.B.
SACERDOS DIVI AVGVSTI. Antonia OR. AR.
SACERDOS VRBIS. Alex. Sévère P.B.
SAC. MON. VRB. AVGG. ET CAESS. NN. Dioclétien M.B. Maximien Hercule M.B.
Constance Chlore M.B. Galère Maximien M.B. Sévère II M.B. Maximin II M.B.
Constantin I M.B.
SAC. M. VRB. AVGG. ET CAESS. NN. Dioclétien M.B.
SACRA MONETA AVGG. ET CAESS. NN. Maximin II M.B.
SACRA MONET. AVGG ET CAESS. NOSTR. Dioclétien M.B. Maximien Hercule M.B.
Constance Chlore M.B. Galère Maximien M.B.
SACRA MONETA VRBIS. Crispus BR.M. Constantin II G.B.M.
SACRA MON. VRB. AVGG. ET CAESS. NN. Dioclétien M.B. Maximien Hercule M.B.
Constance Chlore M.B. Galère Maximien M.B.
SACRA SAECVLARIA. Sept. Sévère OR. (avec S. C.) Caracalla G.B.
SACR. MONET. AVGG. ET CAESS. NN. Constance Chlore M.B.
SACR. MONET. AVGG. ET CAESS. NOSTR. Dioclétien M.B. Maximien Hercule M.B
Constance Chlore M.B. Galere Maximien M B.
SAEC. AVR. P. M. TR. P. COS. III. Adrien OR. AR.
SAEC. FEL. COS. II. Albin AR.
SAEC. FELICIT. Sept. Sévère AR.
SAEC. FELICITAS. Marius OR. B. Tétricus père P.B.
SAEC. FEL. P. M. TR. P. X. IMP. VII. COS. IIII. P. P. Commode AR. (avec S. C.)
G.B.
SAEC. FEL. P. M. TR. P. XI. IMP. VII. COS. V. P. P. Commode AR. (avec S. C)
G.B. M.B.
SAEC. FEL. P. M. TR. P. XI. IMP. VIII. COS. V. P. P. S. C. — VO. DF. Commode G.B.
SAC. FRVGIF. Sept. Sévère OR.
SAEC. FRVGIF. COS. Sept. Sévère OR. AR.
SAEC. FRVGIF. COS. II. Albin AR.
SAECV. FELICIT. Sept. Sévère AR.
SAECVLARES AVG. Gallien B(I). Carausius P.B.
SAECVLARES AVGG. Philippe père OR. AR. Philippe père, Otacilie et Philippe
fils BR.M. Otacilie OR. AR. Philippe fils AR. Trajan Déce (hybride) AR. Hé-
rennius (hybride) AR. Maximien Hercule P.B. (avec S. C.) Philippe père G.B.
M.B. Otacilie G.B. M.B. Philippe fils G.B. M.B.
SAECVLARES AVGG. COS. Maximien Hercule P.B.
SAECVLARES. AVGG. COS. I. Uranius OR.
SAECVLARES AVGG. COS. II. Philippe fils OR. (avec S. C.) G.B. M.B.
SAECVLARES AVGG. COS. III. Philippe père OR. AR. AR.Q. (avec S. C.) G.B. M.B.
SAECVLARIA SACRA. Géta M.B. (avec S. C.) Sept. Sévère G.B. M.B. Caracalla G.B.
Géta G.B. M.B.
SAECVL. FELICIT. Sept. Sévère AR. Julie Domne AR.
SAECVLI FEL. Sept. Sévère AR. Constance Chlore P.B.
SAECVLI FEL. COS. II. Albin AR. (avec S. C.) Sept. Sévère G.B. M.B.
SAECVLI FELIC. AVG. N. Maxence M.B.
SAECVLI FELICI. Carausius P.B.
SAECVLI FELICIT. Faustine jeune OR. AR. Sept. Sévère AR. Maximien Hercule
P.B. Constance Chlore P.B. (avec S. C.) Faustine jeune G.B. M.B.
SAECVLI FELICITAS. Pesc. Niger AR. Julie Domne OR. AR. P.B. Caracalla AR.
Caracalla et Géta OR. Soémias AR. Maesa OR. AR. AR.Q. Mamée AR. Gordien III
AR. Tréb. Galle BR.M. Valérien B. Gallien B. Postume B. M.B. Victorin OR.
B(2). Tétricus père OR. P.B. Quintille P.B. Aurélien P.B. Probus BR.M. Carus
et Carin BR.M. P.B. Carausius P.B. Allectus P.B. (avec S. C.) Sept. Sévère G.B.
M.B. Julie Domne G.B. M.B. Maesa G.B. M.B.
SAECVLI FELICITAS AVG. Licinius fils P.B. Constantin I P.B. Crispus P.B. Cons-
tantin II P.B.

---

(1) Variété avec SAECVLARHS AVG.
(2) Variété avec SACVLI FELICIIAC.

SAECVLI FELICITAS AVG. N. Maxence M.B. P.B.

SAECVLI FELICITAS COS. III. P. P. Sept. Sévère OR. P.B. (avec S. C.) M.B.

SAECVLI FELIC. P. M. TR. P. XV. IMP. VIII. COS. VI. S. C. Commode G.B. M.B.

SAECVLO FRVGIFER. Albin OR.

SAECVLO FRVGIFERO. Pertinax AR. Albin AR. Postume B. M.B. (avec S. C.) Albin G.B.

SAECVLO FRVGIFERO COS. II. Albin OR. BR.M. (avec S. C.) G.B. M.B. Sept. Sévère M.B.

SAECVLO FRVGIFERO TR. P. COS. S. C. Sept. Sévère G.B.

SAECVLO TR. S. C. Sept. Sévère G.B.

SAECVLVM AVGG. Postume G.B.

SAECVLVM NOVVM. Philippe père AR. Philippe père, Otacilie et Philippe fils BR.M. Otacilie OR. Philippe fils AR. BR.M. Etruscille AR. Hostilien AR. Tréb. Galle AR. Volusien AR. (ave S. C. Philippe père G.B. M.B.

SAE. VOTA. MVLT. DD. NN. Constantin I P.B.Q.

SAL. AVG. Postume P.B.Q.

SAL. AVG. P. M. TR. P. COS. III. Adrien OR. AR.

SAL. AVG. P. M. TR. P. XII. IMP. VIII. COS. V. P. P. S. C. Commode G.B.

SAL. AVG. P. M. TR. P. XIII. IMP. Commode OR.

SAL. AVG. P. M. TR. P. XIII. IMP. VIII. COS. V. P. P. S. C. Commode G.B.

SAL. AVG. TR. P. II. COS. II. S. C. Sept. Sévère G.B.

SAL. GEN. HVM. Commode AR. Caracalla AR.

SAL. GEN. HVM. COS. VI. P. P. S. C. Commode G.B. M.B.

SALVATOR REIPVBLICAE. Vétranion OR.

SALV...IE. Honoria P.B.Q.

SALVIS. AVGG. ET CAESS. AVCTA KART. Dioclétien M.B. Maximien Hercule M.B. Constance Chlore M.B. Galère Maximien M.B.

SALVIS. AVGG. ET CAESS. FEL. KART. Dioclétien M.B. Maximien Hercule M.B. Constace Chlore M.B. Galère Maximien M.B Sévère II M.B. Maximin II M.B. Maxence M.B. Constantin I M.B.

SALVIS AVGG. ET CAESS. FEL. ORBIS TERR. Maximien Hercule BR.M.

SALVS. Néron OR. AR. Faustine jeune AR. Lucille AR. (avec S. C.) Lucille M.B. Crispine G.B.

SALVS. A. Tétricus père P.B.

SALVS ANTONINI AVG. Caracalla AR. Elagabale OR. AR. (avec S. C.) G.B. M.B.

SALVS AV. Tétricus fils. P.B.

SALVS AVG. Vespasien AR. Julie de Titus AR. Adrien AR. Antonin OR. AR. Philippe père AR. AR.Q. Otacilie AR. Emilien AR. Gallien B. Salonine B. M.B. Postume OR.Q. B. B.Q. G.B. M.B. Victorin B. Tétricus père OR. P.B. P.B.Q. Tétricus fils P.B. Claude II OR. P.B. P.B.Q. Tacite P.B. Florien P.B. Probus OR. P.B. Carus P.B. Dioclétien M.B. Carausius P.B. Allectus OR. P.B. Constance Chlore P.B. (avec S. C.) Titus M.B. Domitien M.B. Adrien G.B. M.B. Antonin G.B. M.B. Commode G.B. Gordien III G.B. M.B. Philippe père G.B. M.B. Postume G.B.

SALVS. AVG. COS. II. S. C. Antonin M.B.

SALVS. AVG. COS. IIII. Antonin AR. (avec S. C.) G.B. M.B.

SALVS. AVG. Tréb. Galle OR. AR. P.B. Volusien OR. AR. AR.Q. Valérien B. Gallien B. Tétricus père P.B. Tétricus fils P.B. Numérien OR. Carin OR. P.B. Dioclétien P.B. Maximien Hercule OR. P.B. Carausius P.B. Constance Chlore P.B. (avec S. C.) Philippe père G.B. Tréb. Galle G.B. M.B. Volusien G.B. M.B. Valérien G.B. M.B.

SALVS. AVGG. ET CAESS. NN. Constance Chlore OR. Galère Maximien OR.

SALVS AVGGG. Dioclétien OR. Maximien Hercule P.B. Carausius P.B.

SALVS AVGG. NN. Licinius père OR.

SALVS AVG. NOSTRI. Constance II M.B.

SALVS AVG. PARTHICO P. M. TR. P. COS. VI. P. P. S. P. Q. R. Trajan AR.

SALVS AVG. P. M. TR. P. COS. II. Adrien OR. AR.

SALVS AVG. P. M. TR. P. COS. DES. III. Adrien OR. AR.

SALVS AVG. P. M. TR. P. COS. III. Adrien AR.

SALVS AVG. P. M. TR. P. COS. VI. P. P. S. P. Q. R. Trajan OR.
SALVS AVG. PONT. MAX. TR. POT. COS. II. S. C. Adrien G.B. M.B.
SALVS AVG. P. XV. Gallien B.
SALVS AVG. S. C. SENATVS POPVLVSQVE ROMANVS. Trajan G.B.
SALVS AVG. TR. P. VII. IMP. IIII. COS. III. P. P. S. C. Commode G.B. M.B.
SALVS AVG. TR. P VII. IMP. V. COS. III. P. P. S. C. Commode G.B.
SALVS AVG. TR. P. VIII. IMP. V. (ou VI.) COS. IIII. P. P. S. C. Commode G.B.
SALVS AVGVS. Tréb. Galle AR. Volusien AR. (avec S. C.) Hostilien G.B. Tréb. Galle M.B.
SALVS AVGVST. Domitien AR. Mamée AR.
SALVS AVGVSTA S. C. Galba G.B. M.B. Vespasien G.B. Titus G.B.
SALVS AVGVSTI. Elagabale AR. Alex. Sévère AR. Maximin I OR. AR. AR.Q. P.B. Maxime AR. Gordien III AR. (avec S. C.) Galba M.B. Vespasien G.B. M.B. Antonin M.B. Maximin I G.B. M.B. Emilien G.B. Postume P.B.
SALVS AVGVSTI COS. III. S. C. Adrien M.B.
SALVS DD. NN. AVG. ET CAES. — A. ω. Magnence G B. M.B. P.B. Décence G.P. M.B. P.B.
SALVS DD. NN. AVG. T. — A. ω. Magnence P.B.
SALVS ET LIBERTAS. Autonomes de Galba OR. AR.
SALVS ET SPES REIPVBLICAE. Constantin I OR.M. BR.M. Constantin II OR.M. Constant I OR.M. Constance II OR.M.
SALVS EXERCITI. Postume OR. B. Tétricus père P.B.
SALVS GENE. HVMANI. Galba AR.
SALVS GENER. HVMANI. Autonomes de Galba AR.
SALVS GENERIS HVMANI. Autonomes de Galba OR. AR. Galba AR. Trajan OR.
SALVS. GEN. HVMANI. Galba OR. AR.
SALVS III. Carausius P.B.
SALVS ITAL. Gallien B.
SALVS MILITVM Probus P.B.
SALVS MVNDI. Olybrius OR. OR.T. AR.
SALVS P. M. TR. P. VIIII. (ou X.) IMP. VII. COS. IIII. P. P. S. C. Commode G.B.
SALVS P. M. TR. P. XI. IMP. VII. COS. V. P. P. S. C. Commode G.B.
SALVS POSTVMI AVG. Postume OR.B.
SALVS PROVINCIARVM. Postume OR.B. M.B.
SALVS PVBLI. Tacite P.B. Florien P.B. Probus P.B.
SALVS PVBLIC. Autonomes de Galba AR. Probus P.B.
SALVS PVBLICA, Nerva OR. AR. Macrin OR. AR. Alex. Sévère OR. AR. P.B Valérien B. Gallien B. Tacite P.B. Probus P.B. Magnia Urbica P.B. Carausius P.B. (avec S. C.) Adrien M.B. Antonin G.B. M.B. Macrin G.B. M.B. Alex. Sévère G.B. M.B. Balbin M.B. Pupien G.B.
SALVS. PVBL. P. M. TR. P. S. C. Macrin G.B.
SALVS RAEPVBLICAE. Fausta P.B.
SALVS REIP. Valentinien I OR Valens OR. Nepos OR.Q.
SALVS REIPVBLIC. Jean P.B.
SALVS REPVBLICAE. Constantin I AR.M. Fausta OR. P.B. Crispus (hybride) P.B. Constance II P.B.Q. Valentinien I AR.M. Valens AR.M. Valentinien II P.B. P.B.Q. Théodose I P.B.Q Flaccille OR. OR.T. AR. M.B. P.B.Q. Engène P.B. Honorius AR. OR.B.Q. Placidie OR.M. OR. OR.Q. AR. P.B.Q. Jean P.B. Valentinien III OR. OR.Q. P.B.Q. Eudoxie OR. Honoria OR.Q Sévère III OR.Q. Anthémius OR (1). OR.Q. AR. Népos P.B. Augustule P.B.Q. (avec — PAX.) Anthémius OR (2). (avec VOT. X. MVLT. XX.) Valentinien III OR.Q.
SALVS REIPVBLICE. Anthémius OR (3). Placidie P.B.Q.
SALVS ROMANORVM. Eugène AR.
SALVS TR. POT. COS. II. Aelius AR. (avee S. C.) G.B. M.B.
SALVS TR. POT. V. IMP. II COS. II. Vérus AR.M.

___

(1) Variété avec RIEIPVBLICAE.
(2) Variété avec BAS pour PAX.
(3) Variété avec SALVS REPVBLICE.

SALVTARIS. Autonomes de Galba AR.
SALVT. AVG. Carausius P.B.
SALVTI AVG. Pesc. Niger AR. Sept. Sévère AR. (avec S. C.) Faustine mère M.B.
SALVTI AVG. COS. S. C. Sept. Sévère BR.
SALVTI AVG. COS. TRIB. POT. S. Ç. Marc Aurèle G.B. Faustine jeune (*hybride*) G.B.
SALVTI AVG. COS. II. Albin AR.
SALVTI AVG. COS. III. Marc Aurèle AR (avec S. C.) G.B. M.B. Commode G.B.
SALVTI AVG. COS IIII. Antonin AR. (avec S. C.) G B.
SALVTI AVGG. Sept. Sévère AR. (avec S. C.) G.B.
SALVTI AVGVS. Pesc. Niger AR.
SALVTI AVGVSTAE. Faustine jeune OR. (avec S. C) Faustine mère M B. Marc
    Aurèle G.B Faustine jeune G.B. M.B. Vérus (*hybride*) G.B.
SALVTI AVGVSTI. Pesc. Niger AR. Alex. Sévère BR.M. (avec S. C.) Titus G.B. Do-
    mitien M.B.
SALVTI AVGVSTOR. TR. P. II. COS. II. Vérus OR. (avec S. C.) G.B.
SALVTI AVGVSTOR. TR. P. III. COS. II. Vérus OR.
SALVTI AVGVSTOR. TR. P. XVI. (ou XVII.) COS. III. Marc Aurèle OR. (avec S. C.)
    G.B. M.B.
SALVTI AVGVSTOR. TR. P. XVIII. COS. III. Marc Aurèle OR.
SALVTIS. Autonomes de Galba OR.
SANCT. DEO SOLIS ELAGABAL. Elagabale OR. AR.
SANCTO NILO. Autonomes de Julien II P.B.Q. de Julien II et Hélène II P.B.
SAPIENTIA PRINCIPIS. Licinius père P.B.Q. Constantina I P.B Q.
SARAPIDI COMITI AVG. Postume B.
SARMATIA DEVICTA. Constantin I P.B. Crispus P.B. Constantin II P.B.
SARMATIA. — GAVDIVM ROMANORVM. Constantin II OR.Q. AR.
SARMATIS DEVICTIS. Constantin I P.B.
S. C. (*sans autre légende*). Sextus Pompée OR.Q. Auguste OR. AR. G.B. M.B.
    Agrippa M.B. Tibère M.B. Caligula M.B. Claude I G.B. M.B. Britannicus G.B.
    Agrippine jeune G.B. M.B. Néron G.B. M.B. Galba G B. M.B. Vitellius G.B. M.B.
    Vespasien OR. AR. G.B. M.B. P.B. Titus G.B. M.P. P.B. Domitien G.B M.B. P.B.
    Domitia P.B. Nerva P.B. Trajan G.B. P.B. P.B.Q. Adrien G.B. M.B. P.B. P.B.Q.
    Sabine AR. G.B. M.B. P.B. Antonin G.B. M.B. Faustine mère G.B. M.B. Marc
    Aurèle G.B. M.B Faustine jeune BR.M. G.B. M.B. Vérus G.B. M.B. Commode
    M.B. Sept. Sévère M.B. Caracalla M.B. Trajan Dèce P.B. Gallien AR.M. G.B.
    M.B. Tessères P. B.
S. C. S. P. Q. R. Auguste M.B. Néron M.B.
SCYTIA S. C. Antonin G.B. M.B.
SEC. ORB. P. M. TR. P. XIIII. COS. V. DES. VI. Commode OR. AR.
SECORITAS REIPVBLICAE. Jovien OR.
SECVLO FELICI. AVG. N. — VOT XX. MVL. Maxence P.B.
SECVLVM. Tétricus fils P.B.
SECVND. DECEM. ANNALES COS. IIII. S. C. Antonin G.B.
SECVPITAS PEIPETVAE. Constantin I OR.
SECVR. AVG. PONT. MAX. TR. POT. COS. III. S. C. Adrien G.B.
SECVRITAS. Faustine mère BR.M.
SECVRITAS AVG. Adrien OR. Trajan Dèce AR. Volusien AR. Gallien OR. M.B.
    Salonine B. Florien P.B. (avec S. C.) Titus M.B Antonin G.B. M.B. Gordien III
    G.B. M.B. Galllen G.B. M.B. Florien M.B.
SECVRITAS AVGG. Gordien d'Afrique père AR. Gordien d'Afrique fils AR. Hé-
    rennius AR. Hostilien AR Tréb. Galle AR. BR.M. (?) Victorin B. Licinius père
    OR. P.B. Constantin I † P.B. (avec S. C.) Gordien d'Afrique père G.B. Gordien
    d'Afrique fils G.B. Hostilien G.B. Tréb. Galle G.B. Volusien G.B. Gallien G.B.
SECVRITAS AVGVSTI. Néron M.B. (avec S. C.) M.B. Vespasien M.B. Titus M.B. Do-
    mitien M.B.
SECVRITAS AVGVSTI. N. Constantin I BR.M.
SECVRITAS AVGVST. S. C. Titus M.B. Domitien M.B.
SECVRITAS IMPERII. Julie Domne AR. (avec S. C.) Géta M.B.
SECVRITAS IMP. GERMAN. Vitellius OR.

SECVRITAS ORBIS. Philippe père AR. Probus P.B. Dioclétien OR. Galère Maximien AR. (avec S. C.) Gallien G.B.

SECVRITAS PERP. Carausius P.B.

SECVRITAS PERPE. Probus P B.

SECVRITAS PERPETV. Gordien III AR.

SECVRITAS PERPETVA. Caracalla OR. AR. P.B. Gordien III AR. Claude II P.B Probus P.B. Constantin I BR.M. Constant I OR.M. Constance II OR.M. (avec S C.) Caracalla G.B. M.B. Alex. Sévère G.B. M.B. Gordien III G.B.

SECVRITAS PERPETVAE. Constantin I OR.M. Constantin II OR.M.

SECVRITAS P. R. Autonomes de Galba AR. Othon OR. AR. Vespasien OR. Tacite P.B. (avec S. C.) Titus M.B. Domitien M.B.

SECVRITAS P. ROMANI S. C. Galba M B. Vitellius M.B.

SECVRITAS PVB. (ou PVBL.). Gallien B.

SECVRITAS PVBLICA. Sept. Sévère AR. P.B. Caracalla AR. Gordien III OR. AR. Carus P.B. Hanniballien P.B. (avec S. C.) Antonin G.B. M.B. Sept. Sévère G.B M.B.

SECVRITAS PVBLICA. IMP. VI. COS. III. S. C. Marc Aurèle G.B.

SECVRITAS PVBLICA TR. F. VI. (ou VII) IMP. IIII. COS. III. P. P. Commode OR.

SECVRITAS REIP. Constant I P.B.Q. Constance II P.B.Q. Valentinien I AR.M.

SECVRITAS REIPVB. Constant I P.B.Q. Julien II G.B. Procope OR.

SECVRITAS REIPVBL. Constance II P.B.Q.

SECVRITAS REIPVBLICAE. Licinius fils OR.Q. Constantin I OR. OR.Q. Crispus OR. P.B. Constantin II OR. Constant I OR. OR.Q. Constance II OR. P.B.Q. Magnence AR.M. Valentinien I P.B. Valens OR.Q. AR. P.B. Gratien P.B. Valentinien II P.B. (avec VOT. V. MVL. (ou MVLT.) X.) Jovien OR.

SECVRITAS REIPVBLICE. Hélène I OR. P.B. Fausta P.B. Jovien OR. Valentinien I P.B. (avec — VOT. V. MVL. (ou MVLT.) X.) Jovien OR.

SECVRITAS ROMAE. Autonomes de Rome (Constantin) G.B.M.

SECVRITAS SAECVLI. Elagabale AR. Florien P.B. Probus OR.

SECVRITAS SECVLI. Probus P.B.

SECVRITAS TEMPORVM. Caracalla AR. Macrin OR. AR. (avec S. C.) G.B. M.B.

SECVRITATI PERPETVAE. Caracalla OR. Constantin I BR.M. (avec S. C.) Caracalla G.B. M.B.

SECVRIT. AVG. Gallien B (1). Claude II P.B. Quintille P.B. Aurélien P.B. P.B.Q. Numérien P.B.

SECVRIT. AVGG. Dioclétien P.B. Maximien Hercule P.B. Constance Chlore P.B. Galère Maximien P.B.

SECVRIT. IMPERI. Elagabale AR.

SECVRIT. IMPERII. Caracalla AR. Géta OR. AR. AR.Q.

SECVRIT. ORB. P. M. TR. P. XIIII. IMP. VIII. COS. V. P. P. S. C. Commode G.B.

SECVRIT. ORB. P. M. TR. P. XIIII. IMP. VIII. COS. V. DES. VI. S. C. Commode G.B.

SECVRIT. ORBIS. Caracalla OR. AR. Géta AR. Philippe père OR. AR. Otacilie OR AR. Etruscille AR. Gallien OR. B (2) Carausius P.B. (avec S. C.) Philippe père G.B. Gallien B.M.

SECVRIT. PEPRET. DD. NN. Galère Maximien M.B.

SECVRIT. PERP. Gordien III OR. AR. Probus P.B. Dioclétien P.B. Maximien Hercule P.B. Carausius P.B.

SECVRIT. PERPE. Probus P.B.

SECVRIT. PERPET. Valérien B. B.Q. Gallien OR.Q. B. B.Q. M.B. Salonine B. Valérien jeune B. Tacite P.B. (avec S. C.) Gordien III G.B. M.B.

SECVRIT. PERPET. DD. NN. Maximin II †.M.B. Constantin I M.B.

SECVRIT. PVBLICA. Tacite P.B.

SECVRIT. PVB. TR. P. XIIII. IMP. VIII. COS. V. P. P. Commode BR.M.

SECVRIT. PVB. TR. P. XXIX. IMP. VIII. COS. III. Marc Aurèle AR.

SECVRIT. PVB. TR. P. XXX. IMP. VIII. COS. III. S. C. Marc Aurèle M.B.

SECVR. ORB.P. M. TR. P. XIIII. COS. V. P. P. Commode AR.

SECVR. PVB. COS. III. P. P. Adrien AR.

(1) Variété avec SECVRT. AVG.
(2) Variété avec SECVRIT OBIS.

SECVR. TEMPO. Gallien B.
SENAT. P. Q. R. — CL. V. Auguste AR.
SENATVS. Constantin I OR.M.
SENATVS PIETATI AVGVSTI S. C. Galba G.B.
SENATVS POPVLVSQVE ROMANVS S. C. Trajan G.B. M.B. Adrien G.B.
SENATVS POPVLVSQVE ROMANVS VOTA SVSCEPTA Adrien BR M.
SENATVS P. Q. ROMANVS. Auguste AR. Autonomes de Galba AR. Vitellius OR.
SERAPIDI COMITI AVG. Gallien G.B.
SERAPIDI CONSERV. AVG. Commode OR. AR.
SERAPIDI CONSERV. AVG. COS. VI. P. P S C. Commode G.B. M.B.
SERAPI. COMITI AVG. Postume OR. B
SER. GALBA IMP. Galba AR.
SER. SVLPICI GALBAE AVG. Galba AR.
SER. SVLPICIVS GALBA AVG. Galba AR.
SERV. GALBA. Galba OR.
SEVERI AVG. PII FIL. Caracalla OR. AR. BR.M. (avec S. C.) G.B. M.B.
SEVERI PII AVG FIL. Caracalla OR. AR. Géta OR. AR. (avec S. C.) Caracalla G.B.
    M.B. Géta G.B. M.B.
SEVERI TI... Julie Domne AR.
SICILIA. Clodius Macer AR. Adrien G.B.
SICILIA COS. II. P. P. S. C. Antonin G.B. M.B.
SIC X. SIC XX. Maximien Hercule P.B.Q. Galère Maximien P.B.Q. Maximin II
    P.B.Q. Licinius père OR. Constantin I OR. Constance II OR.Q.
SIDERIBVS RECEPTA. Faustine jeune BR.M. (avec S. C.) G.B.
SIGNA P. R Autonomes de Galba OR. AR.
SIGNIS PARTHICIS RECEPTIS. Auguste OR. AR.
SIGNIS RECEPT. DEVICTIS GERM. S. C. Germanicus M.B.
SIGNIS RECEPTIS. Auguste OR. AR. (avec S. C.) Vespasien G.B.
SIGNIS RECEPTIS S. P. Q. R. CL. V. Auguste OR. AR.
SI. ITER. PONTIF. TR. S. C. — PROVIDENT. Drusus M.B.
SIS. (sans autre légende). Constantin II OR. Constant I OR.
SISCIA AVG. Gallien B.
SISCIA PROBI AVG. Probus P.B.
S. M. VRB. AVGG. ET CAESS. NN. Maximien Hercule M.B. Constance Chlore M.B
SOL. AVG. Claude II P.B.
SOL. DOM. IMP. ROMANI. Aurélien M.B.
SOL. DOMINVS IMPERII ROMANI. Aurélien M.B.
SOLE INVICT. Maximin II †.M.B.
SOLE INVICTO. Maximin II OR. M.B. †.M.B.
SOLI COMITI AVGG. NN. Constantin I OR.
SOLI COMITI AVG. N. Constantin I OR.
SOLI COMTI AVG. Gallien B.
SOLI CONS. AVG. Gallien B. Claude II P.B.Q.
SOLI CONSER Tétricus fils P.B.
SOLI CONSERVATORI. Aurélien P.B.
SOLI INVIC. COMITI AVG. COS. IIII. Probus BR.M.
SOLI INVI. COM. AVG. Probus P.B.
SOLI INVICTAE. Galère Maximien M.B. Maximin II †.M.B.
SOLI INVICT. COM. D. N. Constantin I P.B.
SOLI INVICT. CONSERVAT. AVGG. ET CAESS. NN. Maximin II OR Q.
SOLI INVICTO. Gallien OR.Q. B. Aurélien BR.M. P.B. Probus OR. BR.M. P.B. Dio-
    clétien OR. Carausius P.B. Galère Maximien OR.M. OR. Maximin II OR. M.B
    †.M.B. Licinius père †.M.B. Constantin I †.P.B. P.B. Crispus OR.
SOLI INVICTO A. Probus P.B.
SOLI INVICTO AETERNO AVG. Constantin I OR.Q.
SOLI INVICTO AVG. Probus P.B.
SOLI INVICTO COMITI. Maximin II AR. BIL. †.M.B. †.P.B. P B. P.B.Q. Licinius père
    P.B. Constantin I OR.M. OR. †.P.B. P.B. Crispus P.B. Constantin II OR.M. P.B.
SOLI INVICTO COMITI AVG. Probus OR. P.B.

SOLI INVICTO CONSERVAT. AVGG. ET CAESS. NN. Sévère II OR.M.

SOLI INVICTO NK. Maximin II OR.

SOLI INVICTO NK. VL. XC. Maximin II OR.

SOLI INVICTO VMI. Maximin II OR.

SOLI INVICTO P. XV. Gallien B.

SOLI INVICTO VII. C. Gallien B.

SOL. INVICTO. Macrien jeune BIL. Quiétus OR. BIL.

SOLI PROPVGNATORI. Elagabale OR.

SOLVS AVG. Claude II P.B.

SOROR CONSTANTINI AVG. — PIETAS PVBLICA Constantia P.B.

SPE. AVG. COS. II. Albin AR.

SPEI FIRM. Pesc. Niger AR.

SPEI PERPETVAE. Caracalla OR. AR. Géta AR. Elagabale AR Postume B. M.B. Tétricus fils OR. (avec S. C.) Caracalla G.B. M.B.

SPEI TRIB. P. II. COS. II. P. P. Elagabale AR.

SPE. PVBLIC. Carausius P.B.

SPES. Diaduménien OR.Q (avec S. C.) G.B.

SPES AVG. Tétricus père BIL.. P.B P.B.Q. Tétricus fils P.B. Claude II P.B. Tacite P.B. Probus P.B. Carin OR. Carausius P.B. Allectus OR. P.B.

SPES AVG. COS. II. Albin AR.

SPES AVGG. Tétricus père BIL. P.B. Tétricus fils OR OR.Q. BIL P.B. P.B.Q. Numérien OR. Carin OR.

SPES AVGGG. Théodose I P.B.

SPES AVG. N. Probus P.B.

SPES AVGVSTA S. C. Néron Drusus G.B. Claude I G.B. Vespasien G.B. Adrien G.B. Alex. Sévère M.B.

SPES AVGVSTI NOSTRI. Probus P.B.

SPES AVGVSTOR. Philippe fils AR.

SPES FELICITATIS ORBIS. Philippe père AR.

SPES P. R. Adrien OR. AR. (avec S. C.) G.B. M.B. (avec — VOT. V. MVL. X.) Valens OR.

SPES PROBI AVG. Probus P.B.

SPES PVBL. Carausius P.B.

SPES PVBLIC. Claude II P.B.

SPES PVBLICA. Marc Aurèle BR.M. Commode OR. AR. Caracalla OR. AR. Géta OR. AR. Diaduménien OR. AR. Elagabale AR. Elagabale et Aquilia Sévéra BR.M.Alex. Sévère OR. AR. AR.Q.M.B. P.B. Philippe père AR. Philippe fils AR. Hérennius AR.M. AR. Hostilien AR. Emilien AR. Valérien B. Gallien B. B.Q. Salonin B. Macrien jeune BIL. Quiétus BIL. Postume B. Victorin B. Tétricus père OR. BIL. P.B. P.B.Q. Tétricus père et fils P.B. Tétricus fils OR. P.B. Claude II OR. B. P.B. Tacite P.B. Probus P.B. Carus OR. P.B. Numérien P.B. Dioclétien OR. Carausius P.B. Allectus P.B. Licinius fils P.B. Constantin I OR. P.B. (avec S. C.) Commode G.B. M.B. Diaduménien G.B. M.B. Alex. Sévère M.B. Maximin I G.B. Philippe fils M.B. Emilien G.B. M.B.

SPES PVPLI. Tétricus fils P.B.

SPES REIP..... Constance Galle M.B.

SPES REIPVBL. Constantin I P.B.

SPES REIPVBLICAE. Constantin I P.B. Fausta OR.M. OR. P.B. Constantin II AR. Constant I OR. Valens P.B. Valentinien II P.B.Q.

SPES REIPVBLICE. Constant I P.B.Q. Constance II AR. P.B. Julien II AR. P.B.

SPES ROMANORVM. Théodose I AR. Mag. Maximus AR. P.B. Victor AR. P.B. Eugène P.B.Q. Honorius P.B.Q.

SPES R. P. — VOT. V. MVL. X. Valens OR.

S. POMP. Sextus Pompée OR.Q.

S. P. Q. R. Auguste OR. AR. Autonomes de Galba OR. AR. Galba OR. AR. Vespasien OR. AR. Gallien OR. (avec S. C) Adrien G.B. Faustine jeune G.B. Julie Domne G.B.

S. P. Q. R. ADSERTORI LIBERTATIS PVBLIC. (ou PVBLICAE). Vespasien G.B.

S. P. Q. R. AMPLIATORI CIVIVM. Antonin BR.M.

S. P. Q. R. AN. F. F. HADRIANO AVG. P. P. Adrien G.B.M.
S. P. Q. R. AN. F. F. OPTIMO PRINCIPI. Antonin BR.M.
S. P. Q. R. ANN. N. F. F. OPTIMO PRINCIPI PIO S. C. Alex. Sévère M.B.
S. P. Q. R. CL. V. Auguste OR. AR.
S. P. Q. R. EX. S. C. Adrien G.B.
S. P. Q. R. IMP. CAES. Auguste AR.
S. P. Q. R. LAETITIAE C. V. S. C. Commode G.B.
S. P. Q. R. MEMORIAE AGRIPPINAE. Agrippine mère G.B.
S. P. Q. R. OB CIVES SERVAT. Galba M.B.
S. P. Q. R. OB CIVES SERVATOS. Galba G.B. M.B. Vespasien G.B.
S. P. Q. R. OB. CIV. SER. Galba G.B. M.B. Vitellius G.B. Vespasien G.B. Titus M.B. Trajan G.B.
S. P. Q. R. OB C. S. Auguste AR. Autonomes de Galba AR. Galba OR. AR. Vitellius OR. AR. Vespasien OR. AR.
S. P. Q. R. OPTIMO PRINC. Trajan OR. Sept. Sévère OR. Maximin II †.M.B.
S. P. Q. R. OPTIMO PRINCIPI. Trajan OR. OR.Q. AR. AR.Q. Sept. Sévère AR. Gallien B. G.B. M.B. Maximin II P.B. Alexandre (usurpateur) †.M.B. Licinius père P.B. Constantin I OR.Q. P.B. †.P.B. (avec s. c.) Trajan G.B. M.B. Antonin M.B. Sept. Sévère G.B.
S. P. Q. R. PARENT. CONS. SVO. Auguste AR.
S. P. Q. R. P. P. OB CIVES SERVATOS. Caligula G.B. Vespasien G B.
S. P. Q. R. P. P. OB C. S. Caligula OR. AR. Claude I OR. AR. Albin AR.
S. P. Q. R. SIGNIS RECEPTIS IMP. IX. TR. PO. (ou POT.) V. Auguste AR.M.
S. P. R. Q. Auguste AR.
SVMMVS SACERDOS AVG. Elagabale AR.
SYRIA COS. II. S. C. Antonin G.B.
T. CAESAR. Vespasien AR.
T. CAES. DIVI VESP. F. AVG. P. M. TR. P. COS. VIII. — REST. S. C. Auguste G.B.
T. DIVO AVG. DIVI VESP. F. VESPASIANO. Domitien G.B.
TELLVS STABIL. Adrien OR. AR. BR.M. (avec S. C.) G.B. M.B.
TELLVS STABILITA. Faustine jeune BR.M.
TELLVS STABIL. P. M. TR. P. XII. IMP. VIII. COS. V. P. P. Commode BR.M.
TELLVS STAB. P. M. TR. POT. VIII. COS. II. P. P. S. C. Sept. Sévère M.B.
TEMP. FELICITAS. Quintille OR. Probus OR.M.
TEMP. FELIC. P. M. TR. P. XV. COS. VI. Commode AR.
TEMP. FELIC. P. M. TR. P. XV. IMP. VIII. COS. VI. P. P. Commode OR.
TEMP. FELIC. P. M. TR. P. XV. IMP. VIII. COS. VI. S. C. Commode M.B.
TEMPL. DIVI AVG. REST. COS. IIII. Antonin OR. AR.(avec S. C.) G.B. M.B.
TEMPLVM DIV. AVG. RES. COS. IIII. Antonin OR. AR. (avec S. C.) G.B. M.B.
TEMPORA FELIC. Allectus P.B.
TEMPOR. FEL. Constance Chlore P.B.
TEMPOR. FELI. Claude II P.B. Quintille P.B.
TEMPOR. FELIC. Faustine jeune OR. AR. Claude II P.B. Probus P.B. (avec S. C.) Faustine jeune G.B. M.B.
TEMPOR. FELIC. P. M. TR. P. XV. IMP. VIII. COS. VI. S. C. Commode G.B.
TEMPOR. FELICI. Probus OR. AR.
TEMPOR. FELICIT. Probus P.B. Doclétien OR. Maximien Hercule P.B. Constance Chlore P.B. Galère Maximien P.B.
TEMPOR. FELICITAS. Géta AR. Allectus P.B.
TEMPOR. FELICIT. P. M. TR. P. XV. IMP. VIII. COS. VI. P. P. Commode BR.M.
TEMPORVM F. Carausius P.B.
TEMPORVM FEL. Elagabale AR. Maesa AR. Dioclétien P.B. Carausius P.B.
TEMPORVM FELI. Claude II P.B. Quintille P.B. Carausius P.B.
TEMPORVM FELIC. Claude II P.B. Carausius P.B. Allectus P.B.
TEMPORVM FELICIT. Commode BR.M. Carausius AR. P.B (1). Allectus P.B.
TEMPORVM FELICITAS. Adrien BR.M. Marc Aurèle BR.M. Annius Vérus et Commode BR.M. Commode BR.M. M.B.M. Commode et Marcia (?) BR.M. Elagabale

(1) Variété avec TEMPORVM FELILIT.

AR. Alex. Sévère AR. Alex. Sévère et Mamée BR.M. Mamée M.B.M. Gordien III BR.M. Otacilie BR.M. Valérien B. Gallien BR.M. Lélien OR. Marius B. Tacite BR.M. P.B. Florien P.B. Probus BR.M. P.B. Maximien Hercule M.B. Carausius P.B. Galère Maximien M.B. Maximin II M.B. Constantin I M.B.

TEMPORVM FELICITAS AVG. N. Maxence OR. AR.

TEMPORVM FELICITAS COS. IIII. Antonin OR. (avec S. C.) G.B. M.B.

TEMPORVM FELICITAS P. M. TR. P. VIIII. IMP. VII. COS. IIII. P. P. Commode BR.M.

TEMPORVM FELICITAS TR. P. VIII. (ou VIIII.) IMP. VI. COS. IIII. P. P. S. C. Commode G.B.

T. ET DOM. C. EX S. C. Vespasien G.B.

T. ET DOMITIAN CAESARES PRINC. (ou PRIN.) IVVEN. S. C. Vespasien G.B. M.B.

THRACIA COS. II. S. C. Antonin G.B.

TIBERIS S. C. Antonin BR.M. G.B.

TIBERIS TR. POT. COS. III. S. C. Antonin M.B.

TI. CAESAR AVG. F. TR. POT. XV. Auguste OR. AR.

TI. CAESAR DIVI. AVG. F. AVG. P. M. TR. POT. XXIIII. S. C. Livie M.B.

TI. CAESAR DIVI. AVG. F. AVGVST. P. M. TR. POT. XXIII. S. C. Agrippa M.B. Drusus jeune M.B.

TI. CAESAR DIVI AVG. F. AVGVST. P. M. TR. POT. XXIIII. S. C. Auguste G.B. Livie G.B. Agrippa M.B. Tibère G.B.

TI. CAESAR DIVI. AVG. F. AVGVST. P. M. TR. POT. XXXV. S. C. Livie G.B.

TI. CAESAR DIVI. AVG. F AVGVST. P. M. TR. POT. XXXVI. S. C. Auguste G.B. Livie G.B. Tibère G.B.

TI. CAESAR DIVI. AVG. F. AVGVST. P. M. TR. POT. XXXVII. S. C. Auguste G.B. Tibère G.B.

TI. CAESAR DIVI. AVG. F. AVGVST. P. M. TR. POT. XXXIIX. S. C. Auguste G.B. Tibère G.B.

TI. CAESAR. DIVI. AVG. F. IMP. VIII. — TRIB. POT. XXXVIII. PONT. MAX. Tibère M.B.

TI. CLAV. CA. AVG. P. M. TR. P. S. C. Antonia M.B.

TI. CLAVDIVS CAESAR AVG. Claude I P.B. (avec P. N. R.) P.B.

TI. CLAVDIVS CAESAR AVG. GERM. P. M TR. P. IMP. P. P. S. C. Germanicus G.B. M.B Agrippine mere G.B.

TI. CLAVDIVS CAESAR AVG. P. M. TR. P. IMP. P. P. S. C. Drusus l'Ancien G B. Antonia M.B.

TI. CLAVDIVS CAESAR AVG P. M. TR. P. IMP S. C. Drusus l'Ancien G.B. Antonia M.B.

TI. CLAVDIVS CAESAR AVGVSTVS. Claude I P.B.

T. IMP. CAESAR COS. DES. II. CAESAR DOMIT. COS. DES. II. S. C. Vespasien G.B.

T. IMP. CAESAR DOMITIANVS AVG. F. COS DESIG. II. S. C. Vespasien G.B.

TITVS ET CAESAR DOMITIANVS S. C. Vespasien G.B.

TITVS ET DOMITIAN CAESARES PRIN. IVEN. (sic) (IVIN. (sic) ou IVVEN). Vespasien OR. AR.

TITVS ET DOMITIAN. CAES. PRIN. IV. (IVEN (sic) ou IVVEN). Vespasien OR. AR.

TITVS ET DOMITIANVS CAES. PRIN. IV. Vespasien AR.

TITVS ET DOMITIANVS PRINC. IVN. (sic). Vespasien OR.

TITVS IMP. AVG. DOMITIANVS S. C. Vespasien G.B.

TR. (sans autre légende) Constant I OR. Constance II OR. AR.

TRAIANI PARTHICI. Plotine OR.Q.

TRAIECTVS AVG. Gordien III BR.M. M.B.

TRAIECTVS AVGG. Carin BR.M.

TRAIECTVS PONTIF. TR. P. VII. COS. III. Caracalla M.B.M.

TRANQVILLITAS AVG. Antonin AR. Tacite P.B.

TRANQVILLITAS AVG. COS. III. Adrien AR. (avec S. C.) M.B.

TRANQVILLITAS AVG. COS. III. P. P. Adrien AR. (avec S. C) M B.

TRANQVILLITAS AVGG. Philippe père AR. (avec S. C.) G.B.

TRANQ. TR. POT. XIIII. (ou XV.) COS. IIII. Antonin AR.

TR. B P. CONS. IIII. P. P. Constantin I P.B.

TRES GALLIAE. Galba AR.

TRIB. P. COS. II. P. P. Elagabale OR.

TRIB. POT. COS. Antonin OR.Q. AR. (avec S. C.) M.B.
TRIB. POT. COS. DES. II. Antonin AR. (avec S. C.) G.B. M.B.
TRII:. POT. COS. P. P. Gallien OR.
TRIB. POT. COS. II. Aelius OR. Antonin OR. Gallien OR. (avec S. C.) Aelius G.B
TRIB. POT. COS. III. Antonin OR.
TRIB. POT. P. P. S. C. Néron P.B.
TRIB. POT. VIII. COS. III Gallien B.
TRI. PONT. Titus OR.
TRI. POT. Vespasien AR. AR.Q.
TRI. POT. COS. P. P. Probus OR.
TRI POT. II. COS. III. P. P. Vespasien OR. AR.
TRIVMFATOR GENT. BARB. Valentinien I OR. Valens AR.M. Valentinien II AR.M. Théodose I AR.M. Honorius AR.M.
TRIVMFATOR GENTIVM BARBARARVM. Constant I OR.M. AR.M. Constance II AR.M. Magnence AR.M.
TRIVMFVS CAESARVM. Constant I M.B
TRIVMP. AVG. Vespasien OR.
TRIVMPHVS PARTHICVS. Trajan OR.
TRIVNFV. QVADOR. Numérien BR.M.
TR. P. COS. Sept. Sévère OR.Q. AR.Q.
TR. P. COS. II. Antonin AR. (avec S. C.) Trajan G.B.
TR. P. COS. II. P. P. Trajan OR. AR. (avec S. C.) G.B. M.B.
TR. P. COS. III. Antonin OR.Q.
TR. P. COS. III. DES. IIII. Antonin OR.
TR. P. COS. III. (ou IIII.) P. P. Trajan AR.
TR. P. COS. V. P. P. Trajan OR.
TR. P. COS. VII. Domitien AR.
TR. P. COS. VII. DES. VIII. P. P. Titus AR. Domitien OR. AR. (avec S. C.) G.B. M.B.
TR. P. COS. VIII. DES. VIIII. P. P. S. C. Domitien G.B. M.B
TR. P. COS. VIII. P. P. Domitien AR.
TR. P. II. COS. P. P. Commode AR.
TR. P. II. COS. S. C. Commode G.B.
TR. P. II. IMP. COS. P. P. Commode OR AR.
TR. P II. IMP. II. COS. P. P. S. C. Commode G.B. M.B
TR. P. II. IMP. II. COS. S. C. Commode G.B.
TR. P. II. IMP. II. COS. II. P. P. Commode AR.
TR. P. II. P. P. COS. II. Elagabale AR.
TR. P. III. COS. II. Marc Aurèle OR. M.B.M. (avec S. C.) M.B.
TR. P. III. COS. II. P. P. Géta OR. AR. P.B. (avec S. C) G.B.
TR. P. III. IMP. II. COS. P P. Commode OR. AR. (avec S. C.) M.B.
TR. P. III. IMP. II. COS. II. Vérus OR. AR.
TR. P. III. IMP. V. COS. FI. Sept. Sévère AR.
TR. P. III. IMP. V. COS. II. Sept. Sévère AR.
TR. P. III. IMP. V. COS VIIII. P.P. Domitien AR.
TR. P. III. IMP. VI. COS. II. Sept. Sévère AR.
TR. P. IIII. COS. II. P. P. S. C. Géta M.B.
TR. P. IIII. IMP. II. COS. P. P. Commode AR.
TR. P. IIII. IMP. II. COS. II. Vérus OR. AR. AR.Q. (avec S. C) G.B. M.B. (avec VIC. AVG.) OR. (avec VIC. AVG. S. C.) G.B M.B.
TR. P. IIII. IMP. III. COS. II. P. P. Commode OR. AR.
TR. P. V. IMP. II COS. II. Vérus OR. AR. (avec VIC. AVG.) OR.
TR. P. V. IMP. III. COS. II. Vérus OR. OR.Q. AR. P.B. Sept. Sévère OR. AR.
TR. P. V. IMP. III. COS. II. P. P. Commode OR. AR. (avec S. C.) M.B.
TR. P. V. IMP. IIII. COS. P. P. Commode BR.M.
TR. P. V. IMP. IIII. COS. II P. P. Commode OR. OR.Q. AR. (avec S. C) G.B.
TR. P. VI. COS. II. Sept. Sévère AR.
TR. P. VI. IMP. III. COS. II. Vérus OR. AR. BR.M. (avec S. C.) M.B.
TR. P. VI. IMP IIII. COS. II. Vérus OR. (avec VIC. PAR.) OR.
TR. P. VI. IMP. IIII. COS. III. Vérus BR.M. Commode OR.Q.

TR. P. VI. IMP. IIII. COS. III. P. P Commode OR .OR.Q. AR. AR.Q. BR.M. (avec S. C.) G.B. M.B.

TR. P. VII. COS. II. P. P. Sept. Sévère OR.

TR. P. VII. COS. III. Vérus OR.Q. AR.Q.

TR. P VII. IMP. IIII. COS. III. Vérus OR. AR. BR.M. (avec S. C.) G.B. (avec — VIC. PAR.) OR.

TR. P. VII. IMP IIII COS. III. P. P. Commode OR.Q. AR. (avec S. C.) G.B. M.B.

TR. P. VII. IMP. IIII. COS. IIII. DES. V. P. P. S. C. Trajan G.B.

TR. P. VII. IMP IIII. COS. V. P. P S. C. Trajan G.B. M.B.

TR. P. VII. IMP. V. COS. III. P. P. Commode AR. (avec S. C.) G.B. M.B.

TR. P. VIII. IMP. II. COS. IIII. P. P. Commode AR.

TR. P. VIII. IMP. IIII. COS. III. Vérus OR. AR. AR.Q. BR.M. (avec S. C.) M.B.

TR. P. VIII. IMP. V. COS. III. S. C. Vérus M.B

TR. P. VIII. IMP. V. COS. IIII. P. P. Commode OR. AR. BR.M. (avec S. C.) G.B. M.B.

TR. P. VIII. IMP VI COS. IIII. P. P Commode OR. OR.Q. AR. AR.Q. BR.M. (avec S. C.) G.B. M.B.

TR. P. VIIII. IMP. COS. VII. P. P. Titus OR. AR.

TR. P. VIIII. IMP. II. COS. IIII. P. P. Commode AR.

TR. P. VIIII. IMP. V. COS. III. Vérus BR.M. (avec S. C.) M.B.

TR. P. VIIII. IMP. V COS. IIII. P. P. Commode BR.M.

TR. P. VIIII. IMP. VI. COS. IIII. P. P. Commode AR. P.B. (avec S. C.) G.B. M.B.

TR. P. VIIII. IMP. XIIII. COS. VII. Titus OR. AR.

TR. P. VIIII. IMP. XIIII. (ou XV.) COS. VII. P. P. Titus OR. AR.

TR. P. IX. IMP. C. Vespasien AR.

TR. P. IX. IMP. XV. COS. VII. P. P. Titus OR. AR.

TR. P. IX. IMP. XV. COS. VIII. P. P. Titus OR. AR. Domitien AR.

TR. P. X. COS. V. P. P. Postume B.

TR. P. X. IMP. VII. COS. IIII. P. P. Commode AR.Q.

TR. P. XI. IMP. VII. COS V. P. P. S C. Commode G.B.

TR. P. XII. C. VI. P. P. Gallien M.B.

TR. P. XIII. COS. II. Marc Aurèle AR.

TR. P. XV. COS. III. Marc Aurèle AR.

TR. P. XV. IMP. III. COS. II. Vérus BR.M.

TR. P. XV. IMP. VIII. COS. VI. S. C. Commode M.B.

TR. P. XVII. IMP. II. COS. III. S. C. Marc Aurèle G.B. M.B.

TR. P. XVII. IMP IIII. COS. III. S. P. Q. R. — VIC. PARTH. Marc Aurèle BR.M.

TR. P. XVIII. COS. III. Marc Aurèle OR. OR.Q. AR. AR.Q. (avec S. C.) G.B.

TR. P. XVIII. IMP. II. COS. III. Marc Aurèle AR. (avec S. C.) G.B. M.B.

TR. P. XIX. IMP. II. COS. III. S. C. Marc Aurèle AR.

TR. P. XX. IMP. III. COS. III. Marc Aurèle BR.M. (avec S. C.) M.B.

TR. P. XX. IMP. IIII. COS. III. Marc Aurèle OR. AR. (avec S. C.) G.B.

TR. P. XXI. (ou XXII.) IMP. IIII. COS. III. Marc Aurèle OR. AR. BR.M. (avec S. C.) M.B.

TR. P. XXII. IMP. V. COS. III. Marc Aurèle OR. AR.

TR. P. XXIII. IMP. V. COS. III. Marc Aurèle OR. AR. BR.M. (avec S. C.) M.B.

TR. P. XXIIII. COS. III. Marc Aurèle OR.Q. AR.Q.

TR. P. XXIV. IMP. V. COS. III. P. P. S. C. Marc Aurèle M.B.

TR. P. XXVI. COS. III. Marc Aurèle AR.Q.

TR. P. XXVII. IMP. VII. COS. III. S. C. Maic Aurèle M.B.

TR. P. XXIX. IMP. VIII. COS. III. Marc Aurèle OR. AR. (avec S. C.) G.B. M.B.

TR. P. XXX. IMP. VIII. COS. III Marc Aurèle AR. AR.Q. (avec S. C.) G.B. M.B.

TR. P. XXX. IMP. VIII. COS. III. P. P. — FORT. REDVCI. Marc Aurèle AR.

TR. P. XXXI. IMP. VIII. (ou VIIII.) COS. III. P. P. Marc Aurèle AR.

TR. P. XXXII. (ou XXXIII.) IMP. VIIII. COS. III. P. P. Marc Aurèle OR. AR.

TR. P. XXXIII. IMP. X. COS. III. P. P. Marc Aurèle OR. AR. P.B.

TR. P. XXXIIII. IMP. X. COS. III. P. P. Marc Aurèle OR. AR. (avec S. C.) G.B. M.B.

TR. PON. P. P. S. C. Néron P.B.

TR. POT. COS. Commode AR. BR.M. P.B. (avec S. C.) G.B. M.B.

TR. POT. COS. ITER. Vespasien AR.

TR. POT. COS. II. Nerva AR.M. Trajan AR.M. BR.M. Aelius OR. OR.Q. AR. BR.M. Antonin OR. AR. Marc Aurèle OR. AR. Vérus OR. OR.Q. (avec S. C.) Trajan G.B. M.B. Aelius G.B. M.B. Antonin G.B. M.B. P.B. Faustine mère (*hybride*) G.B. Marc Aurèle G.B. M.B. Vérus G.B.

TR. POT. COS. II. COM. ASI. — ROM. ET AVG. Trajan AR.M.

TR. POT. COS. II. P. P. Antonin BR.M. (avec S. C.) Trajan G.B. M.B.

TR. POT. COS. III. Vespasien OR. Antonin OR. OR.Q. AR. (avec S. C.) Trajan M.B. Antohin G B. M B. P.B. Marc Aurèle G.B. M.B.

TR. POT. COS. III. CENSOR. Titus M.B.

TR. POT. COS. III. DES. IIII. Antonin AR. (avec S. C.) G B.

TR. POT. CQS. III. P. P. S. C. Trajan G.B. M.B.

TR. POT. COS. IIII. Antonin OR. OR.Q. AR. AR.Q. (avec S. C.) M.B.

TR. POT. COS. IIII. P. P. S. C. Trajan G.B. M.B.

TR. POT. COS. V. P. P. S. C. Trajan M.B.

TR. POT. COS. VI. CENSOR. S. C. Titus M.B.

TR. POT. COS. VIII. P. P. Domitien AR.

TR. POT. COS. VIIII. Vespasien OR. AR. Domitien AR.Q.

TR. POT. IMP. II. COS. VIII. DES. VIIII. P. P. Domitien OR. AR.

TR. POT. IMP. II. COS. VIII. DES. IX. P. P. Domitien OR.

TR. POT. P. P. S. C. Néron P.B.

TR. POT. II. COS. Commode AR. P.B.

TR. POT. II. COS. P. P. Commode OR.Q.

TR. POT. II. COS. II. Marc Aurèle OR. AR. Vérus OR.Q. (avec S. C.) Marc Aurèle G.B.

TR. POT. II. COS. II. P. P. Elagabale OR.

TR. POT. II. COS. VIIII. DES. P. P. S. C. Titus G.B.

TR. POT. II. COS. VIIII. DES. X. P. P. Domitien OR. AR.

TR. POT. III. COS II. Marc Aurèle OR. OR.Q. AR. BR.M. Vérus OR.Q. (avec S. C.) Marc Aurèle G.B. M B.

TR. POT. IIII. COS. II. Marc Aurèle AR. (avec S. C.) G.B. M.B.

TR. POT. IIII. IMP. II. COS. II. S. C. Vérus M.B.

TR. POT. V. IMP. II. (ou III.) COS. II. S. C. Vérus G.B. M.B.

TR. POT. VI. COS. II. Marc Aurèle OR. AR. (avec S. C.) G.B. M.B.

TR. POT. VI. IMP. III. COS. II. S. C. Vérus G.B. M.B.

TR. POT. VI. IMP. IIII. COS. II. S. C. — VIC. PAR. Vérus G.B. M.B.

TR. POT. VII. COS. II. Marc Aurèle OR. OR.Q. AR. BR.M. (avec S. C.) G.B.

TR. POT. VII. COS. VI. Titus AR.

TR. POT. VII. IMP. IIII. COS. III. Vérus OR. (avec S. C.) G.B. M.B.

TR. POT. VIII. COS. II. Marc Aurèle OR. AR. (avec S. C.) G.B. M.B.

TR. POT. VIII. COS. VII. Titus OR. AR.

TR. POT. VIII. IMP. IIII. (ou V.) COS. III. S. C. Vérus G.B. M.B.

TR. POT. VIIII. COS. II. Marc Aurèle OR. AR. BR.M. (avec S. C.) G.B. M.B.

TR. POT. VIIII. COS. III. S. C. Vérus G.B. M.B.

TR. P. VIIII. IMP. V. COS. III. S. C. Vérus G.B. M.B.

TR. POT. X. COS. II. Marc Aurèle OR. AR. (avec S. C.) G.B M.B.

TR. POT. X. COS. VIIII. Vespasien OR. AR.

TR. POT. XI. COS. II. Marc Aurèle OR. AR. (avec S. C.) G.B. M.B.

TR. POT. XI. COS. III. Sept. Sévère (*hybride*) AR.

TR. POT. XI. COS. IIII. Antonin OR. (avec S. C.) M.B.

TR. POT. XII. COS. II. Marc Aurèle OR. AR. BR.M. (avec S. C.) G.B. M.B.

TR. POT. XIII. COS. II. Auguste OR.Q.

TR. POT. XIII. COS. II. Marc Aurèle OR. AR. BR.M. (avec S. C.) G.B. M.B.

TR. POT. XIIII. Marc Aurèle BR.M.

TR. POT. XIIII. COS II. Marc Aurèle OR. OR.Q. AR. BR.M. (avec S. C.) G.B. M.B.

TR. POT. XIIII. COS. IIII. Antonin BR.M. Vérus (*hybride*) AR. (avec S. C.) Antonin G.B. M.B.

TR. POT. XV. Auguste OR.Q.

TR. POT. XV. COS. Marc Aurèle OR.

TR. POT. XV. COS. II. DESIG. III. Marc Aurèle OR.

TR. POT. XV. COS III. Marc Aurèle OR. AR. (avec S. C.) G.B. M.B.
TR. POT. XV. COS. IIII. Antonin OR. OR.Q. AR. (avec S. C.) G.B. M.B.
TR. POT. XVI. Auguste OR.Q.
TR. POT. XVI. COS. III. Marc Auréle OR.Q.
TR. POT. XVI. IMP. VII. Tibère OR. AR.
TR. POT. XVII. Auguste OR.Q. Tibère OR.Q.
TR. POT. XVII. COS. IIII. S. C. Antonin G.B.
TR. POT. XVII. IMP. VII. Tibère OR. AR.
TR. POT. XVIII IMP. II. COS. III. S. C. Marc Aurèle G.B.
TR. POT. XIX. COS. IIII. Antonin OR. AR. (avec S. C.) G.B. M.B.
TR. POT. XIX. IMP. II. COS. III. S. C. Marc Aurèle G.B M.B.
TR. POT. XX. Tibère OR.Q.
TR. POT. XX. COS. IIII. Antonin OR. OR.Q. AR. BR.M. (avec S. C.) G.B. M.B.
TR. POT. XX. IMP. III. (ou IIII.) COS. III. S. C. Marc Aurèle G.B. M.B.
TR. POT. XX. IMP. IIII. COS. III. S. C. — VIC. PAR. Marc Aurèle G.B. M.B.
TR. POT. XXI. COS. III. Marc Aurèle OR.Q.
TR. POT. XXI. COS. IIII. Antonin OR. AR. BR.M. (avec S. C.) G.B. M.B.
TR. POT. XXI. IMP. IIII. COS. III. S. C. Marc Aurèle G.B M.B.
TR. POT. XXII. Tibère OR.Q.
TR. POT. XXII. COS. IIII. S. C. Antonin G.B.
TR. POT. XXII. IMP. IIII. (ou V.) COS. III. S. C. Marc Aurèle G.B. M.B.
TR POT. XXIII. COS. IIII. S. C Antonin M.B.
TR. POT. XXIII. IMP. V. COS. III. S. C. Marc Aurèle G.B. M.B.
TR. POT. XXIIII. Tibère OR.Q.
TR. POT. XXIIII. COS. IIII. S. C. Antonin M.B.
TR. POT. XXV. Auguste OR.Q. Tibère OR.Q.
TR. POT. XXVI. Tibère OR.Q.
TR. POT. XXVII. Auguste OR.Q.
TR. POT. XXVIII. Tibère OR.Q.
TR. POT. XXVIII. (XXX. ou XXXI.). Auguste OR.Q. Tibère OR.Q.
TR. POT. XXXII. (XXXIIII., XXXV. ou XXXVI.). Tibère OR.Q.
TR. POT. XXXVIII. S. C. Tibère G.B.
TVTELA. Tétricus père P.B. Carausius P.B.
TVTELA AVG. Carausius P.B.
TVTELA AVGVSTI S. C. Vitellius M.B. Vespasien M.B.
TVTELA DIVI AVG. Carausius P B.
TVTELA ITALIAE S. C. Nerva G.B.
TVTELA P. Carausius P.B.
V. Constantin I OR.
VBERITA AV. Carausius AR.
VBERITAS AVG. Trajan Dèce OR. AR. Etruscille AR. Hérennius AR. Hostilien AR. Tréb. Galle AR. Volusien AR. Gallien OR. OR.Q. AR.M. B. Postume B. Tetricus fils P.B. Claude II P.B. Quintille P.B. Aurélien P.B. Tacite P.B. Carausius AR. P.B.
VBERITAS AVGG. Tétricus père OR.
VBERTA AVG. Carausius AR.
VBERTAS AVG. Gallien B. Salonine B. Postume B. Victorin(1) B. Tétricus père P.B. Tétricus fils P.B. Claude II P.B. Tacite P.B. Florien P.B.
VBERTAS SAECVLI. Constantin I P.B. P.B.Q. Constantin II P.B.
VBIQVE PAX. Gallien OR. B. Probus M.B.
VBIQVE VICTOR. Constantin I OR.Q.
VBIQVE VICTORES Constance Chlore OR. Maximin II OR.Q. Licinius père OR. Constantin I OR.M. OR. OR.Q. Crispus OR.T. Constantin II OR.M. OR.T.
VC. VC. Constance Chlore AR.
VEHICVLATIONE ITALIAE REMISSA S. C. Nerva G.B.
VENER. AVG. Carausius P.B.
VENEREM GENETRICEM. Salonine B.

(1) Variété avec IBERTAS AVG.

VENERI AVGVSTAE. Faustine mère OR. Faustine jeune OR. AR. (avec S. C.) Faustine mère G.B. M.B.

VENERI FELICI. Faustine jeune OR. Alex. Sévère (*hybride*) P.B. Mamée OR. AR. AR.Q. (avec S. C.) Antonin G.B. M.B. Mamée G.B. M.B.

VENERI GENETRICI (voir aussi BENERI). Adrien OR. BR.M. Sabine AR (1). Faustine jeune OR. Julie Domne OR. AR. Salonine OR. B. (avec S. C.) Sabine G.B. M.B. Marc Aurèle (*hybride*) G.B. Faustine jeune G.B. M.B. Lucile G.B. Julie Domne G.B.

VENERIS FELICIS. Adrien OR. AR.

VENERI VICT. Julie Domne AR.

VENERI VICTOR. Julie Domne OR.

VENERI VICTR. Julie Domne OR. AR. (avec S. C.) G.B. M.B.

VENERI VICTRI. Numérien P.B.Q.

VENERI VICTRICI. Faustine jeune AR. Caracalla AR. Gallien B (2). Numérien OR. P.B.Q. Carin OR. Magnia Urbica OR. Valérie OR. (AR. ?) M.B. (avec S C.) Faustine jeune G.B. M.B. (avec CMH.) Valérie M.B. (avec NK. VL. XC.) Valérie OR.

VENER. VICTOR. Julie Domne AR.

VENER. VICTRIX S. P. Q. R. Gallien B.

VENVP VICT. (*sic*) Sept. Sévère AR.

VENVS. Faustine jeune OR. OR.Q. AR. BR.M. Lucille OR. AR. BR.M. Crispine OR. OR.Q. AR. (avec S. C.) Faustine mère G.B. Faustine jeune G.B. M.B. Vérus (*hybride*) G.B. Lucille G.B. M.B. Crispine M B.

VENVS AVG Julie de Titus AR. Domitia AR.M. Claude II P.B. Vabalathe P.B.

VENVS AVG. S. P. Q. R. Gallien B. Claude II B.

VENVS AVGVST. Julie de Titus AR.

VENVS CAEL Elagabale AR.

VENVS CAELESTIS. Julie Domne AR. Aquilia Sévéra P.B. Soémias OR. AR. AR.Q. P.B. (avec S. C.) G.B. M.B.

VENVS CELEST. Magnia Urbica P.B.

VENVS CELESTIS. Elagabale P.B.

VENVS FELIX. Faustine jeune AR. BR.M. Lucille BR.M. Crispine OR. AR. Julie Domne OR. AR. AR.Q. Plautille AR.Q. Mamée AR. Gallien B. Salonine OR. B.M.B. Sévérine P.B. Fausta AR.Q. (avec S. C.) Faustine jeune G.B. M.B. Crispine G.B. M.B. Julie Domne G.B. M.B. Aquilla Sévéra G.B. Mamée G.B. M.B.

VENVS GENETRIX. Faustine jeune OR. AR Sept. Sévère (*hybride*) AR. Julie Domne OR. AR. P.B. Orbiane AR. Mamée OR. AR. Magnia Urbica OR. P.B. (avec S. C.) Lucille G.B. Julie Domne G.B. M.B. Mamée G.B.

VENVS VICT. Salonine OR. B. B.Q. (avec S. C.) G.B. M.B.

VENVS VICTRIX. Faustine jeune OR. Lucille AR. P.B. Crispine OR. AR. Julie Domne AR. P.B. Caracalla OR.M. OR. AR. Plautille OR. AR. P.B. Elagabale AR. Paula AR. Maesa AR. Alex. Sévère (*hybride*) AR. Mamée OR.Q. AR. P.B. Gordien III OR.Q. AR. Cornélia Supéra AR. Valérien B. Gallien B. Salonine OR. B. M.B. Valérien jeune B. Magnia Urbica P.B. (avec S. C.) Faustine jeune G.B. Julie Domne M.B Caracalla G.B. M.B. Plautille G.B. M.B. Mamée G.B. M.B. Valérien M.B.

VERITAS AVG. Trajan Dèce AR. Etruscille AR.

VESPASIANVS. Vespasien AR.

VESP. AVG Vespasien AR.

VESP. PON. TR. P. Titus P.B.

VESTA. Néron OR. AR. Vespasien OR. AR. Titus OR. AR. Julie de Titus AR.M. AR. Domitien OR. AR. Plotine OR.Q. Adrien G.B.M. Sabine OR. AR. Faustine mère OR. AR. BR.M. Marc Aurèle et Vérus BR.M. Faustine jeune AR. Lucille AR. Julie Domne OR. AR. M.B.M. P B. Aquilia Sévéra AR. Soémias AR. P.B. Maesa OR. AR. AR.Q. P.B. Etruscille BR M. Cornélia Supéra AR. P.B. Gallien

---

(1) Variété avec VENERI GENTRICI.

(2) Variété avec VENRI.

B. Salonine OR. B. B.Q. (avec S. C.) Germanicus (hybride) M.B. Caligula M.B.
Clande I †M.B. Galba M.B. Vespasien M.B. Titus G.B. M.B. Julie de Titus AR.
M.B. Domitien M.B. Sabine G.B. M.B Faustine mère G.B. M.B. Faustine jeune
G.B. M.B. Lucille G.B. M.B. Julie Domne G.B. M.B. Mae a G.B. M.B. Valérien
G.B. Gallien G.B. Salonine G.B.
VESTA AETERNA. Salonine B.
VESTA COS. V. S. P. Q. R. OPTIMO PRINCIPI. Trajan AR.
VESTAE SANCTAE. Julie Domne AR. (avec S. C.) G.B. M.B.
VESTAE S. C. Faustine jeune BR.M.
VESTA FELIX. Gallien B. Salonine B. (avec S. C.) M.B.
VESTA MATER. Julie Domne OR. AR.M. AR. BR.M. (avec S. C.) BR.M. G.B. M.B.
VESTA P. R. QVIRITIVM. Autonomes de Galba AR. Vitellius OR. AR.
VESTA S. P. Q. R. OPTIMO PRINCIPI. Trajan AR.
VIA TRAIANA. Trajan (Restitution de Gallien?) BIL.
VIA TRAIANA S. P. Q. R. OPTIMO PRINCIPI. Trajan OR. AR. (avec S. C.) G.B M.B.
VIC. AVG. Vespasien OR. AR. Titus OR. Adrien AR Q. Sept. Sévère AR.
VIC. AVG. TR. P COS Sept. Sévère OR. AR.
VIC. GALL. AVG. III. Gallien B.
VIC. GERM. P. M. TR P. V. COS. III. P. P. Postume OR. B.
VIC. PAR. MAX. AVG. S. C. Sept. Sévère M.B.
VIC. PART. Caracalla OR.
VIC. PART. P. M. TR. P. XX. COS. IIII. P. P. Caracalla OR. AR.
VIC. PART. P. M. TR. P. XX. COS. IIII. P. P. VOT. XX. Caracalla OR. AR.
VICT. AETERN. Sept. Sévère AR. Caracalla AR. Géta AR. P.B.
VICT. AETERNAE. Sept. Sévère AR. Caracalla AR.
VICT. AG. Carausius P.B.
VICT. AVG. Néron OR.Q. Vespasien OR. Sept. Sévère AR. P.B. Constant I P.B.Q.
Constance II P.B.
VICT. AVG. COS. II. Albin AR.
VICT. AVG. COS III. Marc Aurèle AR. (avec S. C.) M.B.
VICT. AVG. COS. III. P. P. S. C. Marc Aurèle M.B.
VICT. AVGG. Sept. Sévère AR.Q. Caracalla AR.Q. Géta AR.Q. Valérien jeune B
VICT. AVGG. COS. II. P. P. Sept. Sévère OR. AR.
VICT. AVG. LIB. ROM. ORB. Magnence OR. AR. M.B.
VICT. AVG. P. M. TR. P. III. COS. II. P. P. Sept. Sévère BR.M.
VICT. AVG. TR. P. COS. Sept Sévère OR. AR. (avec S. C.) G.B. M.B.
VICT. AVG. TR. P. S. C. Marc Aurèle G.B Faustine jeune hybride) G.B.
VICT. AVG. TR. P. II. COS. II. Sept. Severe OR. AR. (avec S. C.) G.B M.B.
VICT. AVG. TR. P. III. (ou IIII.) IMP. II COS. II. S. C. Vérus G.B. M.B.
VICT. AVG. TR. P. VI. COS. II. Vérus OR. AR. (avec S. C.) G.B.
VICT. AVG. TR. P. XVIII. IMP. II. COS III. S. C. Marc Aurèle G.B. M.B.
VICT. AVG. TR. P. XX. COS. III. Marc Aurèle OR. AR.
VICT. AVG. TR. POT. COS. III. (ou IIII.) S. C. Antonin M.B.
VICT. AVG. TR. POT. XX. IMP. III. COS III. S. C. Marc Aurèle G.B. M.B.
VICT. BRIT. P. M. TR. P. VIIII. IMP. VII. COS. IIII. P. P. S. C. Commode G.B.
VICT. BRIT. P. M. TR. P. X. S. C. Commode G.B.
VICT. BRIT. P. M. TR. P. XI. IMP. VII. COS. III. P. P. S. C. Commode G.B.
VICT. BRIT P. M. TR. P. XIIII. COS. III. P. P. Caracalla G.B.
VICT. BRIT. P. M. TR. P. XIX. COS. III. P.P. Sept. Sévère AR. (avec S. C.) G.B. M.B.
VICT. BRIT. PONT. MAX. TR. P. III. S. C. Géta G.B.
VICT. BRIT. TR. P. III. (ou IIII.) COS. II. S. C. Géta G.B. M.B.
VICT. BRIT. TR. P. XIIII. COS. III. S. C. Caracalla G.B. M.B.
VICT. CAES. LIB. ROM. ORB. Magnence OR. Décence OR.
VICT. COMES AVG. Postume M.B.
VICT. CONSTANT. AVG. Constance Chlore OR.
VICT. DD. NN. AVG. ET CAES. — VOT. V. MVLT. X. Magnence M.B. †M.B Décence
M.B. P.B. Constance Galle M.B. (avec — VOT. XXX.) Constance II M.B. B.
VICT. DD. NN. AVG. ET CAE. — VOT. V. MVLT. X. Magnence M.B.
VICT. FELI. P. M. TR. P. XIIII. COS. V. P. P. Commode AR

VICT. FELI. P. M. TR. P. XIIII. IMP. VIII. COS. V. P. P. S. C. Commode G.B.
VICT. FEL. P. M. TR. P. XIIII. COS. V. P. P. Commode AR.
VICT. GAL. AVG. Gallien B. Gallien et Salonine OR.
VICT. GALL. AVG. III. Gallien OR. B. BR.M.
VICT. GALLIENI AVG. Gallien B.
VICT. GER. II. Gallien M.B.
VICT. GERM. Gallien B.
VICT. GERMANICA. Gallien OR. OR.Q. B. B.Q. Postume B.
VICT. GERMA. IMP. VI. COS. III. S. C. Marc Aurèle G.B. M.B.
VICT. GERM. IMP. VI. COS. III. Marc Aurèle BR.M. (avec S. C.) G.B. M.B. Marc
Aurèle et Vérus BR.M.
VICT. LAETAE PRINC. PERP. — VOT. P. R. Licinius père P.B. Licinius fils P.B.
Constantin I P.B. Crispus P.B. Constantin II P.B.
VICTO. AVG. Sévère III P.B.Q.
VICTOIA AVGGG. Augustule OR.
VICTOI. AVG. Domitius Domitien OR.
VICTO. IMP. TROPAEA. Pesc. Niger AR.
VICTOR. AETER. Gordien III AR. (avec S. C.) Valérien G.B.
VICTOR. ANTONINI AVG. Elagabale OR. AR. AR.Q. (avec S. C.) M.B.
VICTOR. AVG. Sept. Sévère AR.
VICTOR. AVGVSTI S. C. Vitellius M.B. Maximin I G.B.
VICTOR. CARO. Carus OR. Carin OR.
VICTOR. DD. NN. AVG. ET CAES. — VOT. V. MVLT. X. Magnence P.B.
VICTOR. DD. NN. AVG ET C. — OT. VLT. (sic). Maxence P.B.Q. (avec VOT. V. MVLT.
X.) P.B.
VICTORE AVG. N VOTIS. — VOT. X. MVL XX. Constantin I OR. (avec — X. —
XX.) OR.
VICTORE AVG. N. — X. XX. Constantin I OR,
VICTORES AVGVSTI. Valentinien I OR. Valens OR.
VICTOR. GENTIVM BARBARR. Constantin II BR.M.
VICTOR. GER. (ou GERM). Probus P.B.Q.
VICTOR. GERMAN. Claude II P.B.
VICTORIA. Galba OR. AR. Pesc. Niger AR. Sept. Sévère AR. Tétricus père P.B.
VICTORIA AAAVGGG. Constant (usurpateur) AR.
VICTORIA AAAVGGGG. Constantin III OR. AR.
VICTORIA AAVGGG. Constant (usurpateur) AR. Maxime (usurpateur) AR.
VICTORIA AET. Gallien OR. OR.Q. B. B.Q.
VICTORIA AETER. Gordien III AR. (avec S. C.) G.B. M.B.
VICTORIA AETERNA. Gordien III AR. D oclétien OR. Maxenee M.B. (avec S. C.)
Gordien III G.B. M.B.
VICTORIA AETERNA AVGG. Maxence AR. (avec — VOT. V.) OR.
VICTORIA AETERNA AVGG. NOSTR. Décence BR.M.
VICTORIA AETERNA AVG. N. Maxence OR. M.B. (avec — VOT. X.) OR. P.B. (avec —
VOT. XX.) P.B. (avec — VOT. XX. FEL.) P.B.
VICTORIA ALEXANDRI AVG. N. Alexandre (usurpateur) †M.B.
VICTORIA ANTONINI AVG. Elagabale P.B. (avec S. C.) G.B.
VICTORIA AVG. Vespasien AR. Domitien P.B. Adrien OR. OR.Q. AR. Antonin OR.
Pesc Niger AR. Sept. Sévère AR. Elagabale AR. P.B. Alex. Sévère OR. AR.
Maximin I OR. AR. Gordien III OR. AR. AR.Q. BR.M. Philippe père OR. AR.M.
AR. Jotapien AR(I). Trajan Dèce OR. AR. AR.Q. BR.M. Etruscille (hybride) AR.
Hostilien AR. Tréb. Galle AR. Volusien AR. Emilien OR.AR. Valérien B. Gallien
OR. OR.Q. B.M. B. B.Q. Postume OR. B. G.B. M.B. Lélien B. Victorin OR. AR.
B. Marius OR. B. P.B. Tétricus père OR. P.B. Tétricus fils P.B. Claude II OR.
(OR.Q.?) M.B. P.B. P.B.Q. Quintille P.B. Aurélien OR. (2) P.B. P.B.Q. Vaba-
lathe P.B. Tacite OR. P.B. P.B.Q. Florien P.B. Probus OR. M.B. P.B. P.B.Q.
Carus OR. P.B. Carin OR. M.B. P.B. P.B.Q. Julien (usurpateur) P.B. Dioclétien

(1) Variété avec AVS.
(2) Variété avec IVCTORIA AVG.

OR. P.B. P.B.Q. Carausius P.B. Allectus OR. P.B. Autonomes de Constantinople (Constantin) G.B.M. P.B. Constantin II G.B.M. Constance II BR.M. Magnence OR.M. Jovien AR. Valens P.B.Q. Procope OR. Avitus OR. Sévère III OR. AR. Augustule P.B.Q. (avec S. C.) Vitellius G.B. Vespasien G.B. M.B. Titus G.B. Domitien G.B. Antonin G.B. M.B. Vérus M.B. Macrin M.B. Maximin I G.B. M.B. Gordien III G.B. M.B. Philippe père G.B. M.B. Trajan Dèce G.B. M.B. Emilien G.B. Gallien G.B. M.B. Postume G.B. M.B. — (Avec S. P. Q. R.) Gallien B. B.Q. — (Avec VO. X.) Postume B. -- (Avec VOT. V.) Procope OR.Q. — (Avec VOT. V. MVLT. X.) Valentinien I OR.T. — (Avec VOT. X.) Constance II BR.M. — (Avec VOT. XX.) Constant I BR.M. Constance II BR.M.

VICTORIA AVG. I. Tétricus père P.B.
—   (Avec II.) Gallien OR. B.
—   (Avec III.) Gallien OR. B. M.B. Tétricus père P.B. (avec III. S C. Gallien G.B.
—   (Avec VI. S. C.) Gallien G.B.
—   (Avec VII.) Gallien OR. B. M.B.
—   (Avec VII. C.) Gallien B.
—   (Avec VIII. (ou VIIII.) Gallien B.
—   (Avec LXXII.) Constantin I OR. Constance II OR.

VICTORIA AVG. ET CAES. Magnence M.B. Décence M.B.

VICTORIA AVG. FEL. Carus OR.

VICTORIA AVGG. Caracalla OR. Gordien d'Afrique père AR. Gordien d'Afrique fils AR. Balbin AR. AR.Q. Pupien OR. AR. Philippe père AR. Philippe fils AR. Pacatien (hybride) AR. Hostilien BR.M. Tréb. Galle AR. Volusien OR. AR. Valérien OR. B. BR.M. Gallien OR. B.M. B. B.Q. M.B. Macrien jeune OR. BIL. Quiétus OR. BIL. Postume B. Tétricus père OR. Carus P.B Carus et Carin P B. Numérien P.B. Carin OR. P.B. P.B.Q. Carin et Numérien OR. P.B. Dioclétien OR.M. OR. AR. P.B. P.B.Q. Maximien Hercule AR. P.B. Constance Chlore AR. P.B. Galère Maximien AR. Constantin I P.B Constant I P.B. Constance II P.B. Magnence BR M. Décence BR.M. Constance Galle BR.M. Julien II P.B. Autonomes de Julien II P.B.Q. Valentinien I OR. AR. Valens OR. Gratien OR. AR.M. AR. P.B. Valentinien II OR. Théodose I AR. AR.M. AR. Magnus Maximus OR. M.B. P.B. Eugène OR. P.B. P.B.Q. Honorius OR. AR. AR.Q. Jovin OR. AR. Sébastien AR. Jean AR.Q. Valentinien III AR.Q. P.B.Q. Avitus P.B Glycère OR. (avec S. C.) Macrin M.B. Gordien d'Afrique père G.B. Gordien d'Afrique fils G.B. Balbin G.B. M.B. Pupien G.B. M.B. Philippe père G.B. Tréb. Galle G.B. Volusien G.B. Valérien G.B. M.B. Gallien G.B. M.B. (Avec XXXXX.) Valenlentinien III OR.Q (Avec VOT. X. MVL. XX.) Valentinien II M B. (Avec VOT X. MVLT. XX.) Honorius OR. (Avec VOTIS. X.) Maximien Hercule P.B.

VICTORIA AVGG. ET CAESS. NN. — VOT. XX. Constantin I OR.

VICTORIA AVGGG. Dioclétien P.B. Constantin I †.M.B. P.B. Valentinien I G.B. Valens G.B. P.B.Q. Gratien P.B. Valentinien II AR. AR.Q. BR.M. G.B. P.B. P.B.Q. Théodose I OR. AR. P.B.Q. Magnus Maximus P.B. Honorius OR. AR. P.B. Constance III OR. Placidie OR. Constantin III OR. OR.T. AR. P.B.Q. Jovin AR. Jean OR. Valentinien III OR. OR.T. AR. Pétrone Maxime OR. Avitus OR. Majorien OR. P.B. P.B.Q. Sévère III OR. OR.T. Anthémius OR. Euphémie OR. Glycère OR. AR. Népos OR. P.B. Augustule OR. (Avec — XX. XXX.) Honorius OR.Q.

VICTORIA AVGG. II. GERM. Gallien B.

VICTORIA AVGG. NN. Licinius père P.B. Constantin I AR. P.B. Autonomes de Constantinople (Constantin) G.B.M. Constant I AR. Constance II P.B.Q. (Avec VOT.X.) Constantin I P.B. Constant I BR.M.

VICTORIA AVGG. VO. X. Tétricus père et fils OR.

VICTORIA AVG. LIB. ROMANOR. Magnence OR. AR. G.B. M.B. P.B. Décence OR.M. OR.

VICTORIA AVG. N. Probus P.B. Maxence M.B. Constance II BR.M.

VICTORIA AVG. — ΝΕΙΚΗ ΟΠΛΟΦΟΡΟΣ. Gordien III BR.M. M.B.M.

VICTORIA AVG. NN. Constance II BR.M.

VICTORIA AVG. NOSTRI. Constance II OR. BR.M.

VICTORIA AVGVST. Claude I OR.Q. Néron OR. OR.Q. Vespasien OR. OR.Q. AR.Q. Titus

AR.Q. Domitien OR.Q. AR.Q. Nerva OR.Q. AR.Q. Commode OR. Sept. Sévère AR.M. (avec S. C.) Vespasien M.B. Titus G.B. M.B. Domitien M.B.

VICTORIA AVGVSTI. Autonomes de Galba AR.Q. Vitellius OR. AR. AR.Q. Vespasien AR. AR.Q. Titus AR Q. Domitien AR Q. Adrien G.B Antonin BR.M. Sept. Sévère AR.M. AR. Caracalla AR.M. Alex. Sévère OR. AR. G.B. Gordien III AR. Gallien OR. Constantin I OR.Q. AR. Autonomes de Constantinople (Constantin) G.B.M. Constantin II BR.M. Constant I BR.M. Constance II AR. BR.M M B. Att le OR. (avec S. C.) Néron M.B. Vitellus G.B. M.B. Vespasien G.B. M.B. Titus G.B. M.B. Domitien M.B. Adrien G.B. Antonin G.B. Sept. Sévère G.B. Alex Sévère G.B. M.B. Gordien III G.B.

VICTORIA AVGVSTI COS. P. P. Gordien III BR.M.

VICTORIA AVGVSTI N. Probus BR.M. Constance II OR.T. AR. BR.M. Julien II AR. Jovien BR.M. P.B.Q Valens OR.Q.

VICTORIA AVGVSTI NOSTRI. Constant I OR.M.

VICTORIA AVGVSTI S. C. — OB. CIV. SER. Vespasien G.B.

VICTORIA AVGVSTI. — ΘΕΟC OΠΛΟΦOPOC. Gordien III BR.M. (Avec VOT. X.) Constantin I BR.M. (Avec VOT. XX. MVL. XXX.) Constantin I BR.M. (Avec VOT. XXX.) Constance II OR. (Avec VOT. XXX. MVLT. XXXX.) BR.M. G.B.M. (Avec VOT. XXXX.) OR.M.

VICTORIA AVGVSTORM. VOT. X Constance II OR.T.

VICTORIA AVGVSTORVM Vérus BR M. Philippe père, Otacilie et Philippe fils BR.M. Valérien BR.M. Gallien et Salonin BR.M Carin OR. Constantin I OR. Constant I OR.Q. AR.M. AR. Constance II OR. OR.T. AR.M. AR. AR.Q. BR.M. P.B. Vétranion AR. P.B. Magnence BR.M. Décence BR.M. Constance Galle OR.Q. P.B. Julien II OR.Q Valentinien I AR.M. Valens OR.T. AR.M. Gratien OR.T. AR. Valentinien II OR.T. Théodose I OR.T. Magnus Maximus OR.T. AR. Victor AR. Eugène OR.T. AR. Honorius OR.T. Constance III OR.T. Jean OR OR.T. Valentinien III OR.Q. OR.T. (Avec ROMA. Valentinien I AR.M. (Avec S. C.) Maximin I G.B. Maxime G.B. Hostilien G.B. (Avec — VOT. V.) Constance Galle OR.Q. Julien II OR.Q. Valentinien I OR.T. Valens OR.Q. Valentinien II OR. (Avec VOT. V. MVL. X.) Valentinien I OR. Valens OR. Gratien OR. Valentinien II OR.Q. (Avec — VOT. V. MVLT. X.) Constant I OR. Valentinien I OR.M. Valens OR. OR.Q. AR.M. Gratien OR. OR.Q. Théodose I OR.T. Magnus Maximus OR.Q. Victor OR.Q. (Avec — VOT. X.) Valens OR.Q. Gratien OR Q. (Avec — VOT. X. MVL. XX.) Valens OR. OR.Q. (Avec — VOT. X. MVLT. XV.) Valentinien I AR.M Théodose I OR.Q. OR.T. Honorius OR.Q. (Avec — VOT. X. MVLT. XX.) Constant I OR. Valentinien I OR. Honorius OR.Q. Valentinien III OR.Q. (Avec — VOT. XV. MVLT. XX.) Constance II OR. Valentinien II OR. (Avec — VOT. XX. MVLT. XXX.) Constance II AR.M Honorius OR.Q. (Avec — VOT. XXX.) Constantin I OR. Constant I OR. Constance II OR OR.Q. (Avec — VOT. XXX. MVLT. XXXX.) Honorius OR. OR.Q. (Avec — VOT. XXXX.) Constance II OR.T. (Avec — VOTIS V.) Constance Galle OR.Q. (Avec — VOTIS. X.) OR.Q. Valens OR.Q. Gratien OR.Q. (Avec — XXV.) Constant I OR. Constance II OR.

VICTORIA A. — VOT. Q. Q. MVL. X. Maxence M.B.

VICTORIA BAEATISSIMORVM CAESS. — VOT. X. Crispus BR.M. Constantin II G.B.M.

VICTORIA BEATISSIMORVM CAESS. — VOT. X. Constance Chlore G.B.M. (Avec VOT. XX. MVLT. XXX.) Constantin I BR.M.

VICTORIA BRIT. Caracalla OR.Q. AR.

VICTORIA CAESARIS. Numérien OR. Carin OR. Constance II P.B. Constance Galle AR.

VICTORIA CAESAR NN. Constantin II OR. (avec LXXII.) Constant I OR.

VICTORIA CAESARVM. Constantin II OR. Constance II AR. P.B.Q.

VICTORIA CAES. LIB. ROMANOR. Décence OR.

VICTORIA CAESS. Constantin II OR.T.

VICTORIA CAEES. NN. Licinius fils P.B. Crispus P.B. Constantin II P.B.

VICTORIA CARPICA. Philippe père AR.

VICTORIA CONSTANTI AVG. — VOT. X. MVLT. XX. Constance II OR. (Avec — VOT. XV.) Constance II OR. (Avec — VOT. XX. MVLT. XXX.) Const nce II OR. (Avec — VOT. XXXX.) Constance II OR.T.

VICTORIA CONSTANTI CAES. — VOT. XV. Constance II OR.
VICTORIA CONSTANTINI AVG. Maximin II OR. OR.Q Licinius père OR. Constantin I OR. OR.Q. M.B. Crispus OR. Constantin II BR M. (Avec — LXXII.) Constantin I OR. (Avec — VOT. XX.) Constantin I OR. OR.Q. Constantin II OR. (Avec — VOT. XXX.) Constantin I OR. OR.Q. BR.M. (Avec — VOT. XXXX.) Constantin I OR. OR.T.
VICTORIA CONSTANTINI CAES. — VOT. X. Constantin II OR. (Avec — VOT. XX. Constantin II OR.Q.
VICTORIA CONSTANTIS AVG. Constant I AR. (Avec — VOT. V. MVLT. X.) Constantin II OR. Constant I OR. (Avec — VOT. X.) Constant I OR. (Avec — VOT. XV.) Constant I OR.Q.
VICTORIA CRISPI CAES. — VOT. X. Crispus OR.
VICTORIA D. Magnence P.B.
VICTORIA DDD. NNN. AVGGG. — SIC X. SIC. XX. Constance II OR. (Avec — VOT. V. MVLT. X.) Constant I OR.
VICTORIA DD. NN. Julien II OR.Q.
VICTORIA DD. NN. AVG. Constant I AR. Constance II AR. J lien II AR. Valentinien I OR.Q. Valens P.B. (Avec — VOT. X. MVLT. XX.) Constance II OR.
VICTORIA DD. NN. AVGG. Constantin I OR.Q AR. Constantin II OR. Constant I OR. OR Q. AR. Constance II OR. OR Q. AR. Magnence OR.T. Décence OR.T. Julien II AR. (Avec — VOT. X.) Julien II OR.Q.
VICTORIA D. N. AVG. Valens OR.T.
VICTORIA D. N. AVGVSTI. — VOT. V. MVLT. X. Valentinien I OR.M. Valens OR.M.
VICTORIA D. N. CAES. Décence OR.Q.
VICTORIA D. N. ET PRINCIPVM. — VOT. P. R. Constantin II P.B.
VICTORIAE. Pesc. Niger AR.
VICTORIAE AETERNAE. Claude II P.B.Q.
VICTORIAE AETERNAE. AVGG. S. C. Géta G.B. M.B.
VICTORIAE AVG. Pesc. Niger AR. Sept. Sévère AR.M. AR. Caracalla AR. Gallien B. Postume G.B. Probus OR. P.B. (avec S. C.) Postume G.B. M.B.
VICTORIAE AV. GE. Caracalla AR.
VICTORIAE AVG. II. GERM. Gallien B.
VICTORIAE AVGG. Sept. Sévère OR. AR. Caracalla OR. AR. Valérien OR. B. Gallien OR. B. Numérien OR. Dioclétien OR. AR. Maxence P.B. (avec S. C.) Sept. Sévère M.B. Caracalla G.B. M.B. Géta G.B. M.B.
VICTORIAE AVG. GERMANICA. Gallien OR.
VICTORIAE AVGG. FEL. Sept. Sévère OR. AR. Julie Domne (hybride) AR. Carus OR. (avec S. C.) Sept. Sévère G.B. M.B.
VICTORIAE AVGG. IT. GERM. Valérien B. Gallien B.
VICTORIAE AVGG. NN. — VOT. X. MVL. XX. Constantin I OR.
VICTORIAE AVGVST. Caracalla AR.
VICTORIAE AVGVSTI. Autonomes de Constantinople (Constantin) G.B.M. (avec S. C.) Domitien M.B. (avec — VOT. X.) Florien P.B. Probus OR.M.
VICTORIAE AVGVSTORVM. Marc Aurèle et Vérus BR.M. Phlippe père, Otacilie et Philippe fils BR.M. (avec — ROMA.) Valentinien I G.B. (avec S. C.) Géta G.B.M.B
VICTORIAE AVGVSTT. — VOTIS X. Carus et Carin OR.M.
VICTORIAE BEATISSIMORVM CAESS. — VOT. X. Constance II BR.M.
VICTORIAE BRIT. Sept. Sévère OR. AR. Caracalla OR. AR. P.B. Géta AR.
VICTORIAE RRITANNICAE S. C. Sept. Sévère G.B. M.B. Géta G.B.
VICTORIAE BRITTANNICAE S. C. Sept. Sévère G.B. M.B. Caracalla G.B. M.B. Géta G.B.
VICTORIAE CAESS. AVGG. Q. NN. Constantin II P.B.
VICTORIAE DD. AVGGG. NNN. Valens P.B.
VICTORIAE DD. AVGG Q. NN. Constant I P.B. Constance II P.B.Q.
VICTORIAE DDD. NNN. AVGGG. — VOT XX. MVLTIS XXX. Constantin II OR.
VICTORIAE DD. NN. AVG. ET CAE. — VOT. V. MVLT. X. Constance II (hybride) M.B. Magnence M.B. P.B. Décence M.B. P.B.
VICTORIAE DD. NN. AVG. ET CAES. — VOT. V. MVL. X. Magnence AR.M. AR. M.B. P.B. (avec — VOT. V. MVLT. X.) M.B. P.B. Décence M.B. P.B.

VICTORIAE DD. NN. AVGG. Julien II AR.
VICTORIAE DD. NN. AVGC. AV. — VOT. X. MVL. XX. Conastance II OR. OR.Q.
VICTORIAE DD. NN. AVGG. — VOT. V. MVLT. X. Magnence AR.M. BR.M. (Avec —
VOT. X. MVLT. XV.) Constant I AR.M. (Avec — VOT. X. MVLT. XX.) OR.M. OR.
OR.Q. AR.M. Constance II OR. AR.M. (Avec — VOT. XX. MVLT. XXX.) Constant I
OR. OR.Q. Constance II OR.M. OR. OR.Q. (Avec — VOT. XXX.) OR. (Avec — VOT.
XXX. MVLT. XXXX.) OR.T.
VICTORIAE DD. NN. AVG. — VOTIS V. MVLTIS X. Julien II OR.Q.
VICTORIAE D. N. AVG. Julien II OR.Q. (avec — VOT. V. MVLT. X.) Constant I AR.
(avec — VOT. X. MVLT. XV.) Constant I AR. (avec — VOT. X. MVLT. XX.) Cons-
tant I AR. (avec — VOT. XXV. MVLT. XXX.) Constance II OR. (avec — VOT. XXX.
MVLT. XXXX.) Constance II OR.T. (avec — VOTIS XV. MVLTIS XX.) Constance
II OR.
VICTORIAE FELICI COS. V. P. P. S. C. Commode G.B. M.B.
VICTORIAE FELICI. C. V. P. P. Commode AR.
VICTORIAE GOTHIC. S. P. Q. R. Claude II P.B.
VICTORIAE LAETAE AVGG. NN. — VOT. X. MVL. XX. Constantin I OR.M.
VICTORIAE LAETAE DOM. NOSTR. — P. R. VOT. Constantin I P.B.
VICTORIAE LAETAE PRINC. PERP. — P. R. Constantin I OR. (avec — VOT. P. R.)
Licinius fils P.B. Constantin I P.B. Crispus P.B. Constantin II P.B. (avec —
VOT. X.) Licinius père OR. Constantin I OR. (avec — X.) Licinius père P.B.
Constantin I P.B.
VICTORIAE LAETAE PRIN. P. — VOT. P. R. Constantin I P.B.
VICTORIAE LAETAE PR. P. — VOT. P. R. Constantin II P.B.
VICTORIAE LAET. P. P. — VOT. P. R. Constantin I P.B.
VICTORIAE LAET. PRINC. PERP. — VOT. P. R. Licinius père P.B. Licinius fils P.B.
Constantin I P.B. Crispus P.B. Constantin II P.B.
VICTORIAE LIBERAE. Constantin I P.B.
VICTORIAE MAXIMINI AVG. Licinius père †M.B.
VICTORIAE PERPETVAE. Constantin I P.B.Q. (avec — VOT. XX.) OR.
VICTORIAE SARMATICAE. Dioclétien AR. Maximien Hercule AR. Galère Maxi-
mien AR.
VICTORIAE TVM (sic). Postume G.B.
VICTORIA EXERCIT. Valérien B.
VICTORIA GALBAE AVG. Galba AR.Q.
VICTORIA GER. Probus OR. P.B.Q. Carausius P.B.
VICTORIA GERM. Maximin I OR. OR.Q. AR. AR.Q. Valérien B. Gallien OR. B. B.Q.
Tétricus père OR. Aurélien P.B. Probus OR. M.B. P.B. P.B.Q. (avec S. C) Maxi-
min I G.B. M.B. Valérien G.B. M.B. Gallien G.B. M B.
VICTORIA GERMA. Carausius P.B.
VICTORIA GERMAN. Gallien B. Salonin B. Claude II P.B.
VICTORIA GERMANIC S. P. Q. R. Claude II P.B.
VICTORIA GERMANICA. Caracalla OR. AR. Maximin I AR. BR.M. Maximin I et
Maxime BR.M. Trajan Dèce AR. Hérennius AR. Hostilien AR. Valérien B.
Gallien OR. B. B.Q. BR.M. M.B. Postume B. Carin OR. (avec S. C.) Maximin I
G.B. M.B. Postume G.B.
VICTORIA G. M. Gallien B. B.Q. Claude II P.B. (avec S. C.) Gallien G.B.
VICTORIA GORDIANI AVG. Gordien III AR.
VICTORIA GOTHI. Tacite P.B.
VICTORIA GOTHIC. Probus OR.
VICTORIA GOTHICA. Constantin I BR.M.
VICTORIA GOTTHI. Tacite P.B.
VICTORIA GOTTHICA COS. II. Tacite OR.
VICTORIAI AVGVSTORVM. Honorius OR.
VICTORIAI LAITAI PRINC. PERP. Licinius fils P.B.
VICTORIA IMPERI ROMANI S. C. Galba G.B.
VICTORIA IMP. GERMANICI. Vitellius OR.
VICTORIA IMP. VESPASIANI. Vespasien AR(1).

(1) Variété avec MP. pour IMP.

VICTORIA NAVALIS S. C. Vespasien M.B. Titus M.B. Domitien M.B.
VICTORIA OTHONIS. Othon OR. AR.
VICTORIA PART. Valérien B. Gallien B. Salonin B.
VICTORIA PARTHICA. Macrin AR. P.B. Valérien B. (avec S. C.) Macrin G.B.
VICTORIA PARTHICA MAXIMA. Sept. Sévère AR. Sept. Sévère et Caracalla OR. AR. Caracalla OR.
VICTORIA PARTH. MAX. Sept. Sévère AR. Caracalla AR.
VICTORIA PERPET. — XXX. Florien OR.
VICTORIA PERPETVA. Florien P.B. Probus OR. Julien II AR.
VICTORIA PERPETVA AVG. Tacite P.B.
VICTORIA PERSICA. Galère Maximien BR.M.
VICTORIA P. R. Auguste AR. Galba OR. AR. (avec S. C.) G.B.
VICTORIA PROBI AVG. Probus OR.
VICTORIA ROMANOR. Maxime (usurpateur) AR.
VICTORIA ROMANORVM. Constance II AR.M. BR.M. Constance Galle BR.M. Julien II AR.M. G.B. Jovien G B. Eugène P.B. Constance III AR (1). Attale AR.M. AR. P.B. (avec — VOT. XX.) Julien II OR.Q.
VICTORIA SARM. Dioclétien AR.
VICTORIA SARMAT. Dioclétien AR. Mximien Hercule AR. Constance Chlore AR. Galère Maximien AR.
VICTORIA SARMATI. Constance Chlore AR.
VICTORIA SARMATICA. Dioclétien AR. Maximien Hercule AR.
VICTORI. AV. Carausius P.B.
VICTORI. AVG. Sept. Sévère OR. Postume M.B. Carus OR. Dicclétien OR. Carausius AR. (avec S. C.) Postume G.B.
VICTORI. AVGG. Magnus Maximus M.B.
VICTORI. AVGGG. Sévère III OR.
VICTORI AVGGGG. Sévère III OR.T.
VICTORI. AVGVS. Jovien BR.M.
VICTORIB. AVGG. ET CAESS. NN.. — VOT. XX. Constantin I OR. Constantin II OR.
VICTORIBVS AVGG. NN. VOTIS. — X. Constantin I OR.
VICTORIBVS AVGG. NN. — VOTIS X ET XX. Constantin I OR.M. OR. (Avec — VOTIS XX.) OR. (Avec — VOTIS XXX.) OR M. OR.
VICTORI GENTIVM BARBARR. Constantin II BR.M. Constant I BR.M.
VICTORIOSO SEMPER. Probus OR. P.B. Constantin I OR.
VICTOR. IVST. AV. Julie Domne (hybride) AR.
VICTOR. IVST. AVG. Pesc. Niger AR. Sept. Sévère AR.
VICTOR. LEG Aurélien P.B.
VICTOR OMNIVM GEN. Crispus OR.
VICTOR OMNIVM GENTIVM. Constantin I OR. Constantin II OR. Constant I OR. Constance II OR.
VICTOR OMNIVM GENTIVM AVG. N. Maxence M.B.
VICTOR. SEVER. AVG. Sept. Sévère AR.
VICTOR. SEVER. C. AVG. Sept. Sévère AR.
VICT. PARTHICA. Caracalla AR.
VICT. PARTHICAE. Sept. Sévère AR.
VICT. PARTHIC. AVG.... IMP. VIIII. S. C. Sept. Sévère G.B.
VICT. PARTICA. Valérien jeune B.
VICT. PART. MAX. Sept. Sévère OR. AR. P.B. Caracalla OR. AR. P.B.
VICT. PART. P. M. TR. P. II. COS. II. P. P. Macrin OR. AR. (avec S. C.) G.B. M.B.
VICT. PART. P. M. TR. P. XX. COS. IIII. P. P. — VO. XX. Caracalla OR.
VICT. PROBI. AVG. Probus OR.
VII. DES COS. Gallien OR.
VIRT. Autonomes de Galba AR. Tétricus père P.B.
VIRT. AETER. AVG. P. M. TR. P. XVII. COS. VII. P. P. Commode OR.
VIRT. AVG. Claude II P.B.

___

(1) Vai iété avec VICTORIA POMANORVM.

VIRT. AVGG. Sept. Sévère OR. AR. Caracalla AR.

VIRT. AVG. P. M. TR. P. COS. III. S. C. Adrien G.B.

VIRT. AVG. P. M. TR. P. X. IMP. VII. COS. IIII. P. P. Commode OR. (avec s. C.; G.B.

VIRT. AVG TR. P. COS. Sept. Sévère OR. AR. (avec s. C.) G B. M.B

VIRT. AVG. TR. P. II. COS. II. Sept. Sévère AR. (avec s. C) G.B. M.B.

VIRT. AVG. TR. P. VI. COS. II. P. P. Sept. Sévère OR. (avec s. C.) G.B. M.B.

VIRT. AVG. TR. P. VII. IMP. IIII. COS. III. P. P. Commode OR.

VIRT. AVGVT. NOSTRI. Probus BR.M.

VIRT. EXERC. Licinius père P.B. Licinius fils P.B. Constantin I P.B. Crispus P.B. Constantin II P.B.

VIRT. EXERCIT. GALL. Constantin I P.B.

VIRT. EXERC. ROM. Majorien OR.

VIRT. GALLIENI AVG. Gallien OR.M. OR. B. B Q. G.B.

VIRT. MILITVM. Aurélien P.B.

VIRT. PERP. CONSTANTINI AVG. Constantin I P.B.

VIRTV. AVG. Carausius P.B.

VIRT. VG. Tétricus père P.B.

VIRTVS. Galba OR. AR.

VIRTVS A. Carausius P.B.

VIRTVS AEQVIT. Postume B.

VIRTVS AETERNA AVG. N. Constantin I P.B.

VIRTVS AVG. Antonin AR. Pesc. Niger AR. Sept. Sévère AR. Julie Domne (*hybride*) AR. Alex. Sévère OR. AR. AR.Q. Gordien III OR. AR. AR.Q. Philippe père AR. Philippe fils AR. Trajan Dèce AR. Emilien AR. Valérien B. Gallien OR. OR.Q. B. B.Q. BR.M. Valérien jeune B. Postume B. G.B. M.B. Lélien OR. Victorin B. Marius B. Tétricus père OR. BIL. P.B. Tétricus fils P.B. Claude II B. M.B. P.B. Quintille P.B. P.B.Q. Aurélien OR. P.B. P.B.Q. Vabalathe P.B. Tacite OR. P.B. Florien AR. P.B. P.B.Q. Probus OR. M.B. P.B. P.B.Q Carus P.B. Carin OR. P.B.Q. Dioclétien OR. P.B. P.B.Q. Maximien Hercule P.B. Carausius AR. P.B. Allectus OR. P.B. Constance Chlore AR. P.B. Sévère II BR.M. Licinius père OR. Licinius fils P.B. Autonomes de Rome (Constantin) G.B.M. Constant I BR.M. Constance II BR.M. Constance Galle BR.M. (avec s. C.) Gordien III G.B. M.B. Trajan Dèce G.B. M.B. Emilien G.B. Gallien G.B. M.B. Postume G.B. M.B Florien M.B.

VIRTVS AVG. ET CAESS. NN. Constantin I OR.M.

VIRTVS AVGG. Sept. Sévère AR. Caracalla OR. AR. AR.Q. Gordien d'Afrique fils AR. Philippe père OR. AR. Philippe fils AR. Trébonien Galle AR. Volusien OR. AR. Valérien B. Gallien OR. B. B.Q. Valérien jeune B. Postume B. Victorin B. Tétricus père BIL. P.B. Carus OR. P.B. P.B.Q. Numérien OR. P.B. P.B.Q. Carin OR. M.B. P.B. P.B.Q. Dioclétien OR. M.B. P.B. P.B.Q. Maximien Hercule OR. M.B. P.B. P.B.Q. Carausius AR. P.B. Constance Chlore OR. P.B. P.B.Q. Galère Maximien P.B. Licinius père P.B. Licinius fils P.B. Constantin I P.B. Crispus P.B. Constantin II P.B. Constant I BR.M. Constance II BR.M. Décence BR.M. (avec s. C.) Caracalla M.B. Gordien d'Afrique père G.B. Gordien d'Afrique fils G.B. Philippe fils G.B. Tréb. Galle G.B. M.B. Volusien G.B. M.B. Valérien G.B. M.B. Gallien G.B. M.B. Florien M.B.

VIRTVS AVGG. ET CAESS. Maximien Hercule OR. Sévère II OR. Maximin II OR.

VIRTVS AVGG. ET CAESS. NN. Maximien Hercule M.B. Constace Chlore M.B. Galère Maximien M.B. Sévère II M.B. Maximin II M.B. Constantin I M.B.

VIRTVS AVGGG. Carus P.B. Numérien OR. P.B. Carin OR. P.B. Maximien Hercule P.B. Carausius P.B. Valentinien II P.B. Théodose I P.B.

VIRTVS AVGG. NN. Maximien Hercule OR. Licinius père OR.M. Constant I †.M.B. P.B. P.B.Q. Constance II P.B.

VIRTVS AVGG. PONT. TR. P. IIII. S. C. Caracalla G.B.

VIRTVS AVG. IMP. III. COS II. P. P. S. C. Commode G.B. M.B.

VIRTVS AVG. IMP. IIII. COS II. P. P. S. C. Commode M.B.

VIRTVS AVG. IMP. VI. COS. III. Marc Aurèle OR. (avec s. C.) G.B.

VIRTVS AVG. IMP. X. COS. III. P. P. Marc Aurèle BR.M. (avec s. C) G.B.

VIRTVS AVG. IN AVG. Carausius AR.

VIRTVS AVG. N. Constantin I BR.M. Constant I BR.M. Constance II BR.M. G.B.M. Julien II BR.M. G.B.

VIRTVS AVG. NOSTRI. Constance II BR.M. Magnence AR.M.

VIRTVS AVG. P. M. TR. P. XI. IMP. VII. COS. V. P. P. Commode OR.M.

VIRTVS AVG. P. XV. Gallien B.

VIRTVS AVG. S. P. Q. R. Gallien B. Claude II P.B.

VIRTVS AVG. VII. C. Gallien B.

VIRTVS AVGVST. Vespasien AR. Sept. Sévère AR.

VIRTVS AVGVSTI. Alex. Sévère BR M. Gordien III BR.M. Gallien OR. B. BR.M. Claude II P.B. Aurélien OR. Tacite BR.M. Florien OR. P.B. Probus OR. BR.M. G.B. M.B. P.B. Licinius père OR. Constantin I OR.Q. P.B.Q. Constantin II P.B. Constant I BR.M. Constance II BR.M. (avec S. C.) Alex. Sévère G.B. M.B. Gordien III G.B. M.B.

VIRTVS AVGVSTI N. Constantin I OR. Constance II BR.M. G.B.M.

VIRTVS AVGVSTI NOSTRI. Magnence OR.M. AR.M.

VIRTVS AVGVSTI — VOT. X. Constantin I P.B.

VIRTVS AVGVSTOR. Sept. Sévère AR. Caracalla AR. Caracalla et Géta AR. Géta AR. Carin OR.M. G.B.M. (avec S. C.) Sept. Sévère G.B. M.B. Caracalla G.B. M.B. Géta M.B.

VIRTVS AVGVSTORVM. Sept. Sévère OR. Caracalla OR. Volusien BR.M. Gallien AR.M. Numérien BR.M. Dioclétien P.B. Maximien Hercule OR. P.B. Constance II BR.M. P.B. Vétranion P.B. Magnence BR.M. Constance Galle BR.M. Théodose I G.B.M

VIRTVS AVGVSTORVM NN. Constantin I OR.M.

VIRTVS AV. P. Tétricus père P.B.

VIRTVS CAES. Constantin II BR.M.

VIRTVS CAESARIS. Julien II BR.M.

VIRTVS CAESAR. NN. Crispus OR.

VIRTVS CAESARVM. Constant I G.B.M. Constance II BR.M.

VIRTVS CAESS. Constantin I (hybride) P.B. Crispus P.B. Constantin II BR.M. P.B. Constant I BR.M. Constance II BR.M. G.B.M. M.B. P.B.

VIRTVS CAESS. GLORIA SAECVLI. Constantin I BR.M.

VIRTVS CARI AVG. Cirus P.B.

VIRTVS CARI INVICTI AVG. Carus OR.

VIRTVS CLAVDI AVG. Claude II OR.

VIRTVS CONSTANTI AVG. Constance II OR.M

VIRTVS CONSTANTI CAES. Constance II OR.M. OR.

VIRTVS CONSTANTINI AVG. Constantin II OR.M. OR.

VIRTVS CONSTANTINI CAES. Constantin I M.B. Constantin II OR.M.

VIRTVS CONSTANTINI C. AVS. Constantin II OR.

VIRTVS CONSTANTIS AVG Constant I OR.M.

VIRTVS COS. II. Marc Aurèle AR. (avec S. C.) G.B. M.B.

VIRTVS DD. NN. AVGG. Constant I AR.M. Constance II AR.M.

VIRTVS D. N. CONSTANTINI AVG. Constantin I OR.M.

VIRTVS EQVIT. Postume OR. B. Aurélien OR.

VIRTVS EQVITVM. Postume B.

VIRTVS EXERC. Valentinien II AR.

VIRTVS EXERC. (ou EXERCI.) GALL. Julien II OR.

VIRTVS EXERCIT. Licinius père P.B. Licinius fils P.B. Constantin I P.B. Constantin II P.B. Constance II P.B. Théodose I M.B. (Avec — VOT. X.) Licinius père P.B. Licinius fils P.B. Crispus P.B. Constantin II P.B. (Avec — VOT. XX.) Licinius père P.B. Licinius fils P.B. Constantin I P.B. Crispus P.B. Constantin II P.B. (Avec — VOTIS. XX.) Constantin I P.B.

VIRTVS EXERCITI. Galère Maximien M.B. Magnence AR. Décence AR. Valentinien I M.B.P.B. Valentinien II M.B. Théodose I M.B. Magnus Maximus M.B. Honorius P.B.

VIRTVS EXERCITVM. Constant I OR.M. OR. AR M. Constance II OR.M. Vétranion M.B. P.B.

VIRTVS EXERCITVS. Philippe père AR. Postume OR. Maximien Hercule M.B.

Galère Maximien M.B. Maximin II M.B. Constantin I AR.M. M.B. Constant I AR.M. Constance II AR.M. AR. Vétranion P.B. Magnence P.B. Décence P.B. Constance Galle AR.M. Julien II AR.M. F B. Valentinien I AR.M. Valens AR.M. AR. Gratien AR.M. Valentinien II AR.M. Théodose I AR M. Magnus Maximus AR.M. Eugène AR.M. AR. P.B. Honorius AR.M.

VIRTVS EXERCITVS GALL. Licinius père OR Constantin I OR. OR.Q. Constantin II OR. Constant I OR. Constance II OR.

VIRTVS EXERCITVS ROMANI. Julien II OR.

VIRTVS EXERCITVS ROMANORVM. Julien OR. G.B.

VIRTVS FALERI. Gallien B.

VIRTVS GALLIENI AVGVSTI. Gallien OR.M.

VIRTVS HERCVLI CAESARIS. Constance Chlore OR.

VIRTVS ILLYRICI. Aurélien OR. P.B. Dioclétien OR. Maximien Hercule OR. Constance Chlore OR.

VIRTVS IN. AVG. Carausius AR.

VIRTVS INVIC. AVG. Probus P.B.

VIRTVS INVICTI AVG. Probus P.B.

VIRTVS IOVI CAESARIS. Galère Maximien OR.

VIRTVS IV. AVG. Carausius P.B.

VIRTVS MIL. Gallien B.

VIRTVS MILIT. Aurélien P.B. Dioclétien AR.

VIRTVS MILITVM. Lélien OR. B. Aurélien OR. P.B. Dioclétien OR. AR. Maximien Hercule OR. AR. AR.Q. Constance Chlore OR. AR. Galère Maximien OR. AR. AR.Q. M.B. Maximin II AR. AR.Q. M.B. Maxence AR. Constantin I AR. AR.Q.

VIRTVS MILITVM DD. NN. Licinius fils P.B.

VIRTVS PERPETVA AVG. Constance Chlore M.B. Constantin I M.B.

VIRTVS POSTVMI AVG. Postume M.B.

VIRTVS POSTVMI S. C. Postume G.B.

VIRTVS PROBI AVG. Probus OR. AR (?). BR.M G.B. P.B. P.B.Q.

VIRTVS ROMANI EXERCITVS. Valentinien I AR.M.

VIRTVS ROMANOR. Julien II P.B.Q.

VIRTVS ROMANORVM. Julien II BR.M. Valentinien I OR. Valens OR. Gatien OR. AR. P.B. Valentinien II AR. P.B. Théodose I AR (1). P.B. Magnus Maximus AR. Victor OR. AR. Eugène AR. P B. Honorius OR. AR. Sébastien AR. Attale AR. Valentinien III AR. (Avec – VOT. XX.) Constance II BR.M.

VIRTVS TR. POT. III. COS. II. S. C. Marc Aurèle G.B. M.B.

VIRTVS TR. POT. IIII. COS. S. C. Marc Aurèle G.B. M.B

VIRTVS TR. POT. VI. COS. II. S. C. Marc Aurèle G.B. M.B.

VIRTVS TR. POT. XV. COS. II. S. C. Marc Aurèle M.B.

VIRTVT. AVG. P. M. TR. P. XII. IMP. VIII COS. V. P. P. Commode AR.

VIRTVT. AVG. TR. P. VII. IMP. IIII. COS. III. P. P. Commode OR.

VIRTVTE AVG. Sept. Sévère AR.

VIRTVTI AVG. Adrien OR. Pesc. Niger AR. Albin AR. Sept. Sévère OR. Claude II P.B. Carausius P.B. (avec s. c.) Sept. Sévère G.B.

VIRTVTI AVGG. Sept. Sévère OR. Carin P.B. Dioclétien P.B. Maximien Hercule OR. P.B. P.B.Q. Constance Chlore OR.

VIRTVTI AVGGG. Carausius P.B.

VIRTVTI AVG. P. M. TR. P. XII. IMP. VIII. COS. V. P. P. S. C. Commode G.B. M.B.

VIRTVTI AVG. S. P. Q. R. Gallien B.

VIRTVTI AVG. TR. P. VIII. IMP. V. COS. IIII. P. P. Commode BR.M.

VIRTVTI AVGVSTI. Adrien G.B.M. Gordien III OR. OR.Q. AR. AR.Q. Gallien B. Postume B. Tétricus père OR. Probus OR. (avec s. c.) Domitien M.B. Adrien M.B. Gordien III M.B.

VIRTVTI AVGVSTI TR. P. VII. IMP. IIII. COS. III. P. P. Commode BR.M. (avec s. c.) G.B.

VIRTVTI ET FELICITATI. Trajan OR.

VIRTVTI EXERCITI. Galère Maximien M.B. Maximin II M.B.

---

(1) Quelquefois VRTVS.

VIRTVTI EXERCITVS Galère Maximien M B. Maximin II M.B. †M.B. P.B. Licinius père M.B. †M.B. Constantin I M.B. (avec CMH.) Galère Maximien †M.B. Maximin II †M.B.
VIRTVTI HERCVLIS. Maximien Hercule OR. Galère Maximien OR.
VIRTVTI MILITVM. Galère Maximien AR.
VIT. AVGG. Majorien AR.
VITORIA. Tétricus père P.B.
VITRIA. Majorien AR. AR.Q.
VLTORA AVG. Carausius AR.
VNDIQVE VICTORES. Numérien P.B. Maximien Hercule P.B. Constance Chlore P.B
VN. MR. Constantin I P B.Q.
VOLKANVS VLTOR. Autonomes de Galba AR.
VORIVIVA Carausius AR.
VOT. Tétricus père et fils M.B. Julien II P.B.
VOT. V. Constantin II P.B. Jovien P.B. Valentinien I AR. Valens AR.M. AR. Procope AR. Gratien P.B.Q. Théodose I P.B.Q.
VOT. V. MVL. X. Jovien AR.
VOT. V. MVLT. X. Autonomes de Constantinople (Constantin) OR.T. Crispus P.B.Q. Constance Galle AR. P.B.Q. Julien II AR. Jovien AR. P.B. Valentinien I AR. P.B. Valens AR.M. AR. P.B.Q. Gratien AR.M. AR. P.B.Q. Valentinien II AR. P.B.Q. Théodose I AR. P.B.Q. Magnus Maximus P.B.Q. Eugène AR M. Honorius AR.M. AR. Constance III AR Attale AR. Glycère AR. Népos AR.
VOT. V. MVLT. X. CAESS. Licinius fils P.B. Crispus P.B. Constantin II P.B.
VOT. V. MVLT. X. — VRB. ROM. B. Jovien P.B.
VOT. V. MVLTIS X. Valentinien I AR. Valens AR.
VOT. V. Q. MVLT. X. Maxence P.B.
VOT. X. Constance Chlore OR.Q. P.B. Galère Maximien P.B. Maximin II M.B. Constantin II P.B. Julien II P.B. Valentinien II AR.
VOT. X. AVG N. Constantin I P.B.Q.
VOT. X. CAES. Constance Chlore OR. Constance II OR.
VOT. X. CAESS. Constance Chlore OR. Galère Maximien OR. Sévère II P.B.Q. Maximin II P.B.Q.
VOT. X. CAESS. NN. Maximin II P.B.Q.
VOT. X. ET XV. F. Licinius fils P.B.
VOT. X. ET XV. FEL. RED. CS. Licinius père P.B.
VOT. X. ET XV. F. RED. CS. Constantin I P.B. P.B Q.
VOT. X. ET XV. F. REP. CS. Crispus P.B.
VOT. X. ET XV. F. R. S. Licinius père P.B.
VOT. X. ET XV. F. R. T. Constantin II P.B.
VOT. X. ET XX. Gallien OR. B.
VOT X. FEL. Maxence P.B.
VOT. X. M. XX. Dioclétien P.B. Maximien Hercule P.B. Galère Maximien P.B.
VOT. X. MVLT. X. (sic). Valens P B.Q.
VOT. X. MVL. XX. Constantin I P.B.Q.
VOT. X. MVLT. XV. Valens AR.M. Gratien AR. Valentinien II P.B.Q. Théodose I AR.M.
VOT. X. MVLT. XX. Dioclétien P.B. Maximin II P.B Licinius père P.B. Julien II AR. P.B. Jovien AR. Valentinien I AR. Valens AR. Gratien AR. P.B.Q. Valentinien II OR. AR. P.B.Q. Théodose I AR. P.B.Q. Honorius AR.M. AR. Valentinien III OR.
VOT. X. SIC XX. Constance Chlore AR.Q. Galère Maximien P.B.Q.
VOT. XV. FEL. XX. Licinius père P.B. Licinius fils P.B. Constantin I P.B. Crispus P.B.
VOT. XV. MVLT. XX. Cons'ant I P.B. Constance II P.B.Q. Valentinien I AR. Valens AR. P.B.Q. Gratien AR. P.B.Q. Valentinien II P.B Q. Théodose I AR. P.B.Q. Honorius AR.M. AR.
VOT. VX. MVLT. XX. Valentinien I AR. Valens AR. Gratien AR.
VOT. XV. MVLTIS XX. Constantin I AR. Valentinien I AR.M.
VOT. XV. MVLT. XXX. Gratien AR.

VOT. XX. Dioclétien P.B. Maximien Hercule P.B. Constance Chlore P.B. Galère Maximien P.B.

VOT. XX. AVG. Dioclétien P.B.Q.

VOT. XX. AVGG. Dioclétien OR. Maximien Hercule OR. P.B. P.B.Q. Constance Chlore P.B.Q. Sévère II P.B.

VOT. XX. AVGG. NN. Maximien Hercule OR. Constance Chlore OR. P.B.Q.

VOT. XX. CAES. Constance Chlore P.B.Q.

VOT. XX. MVL. XXX. Valens AR. P.B.Q. Gratien P.B.Q.

VOT. XX. MVLT. XXX. Licinius père P.B. Licinius fils P.B. Constantin I P.B. P.B.Q. Autonomes de Constantinople (Constantin) P.B.Q. de Rome P.B. P.B.Q. Constant I P.B.Q. Constance II P.B.Q. Valens P.B Q Gratien P.B.Q. Valentinien II P.B.Q. Honorius OR. Placidie OR. Honoria OR.

VOT. XX. P. M. TR. P. XV. IMP. VIII. COS. VI. S. C. Commode M.B.

VOT. XX. SIC. XXX. Dioclétien OR. P.B.Q. Maximien Hercule OR. Constance Chlore P.B.Q.

VOT. XXV. Constance Chlore P.B.

VOT. XXX. Constantin I P.B.

VOT. XXX. AVGG. Maximien Hercule P.B. P.B.Q.

VOT. XXX. AVGG. NN. Maximien Hercule P.B.Q.

VOT. XXX. AVG. N. Maximien Hercule P.B.Q.

VOT. XXX. MVLT. XXX. Gratien P B.Q.

VOT. XXX. MVLTIS XXXX. Constance II P.B.

VOT. XXX. MVLT. XXXX. Julien II AR. Honorius OR. Valentinien III OR M. OR. Eudoxie OR.

VOT. XXXX. Constance II AR.

VOTA S. C. Antonin M.B.

VOTA AVGVSTI. Victorin OR. B.

VOTA CAESS. — VOT. XXX. Constantin II BR.M.

VOTA COS. IIII. Antonin OR. (avec S. C.) G.B. M.B.

VOTA DEC. ANN. SVSC. TR. P. VI. IMP. III. COS. III. P. P. S. C. Commode M.B.

VOTA DEC. ANN. SVSC. TR. P. XX. IMP. IIII. COS. III. S. C. Marc Aurèle M.B.

VOTA DECENALIA Gallien B.

VOTA ORBIS. — S. C. Valérien B. Gallien B. Claude II P.B.

VOTA ORBIS ET VRBIS SEN ET P. R. FEL. Licinius père AR.M.

VOTA ORBIS ET VRBIS SEN. ET P. R. — XX.-XXX. AVG. Constantin I AR.M.

VOTA P. M. TR. P. COS. III. P. P. Tétricus père et fils OR. P.B.

VOTA PVBLC. Constantin I P.B.Q.

VOTA PVBLICA. Adrien OR. AR. Faustine mère OR. Marc Aurèle OR. Lucille OR. AR. Crispine et Commode BR.M. Sept. Sévère OR. AR. Caracalla AR. Géta OR. AR. Elagabale AR. P.B. Tétricus père P.B. P.B.Q. Numérien P.B. Carin P.B. Dioclétien M.B. Maximien Hercule OR. M.B. Licinius père P.B.Q. Constantin I OR. P.B. P.B.Q. Crispus P.B. P.B.Q. Constantin II P.B.Q. Constant I P.B.Q. Constance II P.B.Q. Magnence P.B.Q. Constance Galle P.P.Q. Julien II AR.M. M.B. P.B. P.B.Q. Autonomes de Julien II M.B. P.B. P.B.Q. de Julien II et Hélène II †.M.B. d'Hélène II P.B. P.B.Q. Jovien M.B. P.B. P.B.Q. Valentinien I OR. P.B. P.B.Q. Valens OR. M.B. P.B.Q. Gratien OR. AR. P.B.Q. Valentinien II OR P.B.Q. Théodose I OR. Eugène OR. Honorius OR. (avec S. C.) Marc Aurèle G.B. M.B. Sept. Sévère G.B. M.B. Julie Domne G.B. M.B. Caracalla G.B. M.B. Géta G.B. M.B.

VOTA PVBLICA IMP. II. COS. P. P. Commode BR.M. (avec S. C.) G.B.

VOTA PVBLICA IMP. VIIII. COS. III. P. P. S. C. Marc Aurèle G.B. M.B.

VOTA PVBLICA P. M. TR. P. X. IMP. VII. COS. IIII. P. P. Commode BR.M.

VOTA PVBLICA TR. P. II. IMP. II. COS. P. P. S. C. Commode G.B.

VOTA PVBLICA TR. P. III. IMP. II. COS. P. P. S. C. Commode M.B.

VOTA PVBLICA TR. P. VIIII. IMP. VI. COS. IIII. P. P. S. C. Commode M.B.

VOTA PVBLICA TR. POT. XXII. IMP. IIII. COS. III. Commode BR.M.

VOTA PVBLLC. Constantin I. P.B.Q.

VOTA PVBL. P. M. TR. P. Macrin OR. AR. (avec S. C.) G.B. M.B.

VOTA QVICAE. Carausius P.B.

VOTA SOL. DECENN. COS. III. Marc Aurèle OR. AR. (avec S. C.) G.B. M.B.
VOTA SOL. DEC. II. COS. IIII. Marc Aurèle OR. AR. (avec S. C.) G.B. M B.
VOTA SOL DECENN II. COS. IIII. Marc Aurèle OR. AR (avec S. C.) G.B. M.B.
VOTA SOLV. PRO SAL. P. R. Commode AR.
VOTA SOLV. PRO. SAL. P. R. COS. VI. P. P. S. C. Commode G.B.
VOTA SOLVTA DECENNALIVM COS III. S. C. Marc Aurèle G.B.
VOTA SOLVT. DEC. COS. III. Sept. Sévère AR. Caracalla OR. AR.
VOTA SVSC. DECEN. S. C. Sept. Sévère G.B.
VOTA SVSC. DEC. P. M. TR. P. X. IMP. VII. COS. IIII. P. P. S. C. Commode M.B.
VOTA SVSCEP. DEC. III. COS. IIII. Antonin OR. AR.
VOTA SVSCEP. DECEN. S. C. Sept. Sévère G.B. M.B.
VOTA SVSCEP. DECENN. II. COS. III. Marc Aurèle OR. AR. (avec S. C.) G.B. M.B.
VOTA SVSCEP. DECENN. III. COS. IIII. Antonin OR. AR. (avec S. C.) G.B. M.B.
VOTA SVSCEP. DECEN. P. M. TR. P. VIIII. (ou X.) IMP. VII. COS. IIII. P. P. S. C.
Commode G.B.
VOTA SVSCEPTA. Adrien AR. (avec S. C) M.B.
VOTA SVSCEPTA DEC. III. COS. IIII. Antonin OR. (avec S. C.) G.B. M.B.
VOTA SVSCEPTA DECENN. S. C. Commode M.B.
VOTA SVSCEPTA DECENNAL. III. COS. IIII. Antonin AR.
VOTA SVSCEPTA DECENNALIA S. C. Sept. Sévère M.B.
VOTA SVSCEPTA FELICIA P. M. TR. P. XV. IMP. VII. Commode BR.M.
VOTA SVSCEPTA P. M. TR. P. COS. VI. P. P. S. P. Q. R. Trajan OR. AR.
VOTA SVSCEPTA X. Sept. Sévère AR. Caracalla AR. Géta AR. (avec S. C.) Cara-
calla M.B.
VOTA SVSCEPTA XX. Sept. Sévère OR. AR. Julie Domne (hybride) AR. Caracalla
AR. (avec S. C.) Sept. Sévère G.B. M.B.
VOTA TR. P. XXI. IMP. IIII. COS. III. S. C. Marc Aurèle M.B.
VOTA VICENNALIOR. Constantin II P.B.Q. Constance II P.B.Q.
VOTA VIGENNALLIA COS. IIII. Antonin OR. (avec S. C.) G.B.
VOTA X. DD. NN. AVG. ET CAES. — VOT. X. Magnence(?) P.B.
VOT. CAESS. — VOT. XV. Constantin II BR.M.
VOT. DECEN. TR. P. COS. II. Pertinax OR. AR.
VOT. DECE. TR. P. COS. II. S. C. Pertinax G.B. M.B.
VOTIS AVGG. Maximien Hercule P.B.
VOTIS DECENNALIB. Gallien OR. B.
VOTIS DECENNALIBVS. Sept. Sévère OR. AR. Maximin I AR. Balbin OR. AR.
Pupien OR. AR. Gordien III AR. Philippe père AR. Trajan Déce AR. Hé-
rennius AR. Tréb. Galle AR. Volusien AR. Emilien AR. Valérien B. M.B. Gal-
lien B. M.B. Tétricus père OR.Q. Maximien Hercule P.B. (avec S. C.) Maxi-
min I G.B. M.B. Balbin G.B. M.B. Pupien G.B. M.B. Gordien III G.B. M.B. Philippe
père G.B. M.B. Philippe fils G.B. M.B. Trajan Dèce G.B. M.B. Hostilien G.B.
Tréb. Galle G.B. M.B. Volusien G.B. M.B. Emilien G.B. M.B. Valérien G.B.
M.B. Gallien BR.M. G.B. M.B.
VOTIS DECENN. D. N. CONSTANTINI CAES. Constantin II OR.M.
VOTIS FELICIBVS. Commode BR.M. Dioclétien BR.M.
VOTIS MVLTIS. Majorien OR. AR. AR.Q.
VOTIS ROMANORVM. — SIC XX. SIC XXX. Dioclétien OR. OR.Q.
VOTIS VIGENNALIBVS. Alexandre Sévère OR. AR.
VOTIS V. Gratien AR. Magnus Maximus P.B.
VOTIS V. MLTIS X. Magnus Maximus AR.M. P.B.Q.
VOTIS V. MVLTIS X. Licinius père P.B. Constance II AR. Constance Galle AR.
Julien II AR. AR.Q. Jovien AR.M. AR. Valentinien I AR.M. AR. Valens AR.M.
Gratien AR.M. Constance III AR. Jovin AR. (avec — VICTORIA AVG.) Licinius
père OR. Constantin I OR. OR.Q. AR.M.
VOTIS X. Gallien B. Dioclétien P.B Maximien Hercule OR.M. P.B. Constance
Chlore P.B.Q. Galère Maximien P.B. Constantin I P.B. P.B.Q.
VOTIS X. CAES. N. Constantin I OR.M. Constantin II OR.M.
VOTIS X. CAESS. NN. Constantin II OR.M.
VOTIS X. ET XX. Gallien OR. B.

VOTIS X. ET XX. FEL. Probus P.B.
VCTIS X. ET XX. — VOTIS XX. Tacite M.B.
VOTIS X. MVLTIS XV. Valentinien I AR.M. Valens AR.M.
VOTIS X. MVLTIS XX. Constant I AR. Valens AR.M. AR. Gratien AR.M. AR.
VOTIS X. PROBI AVG. ET XX. Probus P.B
VOTIS X. SIC XX. Dioclétien P.B.Q. Constance Chlore P.B.Q. Galère Maximien OR.Q.
VOTIS XV. MVLT. XX. Gratien AR.
VOTIS XV. MVLTIS XY. Valens AR.M. Gratien AR.M. AR.
VOTIS XX. Constantin I AR. P.B.
VOTIS XX. COS. VI. Commode AR.
VOTIS XX. MVLTIS XXX. Constantin I OR.M. AR. Constantin II AR. Constance II AR.
VOTIS XXV. MVLTIS XXX. Constant I AR. Constance II AR.
VOTIS XXX. Maximien Hercule P.B. Constantin I AR.M.
VOTIS XXX. MVLTIS XXXX. Constance II AR. AR.Q. Julien II AR.
VOT. OPTATA ROMAE FEL. Maxence M.B.
VOTO PVBLICO MVLTIS XX. IMP. Carausius AR.
VOT. P. PVB. Valentinien III P.B.Q.
VOT. P. SVSC. PRO SAL. ET RED. I. O. M. SACR. Auguste AR.
VOT. P. SVSC. PR. SAL. ET RED. I. O. M. SACR. Auguste OR. AR.
VOT. PVB. Adrien OR. Valentinien II P.B.Q. Valentinien III P.B.Q. (avec S. C.) Adrien G.B.
VOT. PVBL. Valentinien III P.B Q.
VOT. PVB. P. M. TR. P. COS. II. Adrien AR.
VOT. PVB. P. M. TR. P. COS. DES. III. Adrien AR.
VOT. PVB. P. M TR. P. COS. III. Adrien AR.
VOT. Q. PVB Valentinien III P.B.Q.
VOT. QQ. MVL. X. Maxence P.B.Q.
VOT. QQ. MVL. X. FEL. Maxence P.B.Q.
VOT. QQ. MVL. XX. Maxence P.B.Q.
VOT. SOL. DECEN... III. IMP. VIII. COS. V. P. P. S. C. Commode M B.
VOT. SOL. DEC. P. M. TR. P. XI. (ou XII.) IMP. VIII. COS. V. P. P. Commode AR.
VOT. SOL. DEC. PONTIF. TR. P. XI. COS. III. S. C. Caracalla M.B.
VOT. SOLVTA X. Probus P.B.
VOT. S. PVB. Valentinien III P.B.Q.
VOT. SVSC. DEC. P. M. TR. P. VIIII. IMP. VII. COS. IIII. P. P. Commode OR.
VOT. SVSC. DEC. P. M. TR. P. X. COS. III. P. P. Sept. Sévère AR.
VOT. SVSC. DEC. P. M. TR. P. X. IMP. VII. COS. IIII. P. P. Commode OR. (avec S. C.) M.B.
VOT. SVSC. DEC. PON. TR. P. V. COS. Caracalla AR. P.B.
VOT. SVSC. DEC. III. COS. IIII. Antonin BR.M.
VOTVM PVBLIC. MVLTIS XX. IMP. Carausius AR.
VRBEM RESTITVTAM S. C. Vitellius G.B.
VRBIS ROMA. Avitus AR. Sévère III AR. Eufémie AR. (avec S. C.) Vitellius G.B.
VRBS ROMA. Autonomes de Rome (Constantin) G.B.M. P.B. P.B.Q. Constant I BR.M. Constance II G.B.M Népotien OR. M.B. Magnence M.B. Constance Galle G.B.M. Jovien BR.M. Valentinien I AR. G.B. Valens AR. Gratien AR.G.B. Valentinien II OR. AR. G.B. P.B. Théodose I AR. Eugène AR. Honorius AR. Jean AR. Valentinien III AR. Sébastien AR. Népos AR.
VRBS ROMA BEATA. Autonomes de Rome (Constantin) P.B. Constant I BR.M. Constance II G.B.M.
VRBS ROMA FELIX. Théodose I P.B. Honorius P.B.
V. S. PRO. RED. P. M. TR. P. COS. III. Adrien OR.
VT. XXXV. Théodose I P.B.
VTILITAS PVBLICA. Dioclétien P.B.Q. Maximien Hercule P.B.Q. Constance Chlore P.B. P.B.Q. Galère Maximien P.B.Q. Sévère II P.B.Q. Maximin II P.B. Constantin I P.B.

X. CONSTANTI AVG. Constance Chlore OR.

x. MAXIMINI AVG. Maximin II OR.
XV. VIR. SACR. FAC. Vitellius OR. AR.
XX. Constance Galle AR.M.
XX. DIOCLETIANI AVG. Dioclétien OR.
XX. MAXIMIANI AVG. Maximien Hercule OR.
XXXX. REMISSA S. C. Galba G.B.
XCVI. Dioclétien AR. Maximien Hercule AR. Constance Chlo;e AR. Galère Maximien AR.
♀. Constance II OR. Flaccille OR.T. Placidie OR.T. AR. Avitus P.B.Q. Sévère III AR.Q. P.B. Anthémius AR. Glycère AR.
Sans légende (1). J. César OR. AR. M.B. Brutus AR. AR.Q. Cn. Pompée G.B. M. Antoine AR. AR.Q. Octave-Auguste OR. AR. Tibère G.B. Néron AR. AR.Q. G.B. M.B. Vitellius OR. AR. Vespasien OR. AR. Titus OR. AR.M. AR. G.B. Julie de Titus OR. AR. Domitien OR. AR.M. AR. G.B. P.B. Nerva OR. Trajan OR. BR.M. Adrien OR. OR.Q. AR. BR.M. G B. M.B. Sabine OR. AR. BR.M. Antonin OR. AR. BR.M. M.B. Faustine mère OR. OR.Q. AR. BR.M. Marc Aurèle BR.M. M.B. Marc Aurèle et Vérus BR.M. Marc Aurèle et Commode BR.M. Faustine jeune BR.M. M.B. Vérus OR. BR.M. Lucille BR.M. Commode BR.M. G.B. M.B. Crispine BR.M. Albin PR.M. Elagaba'e BR.M. Philippe père BR.M. Gallien B.Q. Postume BR.M. Claude II P.B. Maximien Hercule P.B.Q. Hélène I P.B. Constantin I OR. P.B.Q. Autonomes de Constantinople (Constantin) P.B. P.B.Q. de Rome G.B.M. P.B. P.B.Q. du Peuple romain P.B.Q. Fausta P.B. P.B.Q. Crispus OR. Constantin II OR. P.B. P.B.Q. Constance II OR. P.B.Q. Constance Galle AR. Julien II OR. AR. G.B. M.B. Procope OR.Q. AR.Q. P.B Q. Théodose I OR.T. Constantin III AR. Jovin AR. A tale P.B Q. Jean OR.T. Valentinien III OR.T. AR. Sévère III P.B. P.B.Q. Glycère P.B.Q. Népos AR.Q. P.B. Augustule AR.

III. INSCRIPTIONS ON THE REVERSES OF ROMAN COLONIAL COINS

ABDERA. *Abdère*. Tibère M.B.
ABDERA D. D. *Abdère*. Tibère G.B.
ACTIA DVSARIA COL. METR. BOSTR. (OU BOSTRA). *Bostra*. Hérennius et Hostilien M.B.
ADVENTVS AVG. COR. *Corinthe*. Néron P.B. ,
ADVENTVS AVGVSTI. *Patras*. Néron P.B. (avec C. P.) P.B.
AELI. MVNICIP. CAEL. *Coela*. Gordien III M.B.
AELI. MVNICIP. COEL. *Coela*. Volusien M.B P.B.
AELI. MVNICIPI COELA. *Coela*. Aelius P.B.
AELL. (sic) MVNICI. COI. (sic). *Coela*. Gallien ·|·M.B.
AEL. MV. COEL. *Coela*. Gallien ┼M B.
AEL. MVN. COEL. *Coela*. Maximin I P.B.
AEL. MVN... COEL. *Coela*. Caracalla P.B.
AEL. MVN. COELA. *Coela*. Maximin I P.B.
AEL. MVN. COEL. ANT. *Coela*. Caracalla P.B.
AEL. MVNIC. COEL. *Coela*. L. Vérus P.B.
AEL. MVNIC. COEL. AN. *Coela*. Gordien III M.B.
AEL. MVNIC. COILA. *Coela*. Adrien P.B.
AEL. MVNIC. CVIL. (sic). *Coela*. Commode P.B.
AEL. MVNIC. CVILA. (sic). *Coela*. M. Aurèle P.B. Commode P.B.
AEL. MVNICI. COEL. *Coela*. Gallien ┼M B.
AEL. MVNICI. COILA. *Coela*. Alexandre Sévère P.B.
AEL. MVNICI. CVILA (sic). *Coela*. Septime Sévère P.B.
AEL. MVNICIP. CO. *Coela*. Tréb. Galle M.B.

(1) Voir aussi COMON. CONOB. CONS. SIS et TR. dans le champ ou à l'exergue.

AEL. MVNICIP. COEL. *Coela.* Caracalla P.B. Alex. Sévère P.B. Tréb. Galle M.B.
AEL. MVNICIP. COIL. *Coela.* Caracalla P.B. Macrin P.B. Elagabale P.B. Gallien †.M.B.
AEL. MVNICIP. COILA. *Coela.* Alex. Sévère P.B.
AEL. MVNICIP. COIL. AN. *Coela.* Elagabale P.B.
AEL. MVNICIPI COEL. *Coela.* Maxime P.B.
AEL. MVNICIPI CVELA (*sic*). *Coela.* Maximin I P B Gordien III M.B.
AEL. MVNI. COEL. *Coela.* Tréb. Galle M.B. Gallien M.B.
AEL. MVNI. COELA. *Coela.* Philippe père †.P.B.
AEL. MVNI. COEL. AI(?). *Coela.* Philippe fils P.B.
AEL. MVNI. COEL. ME. *Coela.* Philippe père †.P B.
AEL. MVNI. COIL. *Coela.* Elagabale P.B.
AEL. MVNI. COILA. *Coela.* Alex. Sévere P.B.
AEL. MVNI. CVELA (*sic*). *Coela.* Maxime P.B.
AESCHINO CAES. L. ITER. PLOTIO PLEB. II. VIR. — ROMA. *Cnosse.* Auguste M.B.
AETERNITATI AVGVSTAE C. A. E. *Emérita.* Auguste M.B. Tibère G.B.
AETERNITATIS AVGVSTAE C. A. E *Emérita.* Auguste M.B.
AETERNITATIS AVGVSTAE C. V T. T. *Tarraco.* Auguste G.B. Tibère G.B.
AETERNVM BENEFICIVM. *Sidon* Elagabale G.B.
AGRIPPINA C. CAESARIS AVG. GERMANICI MATER C. I. C. — αα. *Apamée.* Drusille, Julie et Agrippine M.B.
AGRIPPINA DIVA DRVSILLA IVLIA. C. I. C. *Apamée.* Néron et Drusus M.B.
AIL. MVNIC. COIL. (OU COILA). *Coela.* Commode P.B.
AIL. MVNICIPI COILA. *Coela.* Commode M.B.
AIL. MVNI. COEL. AVG. *Coela.* Antonin P.B.
ALEXAND. TROADA. *Alexandrie Troade.* Tréb. Galle †.M.B.
ALEXAN. TROAC (*sic*). *Alexandrie Troade.* Alex. Sévère M.B.
AN... COLONI. *Antioche Pisidie.* Salonin P.B.
ANT. AVG. GETA. CAES. C. II. L. *Laodicée.* Julie Domne M.B.
ANT. AVG. GET. CAE. C. II. L. *Laodicée.* Sept. Sévère M.B(1).
ANT. AVGVS. GETA COL. L. L. *Laodicée.* Sept. Sévère M.B.
ANT. COL *Antioche Pisidie.* Titus †.M B.
ANTHIO. ANTIOCHI. COL. *Antioche Pisidie.* Philippe père M.B.
ANTHIOS. ANTIOCH. COL. *Antioche Pisidie.* Alex. Sévère M.B.
A.JTHOS. ANTIOCH. COL. *Antioche Pisidie.* Philippe père M.B.
ANTI. CON. AVG. S. R. *Antioche Pisidie.* Gallien †.M.B
ANTIOC. CL. CO. S. R. *Antioche Pisidie.* Volusien M.B.
ANTIOCHAE (*sic*) COLONIAE. *Antioche Pisidie.* M. Aurèle P.B.
ANTIOCH. C. L. S. R. *Antioche Pisidie.* Gallien †.M.B. Salonin †.M.B.
ANTIOCH. CO. *Antioche Pisidie.* Claude II G.B.
ANTIOCH. COL. *Antioche Pisidie.* Philippe père M.B.
ANTIOCH. COL. CAES. *Antioche Pisidie* Alex. Sévère BR.M.
ANTIOCH. COLONIA. *Antioche Pisidie.* Géta P.B.
ANTIOCH. COLONIAE CAES. *Antioche Pisidie.* Sept. Sévère †.P. B
ANTIOCH. COLONIAE S. R. *Antioche Pisidie.* Gordien III P.B.
ANTIOCH. COLON. S. R. *Antioche Pisidie.* Philippe père M.B.
ANTIOCH. COL. S. R. *Antioche Pisidie.* Caracalla G.B. Philippe père M B. Volusien M.B. †.M.B. Gallien †.M.B.
ANTIOCHEAE COLONIAE. *Antioche Pisidie.* M. Aurèle P.B.
ANTIOCHENI COL. CAES. *Antioche Pisidie.* M. Aurèle G.B.
ANTIOCHIA. *Antioche Syrie.* Titus P.B. Domitien P.B.
ANTIOCHIA COLONI. *Antioche Pisidie.* Alex. Sévère P.B.
ANTIOCHIA COLONIA CAESA. (CAESARI. OU CAESARIA.) S. R. *Antioche Pisidie.* Gordien III G.B.
ANTIOCHIA S. R. *Antioche Pisidie.* Gordien III G.B.
ANTIOCHII. C. CL. S. R. *Antioche Pisidie.* Valérien M.B.
ANTIOCHI. CL. (OU CO.). *Antioche Pisidie.* Claude II M.B. †.M.B.

(1) Voir note, Tome IV, page 94.

ANTIOCHI. CO. ANTIOC. S. R. *Antioche Pisidie.* Trajan Dèce M.B.
ANTIOCHI. COL. CA. S. R. *Antioche Pisidie.* Trajan Dèce M.B.
ANTIOCHI. COLONI. S. R. *Antioche Pisidie.* Philippe père M.B.
ANTIOCIII. COLON. S. R. *Antioche Pisidie.* Trajan Dèce M.B.
ANTIOCHI. COLO. S. R. *Antioche Pisidie.* Philippe père M.B. Trajan Dèce M.B.
ANTIOCHI. COL. S. R. *Antioche Pisidie.* Gallien G.B. Volusien †M.B. Valérien †M.B.
ANTIOCHIO CLA. S. R. *Antioche Pisidie.* Volusien ⊹ M.B. Valérien ⊹ M.B.
ANTIOCHIOS... *Antioche Pisidie.* Volusien †.M.B.
ANTIOCII. OC. L. S. R. *Antioche Pisidie.* Gallien M.B.
ANTIOCH. S. R. *Antioche Pisidie.* Gordien III G.B. Volusien M.B.
ANTIO. CL. — T. S. C. *Antioche Pisidie.* Gallien M.B.
ANTIOH. CL. S. R. *Antioche Pisidie.* Gallien M.B.
ANTIOH. O. CL. *Antioche Pisidie.* Gallien ⊹ M.B.
ANTIOSH. IC S. R. *Antioche Pisidie.* Gallien G.B.
ANTONIA BRITANNICVS OCTAVIA. *Corinthe.* Claude I M.B.
ANTONINIANA AL. COL. AVR. METRO. BOSTRA. *Bostra.* Caracalla ⊹.P.B.
ANTONINIANA PVTI. LAV. COL. ET METROP. *Laodicée.* Caracalla G.B.
A. PLAVTIVS. PRO. COS. *Chypre.* Auguste P.B. Livie P.B.
APOLLINI CLAR. C. I. C A. — D. D. *Apamée.* M. Aurèle M.B.
APOLLINI PROPVG. COLON. CAEM. (sic). *Cremna.* Commode G.B.
APOLLINIS SMINTHEI. *Alexandrie Troade.* Caracalla †M.B.
APOLLIN. SMINTHEI. *Alexandrie Troade.* Adrien P.B.
APOLLO AVGVST. C. P *Patras.* Néron M.B.
APOLLONI SANCTO.-S. M. A(1). *Antioche Syrie.* Julien II P.B.
A. P. SID. CO. METR. (OU METRO). *Sidon.* Elagabale M.B.
A. VATRONIO LABEONE II. VIR COR. *Corinthe.* Auguste P.B.
AVG. CAES. M..... *Césarée, Samarie.* Trajan Dèce M.B.
AVG. COL. CREM. *Cremna.* Elagabale M.B.
AVGVSTA. *Italica.* Livie M.B.
AVGVSTA EMERITA. *Emérita.* Auguste G.B. M.B. Livie G.B. Tibère G.B.
AVGVSTA MATER PATRIA (sic). *Leptis.* Tibère G.B.
AVGVSTA MATER PATRIAE. *Leptis.* Auguste G.B.
AVGVSTV. *Thysdrus.* Auguste G.B.
AVGVSTVS. *Césarée-Panias.* Auguste BR.M.
    — *Parium.* Auguste M.B. Caïus César P.B.
AVGVSTVS DIVI F. *Gadès.* Auguste BR.M. G.B.
AVGVSTVS IMP. XXII. COS. XVI. *Parium.* Domitien M.B.
AV. PI. SID. C. MET. *Sidon.* J. Paula P.B.
AVR. PIA SID. COL. METR. CE. PER. IS. OE. *Sidon.* Elagabale G.B.
AVR. PIA SID. COL. METROP. AETER. B. (OU BE). *Sidon.* Elagabale G.B.
AVR. PIA SIDON. COL. METRO. *Sidon.* Elagabale G.B.
AVR. PIA SIDON. COLONIA M..... — III. GAL. *Sidon.* Elagabale G.B. M B.
AVR. PIA SIDON. COLONIA M..... — LEG. III. PAR. *Sidon.* Elagabale G.B
BACC. FRONT. CN. BVCCO IIVIR. II. C. V. I. CEL. *Celsa.* Tibère M.B.
BILBILIS. *Bilbilis.* Auguste M.B.
C. A. *Césarée-Panias.* Auguste BR.M. G B .M.B †.P.B.
C. A. A. PATR *Patras.* Crispine G.B. Sept. Sévère M.B. † M.B.
C. A. A. PATRENSIS. *Patras.* Aelius P.B.
C. A. A. P. PATRIAE. *Patras.* Auguste M.B.
CABE. *Cavaillon.* Lépide AR.Q. M. Antoine P.B. Auguste AR.
C. A. C. *Aelia Capitolina.* Antonin M.B. P.B.
C. A. C. A. COM. P. FEL. *Aelia Capitolina.* Elagabale M.B.
CAE. ANTIOCH. *Antioche Pisidie.* Sept. Sévère †P.B.
CAE. ANTIOCH COL. S. R. *Antioche Pisidie.* Caracalla G.B.
CAE. ANTIOCH. S. R. *Antioche Pisidie.* Gordien III G.B.
CAECILIO NIGRO IIVIR COR. *Corinthe.* Caligula P.B.
C. AE..... CO. P. F. *Aelia Capitolina.* Valérien †.M.B.

---

(1) Quelquefois dans le champ, une des lettres: A. B. Γ. Δ. E. Σ. Z. II. Θ. ou J.

C. A. E. LE. VX. *Emérita.* Auguste P.B.
C. AEM. METO. T. COR. M. ATEL. PRES. C. CAE. CAN. IIII. VIR CLVNIA. *Clunia.* Tibère M.B.
C. AEM. MET. T. COR. M. ATEL. PRES. C. CAE. CAND. IIII. VIR. CLNIA (*sic*). *Clunia.* Tibère M.B.
C. AEM. MET. T. COR. M. ATEL. PRES. C. CAE. CAN. IIII. VIR. CLVNIA. *Clunia.* Tibère M.B.
CAES. ANTI. CL. R. S. *Antioche Pisidie.* Philippe père M.B.
CAES. ANTIOCH. C. L. — S. R. *Antioche Pisidie.* Gordien III M.B.
CAES. ANTIOCH. COL. — S. R. *Antioche Pisidie.* Gordien III BR.M. G.B. M.B. Philippe fils M.B.
CAES. ANTIOCH. CO. S. R. *Antioche Pisidie.* Philippe père M.B.
CAES. ANTIOCHI. C. (OU COL) S. R. *Antioche Pisidie.* Philippe père †.M.B.
CAES. ANTIOCH. S. R. *Antioche Pisidie.* Gordien III BR.M.
CAESAR AVGV. MVN. KANINIO. ITER. L. TITIO IIVIR. *Caesar Augusta.* Auguste M.B.
CAESAR AVGVSTA ALLIAR. T. VERRIO IIVIR. *Caesar Augusta.* Auguste M B.
CAESAR AVGVSTA C. ALLIAR. (OU ALLIARIO.) T. VERRIO IIVIR. *Caesar Augusta.* Auguste M.B.
CAESAR AVGVSTA C. ALSANO T. SERVIO IIVIR. *Caesar Augusta.* Auguste M.B.
CAESAR AVGVSTA CN. DOM. AMP. C. VET IIVIR. *Caesar Augusta.* Auguste M.B.
CAESAR AVGVSTA C. SABINO P. VARO IIVIR. *Caesar Augusta.* Auguste M.B.
CAESAR AVGVSTA L. CASSIO C. VALER. FEN. IIVIR. *Caesar Augusta.* Auguste M.B. P.B
CAESAR AVGVSTA M. PORCI. CN. FAD. IIVIR. *Caesar Augusta.* Auguste M.B.
CAESAR AVGVSTA MVN. KANINIO ITER. L. TITIO IIVIR. *Caesar Augusta.* Auguste M.B.
CAESAR AVGVSTA Q. LVTAT. M. FABI. IIVIR. *Caesar Augusta.* Auguste M.B.
CAESAR AVGVSTA Q. LVTAT. M. FABIO. *Caesar Augusta.* Auguste M.B.
CAESAR AVGVSTA Q. MAXIMO ITER. C. VALENTINO IIVIR. *Caesar Augusta.* Auguste M.B.
CAESAR AVGVSTA Q. STATIO M. FABRICIO IIVIR. *Caesar Augusta.* Auguste M.B.
CAESAR AVGVST. CN. DO. AMP. C. VET. IIVIR. *Caesar Augusta.* Auguste P.B.
CAESAR AV. MVN. KANINIO ITER. L. TITIO IIVIR. *Caesar Augusta.* Augus'e P.B.
CAESARIBVS IIII. VIR CART. *Cartéia.* Cermanicus et Drusus P.B.
CAES. AVGVS. CN. DOM. AMP. C. VET. LANC IIVIR. *Caesar Augusta.* Auguste M.B.
CALAGVRRI. IVLIA. *Calagurris.* Auguste M.B
C. ALEX. AVG. *Alexandrie Troade.* Alex. Sevère †.M.B.
C. A. O. *Olbasa.* Antonin P.B.
C A. PA. *Patras?* ou *Parium?* Domitien P.B.
C. A. PI. MET. SID. *Sidon.* Annia Faustine M.B.
CAPIT. (OU CAPITO) Q. *Cyrénaïque.* Auguste M.B.
C. APRON D. D. P. P. IIVIR. *Utique.* Tibère P.B.
C. ARR. T. CAEL. P. REST. G. CAEL. CAND. IIII. VIR. *Clunia.* Tibère M.B.
C. AVG. CAESAR. *Césarée, Samarie.* Trajan P.B.
C. BAEBIVS. P. F. L. RVSTICELIVS BASTERNA IIVIR. QVINQ. D. D. *Dium.* Tibère P.B.
C. C. A. *Caesar Augusta.* Auguste M.B. Tibère M.B. Caligula M B. P.B.
C. C. A. A. COS. IIII. *Cologne.* Postume P.B.
C. CAEC. SER. M. VAL. QVAD. IIVIR. MVN. TVR. *Turiaso.* Tibère M.B.
C. C. A. IIVIR. — TIB FLAVO PRAEF. GERMAN. L IVENT. LVPERCO. *Caesar Augusta.* Auguste P.B.
C. C. A. IVNIANO LVPO PR. C. CAESAR G. POMPON. PARRA IIVIR. *Caesar Augusta.* Livie M.B.
C. CARRI AQVIL. L. IVNI VETE. IIVIR. — C. C. A. *Caesar Augusta.* Tibère P.B.
C. C. A. SCIPIONE ET MONTANO IIVIR. *Caesar Augusta* Auguste G.B.
C. CASSIVS C. F. IIVIR. C .. DIF. S. C. C. R. *Sinope.* M. Antoine P.B.
C. C. A. TIB. FLAVO PRAEF. GERMAN. L. IVENT. LVPERCO IIVIR. *Caesar Augusta.* Auguste G.B. M.B.
C. C. A. TITVLLO ET MONTANO IIVIR. *Caesar Augusta.* Auguste G.B.
C. CELERE C. RECTO IIVIRI. *Calagurris.* Tibère M.B.
C. CELERE C. RECTO IIVIR. (OU VIRI.) M. C. I. C. *Calagurris.* Tibère M.B.

C. C. I. B. D. D. *Babba*. Claude I M.B. P.B.
C. C. I. B. D. D. PVBL. *Babba*. Claude I M.B.
C. C. I. B. EX. CONSENSV. *Babba*. Néron M.B.
C. COR. FLORO L. CAE. ALACRE IIVIR MVN. ERCAVICA. *Ercavica*. Tibère M.B.
C. CORN. REFEC. M. HELV. FRONT. MVN. AVG. BILBIL. — IIVIR. *Bilbilis*. Caligula M.B.
CEBAC....... *Sébasté*. Domitien (*bilingue*) P.B.
CEBACTHNEON CVP. C. CIE. *Césarée, Samarie*. Commode (*bilingue*) M.B. †.M.B.
CEBACTHNEON CVP. L. CIς *Césarée, Samarie*. Commode (*bilingue*) P.B.
CєBACTHNωON. *Sébast*. Domitien (*bilingue*) P.B. P.B.Q.
CєBACTHNωN L. ѲP. *Sébasté*. Domitien (*bilingue*) M.B.
CєBACTHNωN ѲP. *Sébasté*. Domitien (*bilingue*) P.B.
CEL.. . C... Q. NEV... C. *Corinthe*. Agrippine jeune P.B.
CER. SAC. CAP. OEC. ISEL...... *Héliopolis*. Gallien M.B.
CER. SAC. CAP. OEC. ISEL. HEL. — COL. HEL. *Héliopolis*. Valérien M.B.
CERTO AEFICIO C. IVLIO IIVIR. *Corinthe*. J. César M.B.
C. F. (*sic*) COR. *Corinthe*. Adrien M.B.
C. F. P. D. *Deultum*. Claude I M B. Trajan P.B. Alex. Sévère M.B. Mamée †M.B.
P.B. Maximin I P.B. Maxime P.B. Gordien III P.B. Philippe père P.B. Philippe fils P.B.
C. G. H. I. P. *Parium*. Commode M.B. †.M.B. Caracalla † M.B. P.B.
C G. II. I. PAR. *Parium*. Commode P.B.
C. G. II. PAR. *Parium*. Alex. Sévère †.M.B.
C. G. II. PARI P. IIVII. *Parium*. Gallien M.B.
C. G. I. HAD. PAR. *Parium*. Gallien G.B.
C. G. I. H. P. *Parium*. Adrien P.B. Antonin P.B. M. Aurèle†.P.B. P.B. Commode M.B. P.B. Julie Domne P.B. Caracalla †.M.B. Géta P.B. Macrin P.B. Elagabale P.B. J. Paula † M.B. Maxime P.B. Gordien III M.B. Emilien M.B. Cornélia Supéra † M.B. Valérien †M.B. P.B. Gallien G.B. M.B. †M.B. †P.B. Salonine P.B. Salonin †.M.B. P.B.
C. G. I. H. PA. *Parium*. M. Aurèle P.B. L. Vérus P.B. Commode †.M.B. P.B. Caracalla †.M.B. P.B. Macrin †.M.B. Elagabale †M.B. Alex. Sévère †.M.B. P.B. Gallien G.B. M.B.
C. G. I. H. PAR. *Parium*. M. Aurèle P.B. Commode P.B Philippe père M.B. †M.B. Otacilie M.B. Gallien P.B.
C. G. I. H. PARI. *Parium*. Gallien †.M.B.
C. G. I. H. PARIA. *Parium*. Gallien G.B.
C. G. I. H. PARIA. — IIVII. *Parium*. Gallien G.B.
C. G. I. H. PARRIO (*sic*) CONDIT. *Parium*. Alex. Sévère †.M.B.
C. G. I. H. P. SATVS (*sic*) C. P. *Parium*. Gallien M.B.
C. G. I. P. *Parium*. Tibère P.B. Germanicus P.B. Claude I P.B. Trajan G.B.
C. G. I. PA. *Parium*. Domitien P.B.
C. G. IVL. HA. P. *Parium*. Gallien †.P.B.
C. G. IVL. HAD. PAR. *Parium*. Gallien †.P.B.
C. HEIO POLLIONE ITER C. MVSSIDIO PRISCO IIVIR. *Corinthe*. Auguste †.M.B.
C. HEIO POLLIONE ITER C. MVSSIDI. PRISCO IIVIR. *Corinthe*. Agrippa Posthume P.B.
C. HEIO POLLIONE ITER C. MVSSID. PRISCO IIVIR. *Corinthe*. Tibère M.B. Germanicus M.B.
C. HERENNIVS L. TITVCIVS IIVIR QVIN. *Pella*. Auguste M.B. P.B.
C. I. A. CINOPE (*sic*) AN. CCVII. *Sinope*. Faustine jeune M.B.
C. I. A. DVM. *Dymée*. Auguste P.B.
C. I. AV. SINOP. ANN. CCLII. *Sinope*. Caracalla †M.B
C. I. C. A. *Apamée*. Commode †M.B.
C. I. C. A. APA. *Apamée*. Otacilie † M.B. (avec D. D.) Commode P.B. J. Domne †.M B. Tranquilline P.B. Philippe fils M.B.
C. I. C. A. AP. D. D. *Apamée*. Philippe fils P.B. Tréb. Galle †.M.B.
G. I. C. A. D. D. *Apamée*. J. César P.B. Néron P.B. Trajan P.B. M. Aurèle P.B. Commode P.B. Dide Julien et Manlia Scantilla †.M.B. Julie Domne P.B. Caracalla P.B. Géta P.B. Maxime P.B. Gordien III P.B. Philippe fils P.B.
C. I. C. APA. D. D. *Apamée*. Gallien P.B.

C. I. C. P. I. SP. D. V. SP. IIVIR. — P. P. D. D. *Carthage*. Tibère M.B.
C. I. F. A. C. *Césarée. Samarie*. Adrien P.B.
C. I. F. A. ...CAESA. *Césarée, Samarie*. Antonin P.B.
C. I. F. A. F. C. CAE. MET. — S. P. Q. R. *Césarée, Samarie*. Alex. Sévère M.B.
C. I. F. AN. CXIIX. (ou CXX.). *Sinope*. Titus M.B.
C. I. F. AV. C. *Césarée, Samarie*. Trajan G.B.
C. I. F. AV. CAESAR. *Césarée, Samarie*. Adrien †.M.B.
C. I. F. AVG. CAE. METROPOLI. — S. P. Q. R. *Césarée, Samarie*. Alex. Sévère M.B.
C. I. F. AVG. CAESAR. *Césarée, Samarie*. Adrien P.B.
C. I. F. S. *Sinope*. Tranquilline P.B.
C. I. F. S. A. CCXCIII. *Sinope*. Alex. Sévère M.B.
C. I. F. S. AN. LI. *Sinope*. Auguste P.B.
C. I. F. S. AN. LXXXIII. *Sinope*. Caligula P.B.
C. I. F. S. AN. CXIII. *Sinope*. Néron M.B.
C. I. F. S. AN. C. XIIX. *Sinope*. Titus M.B. Domitien M.B. P.B.
C. I. F. S. AN. CXX. *Sinope*. Titus M.B.
C. I. F. S. AN. CXLI. *Sinope*. Nerva M.B.
C. I. F. S. AN. CXΓIX. *Sinope*. Trajan P.B.
C. I. F. S. AN. CCIII. *Sinope*. Faustine jeune M.B.
C. I. F. S. AN. CCCXI. *Sinope*. Gordien III M.B.
C. I. F. S. AN. CCCXIX. *Sinope*. Philippe fils G.B.
C. I. F. S. AN. CCCXXX. *Sinope*. Gallien G.B.
C. I. F. S. ANN. CXXX. *Sinope*. Domitien P.B.
C. I. F. S. ANN. CLXXVIII. *Sinope*. Adrien P.B.
C. I. F. S. ANN. CCXLIII. *Sinope*. Géta C.B.
C. I. F. S. ANN. CCLVII. *Sinope*. Caracalla G.B.
C. I. F. S ANN. CCXLVIII. (ou CCLX.). *Sinope*. Julie Domne M.B.
C. I. F. S. ANNO. CXXX. *Sinope*. Domitien M.B.
C. I. F. S. ANNO. CCIIII. *Sinope*. M. Aurèle †.P.B.
C. I. F. SINOP. *Sinope*. Sept Sévère P.B. Caracalla P.B.
C. I. F. SINOP. AN. CCLXI. *Sinope*. Macrin M.B. Diaduménien P.B.
C. I. F. SINOP. ANN. CCLII. *Sinope*. Sept. Sévère † M.B. Caracalla † M.B
C. I. F. SINOP. ANN. CCLXVIII. *Sinope*. Sept. Sévère † M.B.
C. I. F. SINOPE. *Sinope*. M. Aurèle P.B.
C. I. F. SINOPE. ANN. CCVII. *Sinope*. M. Aurèle G.B.
C. I. F. SINOPE. ANN. CCLV. *Sinope*. Géta G B.
C. I. F. SINOPES. *Sinope*. Géta P.B.
C. I. G. ACCI. *Acci*. Auguste P.B. Tibère † M.B. Caligula † P.B.
C. I. G. ACCI. — LEG. III. *Acci*. Tibère M.B.
C. I. G. ACCI. — L. III. *Acci*. Caligula M.B.
C. I. G. L. III. ACCI. *Acci*. Auguste M.B.
C. I. L. COR. *Corinthe*. L. Vérus M.B. P.B.
C. I. N. C. N. *Cnosse*. Auguste P.B.
C. I. P. CAES. *Césarée, Samarie*. Trajan P.B.
C. I. P. IIIIVIR. *Clypea*. Auguste G.B.
C. I. SINOP. *Sinope*. Sept. Sévère P.B.
C. I. V. *Vienne*. J. César et Auguste G.B.
C. IV. AVGS. PELLA. *Pella*. Caracalla M.B.
C. IVL. AV. CASSAN. *Cassandrée*. Sept. Sévère P.B.
C. IVL. AVG. CASS. *Cassandrée*. Géta P.B.
C. IVL. HAD. PAR. *Parium*. Gallien ⊹ P.B.
C. IVLI. IIVIR. *Corinthe*. Auguste P.B
C. IVLIO POLYAENO IIVIR COR. *Corinthe*. Néron P.B. (avec ISTHMIA) P.B.
C. IVL. POLYAENO IIVIR QVI. COR. — ADVF. AVG. *Corinthe*. Neron P.B.
CLA. CELERE CN. PVBLI. REG. IIVIR COR. — NE BR. *Corinthe*. Claude I P.B
C. LAETILIVS APALVS IIV. Q. — REX PTOL. *Carthago Nova*. Auguste P.B.
CL. ΔAMS (sic.) *Damas*. Salonine G.B.
CL. ΔAM. S. METRO. *Damas*. Salonine † M.B.
CLEMENS ET LVCRETIVS. — C. C. A. IIVIR. *Caesar Augusta*. Tibère P.B.Q.

CLEMENS ET LVCRETIVS IIVIR. — C. C. A. *Caesar Augusta*. Tibère P.B.
CLEMENTE ET LVCRETIO IIVIR. — C. C. A. *Caesar Augusta*. Tibère P.B.
C. L. I. ... *Corinthe*. J. César P.B.
C. L. I. C. *Corinthe*. Adrien M.B. Sept. Sévère M B.
C. L. I. COR. *Corinthe*. Domitien P.B. Plotine P.B. Antonin M.B. P.B. M. Aurèle
 G.B. M.B. P.B. L. Vérus M.B. P.B. Lucille M.B Commode M.B. †M.B. P.B. Sept.
 Sévère M B. † M.B † P.B. P.B. Julie Domne M.B. † M.B. P.B. Caracalla M.B.
 †M.B. P.B. Plautille M.B. † M.B Géta M.B. † M.B P.B. Élagabale M.B.
C. L. I. CORINT. *Corinthe*. Julie Domne P.B.
C. LOLLI. ITE. M. DOI. IIVRI P. S. S. C. *Paestum*. Tibère P.B.
C. LOLLI. M. DOI. IIVIR. ITE. P. S. S. C. *Paestum*. Tibère P.B.
C. LOLLI M. DOI. IIVIR. P. S. S. C. *Paestum*. Tibère P.B.
C. MAR. CAP. Q. VERSO IIVIR. *Calagurris*, Auguste M.B.
C. MAR. M. VAL. PR. IIVIR. *Calagurris*. Auguste M.B.
C. MET. AV. PI. SID *Sidon* Elagabale P.B.
C. MVSSID. PRISCO IIVIR C. HEIO POLLIONE ITER. *Corinthe*. Tibère M.B. Drusus
 P B. Germanicus M.B.
C. MVSSID. PRISCO IMP. C. HEIO POLLIONE II. R. (*sic*). *Corinthe*. Auguste P.B.
CN. DOM. PROC. A. LAETO IIVIR. *Palerme*. Auguste M.B.
CN. POMP. T. AVO. T. ANTO. M. IVL. SERAN. IIIIVIR. CLVNIA. *Clunia*. Tibère M.B.
CO. AE. CA. *Aelia Capitolina*. Antonin P.B.
CO. AE. CAP. *Aelia Capitolina*. Caracalla P.B.
CO. AE. CAP. COND. *Aelia Capitolina*. Adrien M.B.
CO. AE. CAPI. *Aelia Capitolina*. Antonin P.B.
CO. A. E. VX. *Emérita*. Auguste P.B.
CO. AVG. CO. *Corinthe*. Domitien P.B.
CO. AVGO. (*sic*) TRO. *Alexandrie Troade*. Tréb. Galle M.B.
CO... COR. *Corinthe*. Antonin P.B.
CO. ΔAMAS. *Damas*. Salonine † M.B.
CO. ΔAMAS METRO. *Damas*. Hérennius? M.P.
CO... DIENSIS. *Dium*. Faustine jeune P.B.
COIL. *Coela*. M. Aurèle P.B
COIL. ANT. *Coela*. Caracalla P.B.
CO. IV. CAS. *Cassandrée*. Maesa P.B.
CO. IVL. AV. N....... *Nagidus?* Sept. Sévère G.B.
COL. A. A. PAT. *Patras*. M. Aurèle P.B.
COL. A. A. PATR. *Patras*. Claude I M.B. Domitien M.B. P.B. Adrien M.B. P.B.
 Antonin M.B. P.B. M. Aurèle M.B. † P.B. P.B. L. Vérus M.B. P.B. Commode
 M.B. † M.B. P.B. Sept. Sévère M.B. † M.B. P.B. Julie Domne † M.B. Caracalla
 M.B. † M.B. P.B. Géta M.B. Elagabale M.B. P.B. Gordien III M.B.
COL. A. A. PATRA. *Patras*. Commode † M.B.
COL. A. A. PATRE. *Patras*. Elagabale M.B.
COL. A. A. PATRENS. *Patras*. Auguste M.B. Domitien M.B. Nerva M.B. Adrien
 M.B. † M.B. P.B. Sabine M.B. M. Aurèle M.B. L. Vérus M.B.
COL. A. A. PATRENS. LEG. XXII. *Patras*. Domitien M.B.
COL. A. A. PATR. XXII. *Patras*. Néron M B. Galba M.B. Domitien M.B.
COL. A. A. PAT. XXII. *Patras*. Domitien M.B.
COL. A. A PTAR. (*sic*). *Patras*. M. Aurèle P.B.
COL A. AV. TRO *Alexandrie Troade*. Trajan Dèce P.B.
COL. A. CA. *Aelia Capitolina*. M. Aurèle P.B.
COL. A. CAP. *Aelia Capitolina*. L. Vérus G.B.
COL. A. C. C. P. F. *Césarée, Samarie*. Caracalla M.B.
COL. A. CE? P. F. A. *Aelia Capitolina*. Aquilia Sévéra P.B.
COL. AE. CAP. *Aelia Capitolina*. Adrien P.B. Antonin P.B. M Aurèle et Com-
 mode M.B.
COL. AE. CAP. COMM. P. F. *Aelia Capitolina*. Julie Domne M.B.
COL. AE. CAPIT. *Aelia Capitolina*. Antonin P B.
COL. AE. KA. *Aelia Capitolina*. Trajan Dèce M.B.
COL. AE. KAP. CO. *Aelia Capitolina*. Hérennius et Hostilien M.B.

COL. AEL. ADR. ICONIEN S. R. *Iconium.* Gordien III G.B.
COL. AEL. CAP. *Aelia Capitolina* Adrien G.B. P.B. M. Aurèle M.B. † P.B. P.B. M. Aurèle et L. Vérus G.B. M.B. † M.B. † P.B. P.B. Elagabale M.B.
COL. AEL. CAP. COMM. *Aelia Capitolina.* Diaduménien M.B. † M.B. Elagabale M.B. † M.B. † P.B.
COL. AEL. CAP. COMM. P. F. *Aelia Capitolina.* Pesc. Niger M.B. Elagabale † M.B.
COL. AEL. CAP. COM. P. F. *Aelia Capitolina.* Trajan Dèce P.B.
COL. AEL. CAPITO. *Aelia Capitolina.* L. Vérus G.B.
COL. AEL. CAPIT. — P. F. *Aelia Capitolina.* Elagabale M.B.
COL. AEL. HAD. ICONIENSI S. R. *Iconium.* Gordien III BR.M. Valérien G.B.
COL. AELIA CAP. *Aelia Capitolina.* Antonin P.B.
COL. AELIA CAP. COMM. *Aelia Capitolina.* Sept. Sévère M.B.
COL. AEL. ICONIEN S. R. *Iconium.* Gordien III G.B.
COL. AEL. KA. *Aelia Capitolina.* Trajan Dèce M.B. Hostilien M.B.
COL. AEL. KA. COMM. *Aelia Capitolina.* Trajan Dèce M.B.
COL. AEL. KAP. *Aelia Capitolina.* Trajan Dèce P.B.
COL. AEL. KAP. COMM. *Aelia Capitolina.* Trajan Dèce P B. Hérennius et Hostilien M.B.
COL. AEL. KAP. COMM. P. F. *Aelia Capitolina.* Trajan Dèce M.B.
COA. (sic) AEL. KAP. COM. P. F. *Aelia Capitolina.* Trajan Dèce M.B. P.B.
COL. AEL. KAPIT. COND. *Aelia Capitolina.* Adrien M.B.
COL. AL. AVG. TROA. *Alexandrie Troade.* Alex. Sévère M.B.
COL. AL. AVG. T. TROA. (sic). *Alexandrie Troade.* Alex. Sévère M.B.
COL. AL. AV. TR. *Alexandrie Troade.* Alex. Sévère M.B.
COL. AL. AV. TRO. *Alexandrie Troade.* Alex. Sévère M.B. Gallien † P.B.
COL. ALE. A. TR. *Alexandrie Troade.* Alex. Sévère M.B.
COL. ALE. AVG. (ou AV.) TRO. *Alexandrie Troade.* Alex. Sévère † M.B.
COL. ALE. TRO. *Alexandrie Troade.* Alex. Sévère † M.B. P.B. Mamée † M.B. Volusien M.B.
COL. ALE. TROA. *Alexandrie Troade.* Aquilia Sévéra † M.B. Tréb. Galle † M.B.
COL. ALEX. *Alexandrie Troade.* Caracalla † M.B.
COL. ALEXA. AVG. *Alexandrie Troade.* Caracalla † M.B. Elagabale † M.B.
COL. ALEXAN. AVG. *Alexandrie Troade.* Caracalla † M.B.
COL. ALEXAND. *Alexandrie Troade.* Caracalla † MB.
COL. ALEXAND. AVG. *Alexandrie Troade.* Caracalla † M.B.
COL. ALEXAND. TR. AVG. *Alexandrie Troade.* Caracalla † M.B.
COL. ALEXAN. TPOA. (sic). *Alexandrie Troade.* Alex. Sévère M.B.
COL. ALEXA. TRO. (ou TROAD.). *Alexandrie Troade.* Alex. Sévère M.B. † P.B.
COL. ALEX. AVG. *Alexandrie Troade.* Caracalla † M.B. Elagabale M.B. J. Paula M B. † M.B. Aquilia Sévéra † M.B. Alex. Sévère M.B.
COL. ALEX. AVG. TRO. *Alexandrie Troade.* J. Domne P.B. Alex. Sévère † M.B. Mamée M.B.
COL. ALEX. AVG. TROA. *Alexandrie Troade.* Macrin P.B. Alex. Sévère M.B. Maximin I M.B.
COL. ALEX. TROA. *Alexandrie Troade.* Annia Faustine † M.B. Soémias † P.B. Mamée M.B.
COL. ALEX. TROAD. AVG. *Alexandrie Troade.* Caracalla † M.B.
COL. AL. TRO *Alexandrie Troade.* Alex. Sévère M.B. Maxime M.B.
COL. AL. TROA. *Alexandrie Troade.* J. Domne † M.B. Alex. Sévère M.B.† M.B.
COL. AN... ... *Antioche Pisidie.* M. Aurèle M.B.
COL. AN. PR. CA. *Césarée, Samarie.* Caracalla † P.B.
COL. ANT. BER. *Béryte.* J. Domne † M.B. Caracalla † M.B. P.B.
COL. ANTIOCH. *Antioche Pisidie.* Caracalla † P.B.
COL. ANTIOCHEN. *Antioche Pisidie.* Sept. Sévère † P.B.
COL. ANTIOCHENS. S. R. *Antioche Pisidie.* Elagabale M.B. Maesa M.B.
COL. ANTIOCHII S. R. *Antioche Pisidie.* Philippe père M B.
COL. ANTIOCH. MENLIS. (sic). *Antioche Pisidie.* Julie Domne M.B.
COL. ANTIOCH. S. R. *Antioche Pisidie.* Alex. Sévère G.B.
COL. ANTΩNϬINA (sic) CASSANDRIA. *Cassandrée.* Gordien III M.B.

COL...... APAM. AVG. — D. D. *Apamée*. Philippe père G.B.
COL......A. PIA METR. ... *Sidon*. Annia Faustine † P.B.
COL......A. O. *Alexandrie Troade*. Géta P.B.
COL. A.....TR. *Alexandrie Troade*. Alex. Sévère † M.B
COL. A. TRO. *Alexandrie Troade*. Gallien † M.B P.B.
COL. A. TROA. *Alexandrie Troade*. Mamée † M.B. Tréb. Galle † M.B.
COL. A. TROAD. *Alexandrie Troade*. Caracalla † M.B. Alex. Sévère † M.B.
COL...... AVG. *Béryte*. Vespasien M.B.
COL. AVG. ALE. TROAD. *Alexandrie Troade*. Gallien OR. † P.B.
COL. AVG. ALEX. *Alexandrie Troade*. Maesa M.B.
COL. AVG. (ALEX.) TROA. *Alexandrie Troade*. Valérien † M.B.
COL. AVG. ANTONINIANA ALEX. *Alexandrie Troade*. Caracalla P.B.
COL. AVG. COMAMA. *Comama*. Antonin P.B.
COL. AVG. COMAMENORVM. *Comama*. Caracalla M.B.
COL. AV. GERM. *Germé*. Otacilie P.B
COL. AVG. FEL. HEL. *Héliopolis*. Gallien † M.B.
COL. AVG. FEL. HEL. — CERT. SACR. CAP. OEC. ISE. HEL. *Héliopolis*. Gallien M.B.
COL. AVG FELI. NINI. CLAV. *Ninive*. Trajan M.B.
COL. AVG. F. GERMENO. *Germé*. Commode G.B.
COL. AVG. GERMENO. *Germé*. Diaduménien P.B.
COL. AVG. IVL. COR. *Corinthe*. Gordien III † M.B.
COL. AVG. IVL. PHILIP. *Philippes*. Claude I POT. M.B.
COL. AVG. IVL. PHILIP. — DIVVS AVG. *Philippes*. Trajan M.B. Adrien M.B. Antonin M.B. M. Aurèle M.B.
COL. AVG. IVL. PHILIPP. — DIVVS AVG. *Philippes*. Domitien M.B.
COL. AVG. OL. *Olbasa*. Antonin P.B.
COL. AVGO. TRO. *Alexandrie Troade*. Valérien † M.B.
COL. AVGO. TROA. *Alexandrie Troade*. Tréb. Galle M.B. Volusien † M.B. Gallien † P.B.
COL. AVGO TROAD. *Alexandrie Troade*. Gallien † P.B.
COL. AVG. PELLA. *Pella*. Philippe fils M.B.
COL. AVG. TR. *Alexandrie Troade*. Caracalla † M.B.
COL. AVG. TRO. *Alexandrie Troade*. Commode P.B. Crispine P.B. Caracalla † M.B. P.B. Géta P.B. Elagabale P.B. Alex. Sévère M.B. Maximin I M.B. Maxime M.B. † M.B. P.B. Tréb. Galle P.B. Volusien † M.B. Valérien M.B. † M.B. P.B. Gallien † M.B. † P.B. Salonine † M.B. P.B.
COL. AVG. TROA. *Alexandrie Troade*. Trajan P.B. Adrien P.B. Antonin P.B. M. Aurèle M.B. † P.B. P.B. Commode M.B. † M.B. P.B. Crispine M.B. Sept. Sévère M.B. † M.B. Caracalla M.B. † M.B. Géta † M.B. Elagabale M.B. Alex. Sévère M.B. † M.B. P.B. Maxime M.B. Tréb. Galle M.B. † M.B. Volusien M.B. Valérien † M.B. Gallien † P.B. P.B.
COL. AVG. TROAC. (sic). *Alexandrie Troade*. Alex. Sévère M.B.
COL. AVG. TROAD. *Alexandrie Troade*. Antonin P.B. Commode M.B. † M.B. P.B. Crispine M.B. Caracalla M.B. † M.B. Géta † M.B. Elagabale M.B. Alex. Sévère M.B. Mamée † M.B. Gordien III † P.B. Philippe père M.B. Trajan Dèce P.B. Tréb. Galle M.B. † M.B. P.B. Volusien † M.B. Valérien P.B. Gallien † P.B.
COL. AVG. TRO. ALEX. *Alexandrie Troade*. Elagabale M.B.
COL. AVG. TROAS. *Alexandrie Troade*. Adrien P.B. Sept. Sévère P.B. Caracalla † M.B. Alex. Sévère M.B. Volusien P.B.
COL. AVG. TRO. C. N. *Alexandrie Troade*. Caracalla † M.B.
COL. AVGVSTA EMERITA. *Emérita*. Auguste M.B. Tibère G.B.
COL. AVGV. TROA. *Alexandrie Troade*. Etruscille P.B.
COL. AV. ME. SID. *Sidon*. J. Paula † M.B.
COL. AVP. sic) AEL. CAP. — P. F. *Aelia Capitolina*. Elagabale † M.B.
COL. AV. PIA ME. SIDON. *Sidon*. Maesa M.B.
COL. AV. PIA METRO. SIDO. *Sidon*. Elagabale M.B.
COL. AV. P. M. *Sidon*. Maesa M.B.
COL. AV. P. MET. SIDON. *Sidon*. Maesa M.B.

COL. AV. P. M. MET. SIDONI. *Sidon.* Elagabale M.B.
COL. AVR. ANTONINIAN. (OU ANTONINIANA) ALEX. *Alexandrie Troade.* Elagabale
† M.B.
COL. AVR..... METR. SID. *Sidon.* Alex. Sévère M.B.
COL. AVR. PIA METRO. SID. *Sidon.* Elagabale M.B. P.B. Annia Faustine M.B. P.B.
Maesa G.B. M.B.
COL. AVR. PIA METR. SID. *Sidon.* Elagabale G.B. J. Paula G.B. P.B. Soémias
M.B. Maesa G.B. Alex. Sévère M.B. (Avec CERT. SAC. PER. OECVME. ISELA)
Annia Faustine M.B.
COL. AVR. PIA METR. SIDO. *Sidon.* Alex. Sévère M.B.
COL. AVR. PIA METR. SIDON. *Sidon.* Elagabale M.B. J. Paula G.B. (Avec — CER.
SAC. E. HOCVM. ISELA.) Caracalla G.B. (Avec — CER. SA. PE. HOCVM. ISELA.)
Elagabale G.B. (Avec — CERT. SAC. PER. OECVME. ISELA.) Elagabale M.B.
COL. AVR. PIA MET. SID. *Sidon.* Elagabale M.B. Alex. Sévère M.B. (Avec — IE. PE.
OES. IS.) Elagabale G.B.
COL. AVR. PIA MET. SIDO. *Sidon.* Elagabale G.B. J. Paula G.B.
COL. AV. TRO. *Alexandrie Troade.* Tréb. Galle M.B.
COL. AV. TROA. (OU TROAD.). *Alexandrie Troade.* Caracalla M.B. † M.B.
COL. BER. *Béryte.* Trajan G.B. M.B. P.B. Adrien M.B. P.B Antonin M B. Com-
mode M.B. Sept. Sévère † P.B. Sept. Sévère et Caracalla M.B. † P.B. Julie
Domne † M.B. Caracalla † P.B. P.B. Gordien III † M.B. P.B.
COL. BER. AAT. *Béryte.* Julie Domne M.B.
COL. BER. SEC. SAEC. *Béryte.* Marc Aurèle † P.B. Commode M.B. P.B.
COL. BER. V. VIII. *Béryte.* Claude I P.B.
COL. BOSTRAC (sic)..... *Bostra.* Hérennius et Hostilien P.B.
COL. BOSTR. — N. TR. ALEXANDRIANAE. *Bostra.* Alex. Sévère G.B.
COL. CA. ANTIOCHEN. *Antioche Pisidie.* Géta † M.B.
COL. CA. ANTIOCHI S. R. *Antioche Pisidie.* Trajan Dèce M.B.
COL. CABE *Cavaillon.* Auguste P.B.
COL. CAE. ANTIOCHEN. *Antioche Pisidie.* Elagabale † M.B.
COL. CAE. ANTIOCH. S. R. *Antioche Pisidie.* Sept. Sévère G.B.
COL. CAE. ANTI. S. R. *Antioche Pisidie.* Tibère G.B.
COL. CAES. ANTIOCH. *Antioche Pisidie.* Sept. Sévère G.B. Caracalla † M.B.
COL. CAES. ANTIOCHEN. *Antioche Pisidie.* Julie Domne † M.B. Caracalla † M.B.
COL. CAES. ANTIOCHEN. S. R. *Antioche Pisidie.* Alex. Sévère M.B.
COL. CAES. ANTIOCHIA. *Antioche Pisidie.* Julie Domne † M.B. Gordien III BR.M.
COL. CAES. ANTIOCHO. S. R. *Antioche Pisidie.* Philippe fils M.B.
COL. CAES. ANTIOCH. S. R. *Antioche Pisidie.* Sept. Sévère BR.M. G.B. J. Domne
G.B. Caracalla G.B. Géta BR.M. G.B. Elagabale M.B. Alex. Sévère G.B. Gordien
III BR.M. G.B. † G.B. M.B. Philippe père M.B. Ga'lien G.B.
COL. CAES. ANTIOC. S. R. *Antioche Pisidie.* Gordien III G.B.
COL. CAES. ANTIO. S. R. *Antioche Pisidie.* Sept. Sévère G.B.
COL. CAESAR. ANTIOCH. *Antioche Pisidie.* Julie Domne P.B.
COL. CAESARIA LIB. BΛΦ. *Césarée de Liban.* Macrin M.B.
COL. .....CAP. *Aelia Capitolina.* L. Vérus M.B. Caracalla P.B.
COL. CAP. COM. P. F. *Aelia Capitolina.* J. Domne P.B.
COL. CASS. *Cassandrée.* L. Vérus † M.B. Alex. Sévère M.B.
COL. CASSA. *Cassandrée.* J. Domne † M.B.
COL. C. CASSANDRIAS. *Cassandrée.* Philippe père M.B.
COL. CESAR. (sic). *Césarée de Liban.* Alex. Sévère † M.B.
COL. CESARIA ΛΛΦ. *Césarée de Liban.* Elagabale G.B. M.B
COL. CESARIA BΛΦ *Césarée de Liban.* Alex. Sévère † M.B.
COL. CESARIA LIB. ΛΛΦ. *Césarée de Liban.* Elagabale M.B.
COL. C. LA. COR. *Corinthe.* Auguste P.B.
COL. C. L. AGRIP. COS. IIII. *Cologne.* Postume B.
COL. COR. *Corinthe.* Caïus et Lucius P.B. Domitien M.B. P.B. Sept. Sévère P.B.
Julie Domne P.B. Caracalla † M.B.
COL... COR. *Corinthe.* Domitien M.B. Adrien † M.B. P.B.
COL. CREMNENSIVM *Cremna.* Tranquilline P.B.

COL. CR. VLTRI. *Cremna.* Géta M.B.
COL. ΔAMAC. MET. *Damas.* Alex. Sévère M.B.
COL. DAMAC. METRO. *Damas.* Otacilie G.B.
COL. DAMA. MET. *Damas.* Otacilie G.B.
COL. ΔAMA. MET. — LEG. III. GAL. *Damas.* Volusien † M.B. (Avec — LEG. VI. F.) Otacilie G.B.
COL. ΔAMA. METR. *Damas.* Philippe père M.B. Philippe fils M.B. (Avec — LEG. III. GAL.) Tréb. Galle M.B.
COL. DAMA. METRO. *Damas.* Philippe père M.B. Philippe père et Philippe fils G.B. Otacilie G.B. Philippe fils G.B. M.B.
COL. ΔAMA. METRO. *Damas,* Philippe père G.B M.B. Otacilie G.B. (Avec — CEBACMIA). Tréb. Galle M.B.
COL. DAMA. METRO. — XV. *Damas.* Gallien † M.B.
COL. DAMA. METROP. *Damas.* Otacilie G.B.
COL. ΔAMA. METROP. *Damas.* Philippe fils M.B.
COL. DAMASCO METRO. (ou METROPOL). *Damas.* Tréb. Galle M.B.
COL. ΔAMASCO MET. — CEBACMIA. *Damas.* Volusien M.B.
COL. DAMAS. (ou ΔAMAS.) MET. *Damas.* Tréb. Galle M.B.
COL. DAMAS. METR. *Damas.* Otacilie M.B.
COL. ΔAMAS. METR. *Damas.* Tréb. Galle M.B. Volusien M.B.
COL. DAMAS. METRO. *Damas.* Tréb. Galle M.B. Volusien † M.B.
COL. ΔAMAS. METRO. *Damas.* Philippe père G.B. Tréb. Galle M.B. Salonine † M.B. (Avec — IE.) Tréb Galle M.B. (Avec — IE. CEBACMIA.) Tréb. Galle M.B. (Avec —IEPA CEBACMIA.) Valérien † M.B.(Avec — OAYMIIIA CEBACMIA IE.) Tréb. Galle P.B.
COL. ΔAMAS. MHTRO (sic). IIHΓAI. *Damas.* Otacilie G.B.
COL. DAMAS. METRO. — CEBACMIA. *Damas.* Philippe père et Philippe fils G.B. Otacilie G.B.
COL. ΔAMAS. METRO. — CEBACMIA. *Damas.* Valérien P.B. Gallien † M.B.
COL. ΔAMAS. METROP. *Damas.* Valérien † M.B.
COL. DAMAS. METROP. — XPYCOPOA. *Damas.* Philippe père G.B.
COL. DAMAS. METROPOL. — CEBACMIA. *Damas.* Tréb Galle M.B.
COL. ΔAMASO METROP. — CEBACMIA. *Damas.* Volusien M.B. (Avec — CEBACMIA IE.) Volusien M B.
COL. DAMAT. (sic) MET. *Damas.* Tréb. Galle P.B.
COL. ΔA. METRO. *Damas.* Valérien P.B.
COL. ΔA... METRO. — OΛYMIIIA CEBACMIA. IE. *Damas.* Volusien M.B.
COL. ΔAMS. (sic) MET. *Damas.* Salonine † M.B.
COL. DIENSIS D. D. *Dium.* Philippe fils M.B. Gallien M.B.
COL. Δ. METRO *Damas.* Gallien P.B.
COL. FEL. BER. *Béryte.* Gordien III M.B.
COL. FLA. PAC. DEVLT. *Deultum.* J. Domne M.B. † M.B.
COL. FLAV. AVG. COR. *Corinthe.* Domitien P.B.
COL. FL. AVG. C. CAESA. *Césarée Samarie.* Caracalla † P.B.
COL. FL. PAC. DEVLT. *Deultum.* Julie Domne † M.B. Caracalla † M.B. P.B. Macrin M.B. † M.B. P.B. Diaduménien M.B. † M.B. P.B. Alex. Sévère M.B. Mamée M.B. † M.B. P.B. Maximin I M.B. Maxime M.B. Gordien III M.B. P.B. Tranquilline † M.B. Philippe père M.B. P.B. Otacilie M.B. Philippe fils M.B.
COL. FL. PAC. DEVLTI. *Deultum.* Alex. Sévère M.B.
COL. FL. PA. DEVLT. *Deultum.* Tranquilline † M.B.
COL. GERM. *Germé.* Domitien P.B.
COL. GERME. (ou GERMEN...). *Germé.* Commode P.B.
COL. GERMENORVM. — ACTIA ΔYSARIA. *Germé.* Etruscille P.B.
COL. O. I. H. PA. (ou PARIA). *Parium.* Valérien † M.B.
COL. G. IVL. HAD. PARIA. *Parium.* Gallien † P.B.
COL. G. IVL. H. PAR. *Parium.* Valérien † M.B.
COL. HEL. *Héliopolis.* M. Aurèle (?) P.B. Commode M.B. Sept. Sévère M.B † M.B. † P.B. P.B. J. Domne † M.B. Caracalla † M.B. P.B. Plautille M.B. Géta M.B. P.B. Diaduménien P.B. Elagabale † M.B. Philippe père G.B. Otacilie G.B. Philippe fils P.B. Valérien M.B.

COL. HEL. CERT. SACRV. CAPIT. OECV. ISE. HEL. *Héliopolis.* Valérien G.B.
COL. HEL. I. O. M. H. *Héliopolis.* Sept. Sévère M.B. †M.B. Julie Domne †M.B.
Caracalla M.B. Philippe père M.B. Otacilie G.B.
COL. HEL. LEG. V. MACED. VIII. AVG. *Héliopolis.* Philippe père G.B.
COL. I. AVG. COR. *Corinthe.* Trajan P.B.
COL. I. FLA. AV. F. C. — CAESA. *Césarée Samarie.* Macri) †G.B.
COL. I. FL. AV. CAESARENS. *Césarée Samarie.* Adrien M.B.
COL. I. FL. AV. C. CAESAR. *Césarée Samarie.* Diaduménien P.B.
COL. I. FL. AVG. CAESARENS. *Césarée Samarie.* Adrien G.B.
COL. I. FL. AVG. C. CAE. *Césarée Samarie.* Caracalla P.B.
COL. IV. AV. DIENSIS D. D. *Dium.* Caracalla P.B.
COL. IV. CON. APAM. AVG. D. D. *Apamée.* Gallien G.B.
COL. IV. CONC. AVG. APAM. D. D. *Apamée.* Gallien G.B. M.B.
COL. IVL. *Béryte.* Tibère G.B.
COL. IVL. A. C. *Corinthe.* Domitien P.B.
COL. IVL. AG. (sic) CASSAN. *Cassandrée.* Diaduménien P.B.
COL. IVL. ANT. AVG. FEL. BER. *Béryte* Caracalla †M.B.
COL. IVL. AV. CAS. *Cassandrée.* Marc Aurèle P.B.
COL. IVL. AV. COR. *Corinthe.* Trajan P.B.
COL. IVL. AVG. *Béryte.* Claude I M.B.
COL. IVL. AVG. C. *Cassandrée.* Philippe père M.B.
COL. IVL. AVG. BER. *Béryte.* Adrien M.B.
COL. IVL. AVG. CASS. *Cassandrée.* Marc Aurèle P.B. L. Vérus †M.B. P.B. Elaga-
bale P.B.
CGL IVL. AVG. CASSAN. *Cassandrée.* Titus et Domitien P.B.
COL. IVL. AVG. CASSAND. *Cassandrée* Antonin P.B.
COL. IVL. AVG. CASSANDR. *Cassandrée.* Claude I M.B. Galba M.B.
COL. IVL. AVG. CASSANDREN. *Cassandrée.* Néron M.B. Nerva M.B. Plotine M.B.
M. Aurèle P.B.
COL. IVL. AVG CASSANDRENS. *Cassandrée.* Vespasien M.B. Titus et Domitien
P.B. Domitien M.B. Trajan P.B.
COL. IVL. AVG. CASSANDRIAS. *Cassandrée.* Philippe père M.B. P.B.
COL. IVL. AVG. C. FE. BER. *Béryte.* Nerva G.B.
COL. IVL. AVG. COR. *Corinthe.* Domitien M.B. †P.B. P.B. Trajan P.B. Adrien P.B.
Commode P.B.
COL. IVL. AVG. CREMNA. *Cremna.* Elagabale M.B.
COL IVL. AVG. DIENSIS D. D. *Dium.* Domitien P.B. Adrien †M.B. Emilien M.B.
Gallien †M.B.
COL. IVL. AVG. DIENSIS GLI. *Dium.* Antonin M.B. P.B
COL. IVL. AVG. FE. BER. *Béryte.* Caracalla M.B
COL. IVL. AVG. FE. CREM. MEII. sic. *Cremna.* Gordien III M.B.
COL. IVL. AVG. FE. CREMNA. *Cremna* Etruscille BR.M. G.B.
COL. IVL. AVG. FE. I. O. M. H. — COL. HEL *Héliopolis.* Otacilie G.B.
COL. IVL. AVG. FEL. *Héliopolis.* Otacilie G.B. †M.B.
COL. IVL. AVG. FEL. BER. *Béryte.* Tibère M.B. Caligula M.B. Néron M.B. P.B.
Nerva M.B. Trajan G.B. M.B. Commode M.B. Julie Domne †M.B. Caracalla
G.B. †M.B. Macrin G B M.B. Diaduménien G.B. Elagabale G.B. M.B. Annia
Faustine M.B. Gordien III G.B. †M.B. Otacilie M.B. Hostilien M.B. Valérien
G.B. Gallien G.B. †P.B. Salonine G.B. †P.B.
COL. IVL. AVG. FEL. BER. CAV. *Béryte.* Trajan M.B.
COL. IVL. AVG. FEL. BERY. *Béryte.* Valérien M.B. Gallien G.B.
COL. IVL. AVG. FEL. HE. — CERT. SACR CAP. OECV. ISE. HEL. *Héliopolis* Gallien M.B.
COL. IVL. AVG. FEL. HEL. *Héliopolis* Macrin †M.B. Philippe père G.B. †M.B.
Philippe fils †M.B. Valérien G.B. M.B. Gallien G.B. †P.B. (Avec — CER.
SAC. CAP. OEC. ISE. (OU ISEL.) HEL.) Valérien †G.B. M.B. (Avec — CERTAM.
CAPIT. OECVM. ISELASTI. HELIVP.) Valérien G.B. (Avec — CERT. SACR. CAP. OEC.
ISE. HEL.). Gallien M.B. (Avec — CERT. SACR. CAP. OEC ISEL. HEL.) Caracalla
†M.B. (Avec — CERT. SACR. CAP. OECV. ISEL. HE.). Valérien M.B. (Avec —
CERT. SACR. CAP. OECVME. ISELASTI. HELIVPO.) Valérien M.B.

COL. IVL. AVG. FEL. I. O. M. II. *Héliopolis.* Philippe père M.B.
COL. IVL. AVG. F. HE. *Héliopolis.* Gallien G.B.
COL. IVL. AVGG. F. COMAMENORV. *Comama.* Caracalla G.B.
COL. IVL. AVG. — HEL. *Héliopolis.* Valérien P.B.
COL. IVL. AVG. OLBASE *Olbasa.* Maesa M.B.
COL. IVL. AVG. PEL. *Pella.* Trajan M.B.
COL. IVL. AVG. PELL. *Pella.* Adrien M.B. P.B. M. Aurèle P.B. Macrin P.B.
COL. IVL. AVG. PELLA. *Pella.* M. Aurèle M.B. Caracalla M B. Géta P.B. Macrin
   P.B Élagabale M.B. Paula M B. Alex. Sévère M.B. Mamée † M.B. Maximin I
   M.B. Maxime M.B. Gordien III M.B. Tranquilline M.B. Philippe père M.B.
   Otacilie M.B.
COL. IVL. AVG. PELLV. (sic). *Pella.* Gordien III M.B.
COL. IVL. AVG. PHILIP. *Philippes.* Néron M.B. Vespasien M.B.
COL. IVL. AVG. PHILIP. — DIVVS. AVG. *Philippes.* Caracalla M.B.
COL. IVL. AVSP. CL. LA. *Laodicée.* Maximin I M.B Philippe fils M.B.
COL. IVL. AVS. PEλEA (sic). *Pella.* Macrin M.B.
COL. IVL. AVS. PELLA (sic). *Pella.* Caracalla M.B. Macrin M.B. Mam e M.B.
COL. IVL. BER. VIII. *Béryte.* Nerva M.B.
COL. IVL. CON. A. APA. D. D. *Apamée.* Gallien M.B.
COL. IVL. CON. APAM. AVG. D. D. *Apamée.* Gallien M.B.
COL. IVL. CON. AVG. APAM. D. D. *Apamée.* Trajan Dèce M.B. Volusien M.B.
COL. IVL. CON. AVGV. APAM. D. D. *Apamée.* Gallien † M.B.
COL. IVL. CONC. A. *Apamée.* Alex. Sévère G.B.
COL. IVL. CONC. APAM. AVG. *Apamée.* Caracalla G.B.
COL. IVL. CONC. APAM. AVG. D. D. *Apamée.* Caracalla G.B. Gallien † M.B.
COL. IVL. CONC. APAM. AVG. — LEG. D. D. *Apamée.* Caracalla G.B.
COL. IVL. CONC. APAM. D. D. *Apamée.* Caracalla M.B. Trajan Dèce M.B
COL. IVL. CONC. APAME. *Apamée.* Macrin G.B.
COL. IVL. CONC. AVG. APAM. D. D. *Apamée.* J. Domne M.B. C racalla BR.M. .B.
   M.B. Géta M.B. Valérien M.B. Gallien † M.B.
COL. IVL. CONCORD. APAM AVG. D. D. *Apamée.* Caracalla G.B.
COL. IVL. COR. *Corinthe.* Trajan P.B. Adrien M.B. P.B.
COL. IVL. DIENSIS. *Dium.* Néron M.B
COL. IVL. DIENSIS D. D *Dium.* Trajan P.B. Sept. Sévère M.B. † P.B. P.B. Cara-
   calla † .B Géta † M.B. Élagabale M.B. Soémias M.B. Maesa P.B. Alex. Sévère
   M.B. Maximin I M.B. Maxime M.B. Gordien III M.B. Philippe fils M.B. Gallien
   † M.B. † P.B. Salonine † M.B.
COL. IVL. DIENSIVM D. D. *Dium.* Caracalla M.B. † M.B.
COL. IVL. F. COMAMA. *Comama.* Julie Domne P.B.
COL. IVL. FEIC. (sic) ...LVSTRA. *Lystra.* Auguste M.B.
COL IVL. FEL. GEM. LVSTRA. *Lystra.* M. Aurèle M.B.
COL. IVL. FELI. NINI. C. CLAVD. *Ninive.* Trajan M.B.
COL. IVL. FL. AVG. COR. *Corinthe.* Domitien † P.B.
COL. IVL. FLAV. AVG. COR. *Corinthe.* Domitien M.B. † P.B.
COL. IVL. FLAV. AVG. CORINT. *Corinthe.* Domitien † P.B.
COL. IVL. FLAVIA. AVG. COR. *Corinthe.* Domitien P.B.
COL. IVL. GEM. ACCI. *Acci.* Tibère G.B. Caligula G.B.
COL. IVL. HAD. PAR. *Parium.* Gallien P.B.
COL. IVL. HEL. *Héliopolis.* Nerva P.B (?).
COL. IVLIA AVG. CAS. *Cassandrée.* Géta P.B.
COL. IVLIA AVG CASSA. *Cassandrée.* Maesa † P.B.
COL. IVLIA AVG. CASSAN. *Cassandrée.* Macrin P.B.
COL. IVLIA AVG. COR. *Corinthe.* Trajan M.B.
COL. IVLIAE CONCORD. APMENAE (sic). *Apamée.* Adrien M B.
COL. IVLI. AV. CREMNE. *Cremna.* Aurélien G B.
COL. IVLI. AVG. CASS. *Cassandrée.* Sept. Sévère P.B. Caracalla † M.B
COL. IVL. IVG. (sic) FEL. BER. *Béryte.* Commode M.B.
COL. IVL. L. A. FL. COR. *Corinthe.* Trajan P.B.

COL. IVL. LAV. COR. *Corinthe.* Trajan ✝ M.B.
COL. IVL. LVS. *Lystra.* Trajan P.B.
COL. IVL. NEAP. *Néapolis.* Philippe père et Philippe fils G.B.
COL. IVL. NEAPO. (ou NEAPOL.). *Néapolis.* Philippe père G.B. M.B.
COL. LA. IVL. COR. *Corinthe.* Adrien M.B.
COL. LAODICEAS METROPOLEOS Δ. E. *Laodicée.* Elagabale M.B. Tranquilline M.B.
COL. LAODI. METROPOLEOS D. E. *Laodicée.* Elagabale G.B.
COL. LAOD. METR. ... *Laodicée.* Alex. Sévère M.B.
COL. LAOD. METROPOL. Δ. E. *Laodicée.* Elagabale M.B.
COL. LAOD. METROPOLEOS D. E. *Laodicée.* Elagabale M.B. Philippe père (*bilingue*) M.B. ✝M.B. Philippe fils (*bilingue*) M.B. Tréb. Galle (*bilingue*) G.B. M.B.
COL. LAOD. METROPOLIS D. E. *Laodicée.* Valérien M.B.
COL. LAOD. P. S. METROPOLEOS D. E. *Laodicée.* Elagabale M.B.
COL. LAV. IVL. COR. (ou CORINT). *Corinthe.* Adrien M.B
COL. LAVS. I. COR. *Corinthe.* Adrien M.B.
COL. LAVS. IVL. AVG. COR. *Corinthe.* Trajan M.B. Adrien P.B.
COL. LAVS IVL. COR. *Corinthe.* Adrien M.B. P.B.
COL. LAVS IVL. CORI. *Corinthe.* Macrin M.B.
COL. L. COR. *Corinthe.* Adrien ✝ M.B.
COL. L. I. COR. *Corinthe.* Adrien G.B. Lucille ✝ M.B.
COL. L. IVL. COR. *Corinthe.* Adrien M.B. ✝M.B. P.B. Sabine ✝ M.B. P.B.
COL. L. IVL. COR. AD. AVG. *Corinthe.* Adrien G.B.
COL. L. SEP. SEB. *Sébasté.* Aquilia Sévéra ✝ M.B.
COL. L. SEP. SEBAS. *Sébasté.* Soémias ✝ M.B.
COL. L. SEP. SEBASTE. *Sébasté.* Caracalla ✝ M.B. ✝ P.B.
COL. L. SE. SEBASTE. *Sébasté.* Caracalla ✝ P.B.
COL. L. S. SEBASTE. *Sébasté.* Géta P.B.
COL. ME. ANTONINIAN. *Incertaine de Mésopotamie.* Caracalla P.B.
COL. MEN. ANTIOCH. *Antioche Pisidie.* J. Domne M.B.
COL. MET. ANTON. AVR. ALEX. *Mésopotamie.* Caracalla P.B.
COL. MET. ANTONINIANA. *Mésopotamie.* Caracalla P.B.
COL. MET. ANTONINIANA AV. B. ALEX. *Bostra.* Caracalla ✝ P.B.
COL. MET. ANTONINIANA AVR. ALEX. *Mésopotamie.* Caracalla P.B.
COL. MET. ANTONINIANA AVR. B. *Bostra.* Caracalla ✝ P.B.
COL. MET. (ou METR.) AVR. PIA SID. *Sidon.* Elagabale G.B. M.B.
COL. METR. AVR. PIA SIDON. *Sidon.* Elagabale G.B
COL. METR. BOSTRENORVM ACTIA DVSARIA. *Bostra.* Trajan Dèce M.B.
COL. METRO AVR. PIA SID. *Sidon.* Elagabale G.B.
COL. METROPOL. BOSTRON. (sic). *Bostra.* Trajan Dèce M.B.
COL. METROPOLIS BOSTRA. *Bostra.* Philippe père G.B. Etruscille M.B. (Avec — AKTIA ΔOYCARIA). Philippe père G.B. Philippe fils G.B.|
COL. METROPOL. TYRO. — AKTIA KAICAPIA. *Tyr.* Philippe fils G.B.
COL. METRO TYRO. *Tyr* Gordien III M.B.
COL. MET. SID. — LEG. III. PART. *Sidon.* Annia Faustine ✝ P.B.
COL. MET. TYRO. *Tyr.* Alex. Sévère M.B.
COL. NEAP. NEOCORO. *Néapolis.* Philippe fils ✝ G.B. M.B.
COL. NEAPO. *Néapolis.* Tréb. Galle M.B.
COL. NEAPOL. *Néapolis.* Philippe père G.B. M.B.
COL. NEAPOLI. *Néapolis.* Volusien M.B.
COL. NEAPOLI. NEOCORO. *Néapolis.* Philippe fils M.B.
COL. NEAPOLI. NEOKORO. *Néapolis.* Philippe père et Philippe fils G.B.
COL. NEAPOL. NEOCORO. *Néapolis.* Otacilie M.B.
COL. NEAPOL. NEOKO. *Néapolis.* Philippe père M.B.
COL. NEAPOL. NEOKORO. *Néapolis.* Philippe père et Philippe fils ✝G.B.
COL. NEM. *Nîmes.* Auguste et Agrippa M.B. ✝ M.B.
COL. NINI. CLAVD. *Ninive.* Maximin I G.B. M.B.
COL. NINIVA CLVV. (sic). *Ninive.* Maximin I M.B.
COL. NV. PHOENICES. *Incertaine de Phénicie.* Gordien III M.B.
COLO. AVG. PELLA. *Pella.* Philippe fils M.B

COLO. IV. CASSA. *Cassandrée.* Caracalla M B. P.B. Alex. Sévère M.B.
COLO. IVL. IDENSIS. (*sic*). ꞯꞯ. *Dium.* Macrin M.B.
COL. OLBA..... *Olbasa.* Gordien III †M.B.
COL. OLBASENORVM. *Olbasa.* Volusien M.B.
COLON. ANTIOCH. *Antioche Pisidie.* L. Vérus P.B.
COLON. BOSTRA. *Bostra.* Alex. Sévère P.B.
COLON. CAES. ANTI. S. R. *Antioche Pisidie.* Philippe fils M.B.
COLON. ꞱAMAC S. C. — OAYMHIA. *Damas.* Trajan Dèce BR.M.
COLꞱNEA (*sic*). CASSANDRIA. *Cassandrée.* Gordien III M.B.
COLONIA AELI. CAP. COM. P. FELIK. *Aelia Cafitolina.* † Géta M.B.
COLONIA ANTIOCH. *Antioche Pisidie.* Sept. Sévère P.B.
COLONIA AVG. FELI NINI. CLVV. (*sic*). *Ninive.* Trajan M.B.
COLONIA AVR. PIA METRO SIDON. *Sidon.* Elagabale M.B.
COLONIA BOSTRA. *Bostra.* Alex. Sévère P.B. Mamée †M.B. Tréb. Galle P.B.
COLONIA CAESAR. ANTIOCHIA. — ANTIOCH. COLONIA. S. R. *Antioche Pisidie.* Gordien III G.B.
COLONIA CASSANDRIA. *Cassandrée.* Caracalla et Géta †M.B. Gordien III M.B.
COLONIAE ANTIOCHE. *Antioche Pisidie.* L. Vérus P.B.
COLONIAE PELLENSIS. *Pella.* J. César P.B.
COLONIAE PELLENSIS. — SPES. *Pella.* Auguste P.B.
COLONIA IVL. CONC. AVG. APAM. D. D. *Apamée.* Caracalla G.B.
COLONIA IVL. DIENSIS D. D. *Dium.* Tibère M.B.
COLONIA MALLO S. C. *Mallus.* Etruscille M.B.
COLONIA PATRICIA. *Corduba.* Auguste BR.M. G.B. M.B. P.B.
COLONIA PTOLEMAIS. *Ptolémais.* Caracalla M.B. Alex. Sévère M.B.
COLONIA TYRVS METRO. *Tyr.* Salonine †M.B.
COLONIA TYRVS METROPOLIS AVGVSTA. *Tyr.* Salonine †M.B.
COLONI DAMASCO METROP. — CEBACMIA. *Damas.* Philippe père G.B.
COLONI DAMASCO METROPL (*sic*). — CEBACMIA. *Damas.* Otacilie G.B.
COLONI DAMASCO METROPOL (ou METROPOLI). — CEBACMIA. *Damas.* Philippe fils M.B.
COLONI SEP. S. LA. METROPOLI. *Laodicée.* Trajan Dèce et Etruscille G.B.
COLONI. SEP. TYRVS METR. *Tyr.* Sept. Sévère G.B. Caracalla G.B.
COLON. IVL. AVG. PHILIP. — DIVVS AVG. *Philiftes.* Adrien M.B.
COLON. PTOLEMA. *Ptolémaïs.* Macrin M.B.
COLON. SEP. TYRVS METROP. — LEG. III. GAL. *Tyr.* Julie Domne †M.B.
COLON. SEVER. METROPOLIS SEPT. LAVDIC. *Laodicée.* Sept. Sévère et J. Domne BR.M.
COLO PATR. *Corduba.* Auguste P.B.
COLO. PTOL. *Ptolémaïs.* Caracalla † M.B.
COLO. PTOLE. *Ptolémaïs.* Julie Domne † M.B.
COLO. PTOLEMA. *Ptolémaïs.* Macrin M.B.
COLO. TYRO METROPOL. *Ptolémaïs.* Salonine G.B.
COL. .....PACT. DVLT. (*sic*). *Deultum.* Maxime M.B.
COL. PARIA IVL. AVG. *Parium.* Marc Aurèle M.B.
COL. PATR. *Patras.* Géta P.B.
COL. PATRAE. *Patras.* Domitien M.B.
COL. PATRI. LE. V. X. *Corduba.* Auguste G.B.
COL. ...P. C. CAESAR. S. P. Q. R. *Césarée, Samarie.* Macrin †M.B.
COL. PERM. IMP. *Corinthe.* Domitien M.B.
COL. P. F. AV. F. C. CAES. *Césarée Samarie.* Macrin †M.B.
COL. P. F. AV. F. C. CAESA. *Césarée Samarie.* Hérennius M.B.
COL. P. F. AV. F. C. CAE. METRO. *Césarée Samarie.* Etruscille P.B.
COL. P. F AV. F. C. CAES. METR. (ou METROP.). *Césarée Samarie.* Hostilien P.B.
COL. P. F. AVG. *Césarée Samarie.* Valérien M.B.
COL. P. F. AVG. CAESAR. *Césarée Samarie.* M. Aurèle P.B.
COL. P. F. AVG. CAES. METROP. *Césarée Samarie.* Trajan Dèce P.B.
COL. P. F. AVG. . . CAES. PAL. *Césarée Samarie.* Volusien †P.B.
COL. P. F. AVG. CAES. P. S. P. *Césarée Samarie.* Hérennius P.B.

COL. P. F. AVG. F. C. CAES. MET. PRO PAL. *Césarée Samarie.* Tréb. Galle M.B.
COL. P. F. AVG. F. C. CAES. MET. PR. S. P. *Césarée Samarie.* Tréb. Galle † M.B.
COL. P. F. AVG. F. C. CAES. MET. (ou METR.) PR. S. PAL. *Césarée Samarie.* Volusien † M.B.
COL. P. F. AVG. F. C. FEL. CAES. METR. PR. S. PAL. — L. III. GAL. *Césarée, Samarie* Tréb. Galle G.B.
COL. P. F. AVG. METR. *Césarée, Samarie.* Volusien † P.B.
COL. P. F. AVG. METRO. *Césarée Samarie.* Tréb. Galle † M.B.
COL. P. F. AVG... PR. S. P. *Césarée Samarie.* Tréb. Galle M.B.
COL. P. F. ....CAESAREA. *Césarée Samarie.* Caracalla P.B.
COL. P. F. CAES. MET. PR. S. PAL. *Césarée, Samarie.* Volusien † M.B.
COL. P. F.... CAES. MET. S. P. *Césarée Samarie.* Hérennius M.B.
COL. P. FL. AVG. CAESAREN. *Césarée Samarie.* M. Aurèle † P.B.
COL. P. F... S. METROP. *Césarée Samarie.* Hostilien M.B.
COL. PHILIP. *Philippes.* Gallien P.B.
COL. PR... CAES. METR. *Césarée, Samarie.* Hérennius M.B.
COL. PR. F. AVG. F. CAESAR. METR. P. S. P. *Césarée, Samarie.* Trajan Dèce G.B.
COL. PR. F. AVG. F. C. CAES. *Césarée, Samarie.* Trajan Dèce G.B.
COL. PR. F. AVG. F. C. CAES. ME. *Césarée, Samarie.* Trajan Dèce G.B.
COL. PR. F. AVG. F. C. CAES. MET. (ou METR.) P. S. P. *Césarée, Samarie.* Trajan Dèce M.B.
COL. PR. F. AVG. F. C. CAES. MET. S. P. *Césarée, Samarie.* Trajan Dèce M.B.
COL. PR. F. AVG. F. C. CAES. P. S. *Césarée, Samarie.* Hérennius G.B. M.B.
COL. PR. F.... CAES. *Césarée, Samarie.* Trajan Dèce M.B.
COL. PR. F..... F. C. CAES. METR. P. *Césarée, Samarie.* Trajan Dèce G.B.
COL. PR. FL. AV. CAE. *Césarée, Samarie.* Commode † M.B.
COL. PR. FL. AV. CAES. *Césarée, Samarie.* Antonin M.B. M Aurèle P.B.
COL. PR. FL. AVG. CAES. *Césarée, Samarie.* M. Aurèle P.B. Philippe père G.B.
COL. PR. FL. AVG. CAESA. *Césarée, Samarie.* Philippe père G.B. Philippe fils G.B.
COL. PR. FL. AVG. CAESAR. *Césarée, Samarie.* Macrin M.B.
COL. PR. FL. AVG. CAESAREA. *Césarée, Samarie.* Commode M.B. J. Domne † M.B. Elagabale M.B.
COL. PR. FL. AVG. CAESARENS. *Césarée, Samarie.* Elagabale M.B.
COL. PR. FL. AVG. CAES. MET. S. P. *Césarée, Samarie.* Trajan Dèce G.B. P.B. Etruscille G.B.
COL. PR. FL. AVG. CAES. P. S. P. *Césarée, Samarie.* Trajan Dèce † M.B.
COL. PR. FL. AVG. CAISAR. (sic) *Césarée, Samarie.* Commode † M.B.
COL. PR. FL. AVG... FE. CAESAR. *Césarée, Samarie.* Sept. Sévère M.B.
COL. PR. FL. C. G. CAES. METR. P. S. P. *Césarée, Samarie.* Tréb. Galle M B.
COL. PRI. F. AV. CAESARENS. *Césarée, Samarie.* Trajan M.B.
COL. PRI. FL. AVG. CAESARIENSIS. *Césarée, Samarie.* Trajan M.B.
COL. PRIMA CAESAREA. *Césarée, Samarie.* M. Aurèle P.B.
COL. PRIMAE FL. AVG. CAESAREAE. *Césarée, Samarie.* M. Aurèle M.B.
COL. PRIMA F. AVG. CAES. *Césarée, Samarie.* Commode M.B.
COL. PRIMA FL. AVG. *Césarée, Samarie.* Antonin G.B.
COL. PRIMA FL. AVG. CAES. *Césarée, Samarie.* Antonin P.B.
COL. PRIMA. FL. AVG. CAESAR. *Césarée, Samarie.* M. Aurèle P.B.
COL. PRIMA. FL. AVG. CAESARE. *Césarée, Samarie.* Faustine jeune P.B.
COL. PRIMA FL. AVG. CAESAREA. *Césarée, Samarie.* Antonin M.B. Faustine jeune P.B.
COL. PRIMA FL. AVG. CAESAREN. *Césarée, Samarie.* M. Aurèle † P.B. L. Vérus M.B. † M.B.
COL. PRIMA. FL. CAESARENS. *Césarée, Samarie.* Trajan M.B.
COL. PRIM. ANT. AV. CAE. — M. P. *Césarée, Samarie.* Caracalla M.B.
COL. PRIM. F. AVG. CAESAREN. *Césarée, Samarie.* Lucille M.B.
COL. PR..... MET. PR. S. — PAL. *Césarée, Samarie* Volusien. † M.B.
COL. PTOL. *Ptolémaïs.* Claude I M.B. Trajan M.B. Adrien M.B. P.B. Commode M.B. P.B Sept. Sévère M.B † P.B. P.B. Julie Domne M.B. P.B. Caracalla M.B. † M.B. Géta P.B. Diaduménien M.B. † M.B. Elagabale G B. M B. † P.B. Aquilia

Sévéra M.B. Annia Faustine M.B. Alex. Sévère M.B. Philippe père G.B. M.B.
Otacilie G B. Philippe fils G.B. M.B. Tréb. Galle M.B. Valérien M.B. Gallien
G.B M.B. Salonine M.B. † M B. P.B.
COL. PTOL. BΞC. *Ptolémaïs*. Caracalla M.B
COL. PTOL. DIVOS. CLAVD. *Ptolémaïs*. Néron M.B.
COL. PTOL. HΞC. *Ptolémaïs*. Elagabale G.B. M B.
COL. PTOL. — TER. *Ptolémaïs*. Elagabale G.B.
COL. PTOLE. *Ptolémaïs*. J. Domne † M.B. Alex. Sévère † M.B. P.B.
COL. PTOLEM. *Ptolémaïs*. Alex. Sévere † M.B.
COL. PTOLEMA. *Ptolémaïs*. Philippe père G.B.
COL. ROM. *Romula*. Auguste P.B.
COL. R. P. F. AVG. CAES. METR. *Césarée, Samarie*. Trajan Dèce P.B.
COL. SEBACTE (*sic*). *Sébasté*. J. Domne † M.B
COL. SEP. AVR. LAOD. MATR (*sic*). *Laodicée Séleucide*. Caracalla G.B.
COL. SEP. AVR. LAO. S. METRO. *Laodicée Séleucide*. Caracalla G.B.
COL. SEPT. TYRVS METROP. — LEG. III. GAL. *Tyr*. Sept. Sévère G.B.
COL. SERG. NEAP. *Néapolis Samarie*. Philippe père † G.B. M.B.
COL. SERG. NEAPOL. *Néapolis Samarie*. Philippe père M.B. Philippe père et
Philippe fils † G.B. Otacilie G.B.
COL. SER. NEAP. *Néapolis Samarie*. Philippe fils † G.B.
COL. SER. NEAPOL. *Néapolis Samarie*. Otacilie † G.B.
COL. S. NEAP. *Néapolis Samarie*. Gallien P.B.
COL. TRO. *Alexandrie Troade* Gallien † P.B.
COL. TROA. *Alexandrie Troade*. Caracalla † M.B. Gallien P.B † P.B.
COL. TROADE. *Alexandrie Troade*. Gallien † P.B.
COL. TY....... *Tyr*. Philippe fils G.B. Tréb. Galle M.B.
COL. TYR..... *Tyr* Volusien M.B. Salonine G.B.
COL. TYR. M. (MET. ou METR.). *Tyr*. Gordien III G.B. † M.B.
COL. TYR. METR. — AMBPOCIE IIETRE. *Tyr*. Gordien III G.B. (Avec — IIPA. AKT.)
Philippe père G.B.
COL. TYR. METRO. *Tyr*. Gordien III G.B. (Avec — ΔΙΔω.) G.B.
COL. TYRO MATR. (*sic*). — AKTIA ERACL. *Tyr*. Otacilie G.B.
COL. TYRO ME. *Tyr*. Valérien G.B. Gallien G.B. M.B. Salonine M.B.
COL. TYRO ME... — AKT. KOM. *Tyr*. Volusien M.B.
COL. TYRO MET. *Tyr*. Elagabale M.B. Gordien III G.B. Philippe père G.B. Trajan
Dèce G.B. Tréb. Galle G.B. Volusien M.B. Valérien G.B. † G.B. M.B. Gallien
G.B. Salonine G.B. (Avec — EYPΓIIH.) Gallien G.B. (Avec — LEG. III. GAL.)
Valérien G.B. M.B. (Avec — ΚΛΗ. ΚΛΔ). Philippe père G.B.
COL. TYRO METR. Philippe père G.B. Otacilie † G.B. Tréb. Galle M.B. Va-
lérien † G.B. Gallien G.B. M.B. (Avec — AKTIA ERACL.) Valérien G.B. Gallien
G.B. (Avec — HERACLIA.) Salonine G.B. (Avec — LEG. III. GAL.)Tréb Galle † M.B.
(Avec — .... ΚΛΔ.) Tréb. Galle M.B. (Avec — ωKEAN.) *Tyr*. Valérien G.B.
COL. TYRO METRO. *Tyr*. Maesa M.B. Philippe père G.B. Otacilie M.B. Tréb.
Galle G.B. M.B. Volusien G.B. M.B. Valérien G.B. M.B. Gallien G.B. M.B. Salo-
nine G.B. (Avec — ΘHBE.) Gallien G.B.(Avec — LEG. III. GAL.) Tréb. Galle M.B.
COL TYRO METROP. *Tyr*. Tréb. Galle G.B. Valérien G.B.
COL. TYRO METROPOL. *Tyr*. Volusien M.B. Salonine † P.B.
COL. TYRVS METR. — LEG. III. GAL. *Tyr*. Caracalla G.B.
COL. TYRVS METRO. *Tyr*. Salonine † M.B.
COL. V. IVL. COR. *Corinthe* Adrien M.B.
COL. VL. (*sic*) AVG. PELLA. *Pella* Géta M.B.
COL. XA. TROAC. (*sic*). *Alexandrie Troade*. Alex. Sévère M.B.
COMAM. P. P. COL. IVL. F. *Comama*. Antonin P.B.
COMPOSTO ET MARVLLO IIVIR. — OSCA. *Osca*. Auguste P.B.
COMPOSTO ET MARVLLO IIVIR. V. V. OSCA. *Osca*. Auguste M.B.
CONCORD. AVGVSTOR. COL. ANTIOCH. S R. *Antioche Pisidie*. Caracalla G.B.
Géta G.B.
CONCORDIA BOSTRENORVM. *Bostra*. Hérennius et Hostilien M.B.
CONCORDI. AVGVSTOR. COL. ANTIOCH. S. R. *Antioche Pisidie*. Géta G.B.

COND. — CO. AE. CAP. *Aelia Capitolina*. Adrien M.B.
COPIA. *Lyon*. J. César et Auguste G.B. Auguste P.B.
CO. PR... CAESAR. *Césarée Samarie*. Annia Faustine P.B.
COR. *Corinthe*. Trajan M.B.
COR. PVBLICO REGV..... *Corinthe*. Agrippine jeune P.B.
COR. SE. *Corinthe*. Auguste P.B. Caligula P.B.
C. P. CLEANDRO P. Q. CO... DO... *Patras*. Néron M.B.
C. PETRONIO M. ANTONIO IIVIR. EX. D. D. *Cnosse*. Auguste P.B.
C. PETRONIOS M ANTONIOS IIVIRI EX. D. D. *Cnosse*. Auguste P.B.
C. P. F. AVG. CAESAREA. — S P. Q. R. *Césarée, Samarie*. Caracalla P.B Elagibale M.B.
C. PINNIVS P. AEBVCIVS IIVIR. QVIN. *Corinthe*. M. Antoine M.B.
C. Q? FL. AVG. CAES. METROP. *Césarée Samarie*. Trajan Dèce M.B.
C. R. I. F. S. A. CCCV. *Sinope*. Maximin 1 P.B.
C. R. I. F. S. AN. CCCV. *Sinope*. Maxime P B.
C. R. I. F. S. AN. CCCVIII. *Sinope*. Gordien III M.B.
C. R. I. F. S. AN CCCXI *Sinope*. Gordien III G.B.
C. R. I. F. S. AN. CCCXIV. (CCCXV. ou CCCXVIIII.). *Sinope*. Philippe fils G.B.
C. R. I. F. S. ANNO. CCCX. *Sinope*. Gordien III M.B.
C. R. I. F. SINO. *Sinope*. Maxime P.B.
C. R. I. I. AN. CCCXIX. *Sinope*. Philippe fils G.B.
C. SEMP. BARBA. Q BAEB. FLAVO IIVIR. M. CAL. I. *Calagurris*. Auguste M.B.
C. SEMP. P. ARRI. IIVIR. MVN. CAL. I *Calagurris*. Auguste M.B.
C. SOSIVS Q. ZA. *Zacinthe*. M. Antoine M.B.
C. TARRACINA P. PRISCO IIVIR. V. OSCA. *Osca*. Germanicus M.B.
C. TARRACINA P. PRISCO IIVIR. VRBS VICT. OSCA. *Osca*. Caligula M.B.
C. TARRACINA P. PRISCO IIVIR. — V. V. OSCA. *Osca*. Caligula G.B.
C. TARRACINA P. PRISCO IIVIR. V. V. OSCA. *Osca* Caligula M.B.
C. TER. SVRA L. LIC. GRACILE IIVIR. MVN. ERCAVICA. *Ercavica*. Caligula M.B.
CTOBE. (*sic*). *Stobi* Auguste P B
C. VAL. AEDILES C. SEX. *Calagurris*. Auguste M.B.
C. VALERI. C. FENI. IIVIR. *Calagurris*. Auguste M.B.
C. VAR. RVF. SEX. IVL. POL. IIVIR. Q. *Carthago Nova*. Auguste P.B.
C. VIBIO MARSO PR. COS. C. CASSIVS FELIX A. IIVIR. — D. D. P. P. *Utique*. Tibère M.B
C. VIBIO MARSO PR. COS. DR. (ou DRV.) CAE. Q. PR. T. G. RVFVS F. C. — D. D. P. P. *Utique*. Tibère M.B.
C. VIBIO MARSO PR. COS. II. L. CAECILIVS PIVS IIV. F. C. — M. M. I. V. *Utique*. Tibère M.B.
C. VIBIO MARSO PR. COS. II. L. CAECILIVS PIVS IIVR. (*sic*). — M. M. I. V. *Utique*. Tibère G.B. M.B.
C. VIBIO MARSO PR. COS. II. Q. CAECILIVS PIVS IOVIN. IIV. F. C. — M. M. I. V. *Utique*. Tibère M.B.
C. VIBIO MARSO PR. COS. II. SEX. TADIVS FAVSTVS IIV. — M. M. I. V. *Utique*. Tibère M.B.
C. VIBIO MARSO PR. COS. III. C. CAELIVS PAX A. (AV. ou AVG.) IIVIR. — D. D. P. P. *Utique*. Tibère M.B.
C. VIBIO MARSO PR. COS. III. C. CASSIVS FELIX A. IIVIR. — D. D. P. P. *Utique*. Tibère M.B.
C. VIBIO MARSO PR. COS. III. C. SALLVSTIVS IVSTVS II. (ou IIV.) — M. M. I. V. *Utique*. Tibère M.B.
C. VIBIO MARSO PR. COS. III. M. TVLLIVS IVDEX. — M. M. I. V. *Utique*. Tibère M.B.
C. VIB. MARSO PR. COS. DR. CAE. Q. PR. T. G. RVFVS F. C. — D. D. P. P. *Utique*. Tibère M.B.
C VIB. MARSO PR. COS. NE. CAE. Q. PR. A. M. GEMELLVS F. C. — D. D. P. P. *Utique* Tibère M.B.
C. V. I. CEL. CN. DOMITIO C. POMPEIO IIVIR. *Celsa*. Auguste M.B.
C. V. I. CEL. L. BACCIO MAN. FESTO IIVIR. *Celsa*. Auguste M.B.
C. V. I. CEL. L. SVRA L. BVCCO IIVIR. *Celsa*. Auguste M.B.

C. V. I. F. AV. *Césarée, Samarie.* Trajan G.B.
C. V. MARSO PROCOS. NER. CAES. Q. PR. A. M. GEMELLVS. — **D.** D. P. P. *Utique.* Tibère M.B.
C. V. T. T. *Tarraco.* Auguste G.B. Tibère G.B.
C. V. T. TAR. *Tarraco.* Caïus et Lucius Césars P.B.
DAMACCO (sic) COLONIA METR. S. C. *Damas.* Emilien † M.B.
ΔAMA. METR. *Damas.* Tréb. Galle M.B.
DAMAS. *Damas.* Philippe père et Philippe fils G.B.
ΔAMAS M.... *Damas.* Philippe père G.B.
ΔAMAS METR. *Damas.* Otacilie BR.M.
D. D. *Apamée.* J. César P B. — *Babba.* Claude I P.B.
α. α. *Apamée?* Auguste P.B.
D. D. OPTIMO PRINCIPI C. G. I. P. *Parium.* Trajan P.B.
Δ. E. *Laodicée.* Elagabale P.B.
Δ. E. *(étoile). Laodicée.* Alex. Sévère P.B.
DEANAN. PATR. *Patras.* Domitien M.B.
DECENNALES ANTONINI COS. III. COL. BER. *Béryte.* Sept. Sévère et Caracala M.B.
DECENN. ANT. COS. — COL. BER. *Béryte.* Caracalla † P.B.
DEO AE....... II. PA. *Parium.* Caracalla P.B.
DEO AES. C. G. I. II. P. *Parium.* Gallien P.B.
DEO AESC. SVB. C. G. I. II. P. *Parium.* Commode M.B. Caracalla P.B.
DEO AESCVLAPIO.... COL. H. PAR. *Parium.* Antonin P.B.
DEO AES. SVB. C. G. I. II. P. *Parium.* Alex. Sévère M.B.
DEO CVPIDINI C. G. I, II. P. *Parium.* Otacilie M.B.
DEO CVPIDINI C. G. I. II. PA. *Parium.* Philippe fils M.B.
DEO CVPIDINI COL. GEM. IVL. IIAD. PA. *Parium.* Commode M.B.
D. EX. CONSE. (OU CONSENSV.) C. C. I. B. *Babba.* Néron M.B.
DIANA AVG. LAPIIRIE GAC. *Patras.* Néron M.B.
DIANA ELAEIA. *Elaea.* Sept. Sévère M.B.
DIANAE LAPH..... *Patras.* Domitien M.B.
DIANAE LVCIF. C. I. C. A. D. D. *Apamée.* M. Aurèle M.B.
DIANA LAPIIR. *Patras.* Néron. † M.B. Domitien M.B.
DIVA CLAVD. NER. F. *Incertaine.* Poppée P.B.
DIVA POPPAEA AVG. *Incertaine.* Claudia P.B.
DIVO IVL. AVG. DIVI F. *Philippes.* Auguste. M.B.
DIVOS CLAVD. COL. C. C. S. PTOL. — VI. IX. X. XI. *Ptolémaïs.* Néron M.B.
DIVOS CLAVD. COL. CLA. PTOL. — VI. IX. X. XI. *Ptolémaïs.* Néron M.B.
DIVOS CL... COL. PTOL. *Ptolémaïs.* Adrien M.B
DIVVS AVGVSTVS MVN. TVR. *Turiaso.* Tibère G.B.
DONATIO COL. CRE. *Cremna.* Aurélien M.B.
DVRMIVS M. IIERENNIVS IIVIR. QVINQ. — C. I. A. D. *Dium.* Auguste M.B.
EM. AVG. *Emerita.* Auguste P.B.
E. P. *Incertaine.* Néron M.B.
EΠI KOMINIOY ΠPOKΛOY ANΘY. — KYΠPIΩN. *Chypre.* Claude I (bilingue) M.B.
ERCAVICA. *Ercavica.* Tibère † P.B.
EX CON. C. C. I. B. *Babba.* Néron P.B.
EX CON. D. C. C. I. B. *Babba.* Néron P.B.
EX CONS DEC. C. C. I. B. *Babba.* Galba P.B.
EX CONSENSV D. C. C. I. B. *Babba.* Néron M.B. P.B.
EX. D. D. *Sinope.* Cléopâtre M.B. Auguste P.B.
F. CO. A. CA. ...AV. CO. A. *Aelia Capitolina.* Commode? † M.B.
F. DOMITIO IIVIR. QV. COR. ADVE. AVG. *Corinthe* Néron P.B
FORTVNA COL. ANTIOC *Antioche Pisidie.* Julie Domne † M.B.
FORTVNA COL. ANTIOCH. *Antioche Pisidie.* Sept Sévère M.B. Caracalla G.B.
FORTVNA COL. CAES. ANTIOCH. *Antioche Pisidie.* Gordien III M.B.
FORTVNA COL. CRE... E. *Cremna.* Aurélien G.B.
FORTVNA COLO. ANTIOCH. *Antioche Pisidie.* Sept. Sévère M.B.
FORTVNA COLONIAF ANTIOCH. *Antioche Pisidie.* Antonin M.B. Sept. Sévère P.B. Caracalla P.B

FVLVIANO PRAEF. (OU PRAEFECTO) LVPO IIVIR. C. C. A. *Caesar Augusta.* Tibère M B.
GE. COL. C. ANTIOCH. *Antioche Pisidie.* Sept. Sévère † M.B.
GEN. ANTIOCH. *Antioche Pisidie.* Sept Sévère † P.B.
GEN. COL. ANTIOCH. *Antioche Pisidie.* Sept. Sévère † P.B. P.B. J. Domne † M.B. Caracalla † P.B.
GEN. COL. ANTIOCHE. *Antioche Pisidie.* Sept. Sévère † M.B.
GEN. COL. A. PATRENS. *Patras.* Domitien M.B.
GEN. COL. AVG. TRO. *Alexandrie Troade.* Géta M.B.
GEN. COL. AVG. TROA. *Alexandrie Troade.* Commode M.B.
GEN COL. CA. ANTIOCH. *Antioche Pisidie.* Sept. Sévère † M.B. Caracalla † M.B.
GEN. COL. CAES. ANTIOCHEN. *Antioche Pisidie.* J. Domne M.B.
GEN. COL. C ANTIOCH. *Antioche Pisidie.* Caracalla † M.B.
GEN. COL. C. ANTIOCHE. *Antioche Pisidie.* J. Domne † M.B. Géta † M.B.
GEN. COL. NER. PAT. *Patras.* Néron M.B.
GEN. COL. AVG. TROAD. *Alexandrie Troade.* Commode M.B.
GENI. COL. CAES. ANTIOCH. *Antioche Pisidie.* Sept. Sévère P.B. Julie Domne † M.B Caracalla † M.B.
GENIO ANTIOCHENI. *Antioche, Syrie.* Julien II P.B.
GENIO C. I. C. A. — D. D. *Apamèe.* Antonin G.B.
GENIO CIVITATIS. *Antioche, Syrie.* Julien II P.B.
GENIO COL. CRE... AΣ. *Cremna.* Géta P.B.
GENIO COLON. CAES. ANTIOCHEN. *Antioche Pisidie* Caracalla BR.M.
GENIO COLONIAE ANTIOCH. *Antioche Pisidie.* Antonin M B.
GENIVM C. I. C. *Corinthe.* Agrippine mère P.B.
GENIVS COL. ANTIOCH. S. R. *Antioche Pisidie.* Sept. Sévère G.B. Caracalla G.B.
GEN. POP. ROM. *Italica.* Auguste M.B.
GEN PVBL. D. D. *Babba.* Claude I M.B.
GERM. *Parium.* Domitien P.B.
GERMANICO ET DRVSO. *Cartéia.* Germanicus et Drusus P.B.
GRAECINVS QVINT. TERT. BVTHR. *Buthrote.* Auguste P.B.
HERCVLI AVGVSTO C. P. *Patras.* Néron M.B.
HIBERO PRAEF. *Carthago Nova.* Auguste P.B.
HIPPONE LIBERA. — IVL. AVG. *Hippone.* Tibère G.B.
HOSPITE ET FLORO IIVIR. — V. OSCA V. *Osca.* Tibère † P.B.
HOSPITE ET FLORO IIVIR. V. V. OSCA. *Osca.* Tibère M.B.
ICENO COL. CREAL. (sic). *Cremna.* Géta P.B.
I. C. I. G. AC. *Acci.* Auguste † M.B.
ICONIEN. COLO S. R. *Iconium.* Gallien † M.B. M.B.
ICONIENSI COLO S. R. *Iconium.* Gordien III M.B. Valérien P.B.
ICONIENSIVM COL. S. R. *Iconium.* Gallien † G B.
ICONIENSIVM CO. S. R. *Iconium.* Gordien III M.B. Valérien G.B Gallien G.B. † M.B.
ICONIESI ADRIA COL. *Iconium.* Gordien III M.B.
II. C. I. G. AC. *Acci.* Auguste † M.B.
II. COL. BER. *Béryte.* Elagabale P.B.
III. C. I. G. AC. *Acci.* Auguste M.B.
IIVIR. L. PRISC. C. BROC. *Calagurris.* Auguste P.B.
IIVIR. QVINQ. EX. D. D. *Parium.* J. César P.B.
IKONIEN. COLO. S. R. *Iconium.* Gallien M.B.
I... MIHI... ANTIOCH. COL. *Antioche Pisidie.* Caracalla G.B.
IMP. A. ET. P. G. C. — COL. CRE. *Cremna.* Caracalla BR.M.
IMP. DIVI F. ACTIO. *Pella.* Auguste M.B.
I. O. M. COL. HEL. *Héliopolis.* Alex. Sévère G.B.
IOVI AVG. *Corinthe.* Auguste P.B.
IOVI VICTORI. C. A. *Cologne.* Postume B.
ISTHMIA. *Corinthe.* Domitien G.B. Trajan M.B. Adrien M.B. Antonin M.B Marc Aurèle M.B. L. Vérus M.B. P.B. Commode M.B. P.B. Sept. Sévère M.B.
ISTHMIA C. L. I. COR. *Corinthe.* Caracalla † M.B

ISTHMVS. *Corinthe.* Adrien P.B.
ITALICA. *Bilbilis* Auguste M.B.
IVL. A. COL. PARLAIS. *Parlaïs.* Julie Domne ✝ M.B.
IVL. AVG. COL. PARLA. *Parlaïs.* Commode P.B.
IVL. AVG. COL. PARLAI. *Parlaïs.* Sept. Sévère M.B.
IVL. AVG. COL. PARLAIS. *Parlaïs.* Sept. Sévère M.B. ✝ M.B. ✝ P.B. P.B. Julie Domne M.B. ✝ M.B. P.B.
IVL...... CASSA. *Cassandrée.* Julie de Titus P.B.
IVLIA AVGVSTA. *Parium?* Titus P.B.
IVLIA AVGVSTA C. A. E. *Emérita.* Livie G.B.
IVLIA AVGVSTA C. C. A. *Caesar Augusta.* Tibère M.B.
IVLIA AVGVSTA MVN. ITALIC. *Italica.* Auguste G B.
IVLIA TRAD. *Julia Traducta.* Auguste G B.
IVL. TRAD. *Julia Traducta.* Caïus P.B. Lucius P.B.
IVNIANO LVPO PR. C. CAESAR. C. POMPON. PARRA. IIVIR. *Caesar Augusta.* Livie M.B.
IVNIANO LVPO PR C. CAESAR. C. POMPON. PARRA IIVIR. C. C. A. *Caesar Augusta.* Tibère M.B.
IVPPITER LIBERATOR C. P. *Patras.* Néron M.B.
K. A. C. *Aelia Capitolina?* Antonin P.B.
KOINON KYΠPIΩN. *Chypre.* Claude I *(bilingue)* G.B. M.B.
KOA. CEBACTE. *Sébasté.* J. Domne *(bilingue)* ✝ M.B.
LADICEON. Δ. E. *Laodicée..* Elagabale P.B.
LADIKEΩN *(sic)* Δ. E. *Laodicée.* Alex. Sévère P.B.
LAELIA. *Laelia.* Auguste P.B. Tibère P.B.
L. AEM. MAXVMO M. BAEB. SOBRINO AED. — SAG. *Sagonte.* Tibère P.B.
L. A. FAVSTVS D. C. BASSVS IIVIR. — P. P. D. D. *Carthage.* Tibère P.B.
L. AP. DEC. Q. *Urso.* Auguste G.B. M.B.
L. ARRIO PEREGRINO IIVIR. COR. *Corinthe.* Auguste P.B. (Avec — GENT. IVL.) Livie P.B
L. ARRIVS PEREGRINVS II VIR. COR. *Corinthe.* Auguste ✝ M.B.
LAVDICEON Δ. E. *Laodicée.* Elagabale P.B.
L. AVFID. PANSA SEX. POMP. NIGRO. — AED. C. V. I. CELSA. *Celsa.* Auguste M.B.
L. BACCIO MAN. FESTO IIVIR. — C. V. I. CEL. *Celsa.* Auguste P.B.
L. BACCIO MAN. FLAVIO FESTO. — IIVIR. C V. I. CELSA. *Celsa.* Auguste P.B.
L. BAEBIO P. ANTESTIO IIVIR. *Calagurris.* Auguste M.B.
L. BAEB. PRISCO C. GRAN. BROC. IIVIR. *Calagurris.* Auguste M.B.
L. BENNIO PRAEF. *Carthago Nova.* Agrippa P.B.
L. CAEC. AQVIN. M. CEL. PALVD. IIVIR. MVN. TVR. *Turiaso.* Tibère M B.
L. CASSIO C. NERIO IIVIR. *Incertaine.* Auguste P.B.
L. CASTRICIO REGVLO. IIVIR. COR. *Corinthe.* Tibère M.B.
L. CAN. AGRIPPAE COR. *Corinthe.* Livie M B.
L. CAN. AGRIPPAE IIV. COR. *Corinthe.* Galba P.B.
L. CAN. AGRIPPAE IIVI. (ou IIVIR.). *Corinthe.* Galba P.B.
L. CAN. AGRIPPAE IIVI. COR. *Corinthe.* Galba ✝ M.B P.B.
L. CAN. AGRIPPAE IIVIR. COR. *Corinthe.* Livie M.B.
L. CORN. TERREN. M. IVN. HISPAN. IIVIR. *Celsa.* Auguste M.B.
L. COR. TERR. M. IVN. HISP. IIVIR. *Celsa.* Auguste M.B.
L. DOMI. ROBV. T. OCTAV. METAL. AED. CLVNIA. *Clunia.* Tibère P.B.
LECH. CENCH. *Corinthe.* Adrien ✝ M.B
LEDICEON Δ. E. *Laodicée.* Elagabale P B.
LEG. V. MACED. VIII. AVG. COL. HEL. *Héliopolis.* Philippe fils G.B. ✝ M.B.
LEPI. *Cavaillon.* Lépide AR.Q.
LEPIDO ET GEMELLO IIVIR. C. C. A. *Caesar Augusta* Tibère M.B.
LEPTIS. *Leptis.* J. César G.B.
ΛEΠTIC. B. *Leptis.* Tibère *(bilingue)* G.B.
L. FADI. L. CAE. NIF. *Paestum.* Tibère P.B.
L. FVL. SPARSO L. SATVRNINO. IIVIR M. C. I. *Calagurris.* Tibère M.B.

L. FVRIO C. CRISPO IIVIR. *Corinthe.* Tibère P.B.
L. FVRIO C. CRISPO IIVIR. COR. — AVGVSTVS *Corinthe.* Tibère M.B.
L. FVRIO LABEONE IIVIR. COR. *Corinthe.* Auguste M.B.
L. FVRIO LABEONE IIVIR. COR *Corinthe.* Auguste P.B. (Avec — GENT. IVL.) † M.B.
Livie M.B. Tibère M.B.
L. GRANIO C. VALERIO IIVIR. *Calagurris.* Auguste M.B.
LIBERALITATIS IVL. EBOR. *Ebora.* Auguste G.B.
LIBERALITATIS (OU LIBERAL.) IVLIAE EBOR. *Ebora.* Auguste M.B.
LIBERAT. R. COL. PR. F. *Césarée, Samarie.* M. Aurèle † P.B.
LICINIANO ET GERMANO IIVIR. — C. C. A. *Caesar Augusta.* Caligula G.B M.B.
L. IVL. RVF. T. CAP. L. CON. T. POM. LON. P. IVL. NEP. IIII. VIR. CLVNIA. *Clunia.*
Tibère M.B.
L. KAP. COM. P. F. *Aelia Capitolina.* Trajan Dèce M.B.
L. MANLIO T. PETRON. (OU PETRONIO) IIVIR. C. C. IL. A. *Ilici.* Auguste P.B.
L. MARIO L. NOVIO IIVIR.. — TVRIASO. *Turiaso.* Auguste P.B.
L. MVSSIDI PR. COS. *Corinthe.* Tibère M.B.
LO. (*sic*) AE. CAP. *Aelia Capitolina.* Antonin P.B.
L. PACO FLAM. CH. PV... COR. *Corinthe.* Agrippine jeune P.B.
L. PANSA SEX. NIGRO. — AED. C. V. I. *Celsa.* Auguste P.B.
L. PASS... RVFVS IMP. *Carthage.* Auguste BR.M.
L. POMP. C. IVLI IIVIR. COR. *Corinthe.* Auguste M.B.
L. POMPE. BVCCO L. CORNE. FRONT. *Celsa.* Auguste G.B. M.B.
L. PRISCO. C. BROCCHO (OU BROC.) IIVIR. *Calagurris* Auguste P.B.
L. RVF. PISONE... COR. ADLO. AVG. *Corinthe.* Néron P.B.
L. RVF. PISONE IIVIR. QVI. COR. — ADVE. AVG. *Corinthe.* Néron P.B.
L. RVF. T. CONSI. T. LONG. P. ANTO IIIIVIR. CLVNIA. *Clunia.* Tibère M.B.
L. RVSTICELIVS CORDVS IIVIR QVINQ. D. D. *Dium.* Livie M.B. Tibère M.B.
L. RVTILIO PLANCO IIVIR. — COR. *Corinthe.* Auguste P.B.
L. SE. GEMINO L. VAL. SVRA IIVIR. — SAG. *Sagonte.* Tibère P.B.
L. SEMP. GEMINO L. VALER. SVRA. — SAG. *Sagonte.* Tibère M.B..
L. SEMP. GERMINO L. VAL. SVRA IIVIR. — SAG. *Sagonte.* Tibère M.B.
AT. C. A. *Césarée-Panias.* Auguste M.B.
L. TER. LON. L. PAP. AVIT. IIVIR. Q. C. C. I. A. — IVNCTIO. *Ilici.* Tibère M.B. P B.
L. VALENTINO L. NOVO IIVIR. M. CAL. I. *Calagurris.* Auguste M.P.
L. VAL. FLAVO T. VAL. MERVLA AED. *Calagurris.* Tibère P.B.
L. VOLVSVS SATVR. ACHVL. *Achulla.* Auguste, Caius et Lucius M.B.
M. AC. CANDIDO IIVIR COR. *Corinthe.* Agrippine jeune P.B. Néron P.B. Octavie P.B.
M. AC. CANDIDO IIVIR GEN. COL. COR. *Corinthe.* Claude I P.B. Agrippine jeune
M.B. P.B. Néron P.B. Octavie P.B.
M. AGRIPPA COS. III. MVNICIPI PARENS. *Gadès.* Agrippa G.B.
MALLO COLONIA S. C. *Mallus.* Etruscille M.B. Hostilien G.B. Valérien G.B.
MAN. ACILIO... IIVIR. COR. *Corinthe.* Agrippine jeune P.B.
MAN. SVLP. LVCAN. M. SEMP. FRONT. MVN. TVRIASO,—IIVIR. *Turiaso.* Tibère M.B.
M. ANTONI L. FABI IIVIR. *Calagurris.* Auguste M.B.
MARIO VEGE. LICI. CRES. MVN. TVRIASO — AED. *Turiaso.* Tibère P.B.
M. BARBAT. MAN. ACILIO IIVIR. *Parium.* Auguste M.B
M. BELLIO PROCVLO IIVIR. COR. *Corinthe.* Auguste † M.B. P.B. Germanicus P.B.
Caligula M.B.
M. CATO L. VETTIACVS IIVIR. C. C. A. *Caesar Augusta.* Tibère G.B. M.B. (Avec
— LEG. IV. LEG. VI. LEG. X.) Tibère G.B.
M. EGN. Q. OCT. IIVIR. P. S. S. C. *Paestum.* Tibère P.B.
MENSIS COL. CAES. ANTIOCH. *Antioche Pisidie.* Antonin M.B.
MERC. COL. CR. *Cremna.* Géta P.B.
METRO COA. AV. (*sic*).... *Sidon.* Elagabale † M.B.
M. FICTORI M. SEPTVMI IIVIR. QVINQ. *Pella.* Auguste M.B.
M. FVFIO... O... ER... QVINQ. *Incertaine.* Tibère M.B.
M. GRANIVS MARCELLVS PRO COS. *Incertaine.* Auguste et Livie M.B.
M. H. I. ILERCAVONIA. — DERT. *Dertosa et Ilercavonia.* Tibère M.B.

MID. DEAE COL. ´CREM. *Cremna*. Géta M.B.
M. IVLIVS SETAL L. SEST. CELER IIVIR. — SAL. AVG. — C. I. I. A. *Ilici*. Tibère G.B.
M. IVLIVS SETFAL L. SESTI. CELER IIVIR. — SAL. AVG. — C. I. I. A. *Ilici*. Tibère M.B.
M. LIC. CAP. C. FVL. RVTIL. IIVIR. M. C. I. *Calagurris*. Auguste M.B.
M. LVCR. TER. E. C. CALP. VARO AED. CLVNI. *Clunia*. Tibère P.B.
M. MEMMI L. IVNI *Calagurris*. Auguste M B.
M. M. IVL. VTIC. P. P. D. D. *Utique*. Tibère M.B.
M. M. IVL. VTI. D. D. P. P. *Utique*. Livie P.B.
M. MVN. IVL. VTIC. (OU VTICEN.) D. D. P. P. *Utique*. Tibère M.B.
M. MVN. IVL. VTIC. P. P D. D. *Utique*. Tibère M.B.
M. PLAE. TRANQ. VRSO IIVIR. ITER. *Calagurris*. Auguste M.B.
M. PONT. MARSO C. MARI. VEGETO IIVIR. MVN. TVR. *Turiaso*. Tibère M.B.
M. POR. CN. FAD. IIVIR. *Caesar Augusta*. Auguste P.B.
M. POSTV. ALBINVS IIVIR QVINQ. ITER. V. I. N. K. — AVGVSTO. *Carthago Nova*. Auguste P.B.
M. POSTVM. ALBIN. L. PORC. CAPIT. IIVIR. Q. *Carthago Nova* Auguste M.B. P.B.
M. QVINCTIO Q. ALLIO IIVIR V. V. OSCA. *Osca*. Auguste M.B.
M. SILANO IIVIR COR. *Corinthe*. Agrippine jeune P.B.
M. V. D. D. P. P. *Utique*. Tibère P.B.
MVN. AVGVSTA BILBILIS G. POM. CAPE. II. G. VALE. TRANQ. — IIVIR. *Bilbilis*. Tibère M.B.
MVN. AVGVSTA BILBILIS L. COR. CALDO L. SEMP. RVTILO. — IIVIR. *Bilbilis*. Auguste M.B.
MVN. AVGVSTA BILBILIS L. COR. CAL. L. SEMP. RVTI. — IIVIR. *Bilbilis*. Auguste M.B.
MVN. AVGVSTA BILBILIS M. SEMP. TIBERI L. LICI. VARO. — IIVIR. *Bilbilis*. Auguste M.B.
MVN. AVGVSTA BILBILIS TI. CAESARE III. — COS. *Bilbilis*. Tibère M.B.
MVN. AVGVSTA BILBILIS TI. CAESARE V. L. AELIO SEIANO. — COS. *Bilbilis*. Tibère M.B. † M.B.
MVN. CASCANT. *Cascantum*. Tibère P.B.
MVN. ERCAVICA. *Ercavica*. Auguste M.B. P.B.
MVN. ILERDA. *Ilerda*. Auguste M.B.
MVNICIP. CASCANTVM. *Cascantum*. Tibère M.B. P.B.
MVNICIP. GRACCVRRIS. *Graccurris*. Tibère M.B. P.B
MVNICIPI COELA. *Coela*. Antonin P.B.
MVNICIPI COELA. AVG? *Coela*. Antonin P.B.
MVNICIPII PARENS. *Gadès*. Agrippa BR.M.
MVNICIPII PATRONVS. *Gadès*. Agrippa G.B.
MVNICIPII PATRONVS PARENS. *Gadès*. Agrippa BR.M.
MVNICIP. ILERDA. *Ilerda*. Auguste M.B.
MVNICIPI PARENS. *Gadès* Agrippa G.B.
MVNICIPI STOBEN. *Stobi*. Caracalla † M.B.
MVNICIPI STOBENSI. *Stobi*. Sept. Sévère M.B. Julie Domne G.B. M.B.
MVNICIPI STOBENSIVM. *Stobi* Vespasien M.B. Titus et Domitien M.B. Domitien M.B. Trajan M.B. Géta M.B.
MVNICIPIVM COIL. *Coela*. Antonin P B.
MVNICIPIVM STOBENSIVM. *Stobi*. Vespasien M.B. Géta G.B.
MVNICIP. STOB. *Stobi*. Julie Domne † M.B.
MVNICIP. STOBE. (OU STOBEN). *Stobi*. Caracalla † M.B.
MVNICIP. STOBENS. *Stobi*. Vespasien M.B. P.B. Domitien M.B. Sept. Sévère M.B. Géta P.B.
MVNICIP. STOBENSI. *Stobi*. Caracalla † M.B. Géta G.B. Elagabale M.B.
MVNICIP. STOBENSIV. *Stobi*. Julie Domne † M.B.
MVNICIP. STOBENSIVM. *Stobi*. Elagabale M.B.
MVNICI. STOBE. *Stobi*. Caracalla † M.B. Géta G.B.
MVNICI. STOBEN. *Stobi*. Julie Domne M.B. Caracalla M.B. † M.B. Géta † M.B. Elagabale M.B.
MVNICI. STOBENS. *Stobi*. M. Aurèle M.B. Sept. Sévère M.B. Caracalla † M.B. P.B.
MVNICI. STOBENSI. *Stobi*. Caracalla † M.B.

MVNICI. STOBENSIVM. *Stobi.* Marc Aurèle M.B.
MVNIC. ITALIC. *Italica.* Auguste M.B. P.B. Drusus † P.B. Germanicus P.B.
MVNIC. STO. (ou STOB.). *Stobi.* Caracalla † M.B.
MVNIC. STOBE. *Stobi.* Caracalla † M.B. Géta G.B. Elagabale M.B.
MVNIC. STOBEN. *Stobi.* Sept. Sévère M.B. Julie Domne † M.B. P.B. Caracalla M.B.
MVN. ILERDA. *Ilerda.* Auguste M.B.
MVNI. STOB. *Stobi.* Julie Domne P.B.
MVNI. STOBE. *Stobi.* Trajan G.B. Elagabale G.B.
MVNI. STOBEN. *Stobi.* Julie Domne M.B.
MVNI. STOBENSI. *Stobi.* Sept. Sévère M.B.
MVN. ITAL. PERM. AVG. — PROVIDENT. *Italica.* Auguste M.B.
MVN. KAN. ITE. L. TITIO IIVIR. *Caesar Augusta.* Auguste P.B.
MVNNICI. (*sic*) STOB. *Stobi.* Domitia P B.
MVN. OSIC. (ou OSICERDA) *Osicerda.* Tibère M.B. P.B.
MVN. STOB. *Stobi.* Titus et Domitien M.B. Marc Aurèle M.B. J. Domne M.B.
MVN. STOBENSIVM. *Stobi.* Trajan M.B.
MVN. TVRIA. *Turiaso.* Tibère P.B.
MVN. TVRIASO. *Turiaso.* Auguste G.B. M.B.
MVN. TVRIASO L. FENESTE L. SERANO. *Turiaso.* Auguste M.B.
MVN TVRIASO L. MARCO L. NOVIO. *Turiaso.* Auguste M.B.
NEAPOL. NEOCORO COL. *Néapolis.* Otacilie G.B.
NEPT. AVG. COL. PATR. *Patras.* Domitien M.B.
NINI. C. COLO. *Ninive.* Marc Aurèle P.B.
NONIVS SVLPICIVS IIVIR QVINQ. *Pella.* Auguste M.B
N. TPA (*sic*) BOSTRA. *Bostra.* Elagabale P.B.
N. TR. ALEXAN. BOSTRA. *Bostra.* Mamée G.B.
N. TR. ALEXANDRIANAE COL. BOSTRA. *Bostra.* Mamée G.B.
O. C. S. *Incertaine d'Afrique.* Auguste BR.M.
OCTAVIO LVSCINO IIVIR ITER. COR. *Corinthe.* Claude I † M.B.
OCTAV. LICINIO. IIVIR ITER. *Corinthe.* Auguste † M.B.
OCTAA. (*sic*) Q. DESIG. *Corinthe?* Auguste P.B.
OSCA. *Osca.* Auguste M.B. P.B. Tibère P.B.
PAC. H. PV...? PAC. FLAM. IIV. *Corinthe.* Agrippine jeune P.B.
PAC. H. PV. PAC. FLAM. IIV. — COR. *Corinthe.* Agrippine jeune P.B.
P. AEBVTIO C. NONNIO (?) IIVIR. *Corinthe.* M. Antoine M.B.
P. AEBVTIO C. PINNIO IIVIR. *Corinthe.* M. Antoine M.B.
P. AEBVT. SP. F. C. IVLIO HERAC (ou HER.) IIVIR. QVI. ITER. *Corinthe.* Auguste
   † M.B. P.B.
PALIK. PR. *Cyrénaïque.* Auguste M.B.
P. ALITIO L. MENIO IIVIR. *Corinthe.* M. Antoine M.B.
P. AQVINO C. IVLIO IIVIR *Corinthe.* M. Antoine M.B.
PAX. IVL. *Pax Julia.* Auguste M.B.
P. BAEBIVS IIVIR QVINQ. — D. D. *Dium.* Auguse M.B.
P. CANINIO AGRIPPA IIVIR QVINQ. COR. *Corinthe.* Tibère M.B. P.B.
P. COP. (*sic*) COL. CR. *Cremna.* Géta P.B.
PERM. AVG. COL. ROM. *Romula.* Germanicus P.B.
PERM. CAES. AVG. *Emérita.* Livie G.B. M.B.
PERM. DIVI AVG. MVNIC. ITALIC. — PROVIDENTIAE AVGVSTI. *Italica.* Tibère G B M.B
PERM. DOLABELLAE PRO COS. C. P. G. CAS. *Clypea.* Drusus M.B.
PERM. IMP. *Corinhe.* Domitien G.B.
PERM. IMP. C. L. I. COR. *Corinthe.* Domitien G.B.
PERM. IMP GERM. *Corinthe.* Domitien G.B.
PERMIS. P. CORNELI DOLABELLAE PRO. COS. C. P. CAS. D. D. *Clypea.* Tibère BR.M.
PERMIS. P. DOLABELLAE PRO COS C. P. GAVIO COS. *Clypea.* Tibère BR.M.
PERMIS. P. DOLABELLAE PRO. COS. C. P. G. CAS. — C. P. I. *Clypea.* Tibère M.B.
PERMIS. P. DOLABELLAE PRO. COS. C. P. G. CAS. D. D. — C. P. I. *Clipea.* Tibère
   BR.M.
PERMISSV L. APRONI PRO. COS. III. *Clypea.* Drusus M.B.
PERMISSV L. APRONI PRO. COS. IIII. S. SEX. POM. CELSO. — C. I. P. *Clypea.* Tibère
   M.B. (Avec — C. P. I.) G.B.

PERM. L. VOLVSI PRO. COS. CERC. *Gergis.* Auguste BR.M.
PERM. SIL. *Béryte.* Tibère M.B.
P. FLACCO IIVIR. COR. *Corinthe.* Auguste P.B.
PIETATIS AVGVSTAE C. C. A. *Caesar Augusta.* Livie M.B. Tibère G.B.
P. I. SP. D. V. SP. IIVIR. C. I. C. P. P. D. D. *Carthage.* Auguste M.B. †M.B.
P. MEM. CLEANDRO. — ADVE. AVG. *Corinthe.* Néron P.B.
P. MEM. CLEANDRO IIVIR COR. *Corinthe.* Néron P.B
P. MEM CLEANDRO IIVIR. QVIN. — ADLO. AVG. *Corinthe.* Néron P.B.
P. M. MVN. IVL. VTICEN. D. D. P. *Utique.* Tibère M.B.
P. M. S. COL. VIM.(?) *Viminacium.* Gallien G.B.
P. M. S. COL. VIM. AN. I. *Viminacium.* Gordien III G.B. M.B.
P. M. S. COL. VIM. AN. II. *Viminacium.* Gordien III G.B. M.B.
P. M. S. COL. VIM. AN. III. *Viminacium.* Gordien III G.B. M.B. Philippe père G.B.
P. M. S. COL. VIM. AN. IIII. *Viminacium.* Gordien III G.B. M.B. Philippe père G.B.
P. M. S. COL. VIM. AN. V. *Viminacium.* Gordien III G.B. Philippe père G.B.M.B.
P. M. S. COL. VIM. AN. VI. *Viminacium.* Philippe père G.B.
P. M. S. COL. VIM. AN. VII. *Viminacium.* Philippe père G.B. Philippe fils G.B.
P. M. S. COL. VIM. AN. VIII. *Viminacium.* Philippe père G.B. M.B. Otacilie G.B.
Philippe fils M.B
P. M. S. COL. VIM. AN. VIIII. *Viminacium.* Philippe père G.B. Philippe fils M.B.
P. M. S. COL. VIM. AN. X. *Viminacium.* Otacilie G.B. Trajan Dèce G.B
P. M. S. COL. VIM. AN. XI. *Viminacium.* Philippe père G.B. Otacilie G.B. Trajan
Dèce G.B. M.B. †M.B. Etruscille G.B. Hérennius M.B.
P. M. S. COL. VIM. AN. XII. *Viminacium.* Trajan Dèce G.B. Etruscille M.B. Hé-
rennius G.B. M B. Hostilien BR.M. G.B. M.B. †M.B. Tréb. Galle M.B. Volusien
M.B. Emilien G.B. Valérien? M.B.
P. M. S. COL. VIM. AN. XIII. *Viminacium.* Etruscille M.B. Hostilien G.B. Tréb
Galle M.B. Tréb. Galle et Volusien G.B. Volusien M.B. †M.B.
P M. S. COL. VIM. AN. XIIII. *Viminacium.* Valérien M.B.
P. M. S. COL. VIM. AN. XIV. *Viminacium.* Tréb. Galle M.B. Emilien M.B.
P. M. S. COL. VIM. AN. XV. *Viminacium.* Valérien † M.B. Mariniane †M.B.
P. M. S. COL. VIM. AN. XVI. *Viminacium.* Valérien M.B. Gallien G.B.
PONTIFEX MAXIMVS *Gadès.* Auguste BR.M.
POPVL. COL. COR. *Corinthe.* L. Vérus M.B.
P. POMP. GR. M. PVLLIEN. IIVIR. Q. *Buthrote.* Auguste M.B.
P. QVINCTILI VARI ACHVLLA. *Achulla.* Auguste, Caius et Lucius M.B.
PR. C. COL. CR. *Cremna.* Géta †M.B.
PROCOS..... *Chypre.* Auguste P.B.
PROP. COL. CR. *Cremna.* Géta †M.B. P.B.
PROVIDENT. PER. AVG. *Emérita.* Auguste M.B. Tibère M.B.
PROVIDENT. PERMI. AVG. *Emérita.* Auguste M.B.
PROVINCIA DACIA AN. I. *Dacie.* Philippe père G.B. M B. Otacilie G.B. Philippe
fils G.B. P.B.
PROVINCIA DACIA AN. II. *Dacie.* Philippe père G.B. M.B. Otacilie G.B. Philippe
fils G.B.
PROVINCIA DACIA AN. III. *Dacie.* Philippe père G.B. Otacilie G.B. Philippe fils
G.B. Trajan Dèce G.B. Volusien M.B.
PROVINCIA DACIA AN. IIII. *Dacie.* Trajan Dèce G.B. Etruscille G.B. Hérennius G.B.
PROVINCIA DACIA AN. IV. *Dacie.* Trajan Dèce G.B.
PROVINCIA DACIA AN. V. *Dacie.* Trajan Dèce G.B. Etruscille G.B. Hérennius G.B
Hostilien M.B. Tréb. Galle G.B. Volusien G.B.
PROVINCIA DACIA AN. VI. *Dacie.* Tréb. Galle G.B. Volusien? G.B. Valérien G.B.
Gallien M.B.
PROVINCIA DACIA AN. VII. *Dacie.* Hostilien M.B. Emilien M.B. Gallien M.B.
PROVINCIA DACIA AN. VIII. *Dacie.* Valérien G.B.
PROVINCIA DACIA AN. VIIII. *Dacie.* Valérien G.B.
PROVINCIA DACIA AN. X. *Dacie.* Gallien G.B.
PROVINCIA DACIA AN. XI. *Dacie.* Gallien M.B.
P. TVRVLIO IIVIR QVINQ. VR. I. N. K. *Carthago Nova.* Auguste P.B.

P. VEN. FRONTONE IIVIR COR. *Corinthe.* Néron P.B.
P. VENTIDIO FRONTONE IIVIR COR. *Corinthe.* Néron P.B.
P. VIBIO SAEC. CAES. — Q. BARBA PRAEF. PRO. IIVIR. *Parium.* Auguste M.B.
P. VINIRIO IIVIR COR. *Corinthe.* Néron P.B.
P. VIPSANIO AGRIPPA IIVIR COR. *Corinthe.* Auguste ┼M.B. Antonia P.B. Caligula M.B.
P. VIPSANO (*sic*) AGRIPPA IIVIR COR. *Corinthe.* Caligula M.B.
Q. AEM. C. POST. MIL. *Calagurris.* Auguste M.B.
Q. AE. PROCVLO M. AEL. MAXVMO IIVIR. — OSCA. *Osca.* Tibère ┼P.B.
Q. ANTONI. (OU ANTON.) L. FABI. *Calagurris.* Auguste M.B.
Q. FLACC. L. ANNIO IIVIR COR. *Corinthe.* Néron P.B.
Q. FLACCO IIVIR COR. *Corinthe.* Agrippine jeune P.B.
Q. FVL. FLACCO IIV. COR. *Corinthe.* Néron P.B.
Q. FVL. FLACCO IIVIR COR. *Corinthe.* Claude I P.B. Agrippine jeune P.B. Néron M.B. P.B Octavie P.B.
Q. FVL. FLACCO IIVIR GEN. COL. COR. *Corinthe.* Agrippine jeune M.B. Néron P.B. Octavie P.B.
Q. FVLVIO L. ANNIO IIVIR COR. *Corinthe.* Agrippine jeune P.B.
Q. IVLI... CO... IIVIR. COR. *Corinthe.* Agrippine jeune et Néron P.B.
Q. LVCRETI L. PONTI IIVIR. *Parium.* J. César P.B.
Q. LVCRETI (OU LVCRETIO) L. PONTI. (OU PONTIO.) IIVIR M. TVRIO LEG. *Parium.* J César P.B.
Q. LVCRET. L. PONTI IIVIR COL. DED. P. *Parium.* J. César P.B.
Q. NAEV. SVRA A. HIRTVL. NIGER IIVIR. — B. *Buthrote.* Auguste P.B.
Q. OPT. IIVIR. *Paestum.* Tibère P.B.
Q. OPT. IIVIR P. S. S. C. *Paestum.* Tibère P.B.
Q. PAPIR. CAR. Q. TERE (OU TER.) MONT. IIVIR. Q. C. A. IL. A. — IVNONI. *Ilici.* Auguste P.B.
Q. PAQVIVS RVF. C. D. — LEG. *Parium.* M. Antoine M.B.
Q. PAQVIVS RVF. LEG. C. D. *Parium.* M. Antoine M.B. Claude I M.B.
Q. TERENTIO CVLLEONE PRO. COS. (IIVIR) ? *Corinthe.* Auguste M.B.
QVIETO ET PEREGRINO IIVIR V. V. OSCA. *Osca* Tibère M.B.
RECTO ET MACRINO AED. — TVRIA. *Turiaso.* Tibère P.B.
ROMA. *Italica.* Auguste M.B.
ROMAE FEL. *Laodicée.* Caracalla G.B. Macrin G.B. Diaduménien G.B.
ROM. ET AVG. *Lyon.* Auguste BR M. G.B. M.B. P.B. Tibère G.B. M.B. P.B. Claude I M.B. P.B. Néron M.B.
SAC. CAP. OIC. ISE. — COL. HEL. *Héliopolis* Gallien M.B.
SALASSO COMITIAE SEX. REO. IIVIR. — L. CLODIO RVFO PROCOS. *Agrigente.* Auguste M.B.
SAIVS (*sic*) C. P. C. G. I. H. P. *Parium.* Galllien ┼M.B.
S. C (I). *Antioche* (*Syrie*). Auguste M.B. Tibère G.B. M.B. ┼M.B. Claude I M.B. P.B. Néron G.B. M.B. ┼P.B. P.B. Galba ┼G.B. M.B. ┼P.B. Othon G.B. M.B. ┼P.B. Vespasien M.B. ┼M.B. P.B. Titus M.B. Domitien G.B. M.B. ┼M.B. P.B. Nerva G.B. M.B.
SCATO PR. *Cyrénaïque.* Auguste M.B.
SCIPIONE ET MONTANO IIVIR. — C. C. A. *Caesar Augusta.* Germanicus M.B. Agrippine mère M.B. Caligula G.B.
SCIPIONE ET MONTANO IIVIR C. C. A. *Caesar Augusta.* Agrippa M.B. Germanicus M.B. Caligula M.B.
SEGOBRIGA. *Ségobriga.* Auguste M.B. Tibère M.B. P.B. Caligula M.B P.B.
SEP. COL. LAVD. METPO. (*sic*). *Laodicée.* Géta ┼ M.B.
SEPT. COLON. METROP. TYRI. *Tyr.* Elagabale et Maesa G.B.
SEPTIM. TYRO COL. *Tyr.* Elagabale G.B.
SEPTIM. TYRO COLON. *Tyr.* Caracalla G.B. Elagabale G.B. M.B.
SEPTIM. TYRO LEG. III. GAL. *Tyr.* Elagabale M.B.

(1) Les sigles s. c. sont accompagnés des lettres numérales grecques suivantes : sous Domitien : A. E. Θ.; sous Nerva: A. B. Γ. Δ. E. Z. H. Θ. I. K.

SEPT. TYRVS METRO. COL. *Tyr.* Caracalla G.B.
SEPT. TYRVS METRO. COLONIA ACTIA FRACLIA. *Tyr.* Caracalla M.B.
SEP. TYR. MET. COL. *Tyr.* Elagabale † P.B.
SEP. TYR. METR. COLO. *Tyr.* Macrin M.B.
SEP. TYRO C. . *Tyr.* Caracalla M.B.
SEP. TYRO COL. — LEG. III. GAL. *Tyr.* Elagabale M.B.
SEP. TYRO METRO. *Tyr.* Elagabale † P.B.
SEP. TYRO METRO. COL. *Tyr.* Alex. Sévère G.B.
SEP. TYRO METROP. COLON. — LEG. III. GAL. *Tyr.* Macrin M.B.
SEP. TYRO METROP. COL. PENIC. *Tyr.* Alex. Sévère † M.B.
SEP. TYRVS MET. COLONIA. *Tyr.* J. Domne G.B.
SEP. TVRVS METR. COLON. *Tyr.* Géta G.B.
SEP. TYRVS METRO COLON. *Tyr.* Macrin P.B.
SEP. TYRVS METRO COLONI. *Tyr.* J. Domne † M.B. Caracalla M.B. † M.B.
SEP. TYRVS METRO. COLON. — LEG. III. GAL. *Tyr.* Caracalla M.B. Géta G.B.
SEP. TYRVS METROP. *Tyr.* Plautille M.B.
SEP. TYRVS METROP. COLON. (ou COLONI.). *Tyr.* Diaduménien P.B.
SEP. TYRVS METROP. COLONIA. *Tyr.* Plautille G.B.
SEP. TYRVS METROP. COLONI. — LEG. III. GAL. *Tyr.* Géta † G.B.
SEVERO ET AQVILO IIVIR. — TVRIASO. *Turiaso.* Auguste P.B.
SEX. AEBVTIVS L. LVCRETIVS IIVIR. — C. C. A. *Caesar Augusta.* Tibère P.B.
SEX. CETHEGO Q. POMP. SEGVNDINO. *Celsa.* Auguste M.B.
SID. COL. MET. AVR. PIA. *Sidon.* Elagabale M B.
SILVA. COL. CREM. *Cremna.* Hostilien P.B.
SISENNA PR. COS. L. SAT. I. *Corinthe.* Auguste † M.B.
SOSIVS IMP. *Zacinthe.* M. Antoine P.B.
SPARSO ET CAECILIANO IIVIR. VRB. VIC. OSCA. *Osca.* Auguste M.B.
STOBENSIVM. *Stobi.* M. Aurèle M.B. Faustine jeune P.B.
T. CAECILIO LEPIDO C AVFIDIO GEMELLO IIVIR. — C. C. A. *Caesar Augusta.* Tibère G.B.
T. CAECILIO LEPIDO C. AVFIDIO GEMELLO IIVIR. C. C. A. *Caesar Augusta.* Tibère M.B.
T. COELIVS PROCVLVS M. AEMILIVS SEVERVS Q. — C. I. I. A *Ilici.* Tibère M.B.
T. COELIVS PROCVLVS M. AEMILIVS SEVERVS — Q. I. I. A. *Ilici.* Tibère † M.B.
THAPSVM IVN. AVG. *Thapsus.* Tibère M.B. Tibère et Livie M.B.
TIB. FLAVO PRAEF. GERMAN. L. IVENT. LVPERCO. — C. C. A. IIVIR. *Caesar Augusta.* Auguste P.B.
TI. CAESAR L. CAEL. CLEM. FLA. *Paestum.* Tibère P.B.
TI. CLA. (ou CLAVD.) ANAXILAO IIVIR. COR. *Corinthe.* Néron P.B.
TI. CLAVDIO OPTATO IIVIR. COR. *Corinthe.* Néron P.B. (Avec ISTHMIA). P.B.
TI. CLAVDIO Q. ADV. AVG. COR. *Corinthe.* Néron P.B.
TI. CLAVDIVS. *Gadès.* Néron BR.M. G.B.
TI. CLAVDIVS NERO. *Gadès.* Néron G.B.
TI. CLAVD. OPTATO IIVIR. COR. *Corinthe.* Claude I P.B.
TITVLLO ET MONTANO IIVIR. — C. C. A. *Caesar Augusta.* Germanicus M.B. Agrippine mère M.B.
TITVLLO ET MONTANO IIVIR C. C. A *Caesar Augusta.* Agrippa M.B. Caligula M.B.
TRIB. POT. COS. III. C. G. I. P. *Patras.* Adrien † M.B.
TROA. — AV. C. *Alexandrie Troade.* Gallien † M.B.
TROA. — AV. C. C. *Alexandrie Troade.* Gallien M.B.
TROAC. — AV. CO. *Alexandrie Troade.* Gallien M.B.
TROAD. — AV. CO. *Alexandrie Troade.* Gallien G.B.
TROAS. — AV. CO. *Alexandrie Troade.* Gallien M.B.
T. SVLP. Q. VAR. Q. PONT. PILA. MVN. TVRI. — AED. *Turiaso.* Tibère P.B.
T. VALE. GRACILLE..... AED. CLVNIA. *Clunia.* Tibère P.B.
TVRIASO M. CAECIL. SEVERO C. VAL. AQVILO. — IIVIR. *Turiaso.* Auguste M.B
TYR... COL. *Tyr.* Alex. Sévère M.B.
TYR. COLONI. *Tyr.* Gordien III G.B.
TYRIORVM. *Tyr.* Elagabale G.B. M.B. Aquilia Sévéra G.B. M.B. Maesa G B. M B

Mamée M.B. Etruscille G.B. (Avec — AMBPOCIE IIETPE.) Maesa M.B. (Avec — ΔΕΙΔωΝ.) Elagabale † M.B. (Avec — HRAKAIA OAYMIIIA. — B.) Elagabale G.B.
TYR. METR. COL. *Tyr.* Diaduménien M.B.
TYR. METRO. COL. *Tyr.* Gordien III G.B.
TYRVS M. COLONI. *Tyr.* Sept. Sévère G.B.
TYRVS SEPT. COL. METROPOL. *Tyr.* Valérien et Gallien M.B.
VENVS C. I. C. A. AVG. D. D. *Apamée.* J. Domne M.B.
VENVS C. I. C. APAM. D. D. *Apamée.* Commode M.B.
VETILIO BVCCONE C. FVFIO — AED... CELSA. *Celsa.* Tibère P.B.
VICT. AVG... COR. *Corinthe.* Domitien M.B.
VICT... COL... A. AP. *Apamée.* J. César M.B.
VICT. D. N. COL. ANTIOCII. S. R. *Antioche Pisidie.* Caracalla BR.M.
VICTORIA AVG. CAPITONE ITER. IIVIR. *Corinthe.* Auguste M.B.
VICTORIA AVG. CYTHERO ITER. IIVIR. *Corinthe.* Auguste M.B.
VICTORIA DOMINI ANTI. COΓONII (sic) S. R. *Antioche Pisidie.* Gordien III G.B.
VICTORIAE AVGVSTORV. COL. ANT. S. R. *Antioche Pisidie.* Géta G.B.
VICTORIAE DDD. NNN. CO. AN. S. R. *Antioche Pisidie.* Caracalla BR.M.
VICTORIAE DD. NN. COL. ANT. S. C. *Antioche Pisidie.* Géta G.B. †G.B.
VICTORIAE DD. NN. COL. ANT. S. R. *Antioche Pisidie.* Sept. Sévère BR.M. G.B. Géta G.B.
VICTOR. AVG. *Parium?* Domitien P.B.
VIRT. AVG. COL. ANTIOCH. S. R. *Antioche Pisidie.* Gordien III G.B.
VIRT. AVGG. COL. ANTIOCII. S. R. *Antioche Pisidie.* Géta G.B.
VRBS VIC. OSCA. D. D. *Osca.* Tibère M.B.
VRSONE. *Urso.* Auguste M.B.
V. VIII. *Béryte.* Claude I P.B.
V. V. *Osca.* Auguste M.B. Tibère M.B. Caligula M.B.
Sans légende. (*Deux colons labourant avec deux bœufs*). *Parium.* Auguste P.B. Tibère P.B. Claude I P.B.

IV. INSCRIPTIONS ON

TESSARAE AND CONTORNIATES

ACCIVS. *Contorniates.* Horace.
AC... LL.. — PEINTSI. (sic). *Contorniates.* Trajan.
AELIANE NICA. *Contorniates.* Miscellanées.
AENEAS. *Contorniates.* Néron. Trajan.
ALEXANDER. *Contorniates.* Alexandre.
ALEXANDER MAC. *Contorniates.* Alexandre.
ALEXANDER MACEDO. *Contorniates.* Alexandre.
ALEXANDER MACID. *Contorniates.* Alexandre.
ALEXANDER. MAG. *Contorniates.* Alexandre.
ALEXANDER MAG. MACEDON. *Contorniates.* Alexandre
ALEXANDER MAGNVS. *Contorniates.* Alexandre.
ALEXANDER MAGNVS MACEDON. *Contorniates.* Alexandre
ALEXANDER MAGNVS MHCEDON. *Contorniates.* Alexandre.
ΑΛΕΞΑΝΔΡΟΣ ΙΙΑΣΙΛΕΥΣ. *Contorniates.* Alexandre.
ALEXSΔPI. *Tessères mystiques.*
ALEXXANDER MAC. *Contorniates.* Alexandre
ALEXXANDR. *Tessères mystiques*
ΑΛΙΙΙΛΟΟΣ. *Contorniates.* Demosthène.
ALLIGER. *Contorniates* Miscellanées.
AMOR. *Contorniates.* Miscellanées.
ANNONA AVGVSTA CERES. *Contorniates.* Rome. (avec S. C.) Trajan.
ANTINOΩ IIANI. *Contorniates.* Antinoüs.

APOLLONIVS TFANEVS (sic). *Contorniates.* Apollonius de Tyane.
APOLLO PITIVS. *Contorniates.* Apollon.
A. P. P. F. *Tessères des jeux.*
APVLEIVS. *Contorniates.* Apulée.
ARBELAS HAREMATVS (ou PAREMATVS). *Contorniates.* Apollon.
ARTEMI VINCAS. — IVCVNDATOR PENNA. *Contorniates.* Honorius.
ASINA. *Tessères mystiques.*
ASTVRI NICA. *Contorniates.* Miscellanées.
ASTVRI NIKA. — BROTOCALES. *Contorniates.* Miscellanées.
ASTVRI NIKA. — CVPIDO. *Contorniates.* Miscellanées.
ASTVR : N:: *Contorniates.* Miscellanées.·
AVG. *Tessères.* Auguste. Claude I. *Tessères des jeux.*
AVGGG. *Poids.* Théodose, Honorius et Arcadius.
AVG. I. *Tessères.* Auguste.
AVGVST. S. C. PORT. OST. *Contorniates.* Trajan.
AVRELIANVS. *Contorniates.* Néron. Trajan.
A. XV. *Tessères des jeux.*
A. XVI. *Tessères des jeux.*
BABVLIVS. *Contorniates.* Miscellanées.
BALAMS.... IVS. *Contorniates.* Horace. Térence.
BAL. LORVS. *Tessères des jeux.*
BETOYPIOC. *Contorniates.* Antinoüs.
BONIFATI VINCAS VRSI. *Contorniates.* Trajan.
BONIFATIVS. *Contorniates* Julien II. Valentinien III
BONONIA OCEANEN. *Contorniates.* Constant I.
BROTOCALE. *Contorniates.* Miscellanées.
CALODVANI. *Contorniates.* Auguste.
CASIBANVS. *Contorniates.* Commode
CERVOMTIVS. *Contorniates.* Caracalla.
C. MITREIVS L. F. MAG. IVVENT. *Tessères des jeux.*
COLENDVS *Contorniates.* Néron. Trajan. Miscellanées
COLONIA DEDVCTA. *Contorniates.* Caligula. Miscellanées.
COS. IIII. *Tessères.* (Trajan ?) P.B.
COSMVS. *Contorniates.* Miscellanées.
C. S. *Contorniates.* Faustine mère.
CVPIDO. *Contorniates.* Miscellanées.
D. *Tessères des jeux.*
D. CALODVANI. *Contorniates.* Néron. Trajan.
DD. NN. *Poids.* Gratien et Valentinien II.
DD. NN. O. B. N. *Poids.* Valentinien III.
DECVRSIO. *Contorniates.* Néron.
ΔΗΜΟΣΘΕΝΗΣ. *Contorniates.* Démosthène.
DEO SERAPIDI. *Contorniates.* Serapis.
ΔΙΑΠΕΠΩΝ. *Contorniates.* Alexandre. Euripide.
DIVA FAVSTINA. *Contorniates.* Faustine mère.
DIVA FAVSTINA PIA. *Contorniates.* Néron.
D. N. IHV. XPS. DEI. FILIVS. *Tessères mystiques.*
DOMINVS FYLOBACVS. *Contorniates.* Miscellanées.
DOMINVS IN VENE. *Contorniates.* Miscellanées.
DOMINVS IN VENETO. *Contorniates.* Alexandre. Trajan.
DOM. N. N. S. *Contorniates.* Trajan.
ELIANVS. *Contorniates.* Miscellanées.
EPEPN. *Contorniates.* Miscellanées.
EIII CTPATHΓOY KV. AICIMOY PE. *Contorniates.* Aelius.
ETERNIT. P. R. *Contorniates.* J. César.
EVGENIVS. *Contorniates.* Miscellanées.
EVGENIVS ACHILLES SIDEREVS SPECIOSVS DIGNVS. *Contorniates.* Trajan.
EVGENIVS ACHILLIS (sic) SIDEREVS SPECIOSVS DIGNVS. *Contorniates.* Miscellanées.
Honorius.

EYPIIIIΔHC. *Contorniates.* Euripid .
EVSTORTIVS IN PRASINO. *Contorniates.* Alexandre.
EVTEIMI NICA. — TVRIFICATOR ASTVTVS. *Contorniates.* Trajan.
EVTIMI VINCAS. *Contorniates.* Honorius. Miscellanées.
EVTIMI VINCAS. — RVS ALLIGER. *Contorniates.* Théodose I. Honorius.
EVTIMVS MATVNDVS? *Contorniates.* Néron.
EVTIMVS MIRANDVS. *Contorniates.* Néron.
EVTYMIVS. *Contorniates.* Trajan.
EXAGIVM SOLIDI. *Poids.* Honorius. Honorius, Arcadius et Théodose II.
EXAGIVM SOLIDIS. *Poids.* Honorius et Arcadius.
EXAG. SOL. SVB. VI. INL. IOHANNI COM. S. L. *Poids.* Honorius, Arcadius et Théo-
dose II.
EXVPERANTI VINCAS. *Contorniates* Néron.
FILINVS. *Contorniates.* Néron. Trajan.
FLAVIANVS. *Contorniates.* Caligula. Néron.
FLIANE NICA. *Contorniates.* Apollonius de Tyane.
G. *Tessères des jeux.*
GERONTIVS. *Contorniates.* Trajan. Caracalla.
GLORIA ROMANORVM. *Poids.* Honorius, Arcadius et Théodose II. *Contorniates.*
Constance II.
H. *Tessères.* Julie.
HORATIVS. *Contorniates.* Horace.
YΨIIIYAII. *Contorniates.* Trajan. Miscellanées.
I. *Tessères.* Auguste. Julie. Tibère.
II. *Tessères.* Auguste. Julie. Tibère. *Tessères des jeux.*
III. *Tessères.* Auguste. Tibère. Antonia. Drusille. Julien II. *Tessères des jeux.*
IIII. *Tessères.* Auguste. Caïus et Lucius. Tibère. Antonia. Caligula. Honorius.
Tessères des jeux.
IЭTPRED. *Contorniates.* M. Aurèle.
IM..... DATOR PENNA VINCAS. *Contorniates.* Honorius.
IMP. III. *Tessères.* (Trajan?) P.B.
INVICTA ROMA FELIX SENATVS. *Contorniates.* Rome.
IOHANNES NICAS. *Contorniates.* Valentinien III
I O. IO. TRIVMP. *Tessères.* (Domitien ?) P.B.
IPODROMOS HERACLEOS ANDREA. *Contorniates.* Anthémius.
LAVRENTI NIKA. *Contorniates.* Néron.
LIBERTAS PVBLICA S. C. *Contorniates.* Galba.
LISIFONVS. *Contorniates.* Auguste. Néron. Trajan.
L. SEXTILI † F. IIII. *Tesssères des jeux.*
M. *Tessères des jeux.*
MARGARITA VINCAS. *Contorniates.* Théodose I. Valentinien III.
MATRI DEVM SALVTARI. *Contorniates.* Alexandre. Agrippine mère. Faustine
mère.
MORA. *Tessères des jeux.*
M. VINCAS. *Contorniates.* Théodose I. Valentinien III.
N. *Tessères des jeux.*
NIKOKPEΩN ANAΞAPXOC. *Contorniates.* Nicocréon et Anaxarque.
NVSMAGCON MONINVS. *Contorniates.* Alexandre. Salluste. Caracalla. Miscellanées.
O. C. S. C. *Tessères des jeux.*
OLEXIVS. *Contorniates.* Caracalla.
OLINPICVS. *Contorniates.* Néron.
OAYMIIIAC. *Contorniates.* Olympias.
OLYMPIAS REGINA. *Contorniates.* Alexandre. Trajan.
OLYMPI NIKA. *Contorniates.* Neron.
OLYMPIODORVS. *Contorniates.* Miscellanées.
OLYNPIVS. *Contorniates.* Miscellanées.
ΩMHPOC. *Contorniates.* Homère.
ORATIVS. *Contorniates.* Horace.
OYΔEN EMOY ΣOY EΣTAI AKKIZOMENOY. *Contorniates.* Anacréon et Anaxarque.

PACE P. R. VBIQ. PARTA IANVM CVLSIT. S. C. *Contorniates.* Néron.
PANNONI NIKA. *Contorniates.* Miscellanées.
ΠΑΡΘΕΝΟΠΕ. *Contorniates.* Alexandre.
P. E. *Contorniates.* Miscellanées.
PETRONI PLACEAS. *Contorniates.* Salluste.
PETRONIVS MAXSVMVS V. C. CONS. *Contorniates.* Valentinien III.
P. L. *Tessères des jeux.*
PLACEAS PETRI. *Ccntorniates.* Valentinien III.
POLISTEFANVS. *Contorniates.* Trajan.
ΠΥΘΑΓΟΡΗΣ. *Contorniates.* le Soleil.
QVI. LVDIT. ARRAM. DET. QVOD. SATIS. SIT. *Tessères des jeux* M.B.
REGINA. *Contorniates.* Alexandre. Néron. Trajan. Caracalla.
REPARATIO MVNERIS FELICITER. *Contorniates.* Rome.
ROMA. *Tessères des jeux.*
ROMAE AETERNAE. *Contorniates.* Rome.
ROMA S. C. *Contorniates.* Olympias. Néron. Vespasien.
ROSCIVS. *Contorniates.* Néron.
SABINAE. *Contorniates.* Alexandre. Néron Trajan. Adrien.
SABVCIVS PINIAN..... (SIVOS)? *Contorniates.* Caracalla.
SALLVSTIVS AVTOR. *Contorniates.* Salluste.
SAPIENTIA. *Contorniates.* Honorius.
S. C. *Contorniates.* Agrippine mère, Néron, Galba, Trajan. *Tessères des jeux.*
S. E. *Contorniates.* Néron.
SELEVCVS. *Contorniates.* Miscellanées.
SERACVSVS. *Contorniates.* Miscellanées.
SOLI INVICTO. *Contorniates.* Alexandre.
SOL. ORIENS. *Contorniates.* Salluste.
S. P. Q. R. *Contorniates.* Agrippine mère. Trajan.
STEFANAS. *Contorniates.* Alexandre. Néron.
STEFANVS DOMINATOR. *Contorniates.* Trajan.
T. *Tessères des jeux.*
TERENTIVS. *Contorniates.* Térence.
ΘΕωΦΙΛΕ NIKA. *Contorniates.* Valentinien III.
TITIVS. *Contorniates.* Trajan.
TOXXOTES. *Contorniates.* Miscellanées.
TR. *Tessères des jeux.*
TVRRANIVS. *Contorniates.* Trajan.
V. *Tessères.* Auguste. Octavie. Tibère. Claude I. Julien II. *Tessères des jeux. Tessères mythologiques.*
VI. *Tessères.* Auguste. Tibère. Caligula. Claude I.
VII. *Tessères.* Auguste. Tibère. *Tessères mythologiques,*
VIII. *Tessères.* Auguste. Auguste et Livie. Tibère. Caligula. Caligula et Agrip pine jeune. Julien II. Honorius.
VIIII. *Tessères.* Auguste. Caïus et Lucius. Caligula. Constance Calle. *Tessères des jeux.*
VAL. NOB. C. *Contorniates.* Néron.
VICTORIA AVG. *Contorniates* Antinoüs.
VICTORIA AVGG. *Contorniates.* Constant I.
VICTORIA CONSTANTI AVG. *Contorniates.* Constantin I.
VIRTVS AVGG. *Contorniates.* Constant I.
VL. *Tessères des jeux.*
VOTA PVBLICA. *Contorniates.* Trajan.
VOTA XXE. *Contorniates.* Valentinien III.
Vot. IS. ...X MVLTIS. *Contorniates.* Majorien.
VRANI NICA MVNIO. *Contorniates.* Trajan.
VRBS ROMA. *Contorniates* Rome.
VRBS ROMA AETERNA. *Contorniates.* Adrien.
VRBS ROMA HETERNA. *Contorniates.* Trajan.
VRSE VINCAS. *Contorniates.* Miscellanées.

x. *Tessères*. Auguste. Tibère. Caligula.
XI. *Tessères*. Auguste. Tibère. Caligula. *Tessères des jeux*.
XII. *Tessères*. Auguste. Tibère. Caligula. Théodose I. *Tessères des jeux*.
XIII. *Tessères*. Auguste. Tibère. Caligula. Caligula et Agrippine jeune. Julien II. *Tessères des jeux*.
XIIII. *Tessères*. Auguste. Tibère. Caligula et Agrippine jeune. Drusille.
XV. *Tessères*. Auguste. Tibère. Caligula. Caligula et Agrippine jeune. Claude I.
XVI. *Tessères*. Auguste. *Tessères des jeux*.
x. VIIII. *Tessères*. Claude I.
XIX. *Tessères*. Auguste.
XXVI. *Tessères mythologiques*.
SANS LÉGENDE. *Tessères* Caius César. Néron. *Tessères des jeux*. *Tessères mystiques*. *Poids*. Gratien et Valentinien II. Honorius, Arcadius et Théodose II. *Contorniates*. Serapis. Mercure. Hercule. Minerve. Rome. Alexandre. Apulée. Homère. Horace. Olympias. Salluste. J. César. Auguste. Agrippine mère. Caligula. Néron. Galba. Vespasien. Trajan. Adrien. Antinoûs. Antonin. Faustine mère. Lucille. Julie Domne. Caracalla. Constant I. Julien II. Théodose I. Honorius. Valentinien III. Majorien. Miscellanées.

ABRÉVIATIONS

OR.M.	Médaillon d'or.
OR.	Sou d'or.
OR.Q.	Quinaire, demi-sou.
OR.T.	Tiers de sou.
AR.M.	Médaillon d'argent.
AR.	Denier.
AR.Q.	Quinaire et petites divisions.
POT.	Potin.
BIL.M.	Médaillon de billon.
BIL.	Billon.
BIL.Q.	Billon quinaire.
B.	Billon ou petit bronze.
B.Q.	Billon ou petit bronze quinaire.
BR.M.	Médaillon de bronze.
G.B.M.	Grand bronze médaillon.
M.B M.	Moyen bronze médaillon.
G.B.	Grand bronze.
†G.B.	Grand bronze inférieur.
M.B.	Moyen bronze.
†M.B.	Petit moyen bronze.
†P.B.	Petit bronze excédant.
P.B.	Petit bronze ordinaire.
P.B.Q.	Petit bronze quinaire.
*	Médaille unique.
B.	Musée Britannique.
F.	Cabinet de France.
P.	Musée de Berlin.
T.	Musée de Turin.
V.	Musée de Vienne.
℞.	Revers.

TABLES

I

TABLE EXPLICATIVE

DES LETTRES ET DES SYLLABES QUI SE RENCONTRENT A L'EXERGUE
(ET QUELQUEFOIS DANS LE CHAMP) DES MÉDAILLES ROMAINES SURTOUT
A PARTIR DE DIOCLÉTIEN.

———

Plusieurs des interprétations qui ont été données de ces lettres sont parfaitement sûres; quelques-unes sont probables, d'autres sont possibles; beaucoup enfin sont conjecturales, sans parler de celles qui sont absurdes. Je ne donnerai ici que les interprétations certaines, probables et possibles. Du reste, je ferai observer que ce n'est que depuis une cinquantaine d'années que l'interprétation de ces lettres, tentée par Hardouin, Vaillant et Jobert, et et améliorée par le baron Bimard de la Bastie et Eckhel, a enfin atteint un certain degré de perfection, grâce aux recherches des savants de ce siècle.

Pour comprendre cette table, il faudra se rappeler que toutes les interprétations qui ne seront suivies d'aucune indication sont positives; que celles qui seront suivies d'un point d'interrogation sont probables, et que celles qui ne sont que possibles seront suivies de deux points d'interrogation.

A. Premier atelier de Lyon jusqu'à Dioclétien.

A *Prima*, lorsqu'il précède ou suit un nom de ville, telle que ASIS, ASIRM, ALEA, ANTA(1).

AL., ALE. Alexandria (Alexandrie).

AMB. Ambianum (Amiens).

AN, ANT. Antiochia (Antioche).

AQ. Aquileia (Aquilée).

AR, ARL. Arelatum.

AVG. Augusta (Londres).

B *Secunda*. Cette lettre précède ou suit les noms de villes, comme BTR, BSIRM, ALEB, HERACLB (2).

C. Constantinopolis ?? Ce C est généralement suivi d'une lettre numérale grecque, séparée par une étoile (Constantinople) (3).

---

(1) Toutes ces lettres A, B, Γ, Δ, E, etc , ont la même signification lorsqu'elles suivent une légende, telle que CONCORDIA AVGGA, VOT. XX. MVLT. XXXE.
(2) Cette même lettre indiquait le second atelier de Lyon.
(3) Cette même lettre indiquait le troisième atelier de Lyon.

CON. ou CONS. Constantina (Arles) ou Constantinopolis.

CON. CONS. ou CONST. Suivi de A. B. Γ. Δ. E. Σ. Z. H. Θ. I. O·I IA. Constantinopolis, qui avait même plus de onze ateliers.

CON. CONS. ou CONST. précédé de P. S. T. Q. Constantina (Arles), qui avait quatre ateliers que nous retrouvons sur les monnaies signées ARL.

CVZ ou CYZ, CVZIC ou CYZIC. Cyzicus (Cyzique).

Γ *Tertia*, précédant ou suivant un nom de ville, comme ΓSISC, ALEΓ.

D. Quatrième atelier de la ville de Lyon jusqu'au règne de Dioclétien.

Δ *Quarta*, précédant ou suivant un nom de ville, tels que ΔSIRM, ALEΔ.

E *Quinta*. Cette lettre précède ou suit les noms de villes, comme ESIRM. ANTE.

H. Heracleia ? (Héraclée).

H *Octava*, précédant ou suivant un nom de ville, tel que HTR, ANTH.

HERAC. Heracleia.

HT. Heracleia ??

I. *Decima*, précédant ou suivant un nom de ville, comme ITR, ANTI.

K. Carthago (Carthage).

KA. Constantinopolis ??

KART. Carthago.

KON, KONS, KONST, KONSTANT (TAN en monogramme). Constantinopolis.

KY. Cyzicus.

LD Lugdunum (Lyon).

L. LN. Londinum ? (Londres).

LG. Lugdunum ? (Les lettres PLC, si fréquentes sous Dioclétien, Maximien Hercule. etc., paraissent donc en conséquence devoir se lire PLG.)

LON. Londinum.

A *Vigesima*. comme CONCORDIA AVGGA à Honorius.

M *Moneta*, comme dans MKVA (Moneta Cyzici primâ, *officinâ* sous-entendu).

MD, MED. Mediolanum (Milan).

N. Nicomedia ? (Nicomédie) ou Narbona (Narbonne) selon M. Sabatier.

OB. Voyez à la page 83 de ce volume.

OF, OFF. *Officina*.

OST. Ostia. (Ostie).

P *Percussa* ou *Prima*. Cette lettre précède ou suit souvent les noms de villes, comme PARL, PCONST, AQP, CONSP.

Q *Quarta*, précédant ou suivant un nom de ville, comme QARL. MOSTQ.

R. Roma? Rome.

RM ou ROM. Roma.

RV. Ravenna (Ravenne). Peut-être que RVPS signifie Ravennae pecunia signata.

S. Siscia ??

S *Secunda*. Précédant ou suivant un nom de ville, tel que SARL, SCONST, AQS.

S. *Signata*.

SD. Serdica (Sardique).

SER. Serdica.

SIRM. Sirmium (Sirmich).

sisc ou sis. Siscia.

sm (dans le champ). Sirmium.

sm (à l'exergue). *Signata* ou *sacra moneta*. Les plus grandes complications de lettres s'expliquent par cette interprétation : smanta. Signata moneta Antiochiæ primâ. smnd. Signata moneta Nicomediæ secundâ.

ϛ. *Sexta*, comme concordia avggϛ.

t. Tarragona ? (Tarragone) ou Thessalonica ? (Thessalonique).

t. *Tertia*, lorsqu'il précède ou suit un nom de ville, comme tarl, aqt.

tes. Thessalonica.

th. Thessalonica.

tr. Treviri (Trèves).

ts. Thessalonica ?

Θes. Thessalonica.

Θ. *Nona*, suivant un nom de ville, tel que smanΘ.

z. *Septima*, suivant un nom de ville, tel que siscpz.

BIBLIOTHECA AEGYPTIACA

ARES PUBLISHERS presents for the first time a new program of reprinting at LOW BUDGET PRICES all the most important works on the LANGUAGE, HISTORY and CIVILIZATION of the ANCIENT EGYPTIANS. The volumes listed below ARE ALL AVAILABLE and you may order them directly from us (ALL PREPAID ORDERS mailed in 48 hours from receipt), or from your bookseller or book supplier.

ANCIENT EGYPTIAN MEDICINE: THE PAPYRUS EBERS. *Cyril Bryan.*
   All sorts of remedies for ailments still plaguing the human race in this original work on ancient Egyptian medicine, as written by an ancient physician. The best information source known on Egyptian medical practices.
   ISBN 0-89005-004-X. 208pp. *$10.00*

EGYPTIAN LANGUAGE: EASY LESSONS IN EGYPTIAN HIEROGLYPHICS.
E.A. Wallis Budge.
   An easy introduction to the study of the ancient Egyptian language and hieroglyphic inscriptions. A lengthy list of hieroglyphic characters, telling both their value as idiograms and as phonetics. Shows how to decipher the ancient hieroglyphics.
   ISBN 0-89005-095-3 . . . . *$10.00*
   Student edition *$6.00*

EGYPTIAN HIEROGLYPHIC GRAMMAR: With Vocabularies, Exercises, Chrestomathy (A First Reader) Sign-List and Glossary. *S.A.B. Mercer.*
   Mercer's grammar was a product of his experience in teaching Oriental Languages. His basic idea in writing was that "the beginner needs a textbook which is both simple and a so supplied with exercises" and that "the larger grammars are reference books and unsuited for the use of beginners."
   Mercer divided his 'Grammar' into chapters or lessons, and supplied each chapter with copious exercises. He supplied also a fine selection of hieroglyphic texts forming a reader for the student, added a Sign-List with explanations of the signs and finally a Glossary translating the Egyptian words in English.
   For the student who wishes to learn how to read and write the hieroglyphics and understand also the words and sentences formed by them, Mercer's book is an invaluable help.
   ISBN 0-89005-203-4, viii + 184pp. *$12.50*

CATALOGUE OF THE EGYPTIAN HIEROGLYPHIC PRINTING TYPE.
Alan H. Gardiner.

An amazing collection of tables which provide instant identification of all the Egyptian hieroglyphs. Arranged by type, such as "Gods," "Goddesses," "Birds," "Parts of Animals," a glance at the index shows exactly where to find the hieroglyphs which you wish to decipher. Useful introductory section and listing of Egyptian alphabet.

ISBN 0-89005-098-8 . . . . **$6.00**

EGYPTIAN READINGBOOK: Exercises and Middle Egyptian Texts. *Selected & Edited by Dr. A. De Buck.*

The Egyptian Readingbook, compiled by one of the best Egyptologists of the University of Leyden, is a unique collection of literary, religious, and private texts written in hieroglyphics. The student who has worked with Budge's, *Egyptian Language* or Mercer's *Grammar* needs the texts in the 'Readingbook' for study and practice.

ISBN 0-89005-213-1, 220pp. 8½ x 11 . . . . **$20.00**

PAPER AND BOOKS IN ANCIENT EGYPT. *J. Cerny.*

The revolution that the invention of the book brought to the cultures of the ancient people of the Near-East and the Mediterranean started in Egypt. It was under the shade of the Megalithic Egyptian temples, that the first 'papyrus scroll' was developed and in the great libraries of the Ptolemaic period that the idea of the 'papyrus codex' was born many centuries later. Without the Egyptian thought and thinkers, writing could still be limited to materials that could have delayed considerably the expansion of information, education and learning.

Prof. Cerny's account of 'Paper and Books in Ancient Egypt,' is the most complete, documented and dependable study available. In its compact form, it contains more information and facts than any other reference work on the subject.

ISBN 0-89005-205-0, 37pp. **$5.00**

TEN YEARS DIGGING IN EGYPT. *Flinders Petrie.*

A most fascinating account by the premier Egyptologist describing some of the most important discoveries in Egypt at the end of the 19th century. Illustrated with the drawings of the author.

ISBN 0-89005-107-0. 250pp. **$10.00**

Student edition **$6.00**

HISTORICAL SCARABS. *Flinders Petrie.*

The pocket handbook for the historian and collector of scarabs, with original drawings by Petrie. A useful primer to Newberry's *Ancient Egyptian Scarabs*. Includes 69 plates.

ISBN 0-89005-122-4. 84pp. **$10.00**

Student edition **$6.00**

ANCIENT EGYPTIAN SCARABS. *P. Newberry.*

A concise work covering all aspects of scarabs, cylinder seals, signet rings and other seals used by the ancient Egyptian. Indispensable reference work for scholars and collectors.

ISBN 0-89005-092-9 .... *$10.00*

Student edition *$6.00*

CULTS AND CREEDS IN GRAECO-ROMAN EGYPT. *H. Idris Bell.*

Valuable information from ancient papyri on the previously confused history of the religions and cults of Graeco-Roman Egypt. Special selections on the pagan amalgam, Jews in Egypt and the rise of Christianity.

ISBN 0-89005-088-0. x + 117pp. *$10.00*

Student edition *$6.00*

INSCRIPTIONES GRAECAE AEGYPTI: INSCRIPTIONES NUNC CAIRO IN MUSEO. *G. Milne.*

The Greek inscriptions of Egypt included in this volume, originally published in the *Catalogue General des Antiquities Egyptiennes du Musee du Caire,* are here for the first time technically incorporated in the *Inscriptiones Graecae* along with the author's excellent commentaries.

ISBN 0-89005-111-9. 169pp. *$25.00*

INSCRIPTIONES GRAECAE PTOLEMAICAE I. *Max L. Strack.*

The first collection of Ptolemaic inscriptions not limited to the political boundaries of the Empire, but including inscriptions from all areas which came under the radiating influence of its culture. Also appearing is an appendix which includes tables for the "Names and Epithets of the Kings," his "Chronological List of the Kings," plus several commentaries.

ISBN 0-89005-171-2. 120pp. *$10.00*

The new series of the BIBLIOTHECA AEGYPTIACA is only a part of our publishing program of reprinting and publishing new books on the ANCIENT WORLD. Our 1977 catalogue lists more than 150 books in this special area, with emphasis on the ANCIENT NEAR EAST, the ANCIENT MEDITERRANEAN, ANCIENT GREECE, the HELLENISTIC WORLD and the WORLD OF ROME. If you are interested, send us a postcard with your name and address. We will mail to you a FREE copy.

ARES PUBLISHERS Inc.
612 NORTH MICHIGAN AVE., SUITE 216
CHICAGO, ILLINOIS 60611